LISP

A Gentle Introduction to Symbolic Computation

DAVID S. TOURETZKY
Computer Science Department
Carnegie-Mellon University

Sponsoring Editor: John Willig

JOHN WILEY & SONS
New York • Chichester • Brisbane • Toronto • Singapore

To Phil and Anne

The names of all computer programs and computers included herein are registered trademarks of their makers.

Reproduction of M.C. Escher's "Drawing Hands" courtesy of The Vorpal Gallery, New York City, San Francisco and Laguna Beach, California.

Library of Congress Cataloging in Publication Data
Touretzky, David S.
LISP: a gentle introduction to symbolic computation.
Copyright © 1984 John Wiley & Sons, Inc.
Includes index.
1. LISP (computer program language) I Title.
II Title: L.I.S.P.
QA76.73.L23T67 1984 001-64'24 83-12712

ISBN 0-471-60349-X

9 8 7 6 5

Contents

Preface

This book is about learning to program in Lisp. About twenty-five years old, Lisp is one of the oldest computer languages, yet its importance and popularity are increasing today as never before. One reason Lisp is so important is that it is the *lingua franca* of artificial intelligence research, or "AI." AI is moving from the laboratory to the everyday world, and tremendous changes are in store for our society as a result. Lisp's popularity is also growing because it offers a friendly, interactive programming environment, an invaluable aid to beginning programmers.

When I wrote the book I had three types of readers in mind, and I would like to address each in turn:

- The humanities student taking his or her first programming course. For you, let me stress the word *gentle* in the title. I assume no prior mathematical background beyond arithmetic. Even if you don't like math, this book may teach you to enjoy computer programming. I've avoided technical jargon. There are many examples. Plenty of exercises are interspersed with the text, the answers to which may be found in appendix D.

- Psychologists, linguists, and other persons interested in AI and cognitive science. As you begin your inquiry into artificial intelligence, you will see that almost all research in this field is carried out in Lisp. This book can be your doorway to a deeper understanding of the technical literature as well as a quick introduction to the central tool of AI.

- Computer hobbyists. Several high-quality mini-Lisp systems are available today for personal computers, such as the Apple and many Z-80

> based machines. These systems are adequate for learning Lisp and writing simple programs, but currently their power is limited by a lack of memory. When more powerful personal computers become affordable—for example, those with 24- or 32-bit address spaces and virtual memory capability—hobbyists will be able to run the same Lisp software that is used in today's AI research labs. The prospect of putting research-quality Lisp systems into the hands of computer hobbyists is truly exciting. This book will teach you to use the Lisp systems available today, but more important it will help you prepare for the technology that is coming tomorrow.

There has never been a standard Lisp. Throughout its history the language has been evolving and gradually maturing; the end of this process is not yet in sight. Consequently there are a large number of Lisp dialects around. Lisp 1.5 is the closest thing there is to a "standard" Lisp, but it's a 1962 dialect that lacks much of the power of modern Lisp. The major dialects today are MacLisp, Interlisp, UCI Lisp, and Lisp Machine Lisp; Franz Lisp and Common Lisp are MacLisp offshoots that are developing rapidly and will soon be important in their own right. This book is based primarily on MacLisp and Common Lisp, with a few borrowings from other dialects. Appendix C gives information on how to make virtually any Lisp system compatible with the one used in the book.

Acknowledgments

This book began as a set of notes for a Lisp-based programming course for humanities students at Carnegie-Mellon University. I am very much indebted to Phil Miller for the administrative support that made the course possible. John McDermott and Scott Fahlman also helped in administrative matters.

My second great debt is to Anne Rogers, who took it upon herself to edit early drafts of the manuscript. Anne was an irrepressible source of encouragement; her enthusiasm kept the book alive through some difficult times.

Gail Kaiser, Mark Boggs, Aaron Wohl, and Lynn Baumeister all taught the new Lisp course using my notes. Their feedback helped improve succeeding drafts. Gail was an especially generous contributor; I have adopted several of her exercises.

Richard Pattis, author of another fine programming text, was an able publicity agent and ultimately helped me find a publisher. Abby Gelles also helped publicize the book.

Loretta Ferro, Maria Wadlow, and Sandy Esch kindly served as test subjects in my first pedagogical experiments. I also thank my students in the first actual Lisp course for the time and energy they put into it.

The Computer Science Department at Carnegie-Mellon provided superb computer facilities and, equally important, the intellectual environment that made this work possible. Throughout the project I was most fortunate to be supported by a graduate fellowship from the Fannie and John Hertz Foundation.

Introduction: Getting Acquainted

1. BEAUTY AND THE BITS

There are literally hundreds of books on the market today about how to program a computer. What distinguishes this one from the rest, besides the fact that it uses Lisp, is its treatment of computer programming as an *aesthetic* activity. The computer is not a musical instrument, but at a slightly more abstract level one could truthfully call it the greatest keyboard instrument of the twentieth century. Just as the piano allows us to create beauty in structured patterns of sound, the computer is a tool for finding beauty in information structures. Much of the beauty of computer science is mathematical in flavor, but don't be put off by that fact. Programming is very different from ordinary pencil-and-paper mathematics.

I believe there is something in common between what programmers do and what musicians do. Therefore in writing this book I have borrowed some ideas from the format of an introductory piano book.

There are two components to piano books: theory and keyboard exercises. Music theory is a mathematical description of some of the elements of music. It contains formal descriptions of harmony, chord structure, counterpoint, and rhythm. Computer science theory deals with another set of formal elements: information structures, control structures, algorithms, and representation languages.

Exercises are what convert purely theoretical understanding into demonstrable skill. There is a long way to go from understanding the properties of a theoretical piano (or computer) to getting a real one to do something interesting. Pianists and programmers put in lots of practice at their respective keyboards in order to achieve proficiency. The exercises that appear throughout this book will help you improve your own programming skills, until you are a computer "virtuoso."

2. PRACTICAL REASONS FOR LEARNING ABOUT COMPUTERS

Computer courses are one of the most rapidly growing areas in the modern college curriculum. Everyone needs some knowledge of computer basics because of the major role computers play in a technological society. Computer programming is also an excellent way to develop formal reasoning skills. People have traditionally learned formal reasoning by studying mathematics (especially geometry and logic), but for many these subjects are too difficult and tedious to be enjoyable. Programming, on the other hand, is fun—even addictive. Students can say things to the computer (in a computer language), and the computer talks back to them.

A computer that talks back helps students to explore new ideas, for they can see immediately whether the ideas work or not. Students can learn, and are encouraged to learn, by experimenting and discovering new things in a personal dialog with the machine. Computers can put animation into a subject that mere pencil and paper leave abstract and lifeless.

3. COMPUTERS ARE EVERYWHERE

Computers exist in a great variety of forms, from $10 microprocessors no larger than a thumbnail to $10 million dynamos that can easily fill a house. There are many ways the most versatile of all machines is put to use in our society. Here are a few:

- *Data Processing.* Perhaps the most well-known computer application, data processing is the primary purpose for which businesses buy computers. Computers are used to automate routine paperwork by doing such things as recording customer orders, sending out bills, managing inventory, printing paychecks, and keeping personnel records.

- *Embedded Applications.* Small computers are often placed inside other machines, such as video games, pocket calculators, electronic banking machines, and programmable microwave ovens. Even some cars now include a computer: it controls carburetion, assures even braking, and provides for a more informative instrument panel.

- *Communication.* Our telephone system would be impossible without computer-controlled switching equipment. Computers also run communications satellites and electronic communication networks. One such network, the ARPANET, spans half the globe and connects over a hundred universities, research centers, and government installations. A person with access to this network can send electronic mail to anyone else on the network in just seconds, instead of the days it takes for regular mail. Airline reservation systems are another example of how computers make communication speedier.

- *Text Processing.* Computers have revolutionized the process of composing and editing text. Far more versatile than an ordinary typewriter, a computerized "word processor" lets an author correct misspellings, change wording, and cut and paste sentences or even entire paragraphs simply by pushing a button. By the way: The page you're reading now was composed, edited, typeset, and printed using a network of cooperating computers.

- *Information Retrieval.* Computers are very good at searching through a large body of information quickly. Major libraries have links to computers that can electronically search a database of medical or legal abstracts. Tens of thousands of entries can be examined in a few minutes, saving researchers many hours of manual work. Similar information retrieval techniques are used by large businesses or utility companies to immediately retrieve a customer's record when he or she calls in with a question about service. The telephone company uses computers to help directory assistance operators look numbers up quickly.

- *Personal Computing.* As their prices keep dropping and their capabilities increase, computers are moving into more and more homes. People use home computers to play games ranging from the traditional chess, backgammon, and blackjack, to Space Invaders and Pac-Man. Home computers also do useful things such as budget planning and maintaining Christmas card lists. People who learn to program their own computers have an unlimited opportunity for creative play.

4. COMPUTERS AS RESEARCH TOOLS

There are several different ways in which computers can be used as research tools. These may be classified as processing data, viewing data, and producing data.

An example of *processing* data is statistical analysis, such as linear regression or analysis of variance. Such procedures are difficult and tedious to do by hand but can be done quite quickly and accurately by standard statistical computer programs such as SPSS or BMD.

When the computer is used to *view* data, it generates an organized view by maintaining lists in alphabetical order or generating indices or cross-reference listings on demand. Sophisticated systems now accept queries such as "list the names and addresses of all employees who work in plant #3 and make more than $15,000 a year"; the computer then selects from a large file of information only those records that satisfy the request. Another way in which computers help people view data is by generating plots and graphs automatically.

A computer can *produce* data by acting out some theory or model that a researcher is investigating. A physicist, for instance, might program a computer with detailed equations describing the behavior of a nuclear reactor. Then, after the initial conditions haven been established, the computer could solve the equations and say what the reactor would do. This is both faster and cheaper than actually building the reactor. If the physicist wanted to study core meltdowns or massive cooling system failures, a computer model might be the only way to safely conduct the research.

In practice, research computing usually involves a combination of all three of these activities.

5. COMPUTERS AND FORMAL REASONING

Formal reasoning is one way of dealing with the world around us. Other reasoning styles are not "formal," but they are equally important, such as the kinds that let us interpret poetry, invent a recipe, or mentally visualize a three-dimensional object. Formal reasoning is important because it is the foundation for modern-day science and mathematics, fields with which every educated person should be familiar.

How do we learn formal reasoning? Usually by studying logic or geometry and learning to prove theorems. A beginning student of logic might be asked to prove a theorem such as

$$((p \Rightarrow q) \Rightarrow r) \Rightarrow (p \Rightarrow (q \Rightarrow r))$$

Or, in a geometry class, the task might be to "prove that the alternate interior angles formed by a line intersecting two parallel lines are equal." The *formal* part of the process is the way in which the student is allowed to prove the truth of a theorem. One can't say, "Well, those angles look about equal in the diagram, so the theorem must be true." One can't argue from aesthetics, either, such as saying that alternate interior angles *ought* to be equal because that leads to pleasant symmetries. The only way to show formally that a statement is true is to produce a step-by-step *logical* proof that it is true.

Many people discover they have trouble proving theorems and therefore become convinced that they can't do formal reasoning. This is unfortunate, because they are cutting themselves off from a large body of fascinating intellectual material. Theorem proving is not the only way to learn formal reasoning, and it isn't even the most useful way to apply it. After all, when was the last time you needed to prove a theorem outside of a classroom? We shall consider a different approach to formal reasoning: computer programming.

In computer programming, the object is not to prove theorems but rather to write programs to make the computer do something. The difference between a program and a theorem is that a program is more lively, more animated. The computer will act out the instructions in the program, and the programmer can monitor the computer's behavior to see if it is doing the right thing.

The formal part of computer programming is in the specification of the program. Programs are written in a concise logical notation called a **programming language**. Because the computer actually interprets the program and follows out its instructions, finding mistakes in programs is far easier than finding mistakes in proofs. Also, the subject matter of elementary computer programming is generally less abstract than that of elementary mathematics, which makes programming more intuitive and easier to learn.

6. PROGRAMS ARE DESCRIPTIONS

A computer program is a *description* of something. For instance, a program can be a description of a *procedure*. Suppose we needed a procedure for making toast. If our instructions were to be read by a human being, they could be very informal. We might describe the "make toast" procedure as:

1. Go to the breadbox.
2. Remove as many slices of bread as you want pieces of toast.
3. Put the bread in the toaster and press the handle down.
4. Wait for the toast to pop up.

Any intelligent person could follow this procedure, but a computer cannot because the procedure is too vague. For example, the procedure doesn't tell how to recognize a breadbox or a toaster if you've never seen one before. It doesn't say what to do if the toaster is not plugged in. It doesn't say what to do if you want four slices of toast but the toaster can only hold two. And it doesn't say what to do if you want dark toast but the toaster produces light toast. In fact, it doesn't even say what "toast" is!

The procedures we write in Lisp will deal with abstract things called numbers and symbols, not toasters and pieces of bread, but the point is the same: our descriptions must be precise and complete if the computer is to follow them properly.

Another possible answer to the question "What do programs describe?" is that programs describe machines. Suppose we construct a computer program to figure income tax. We could think of that program as a description of a hypothetical *income-tax-figuring machine*. A computer, then, is just a general-purpose machine that can act like any special-purpose machine, given an adequate description of the special-purpose machine.

Whether we view programming as procedure-writing or machine-building, our descriptions must be carefully thought out if the computer is to interpret them successfully. Programming languages, unlike ordinary human languages, are specially designed for writing precise (yet concise) descriptions.

7. ARTIFICIAL INTELLIGENCE: CAN MACHINES REALLY THINK?

Back in the fifties and sixties it was fashionable to refer to computers as "electronic brains." This makes about as much sense as calling an automobile "mechanical feet." Today's computers, even the very largest models, are childishly simple when compared with the human brain. They do not think, feel, or experience the world any more than an automobile does—they simply calculate things, like super-fast adding machines, and display the results.

This does not mean that computers are fundamentally incapable of thought. Whether they are or not is a topic of much heated debate. However, none of the computers that exist today are anywhere near large enough or complex enough for there to be serious consideration given to their sentience.

The field of artificial intelligence, a subdiscipline of computer science, is concerned with making computers do intelligent things such as play chess, understand spoken language, solve puzzles, or diagnose diseases. Today's computers can do all of these things (with varying degrees of success), but "thought," in the deep significant human sense, is beyond them.

Exercises

1. List five ways you use or come in contact with computers in your daily life.

2. Walk into your nearest computer store (any Sears or Radio Shack will do) and ask the salesperson why you should buy a home computer. Are his or her arguments convincing? Did you buy one?

3. Consider an economist who uses a computer to model a pet theory about monetary supply. She writes a computer program, feeds it some current data, and gets back a prediction of the state of her country's economy six months from now. The prediction turns out to be dead wrong. List as many factors as you can think of that could be responsible for this.

4. Some people have argued (fallaciously) that computers will never be able to think because "after all, a computer can only do what it's told to do." Is it possible to write down a set of instructions that *tell* a computer how to think? Take a position and defend it briefly.

1 Functions and Data

1. INTRODUCTION

This chapter begins by introducing a notation for **functions** and **data**. The term data means *information*, such as numbers, words, or lists of things. You can think of a function as a box that data passes through. The function operates on the data in some way, and the **result** is what flows out.

After covering some of the built-in functions provided by Lisp, we will learn how to put functions together to make new ones—the essence of computer programming. Several useful techniques for making new functions will be presented at the end of the chapter.

2. FUNCTIONS ON NUMBERS

Probably the most familiar functions are the simple arithmetic functions of addition, subtraction, multiplication, and division. Here is how we represent the addition of two numbers:

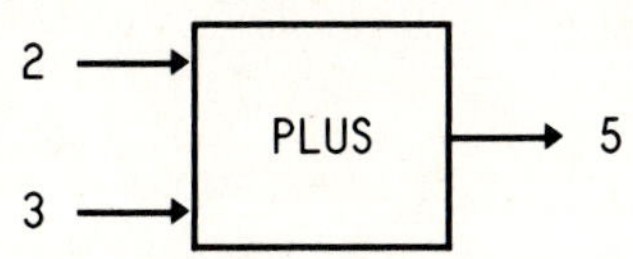

The name of this function is "PLUS." It took the numbers 2 and 3 as input and produced 5 as its result.

Here is a table of Lisp functions that do useful things with numbers:

PLUS	adds two numbers
DIFFERENCE	subtracts the second number from the first
TIMES	multiplies two numbers
QUOTIENT	divides the first number by the second; returns the quotient (an integer)
REMAINDER	divides the first number by the second; returns the remainder
ADD1	adds one to a number
SUB1	subtracts one from a number

Let's look at another example of how data flows through a function:

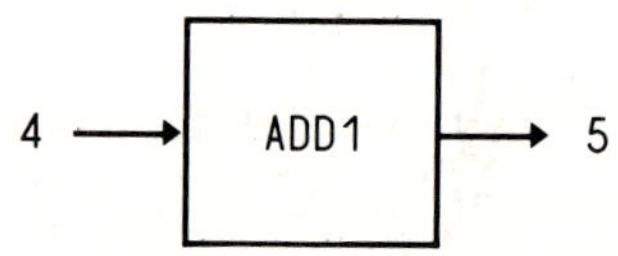

The number 4 enters ADD1, which adds 1 to it (just as the name says) to produce a result of 5.

3. INTEGER DIVISION

In this book we will work only with integers (whole numbers). When we divide one integer by another, we always get an integer result. If there is a remainder from the division, it is discarded. However, the REMAINDER function can be used to compute the remainder. Example:

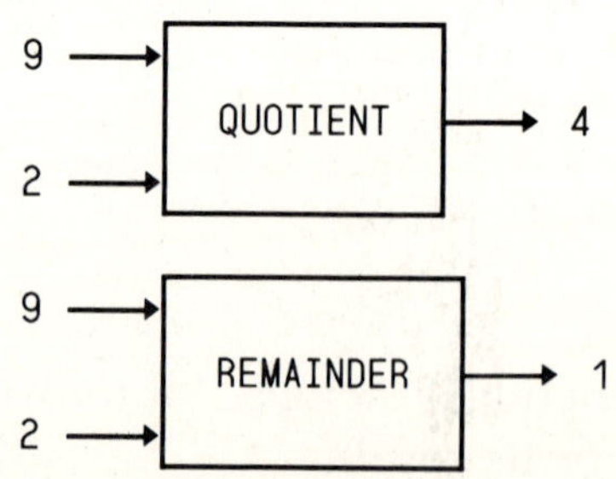

4. ORDER OF INPUTS IS IMPORTANT

The pieces of data that flow into a function are called **inputs**, and the result of the function is called its **output**. The order in which inputs are supplied to a function can be important. For example, dividing 9 by 2 is not the same as dividing 2 by 9:

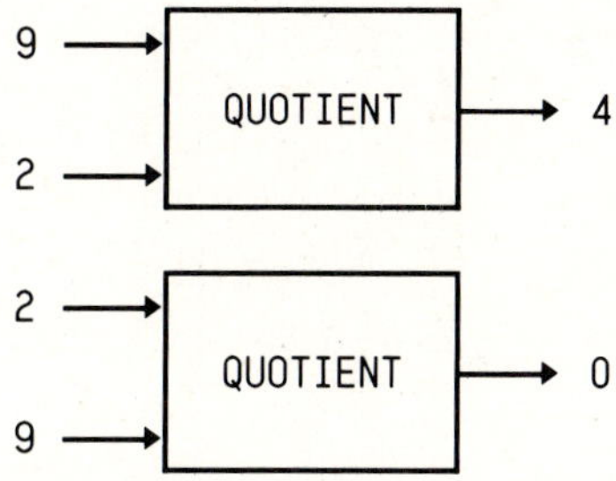

When we divide 9 by 2 we get 4 (with a remainder of 1). When we divide 2 by 9 we get 0 (with a remainder of 2).

Exercise

Here are some function boxes, with inputs and outputs. In each case one item of information is missing. Use your knowledge of arithmetic to fill in the missing item:

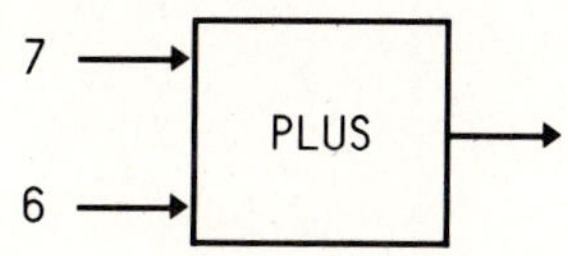

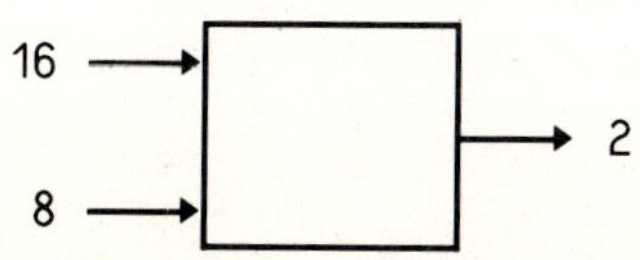

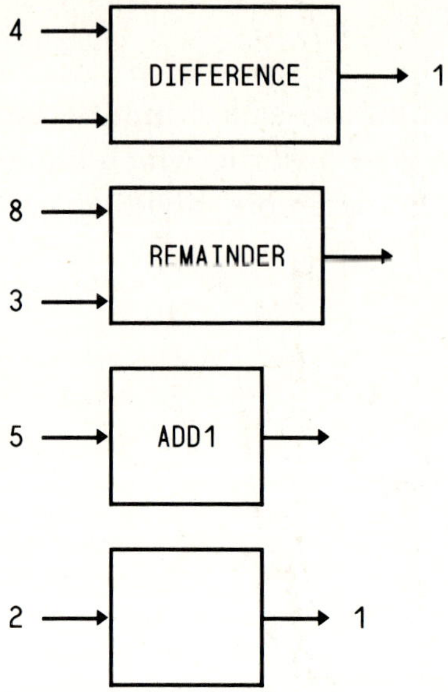

Here are a few more challenging problems. Remember that the **QUOTIENT** function always returns an integer. I'll throw in some negative numbers just to make things interesting.

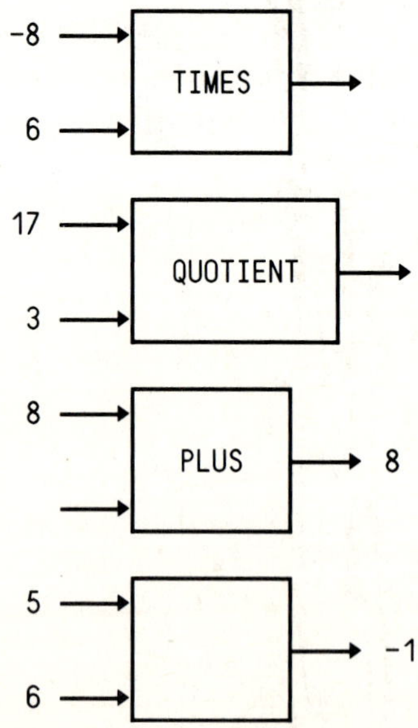

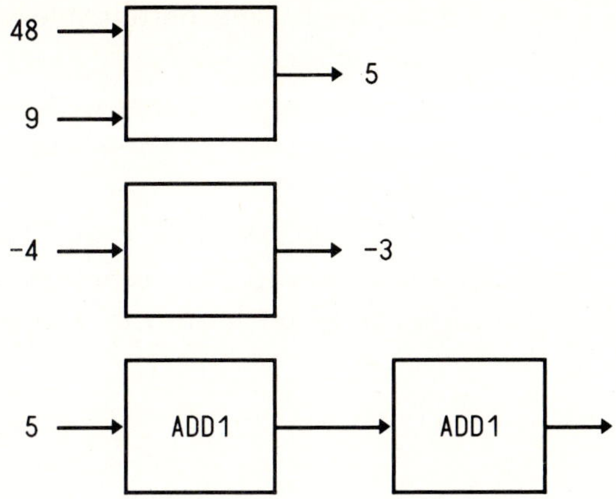

5. SYMBOLS

Symbols are another type of data in Lisp and are more interesting than numbers. We can use symbols to represent manys kinds of things: English words, people's names, even the names of Lisp functions. Symbols are made up of combinations of letters and numbers plus a few special characters such as hyphens. Here are some examples of Lisp symbols:

A	R2D2
ZORCH	BANANAS
NANOO-NANOO	COMPUTER
MARYANNE	WARP-ENGINES
ADD1	TUESDAY
YEAR-TO-DATE	XYZZY

and even

ANTIDISESTABLISHMENTARIANISM

Notice that symbols may include digits in their names, as in "ADD1" or "R2D2," but this does not make them numbers. It is important that you be able to tell the difference between a number and a symbol.

number A sequence of digits "0" through "9," or such a sequence preceded by a plus sign or a minus sign.

symbol Any sequence of letters, digits, and permissible special characters that is not a number.

Exercise

Next to each of the following, put an "S" if it is a symbol or an "N" if it is a number. Remember: English words may sound like numbers, but a true Lisp number contains only the digits 0–9, with an optional sign.

_______ AARDVARK
_______ 87
_______ PLUMBING
_______ 1–2–3–GO
_______ 1492
_______ 314159265358979
_______ TIMES
_______ ZEROP
_______ ZERO
_______ 0
_______ −12
_______ SEVENTEEN

6. THE SPECIAL SYMBOLS T AND NIL

Two Lisp symbols have special meanings attached to them. They are:

`T` truth, "yes"
`NIL` falsehood, emptiness, "no"

T and NIL are so basic to Lisp that if you ask a really dedicated Lisp programmer a yes-or-no question, he may answer with T or NIL instead of English. ("Hey, Jack, want to go to dinner?" "NIL. I just ate.") More important, certain Lisp *functions* answer questions with T or NIL. Such yes-or-no functions are called **predicates**.

7. SOME SIMPLE PREDICATES

A predicate is a question-answering function. Predicates output the symbol T when they mean *yes* and the symbol NIL when they mean *no*. The first predicate we will study is the one that tests whether its input is a number or not. It is called NUMBERP (pronounced "number-pee," as in "number predicate") and it looks like this:

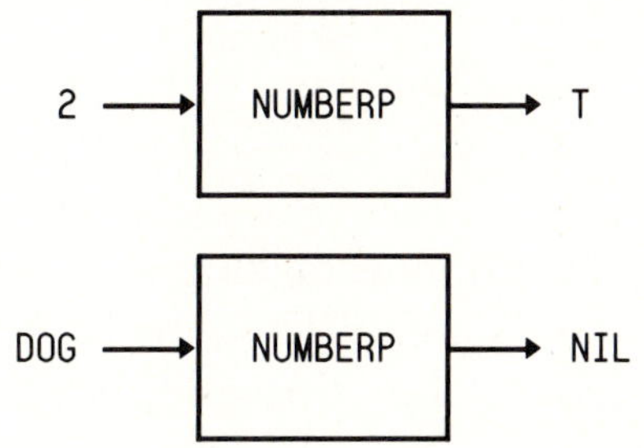

Similarly, the SYMBOLP predicate tests whether its input is a symbol. SYMBOLP returns T when given an input that is a symbol; it returns NIL for inputs that are not symbols.

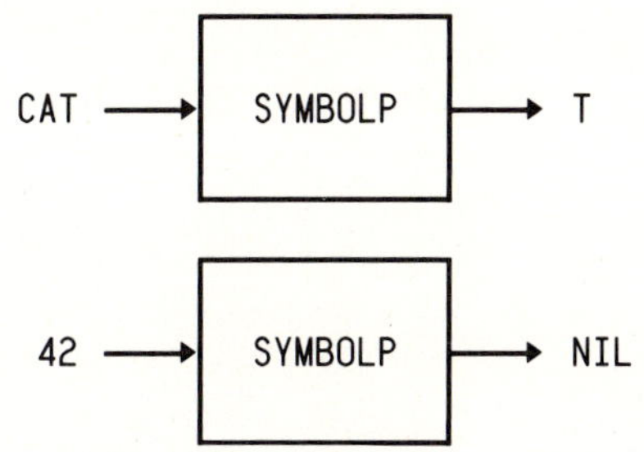

ZEROP and ODDP are two predicates that work only on numbers. ZEROP returns T if its input is zero. ODDP returns T if its input is an odd number.

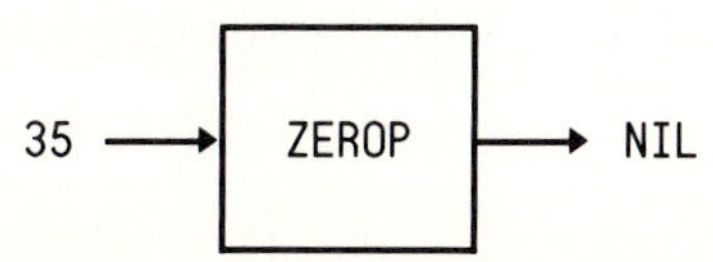

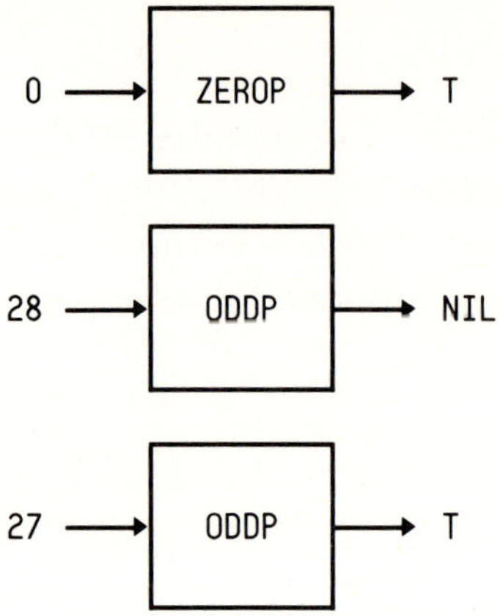

By now you've caught on to the convention of tacking a "P" onto a function name to show that it is a predicate. ("Hey, Jack, HUNGRYP?" "T, I'm starved!") Not all predicates obey this rule, but many do.

Here are two more predicates: LESSP returns T if its first input is less than its second, while GREATERP returns T if its first input is greater than its second.

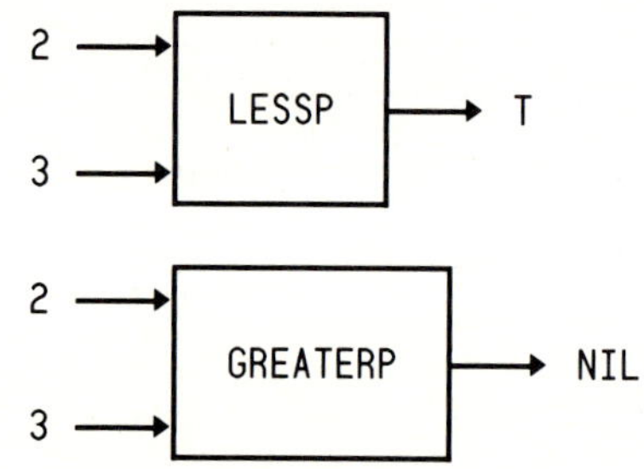

8. THE EQUAL PREDICATE

EQUAL is a predicate for comparing two things to see if they are the same. (EQUAL is also our first exception to the convention that predicate names end with a "P.") EQUAL returns T if its two inputs are equal; otherwise it returns NIL.

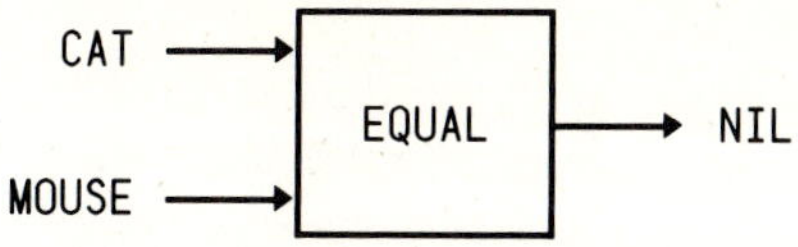

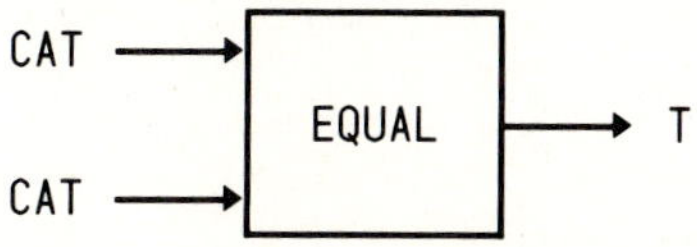

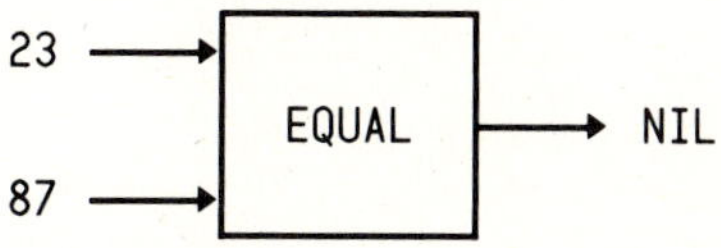

Exercise

Fill in the result of each computation:

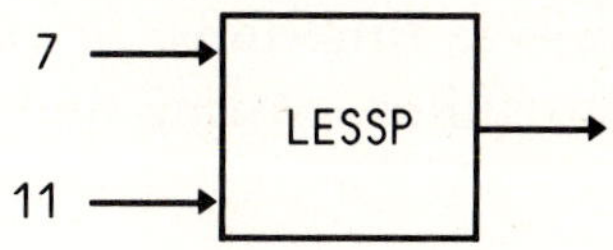

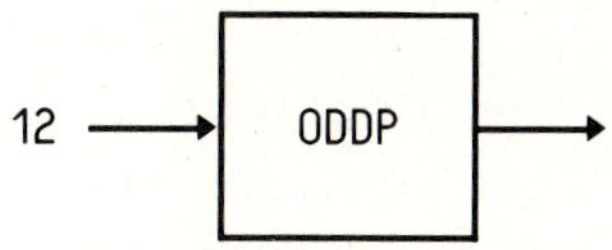

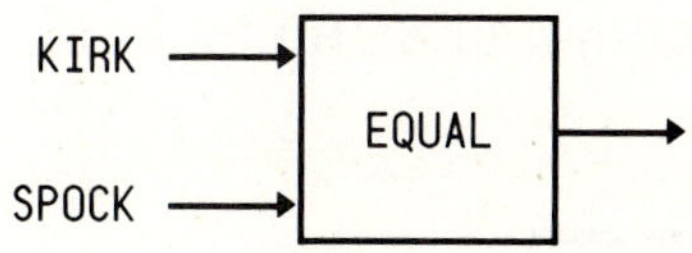

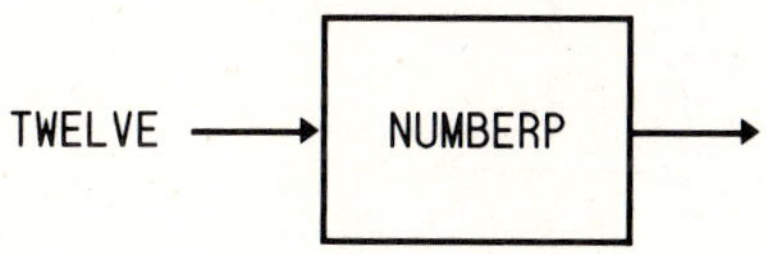

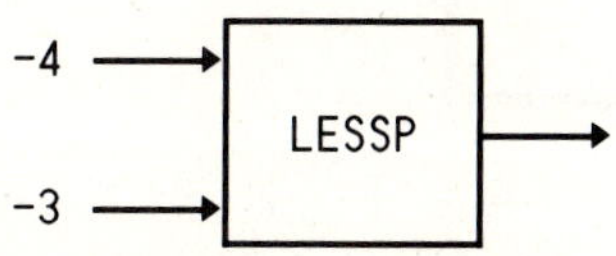

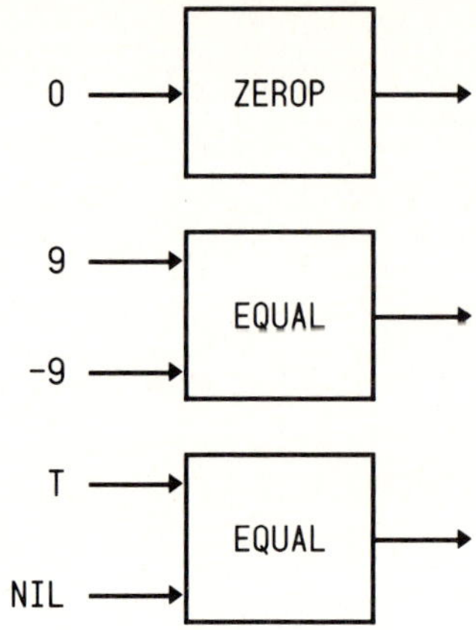

9. PUTTING FUNCTIONS TOGETHER

So far we've covered fourteen simple functions that are built into Lisp. These built-in functions are called **primitive functions**, or **primitives**. We can make new functions by putting together existing ones.

9.1. Defining SUB2

Suppose we would like to define a function that subtracts 2 from its input. We have a primitive function that subtracts 1—it's called SUB1—so if we put two SUB1's together, we'll have a function that subtracts 2. We'll call it SUB2. The definition of SUB2 looks like this:

Definition of SUB2:

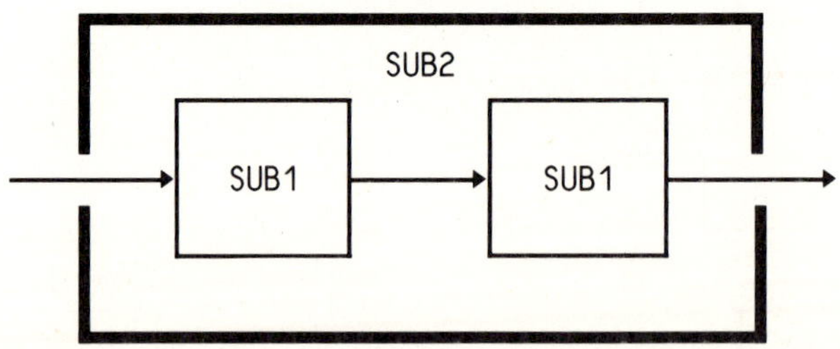

After a function has been defined, we need only write its name in order to use it. For example, since we have defined SUB2, we can now subtract 2 from 6 by writing:

Remember that the SUB2 box actually has smaller boxes inside of it; the smaller boxes are the two SUB1 functions we hooked together in SUB2's definition. Here is what the call to SUB2 looks like from the inside:

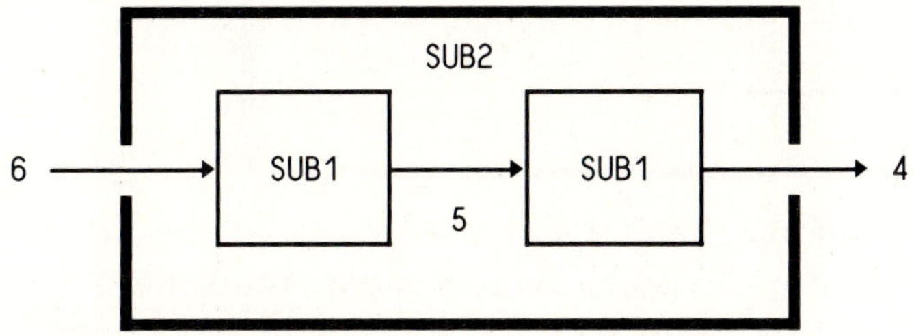

9.2. Defining ONEMOREP

Let's try defining another function. How might we define ONEMOREP, a predicate that tests whether its first input is exactly one greater than its second input? Here is one way:

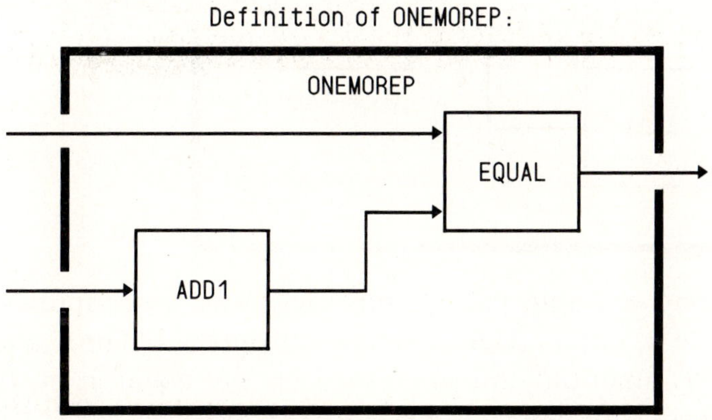

Do you see how ONEMOREP works? If the first input is one greater than the second input, adding 1 to the second input should make the two equal. In this case, the EQUAL predicate will return T. On the other hand, if the first input to ONEMOREP isn't one greater than the second input, the inputs to EQUAL won't be equal, so it will return NIL. Example:

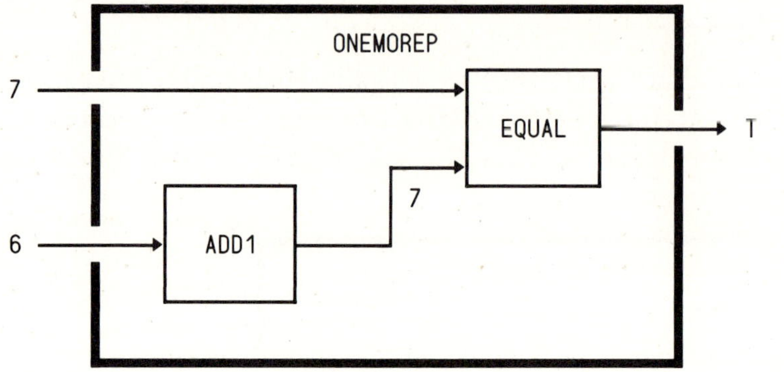

In your mind (or out loud if you prefer), trace the flow of data through ONEMOREP for the preceding example. You should say something like this: "The first input is a 7. The second input, a 6, enters ADD1, which outputs a 7. The two 7's enter the EQUAL function, and since they *are* equal, it outputs a T. T is the result of ONEMOREP." Here is another example to trace:

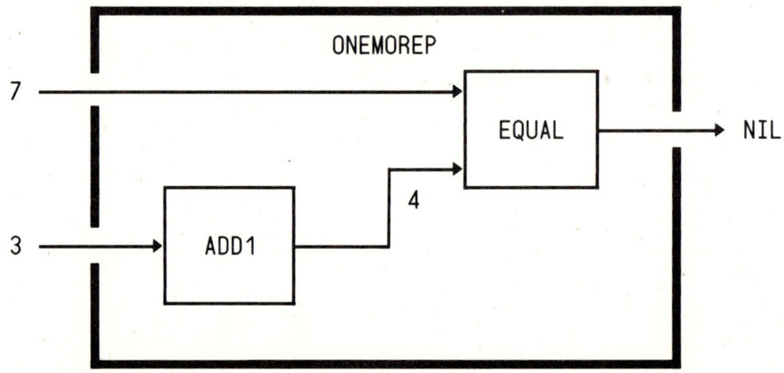

For this second example you should say, "The first input is a 7. The second input, a 3, enters ADD1, which outputs a 4. The 7 and the 4 enter the EQUAL function, and since they *are not* equal, it outputs a NIL. NIL is the result of ONEMOREP."

9.3. Using Constants in Functions

A **constant** is a piece of data that is built into a function, rather than being supplied as an input to it. For example, suppose we wanted to make a function called HALF that divided its input by 2. HALF should take only one input, the number to be halved, but the QUOTIENT primitive must receive *two* inputs. The second input to QUOTIENT is the constant 2 that appears inside the HALF function.

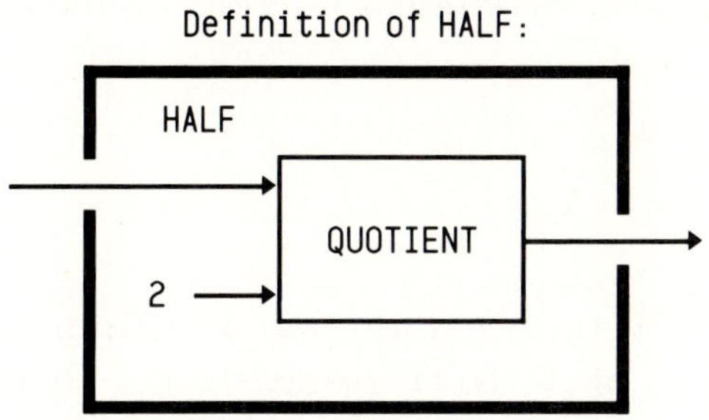

Here are some examples of HALF:

Exercises

1. Write a predicate TWOMOREP that returns T if its first input is exactly two more than its second input. Use the ADD2 function in your definition of TWOMOREP. Since ADD2 is not built into Lisp, you must give a definition for ADD2.

2. Find a way to write the TWOMOREP predicate using SUB2 instead of ADD2.

3. If we reached into the definition of HALF and changed the constant 2

to 3, we'd have a function we could call THIRD. What would we have if we changed the constant to be negative one?

4. Write the ADD50 function, which adds 50 to its input.

5. Write a POSITIVEP predicate that returns T if its input is greater than 0.

6. Write the predicate FREDP, which returns T if its input is the symbol FRED.

10. THE NOT PREDICATE

NOT is the "opposite" predicate: it turns *yes* into *no*, or *no* into *yes*. In Lisp terminology, given an input of T, NOT returns NIL. Given an input of NIL, NOT returns T. The neat thing about NOT is that it can be attached to any other predicate to derive its opposite; for example, we can make a "not equal" predicate from NOT and EQUAL, or a "not odd" predicate from NOT and ODDP. We'll see how this is done in the next section. Examples of NOT:

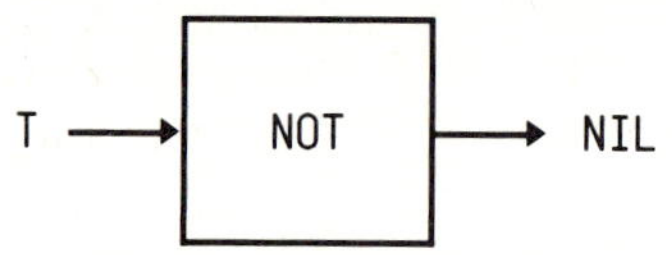

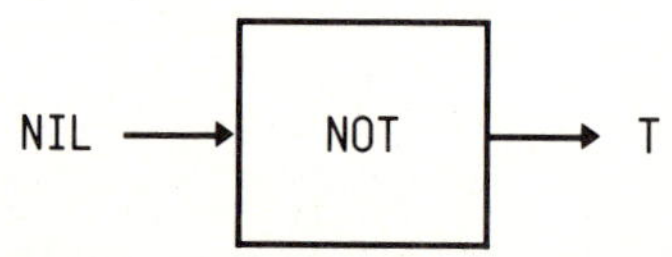

By convention, NIL is the only way to say *no* in Lisp. Everything else is treated as *yes*. Thus NOT will return NIL for every input except NIL.

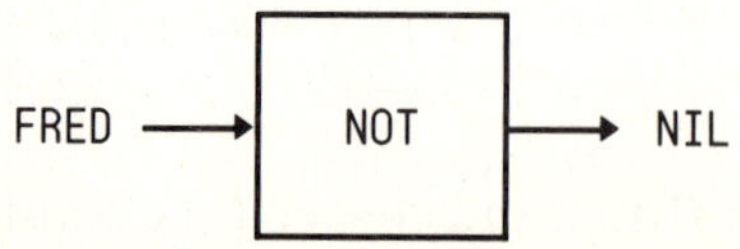

Exercises

Fill in the results of the following computations:

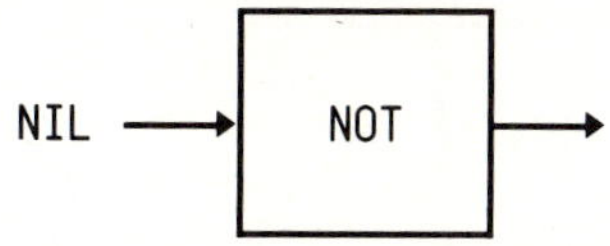

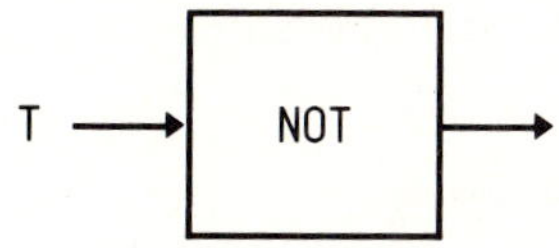

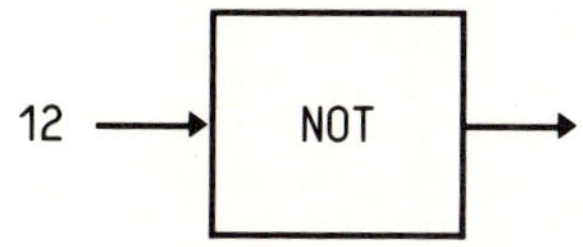

10.1. Negating a Predicate

Suppose we want to make a predicate that tests whether two things are not equal—the opposite of the EQUAL predicate. We can build it by starting with EQUAL and running its output through NOT to get the opposite result:

Definition of NOT-EQUAL:

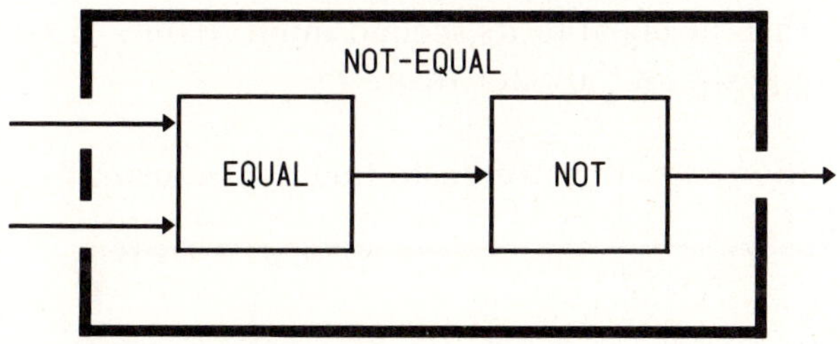

Because of the NOT function, whenever EQUAL would say "T" NOT-EQUAL says "NIL," and whenever EQUAL would say "NIL" NOT-EQUAL says "T." Here are some examples of NOT-EQUAL. In the first one, the symbols PINK and GREEN are different, so EQUAL outputs a NIL and NOT changes it to a T.

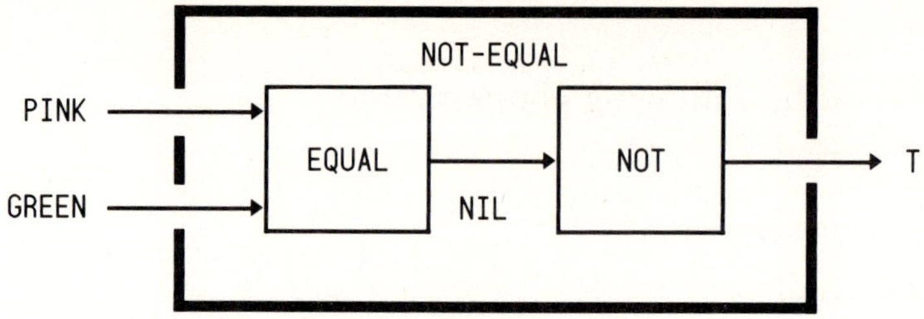

In the second example, PINK and PINK are the same, so EQUAL outputs a T. NOT changes this to NIL.

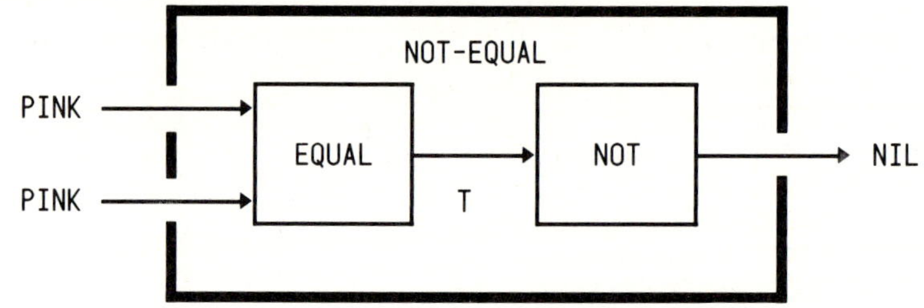

Exercises

1. Write a NOT-ONEP predicate that returns T if its input is not 1.

2. Write a predicate called EVENP that is the opposite of ODDP (it should return T if its input is an even number).

3. Write the predicate LESS-THAN-OR-EQUAL that returns T if its first input is less than or equal to its second input. (Hint: "Less than or equal" is the opposite of "greater than.")

4. Under what condition does this predicate function return T?

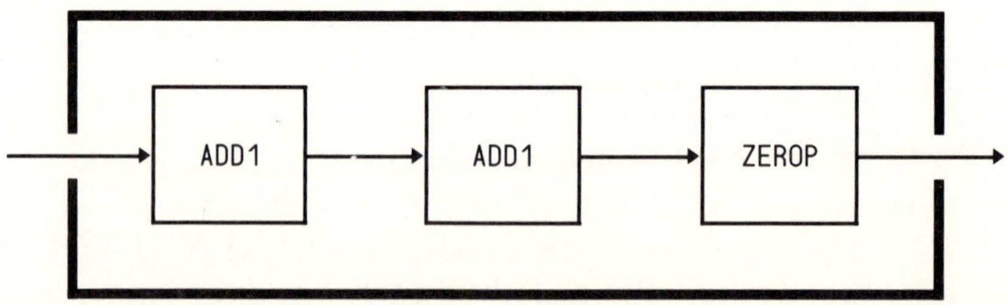

5. Consider the following function:

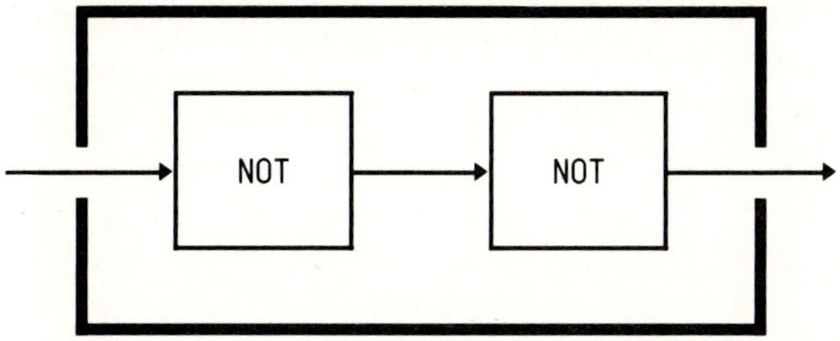

What result does the function produce when given the input NIL? What result does it produce when given T? Will all data flow through this function unchanged? What result is produced for the input RUTABAGA?

6. A **truth function** is a function whose inputs and output are truth values—that is, *true* or *false*. NOT is a truth function. Write XOR, the exclusive-or truth function, that returns T when one of its inputs is NIL and the other is T, but returns NIL when both are NIL or both are T. (Hint: This is easier than it sounds.)

11. CASCADING OF FUNCTIONS

Cascading of functions is another useful programming trick. Suppose we want to write a function that adds three numbers together. Assuming that PLUS can add only two numbers at a time, the solution is to cascade two PLUS functions together. We'll call the resulting function TRI-PLUS.

Definition of TRI-PLUS:

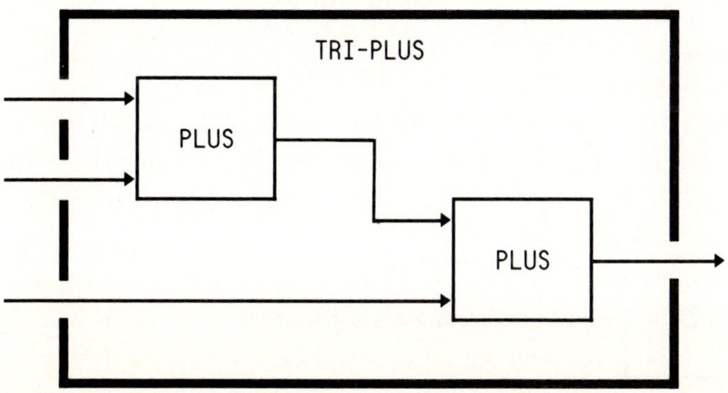

Here is an example of the use of TRI-PLUS. You should be able to use the *definition* of TRI-PLUS to sketch out the details of what goes on inside the TRI-PLUS box:

12. ERRORS

Even though our system of functions is a very simple one, we can already make several types of errors in it. One error is to give a function the wrong type of data. For example, the PLUS function can add only numbers; it cannot add symbols:

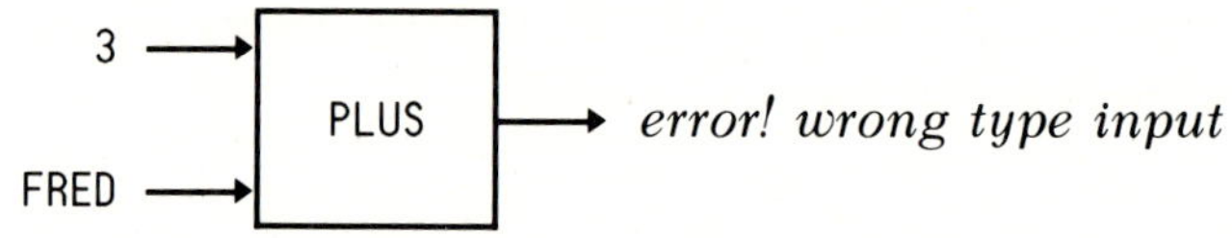

Another error is to give a function too few or too many inputs:

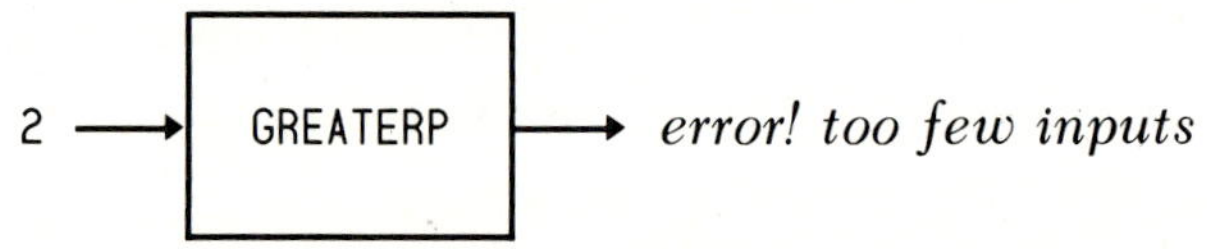

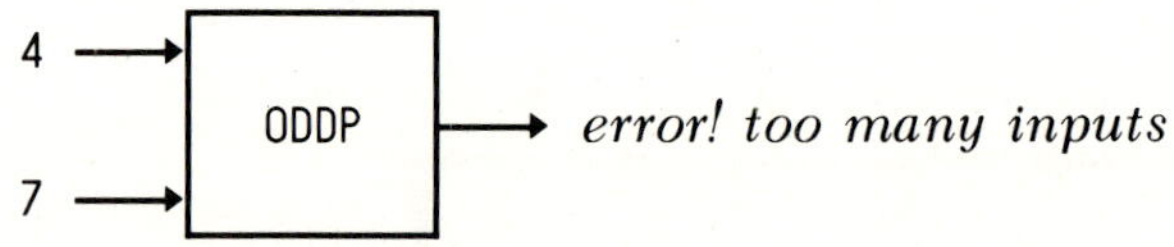

Last, an error may occur because the function cannot do what is requested of it. This is what happens when we try to divide a number by zero:

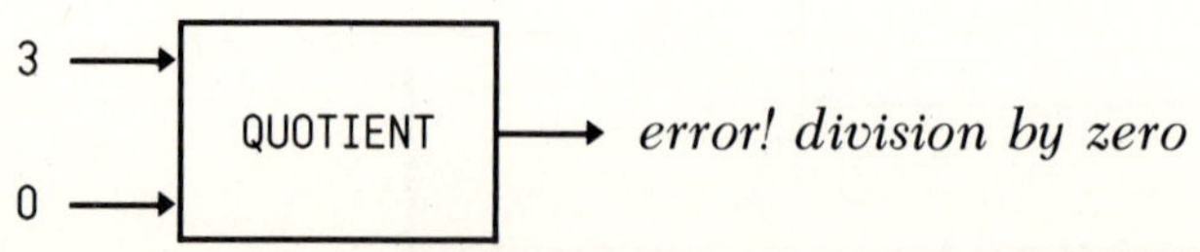

Learning to recognize errors is an important part of programming. You will undoubtedly get lots of practice in this art, since few computer programs are ever written correctly the first time.

Exercises

1. Use the cascading of functions trick to write a function that divides its first input by its second, third, and fourth inputs. Example: 120 divided by 2, then 3, then 5 yields a result of 4.

2. What is wrong with this function?

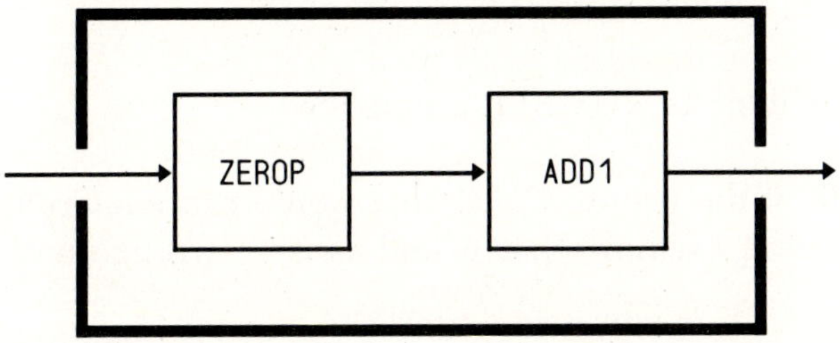

3. What is wrong with this function?

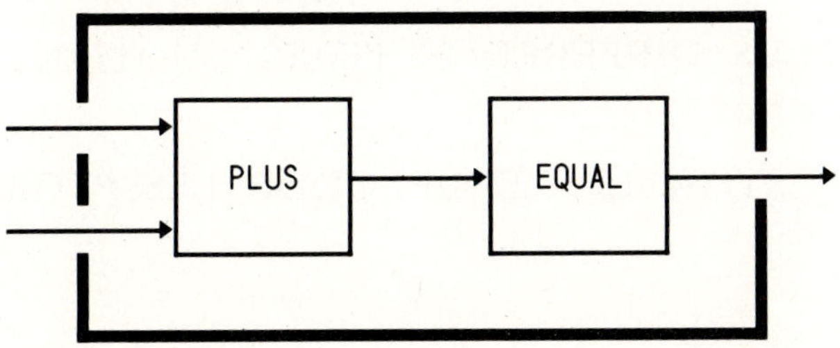

13. SUMMARY

In this chapter we covered two types of data: numbers and symbols. We also learned several built-in functions that operate on them.

Predicates are a special class of functions that use T and NIL to answer questions about their inputs. The symbol NIL means *false* and the symbol T means *true*. Actually, everything other than NIL is treated as *true*.

A function must have a definition before we can use it. We can make new functions by putting old ones together. A constant is a piece of data included in a function's definition. Two useful tricks for making new functions are (1) negating a predicate to get an opposite predicate, and (2) cascading functions to handle larger numbers of inputs.

Review Exercises

1. Are all functions predicates?

2. Which two built-in predicates introduced in this chapter have names that do not end in "P"?

3. Is SYMBOL a symbol? Is NUMBER a number?

4. Give an example of the use of ADD1 that would cause a wrong-type input error. Give an example that would cause a wrong-number-of-inputs error.

Functions Covered in This Chapter

Arithmetic functions: PLUS, DIFFERENCE, TIMES, QUOTIENT, REMAINDER, ADD1, SUB1

Predicates: NUMBERP, SYMBOLP, ZEROP, ODDP, LESSP, GREATERP, EQUAL, NOT

Advanced Topics 1

Computer programming is based on a rich tradition of mathematics and philosophy that has been developing for several hundred years. Much of this material is accessible to the beginning student. The Advanced Topics sections at the end of each chapter have been added not only to introduce advanced programming material, but also to show computer programming in its broader mathematical perspective.

1. TYPES OF OBJECTS

In Lisp, everything has a **type**. Two types of data we know about are numbers and symbols. Numbers in turn come in different types, such as integers and reals.

Another type of object we have encountered is functions. We can divide functions into subtypes too, according to the types of their inputs and outputs. For example, ADD1 is a function that takes a number as input and produces a number as output. The type of ADD1 is:

```
number → number
```

Another function of the same type is SUB1, since SUB1 also takes a number as input and produces a number as output. ODDP, however, is a different type of function. ODDP takes an integer (not any other kind of number) as input. Since ODDP is a predicate, its output is either T or NIL. We denote the type of ODDP as:

```
integer → {T, NIL}
```

GREATERP is an example of a predicate requiring two inputs. The type of GREATERP is therefore written:

```
number × number → {T, NIL}
```

Yet another type of function is exemplified by NOT. The input to NOT can be any kind of object at all. We denote this by:

```
any → {T, NIL}
```

What this notation tells us about a function is its **domain** and **range**. The domain of a function is its set of possible input values; the range is its set of possible output values. Thus, for example, the domain of ODDP is the integers, and the range of ODDP is the set {T, NIL}.

2. CLOSURE

Some functions possess the interesting property that they are **closed** over their domains. This means that any value the function produces as output is guaranteed to be in its set of valid inputs. For example, since ADD1 takes a number as input and produces a number as output, it is closed over the set of all numbers. In other words, if you feed a number to ADD1 you'll get a number back, and this number can in turn be fed to ADD1 and you'll get another number back, and so on.

Not all functions are closed over their domains. ODDP, for example, takes a number as input but produces T or NIL as output. Thus the output of ODDP is not contained in its set of valid inputs. You cannot use T or NIL as input to ODDP, because the ODDP function is only defined over the integers.

Most common arithmetic functions are closed over the set of real numbers, but some are not. Consider the reciprocal function, 1/x. This function is undefined for the input zero but is defined for all other real numbers. Moreover, the output of this function will never be zero when the input is not zero. (The output is undefined when the input is zero.) Therefore, reciprocal is closed over the set of reals *except for* zero.

Now let's consider some real-world functions. We may imagine a function called Age-of that takes a person as input and returns his age, in years, as output. For example, we might write Age-of(John) = 27. The type of Age-of would be:

```
person → number
```

Is Age-of closed over its domain? Obviously not, since the output of Age-of is a number but the input to Age-of must be a person. It makes no sense to ask about the age of a number.

Another real-world function might be Father-of—for example, Father-of(John) = Harry. The type of this function is:

```
person → person
```

Is Father-of closed over its domain? Yes, because the output of Father-of can be used as input to Father-of. The father of John is Harry, the father of Harry is Fred, the father of Fred is Elmo, the father of Elmo is Ludwig, and so forth.

In general, a function is closed over its domain if and only if its range is contained in its domain. In the case of ADD1, for example, its range (the set of all numbers) is contained in its domain (the set of all numbers), so ADD1 is closed over its domain. For ODDP, however, the range (the set {T, NIL}) is not contained in the domain (the set of all integers), so ODDP is not closed over its domain.

A function can also be closed over a subset of its domain, as long as its range for that subset is contained in the subset. Thus, while NOT is closed over **any** because its range is contained in **any**, NOT is also closed over symbols, because symbols are in its domain and {T, NIL} is contained in the set of symbols. However, even though integers are in its domain, NOT isn't closed over the set of integers, because {T, NIL} isn't contained in that set.

When talking about a function being closed, we normally give the *largest* domain over which it is closed. For NOT this domain is **any**. The smallest domain over which NOT is closed is the set {T, NIL}. For ADD1, the largest domain over which it is closed is **number**, but it is also closed over certain subsets of **number** such as the positive integers. ADD1 is not closed over any finite subset of the integers (why?), so there is no *smallest* set over which ADD1 is closed.

3. INVERSES

The inverse of a function is another function that, given the output of the first function, computes the input that would produce that output. In other words, the inverse "undoes" the effect of the original function. For example, the inverse of ADD1 is SUB1. If you give ADD1 the input 4 and it produces 5 as the result, then you know that giving 5 to SUB1 will produce 4 as the result. Similarly, if Wife-of(John) = Mary, then Husband-of(Mary) = John. Wife-of and Husband-of are inverses of each other.

Some functions are their own inverses. For example, the inverse of Reciprocal is Reciprocal, because $1/(1/x) = x$. Spouse-of is another function that is its own inverse. If Spouse-of(John) = Mary, then Spouse-of(Mary) = John.

If a function F is its own inverse, then $F(F(x)) = x$—for example, Spouse-of(Spouse-of(John)) = John. The negation function, $Minus(x) = -x$, is another function that is its own inverse. $Minus(Minus(x)) = --x = x$.

Not all functions have inverses. ODDP, for example, takes an integer as input and produces either T or NIL as a result. There is no way to go in the opposite direction, to start from T or NIL and figure out what input to ODDP produced that result.

4. FORMAL DEFINITIONS SHOULD ALSO BE CONSTRUCTIVE

When we first learned to put functions together to make new functions, the importance of an explicit definition was emphasized. The definition tells exactly *how* a function is put together, by describing the boxes and connections of which it is composed.

Consider this definition of the Square-Root function:

Square-Root(x) A number y such that $y^2 = x$.

This definition tells us exactly what the Square-Root function does; a mathematician would have no quarrel with it. But as computer programmers, we object on the grounds that it tells us nothing about how to *construct* a square root function. An adequate definition from our point of view must not only say what a function does but also how it does it.

A satisfactory function definition is one that reduces the function to a well-defined arrangement of primitives. The primitives themselves are defined a priori by the design of the computer's circuitry.

5. REAL-WORLD SENSE; COMPUTER NONSENSE

Finally, we examine some problems that arise when formal mathematical systems (like computer programs) are used to describe informal but complex real-world relations. These relations are filled with subtlety and hidden assumptions, so that while a computer program may appear to model them, the model breaks down when we take a closer look.

For instance, it might appear that Age-of is a very elementary function. All it has to do is subtract the time a person was born from the time at which his age is being measured. If a person was born on May 3, 1961, and we ask his age on May 3, 1981, for example, he is clearly twenty years old.

But what is the age of a baby an hour before it is born? Should we say that it is -1 hours old? Or should we say that the concept of age is undefined for persons who haven't been born yet?

If we programmed a computer to calculate age by subtracting time of birth from time of inquiry, we might very well get a negative number as the computed age of an unborn child. On the other hand, depending on how the computer was programmed, we might get an "error message," an indication that the programmed concept of age could not be applied to this problem. No matter what the computer said, however, its opinion on the matter would be worthless. Age is a concept defined by human beings. The most the computer can do in this case is implement whatever decision we reach about its meaning.

Here is another example of how real-world sense can become computer nonsense. We normally calculate age in years. With a little more work, we could calculate it in days instead. Getting the answer exactly right would be a bit tricky because of leap years, but it could be done. But why stop there? Using the brute power of the computer, we could calculate age in hours, in seconds, or even in milliseconds. (Wouldn't you be impressed if a computer told you that you were exactly 662,256,483,647 milliseconds old?) But this is nonsense!

The problem lies not in the computer's calculations, which we assume are accurate, but in the reduction of a fuzzy real-world concept to a rigid mathematical one. How can we define *exactly* when a person is born? We might give the time in hours with a fair degree of assurance, or even in minutes if we admit that someone whose birth certificate read "1:47 A.M." might actually have been born at 1:46 or 1:48. But the exact *down-to-the-millisecond* time that birth takes place is not defined in our culture. It is considered meaningless to speak of time of birth with millisecond accuracy; thus it is impossible to calculate someone's age in milliseconds.

This illustrates the truth of GIGO, the first law of computer programming. GIGO stands for "Garbage In, Garbage Out." In other words, if the inputs to a computer are inaccurate or ill conceived, the results are guaranteed to be equally worthless.

Exercises

1. What are the domain and range of the negation function Minus? Over what set is Minus closed? The set {0} is a non-empty *finite* set over which Minus is closed. What are some others?

2. Is NOT closed over the domain {FOO,NIL}?

3. What is the type of the EQUAL function? What is the type of TRI-PLUS, the three-input cascaded PLUS function defined in the text?

4. Why would you have difficulty writing a QUOTIENT function using only the primitives described in this chapter? What sorts of additional primitives would you need in order to write QUOTIENT?

5. In an earlier exercise we introduced the notion of a truth function—a function whose inputs and outputs are limited to T or NIL. All truth functions are predicates. Are all predicates truth functions?

6. Two functions are "the same" if for every possible input they produce the same output. It does not matter whether they have the same name or not. How many distinct one-input truth functions could there be? (NOT is an example of a one-input truth function.) How many two-input truth functions could there be?

2 Lists

1. LISTS ARE AN IMPORTANT DATA TYPE

Lisp was originally known as a list processing language. In fact, the name Lisp is an acronym for List Processor. Lists are still the central data type of Lisp. They are important because they can be made to represent practically anything, from abstract sets to English sentences. Even functions can be represented as lists, as we'll see in the next chapter.

2. WHAT DO LISTS LOOK LIKE?

Every list has two forms: a printed representation and an internal one. The printed representation is most convenient for people to use; the internal one is the way the computer stores the list in its memory.

The printed representation of a list always begins with a left parenthesis. Then comes zero or more pieces of data (called the **elements** of the list) and a right parenthesis. Here are some examples of lists in printed form:

```
(RED YELLOW GREEN BLUE)

(AARDVARK)

(2 3 5 7 11 13 17)

(3 FRENCH HENS 2 TURTLE DOVES 1 PARTRIDGE 1 PEAR TREE)
```

A list may contain other lists as elements. Given the three lists

```
(BLUE SKY)
(GREEN GRASS)
(BROWN EARTH)
```

we can make a list of them by enclosing them within another pair of parentheses. The result is shown below. Note the importance of having two levels of parentheses: this is a list of *three lists,* not a list of six symbols.

```
((BLUE SKY) (GREEN GRASS) (BROWN EARTH))
```

We can display the three elements of this list vertically instead of horizontally if we choose. Spacing and indentation don't matter as long as the elements themselves and the parenthesization aren't changed. For example, the list of three lists could have been written like this:

```
((BLUE SKY)
    (GREEN GRASS)
        (BROWN EARTH))
```

The first element of this list is still the list (**BLUE SKY**).

Here's another list of lists:

```
((JOHN F KENNEDY)
 (LYNDON B JOHNSON)
 (RICHARD M NIXON)
 (GERALD R FORD)
 (JAMES E CARTER))
```

This list has five elements. Each of its elements is a list containing a first name, a middle initial, and a last name. Thus each element is a list of three elements.

Exercise

Which of these are well-formed lists? That is, which ones have properly balanced parentheses?

```
)A B(
(A B (C
A B )(C D)
((A) (B))
(A (B (C))
(A (B (C)))
```

3. LENGTH OF LISTS

The length of a list is the number of elements it has. Length is independent of the complexity of the elements. The following lists all have exactly three elements, even though in some cases the elements are themselves lists. The three elements are shown by underlining.

```
(ALPHA BRAVO CHARLIE)

((A A) (B B) (C C))

(A (B X Y Z) C)

(FOO 937 (GLEEP GLORP))

(((ROY)) ((TWO WHITE DUCKS)) ((MELTED BUTTER)))
```

Exercise

How many elements do each of the following lists have?

```
_______   (OPEN THE POD BAY DOORS HAL)

_______   ((OPEN) (THE POD BAY DOORS) HAL)

_______   ((1 2 3) (4 5 6) (7 8 9) (10 11 12))

_______   ((ALL) FOR ONE (AND (TWO (FOR ME))))

_______   ((Q SPADES)
           (7 HEARTS)
           (6 CLUBS)
           (5 DIAMONDS)
           (2 DIAMONDS))
```

```
_______   ((PENNSYLVANIA (THE KEYSTONE STATE))
           (NEW-JERSEY (THE GARDEN STATE))
           (MASSACHUSETTS (THE BAY STATE))
           (FLORIDA (THE SUNSHINE STATE))
           (NEW-YORK (THE EMPIRE STATE))
           (INDIANA (THE HOOSIER STATE)))
```

4. NIL: THE EMPTY LIST

A list of zero elements is called an **empty list**. It is written as an empty pair of parentheses:

```
()
```

The empty list can also be written as the special symbol NIL. This is a somewhat tricky point: NIL is a symbol but at the same time it is a list. NIL *is* the empty list; we are always free to write NIL instead of (), and vice versa. Thus a list like (A NIL B) can also be written (A () B). It makes no difference which form is used.

Exercise

Match each list on the left with a corresponding list on the right by substituting NIL for () wherever possible. Pay careful attention to levels of parenthesization.

```
()              ((NIL))
(())            NIL
((()))          (NIL)
(() ())         (NIL (NIL))
(() (()))       (NIL NIL)
```

5. INTERNAL REPRESENTATION OF LISTS

Lists are represented by the computer internally as chains of **cons cells,** as in figure 2.1a and 2.1b. A single cons cell is shown in figure 2.2. It consists of a CAR half and a CDR half. CAR stands for *c*ontents of *a*ddress portion of *r*egister, while CDR, pronounced "could-er," stands for *c*ontents of *d*ecrement portion of *r*egister. (These are bits of technical jargon from the early days of computers.)

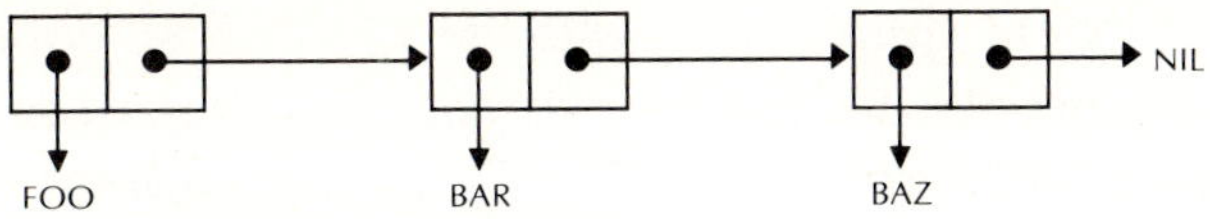

Figure 2.1a Cons cell representation of the list (FOO BAR BAZ).

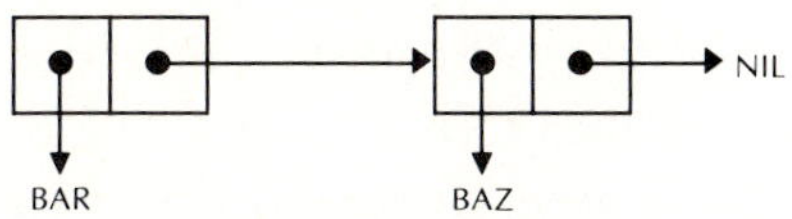

Figure 2.1b The list (BAR BAZ).

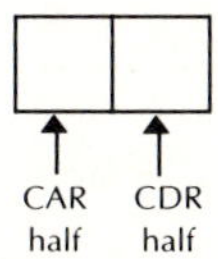

Figure 2.2 A cons cell.

In order to understand how cons cells are actually strung together into chains, we must first understand the notion of an **address.** Every piece of data, be it a number, a symbol, or a cons cell, exists at a unique location in the computer's memory. The number associated with this location is its address. Thus a cons cell can point to any object, including another cons cell, by storing that object's address in its CAR or CDR half. Stored addresses are known as **pointers.** Remember that pointers are numbers. In the computer's circuitry, then, a cons cell is just a place in memory where two numbers that refer to other places in memory are stored.

When we want to discuss the representation of some particular list, a page full of numbers makes for dull reading. That's why we draw pictures such as the one in figure 2.1a. We show each cons cell as a box with two halves (the CAR and CDR), and we draw each pointer as an arrow. This method allows us to display the internal representation of a Lisp object without having to write down, or even know, any addresses.

Figure 2.1a shows the list (FOO BAR BAZ) drawn as a chain of three cons cells. The CAR half of each cell points to an element of the list, that is, to the symbol FOO, BAR, or BAZ. The CDR half of each cell points to the next cell in the chain, or to NIL in the case of the last one.

The address of a list is simply the address of its first cons cell. Remember that NIL represents the empty list. Another way to say it is: NIL is the list consisting of zero cons cells. Thus the address of the empty list is the address of the symbol NIL.

Figure 2.3 shows the list (BUY ONE GET ONE FREE) in cons cell notation. This list consists of five elements; hence it is represented by a chain of five cons cells. As always, the CDR of the last cell in the chain points to NIL. Note that although the symbol ONE appears twice in this list, there is only a single symbol by that name stored in the computer. The second and fourth cons cells making up the list (BUY ONE GET ONE FREE) point to the same symbol.

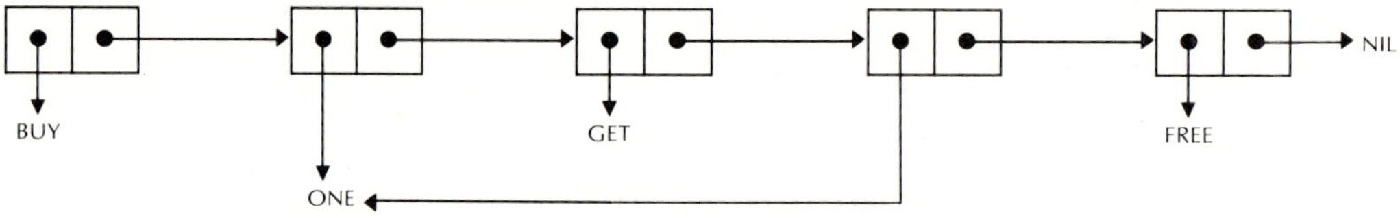

Figure 2.3 The list (BUY ONE GET ONE FREE).

We have already seen examples of nested lists in printed form. In cons cell notation, nested lists have multiple levels of cons cells corresponding to their multiple levels of parentheses. For example, figure 2.4 shows the cons cell representation of the list (A (B C) D). The second element of this list is the list (B C), represented by a chain of cons cells one level below the top level.

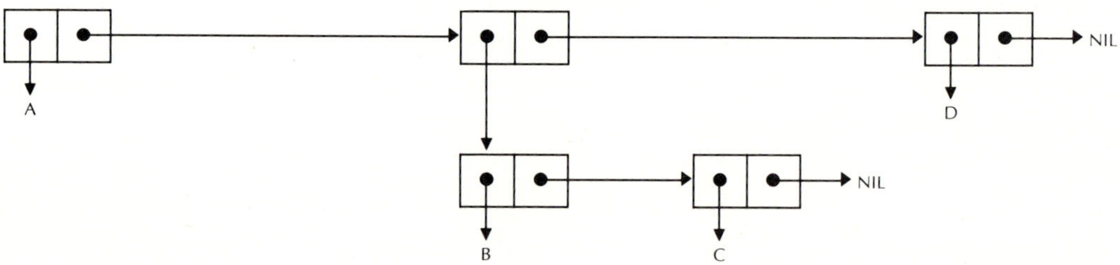

Figure 2.4 The list (A (B C) D).

Figure 2.5a shows the two lists (BLUE CUBE) and (RED PYRAMID). If we make a list of these, we get the nested list ((BLUE CUBE)(RED PYRAMID)) shown in figure 2.5b. The top level structure is a list of two elements. Each element is itself a list, in this case a list of two symbols.

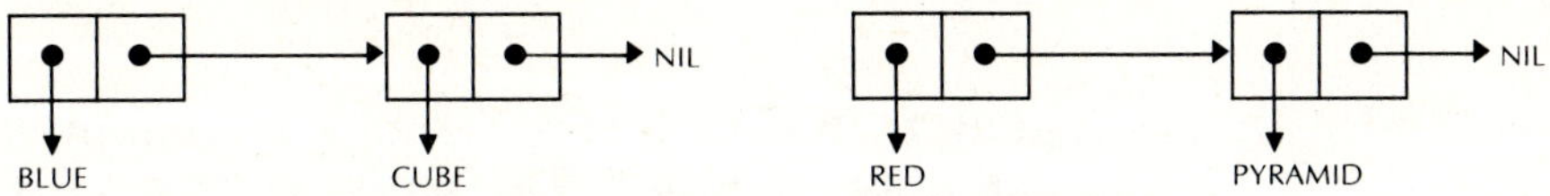

Figure 2.5a The lists (BLUE CUBE) and (RED PYRAMID).

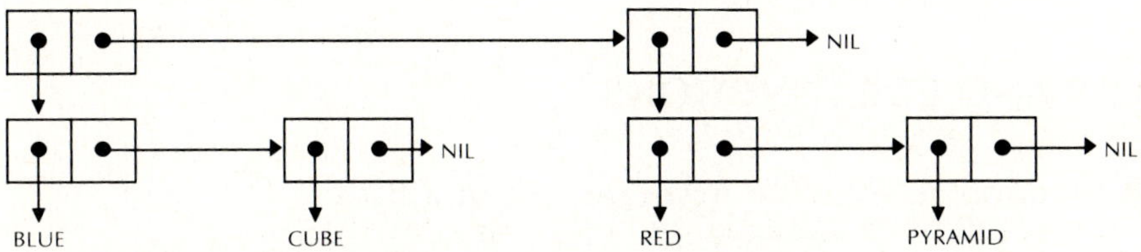

Figure 2.5b The list ((BLUE CUBE) (RED PYRAMID)).

Figure 2.6 shows how cons cell structure gets deeper as depth of parenthesization increases. The lists (PHONE HOME), ((PHONE HOME)), and (((PHONE HOME))) require one, two, and three levels of cons cells, respectively.

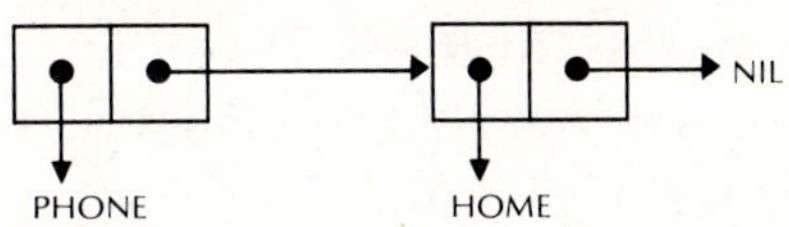

Figure 2.6a The list (PHONE HOME).

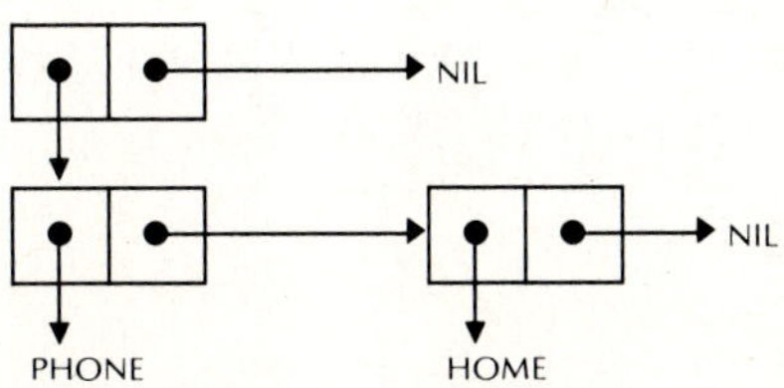

Figure 2.6b The list ((PHONE HOME)).

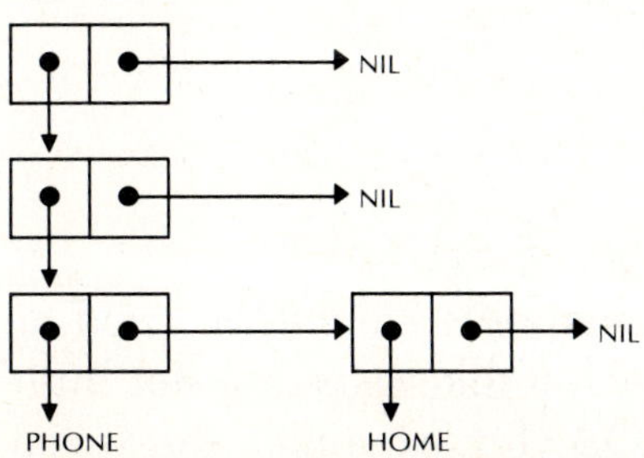

Figure 2.6c The list (((PHONE HOME))).

Exercise

Show how the list (ALAS POOR YORICK) is represented in computer memory by drawing its cons cell representation. Do the same for the list (TO BE OR NOT TO BE).

6. THE CAR AND CDR FUNCTIONS

The CAR function returns the first element of a list:

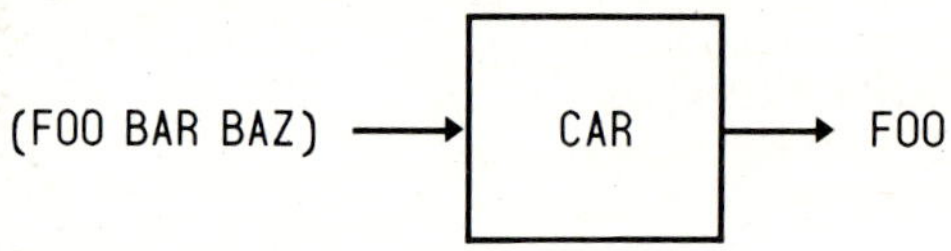

A better name for this function would be FIRST, but "CAR" is suggestive of the way the function actually works: given a pointer to a cons cell, it returns the CAR half of that cell. This amounts to returning to the first element of a list, given a pointer to the list itself. If you look at the list (FOO BAR BAZ) in figure 2.2a you will see that the CAR half of the first cons cell points to the symbol FOO.

Figure 2.7 shows the list (FROB) in cons cell notation. This list is represented by a single cell whose CAR half points to the symbol FROB and whose CDR half points to NIL. Now that you know how CAR works, you should be able to guess what CAR of (FROB) is.

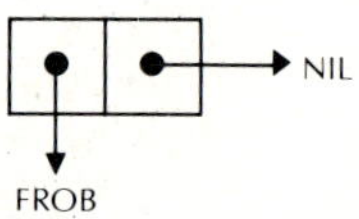

Figure 2.7 The list (FROB).

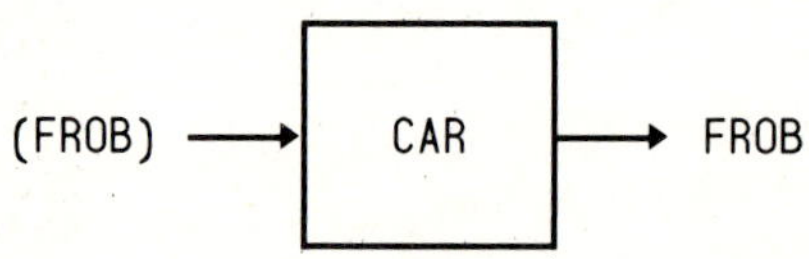

In our dialect of Lisp, numbers and symbols cannot be used as inputs to CAR because numbers and symbols, unlike lists, are not built out of cons cells. Taking the CAR of FROB, for example, causes an error.

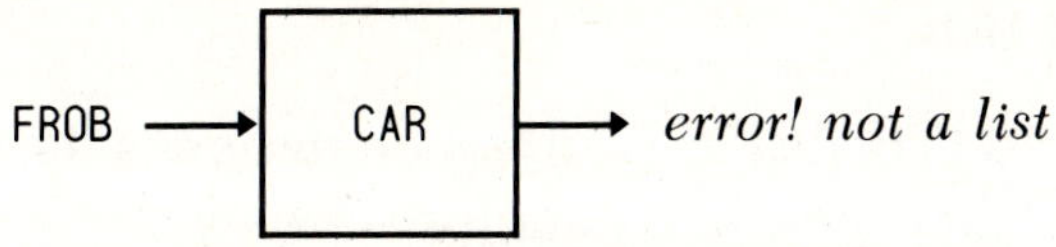

The not-a-list error is a more specific version of the wrong-type input error we saw in chapter 1. Different Lisp dialects may phrase the error message slightly differently.

The CDR function is defined analogously to CAR: it returns the CDR half of the cons cell it is given as input. CAR and CDR are complementary: if CAR were called **FIRST**, CDR would be called **REST**. In figure 2.1a, for example, the CDR of (**FOO BAR BAZ**) is the list (**BAR BAZ**). The cons cell representation of (**BAR BAZ**) is shown in figure 2.1b.

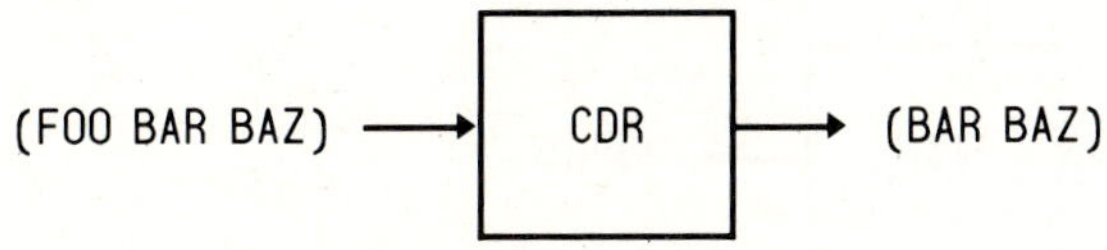

Another example:

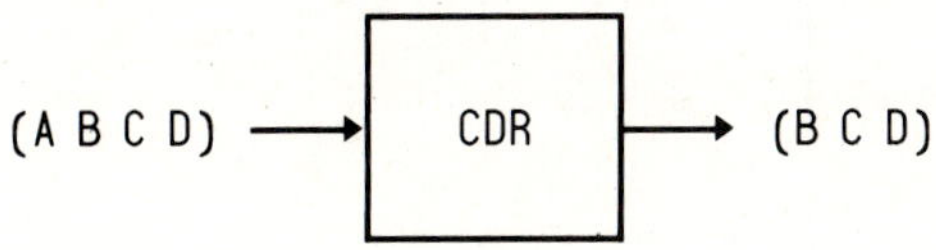

The CDR of a single-element list is the empty list, NIL. Let's take the CDR of (**FROB**), shown in the following example and in figure 2.7:

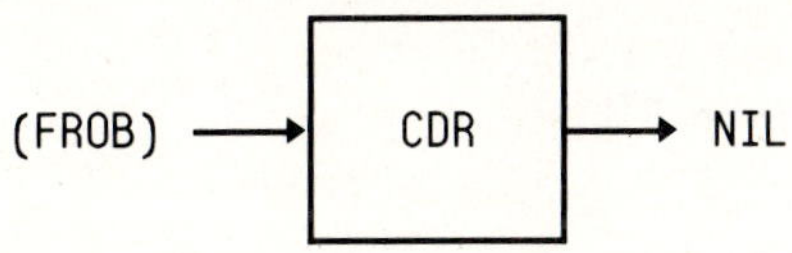

In our dialect of Lisp, CDR will not work on inputs that are not lists.

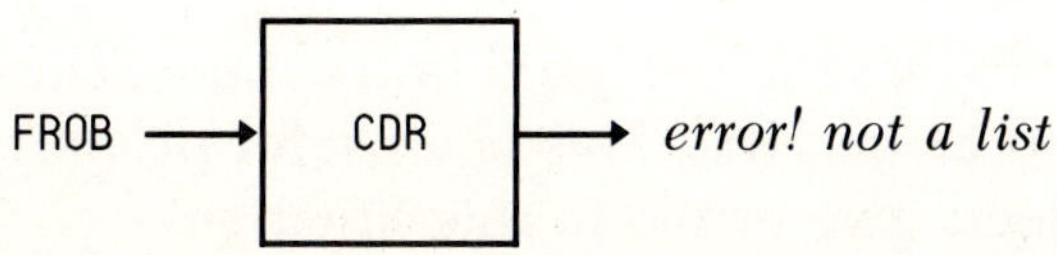

6.1. CAR and CDR of Nested Lists

CAR and CDR work on nested lists just as easily as on flat ones. Refer to figure 2.5b as you follow the first pair of examples:

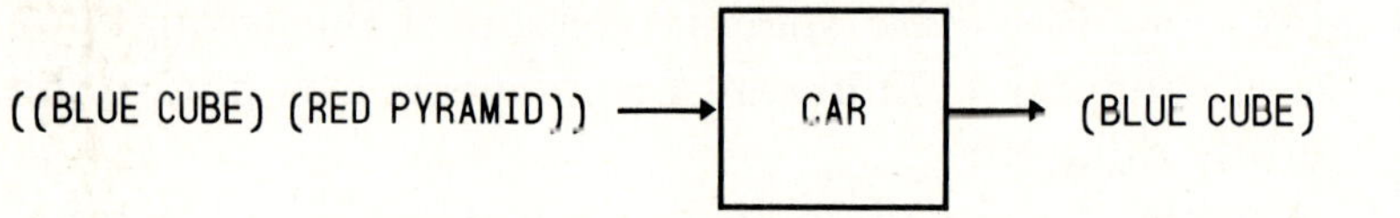

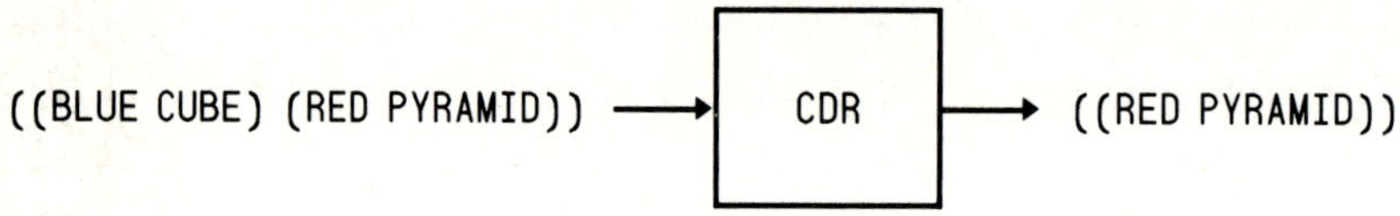

Here are two more pairs:

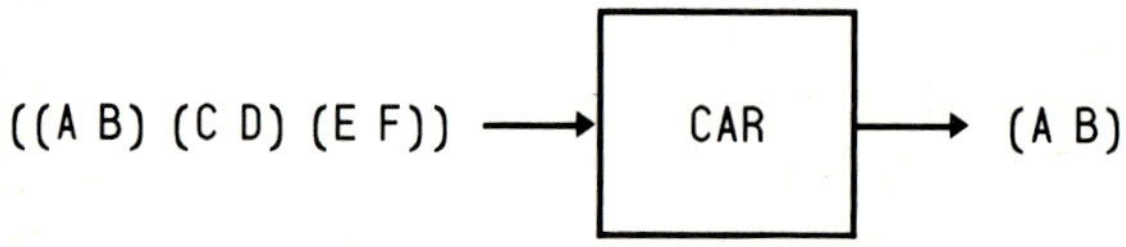

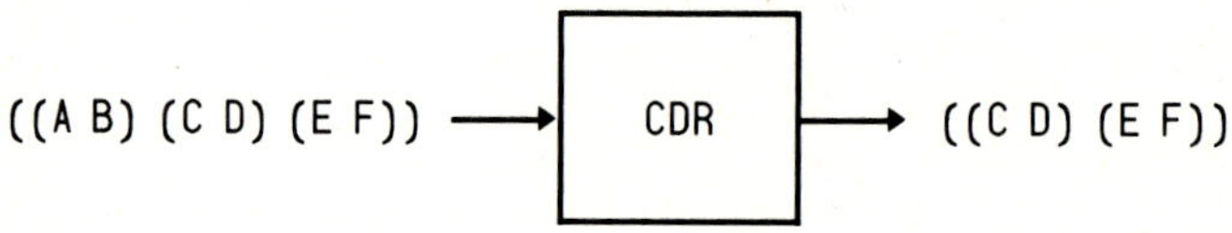

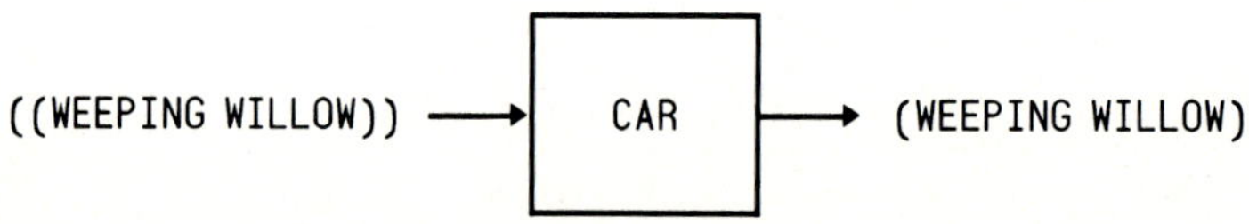

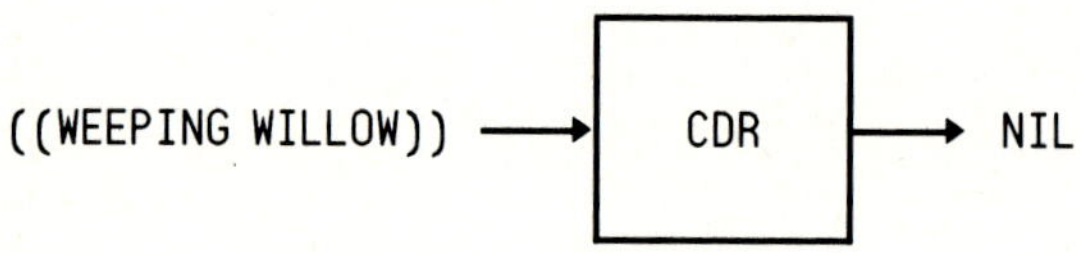

6.2. CAR and CDR of NIL

In many versions of Lisp, including the one used in this book, the CAR and CDR of NIL are defined to be NIL. This is a useful property for NIL to have. Some Lisp dialects give errors in this situation.

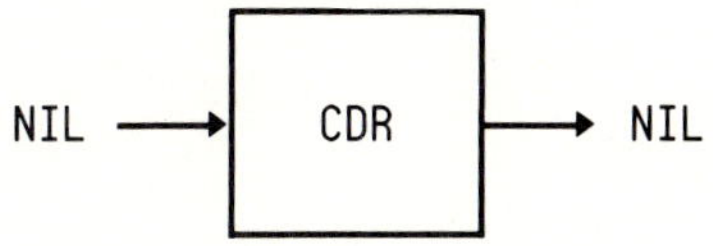

Review

The important points about CAR and CDR as they are used in this book are:

- CAR returns the first element of a list.
- CDR returns the rest of the list, that is, whatever appears *after* the first element.
- The CAR and CDR of NIL are both NIL.
- CAR and CDR accept only lists as input.

Exercise

Fill in the results of the following computations.

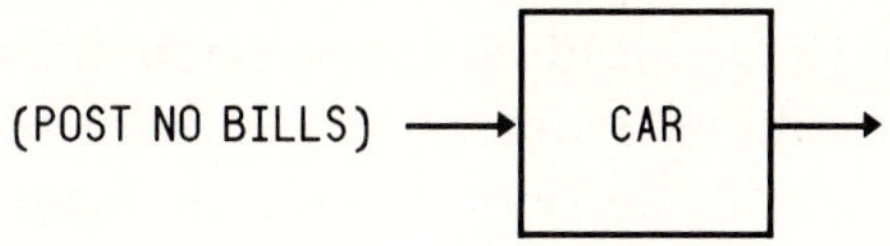

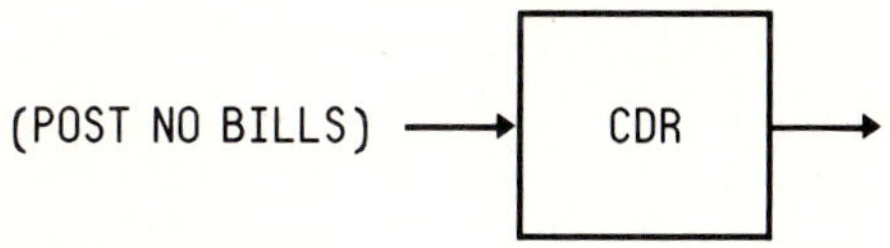

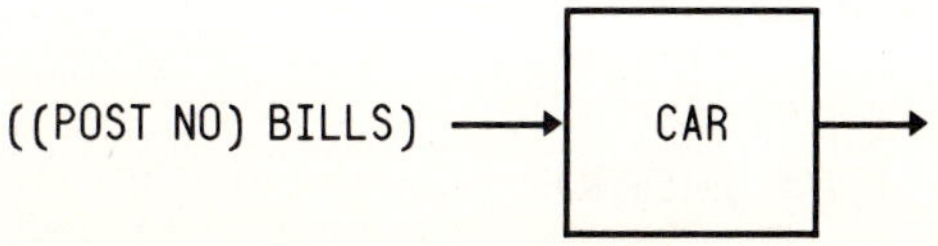

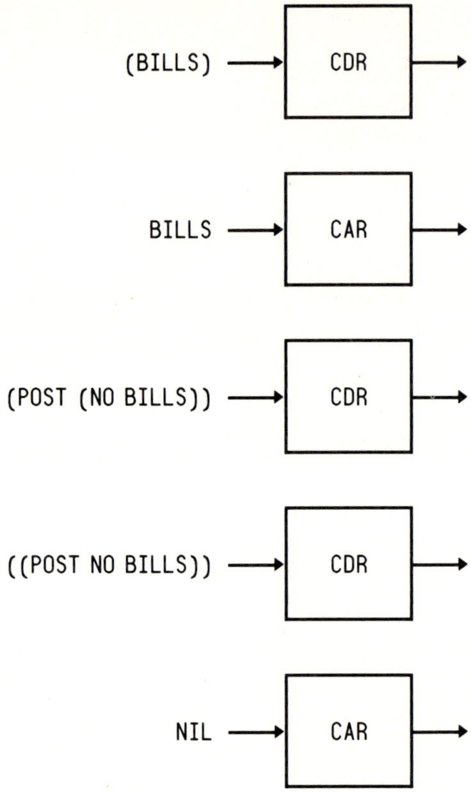

7. CONS

The CONS function is used to build new list structure. CONS is short for CONStruct. If we look only at the printed representation of lists, the effect of CONS appears to be to add an element to the front of a list. For example, we can use CONS to add the symbol A to the front of the list (B C D):

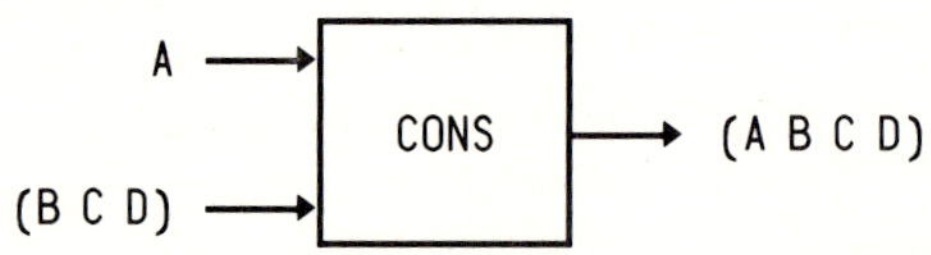

Another example: adding the symbol SINK onto the list (OR SWIM).

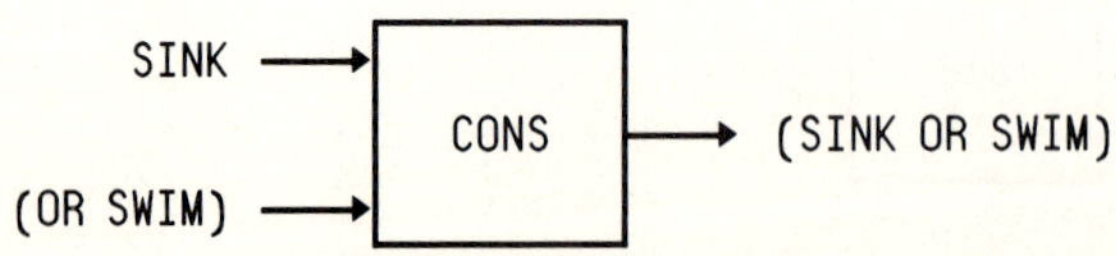

Here is a function GREET that adds the symbol HELLO onto whatever list it is given as input:

Definition of GREET:

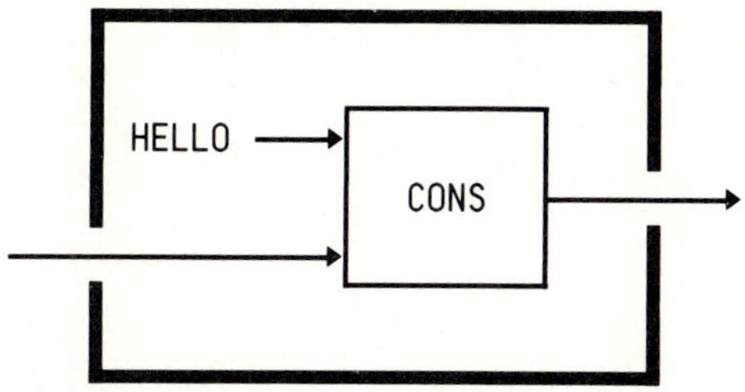

Examples of GREET:

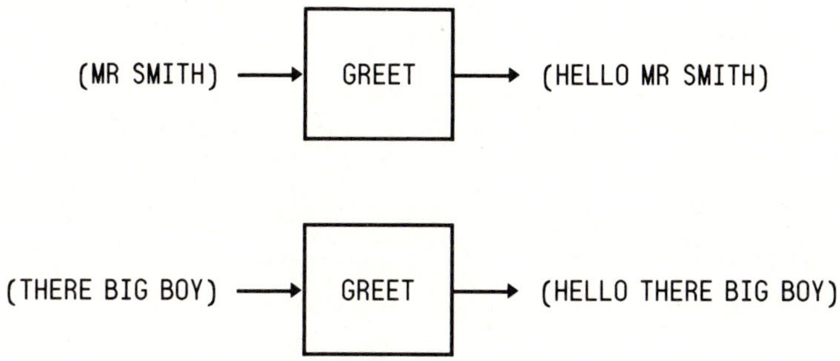

CONS actually works by allocating a new cons cell and filling the cell's CAR and CDR halves with pointers to its first and second inputs. Figure 2.8 shows how CONS generates the list (HELLO THERE BIG BOY) from the inputs HELLO and (THERE BIG BOY). In figure 2.8a we see just the two inputs to CONS. In figure 2.8b the new cell that CONS has allocated appears. In figure 2.8c CONS has filled in the CAR and CDR halves of the cell. Figure 2.8d shows the same list as figure 2.8c, but drawn in the conventional way.

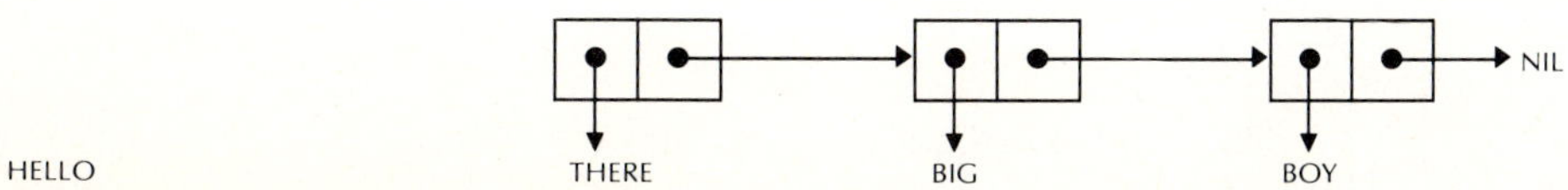

Figure 2.8a The inputs to CONS.

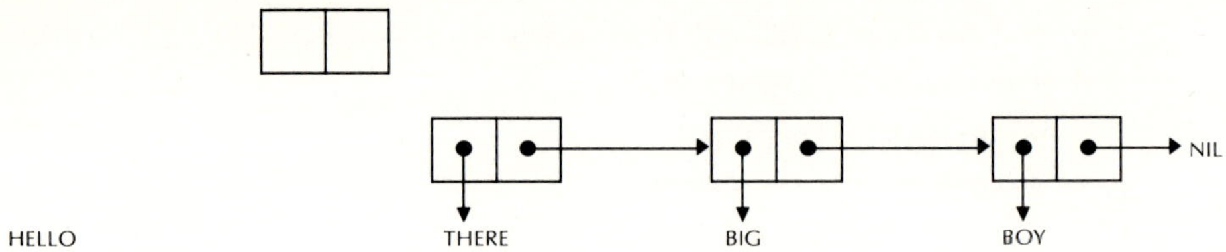

Figure 2.8b A new cons cell is allocated.

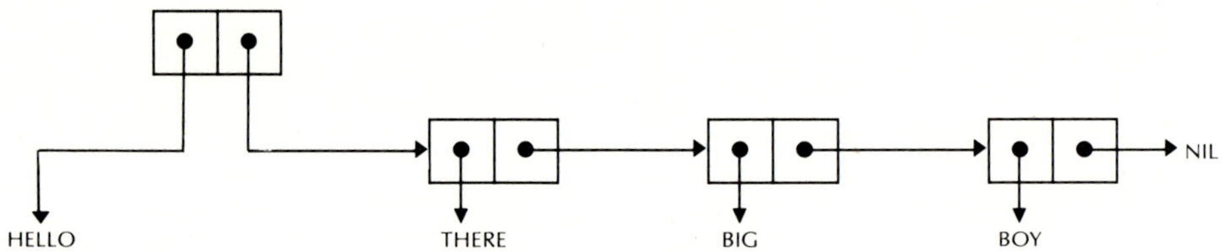

Figure 2.8c The CAR and CDR halves are filled in.

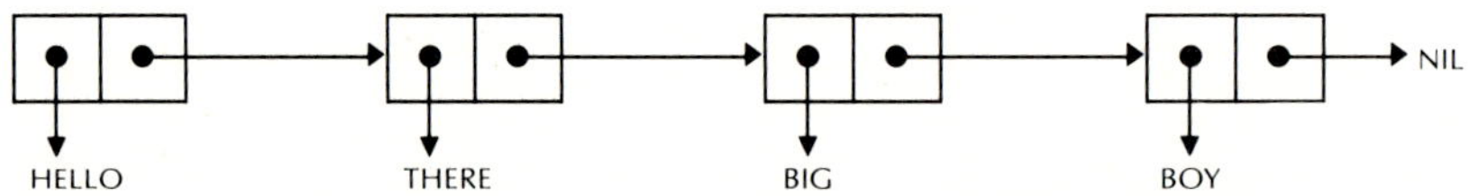

Figure 2.8d The previous figure redrawn in conventional form.

7.1. CONS and the Empty List

Since NIL is the empty list, if we use CONS to add something onto NIL we get a list of one element.

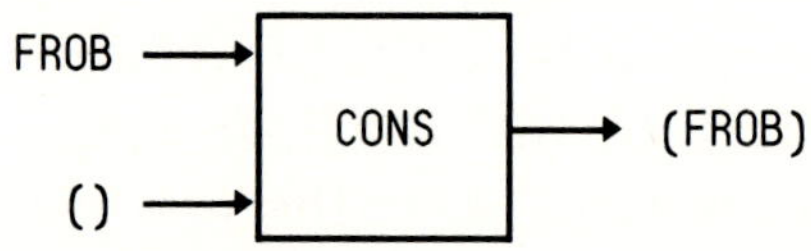

You should be able to confirm this result by looking at figure 2.7. The CAR of (FROB) is the symbol FROB and the CDR of (FROB) is NIL, so CONS must have built the list from the inputs FROB and NIL. Here's another example that's very similar, except that NIL has been substituted for FROB:

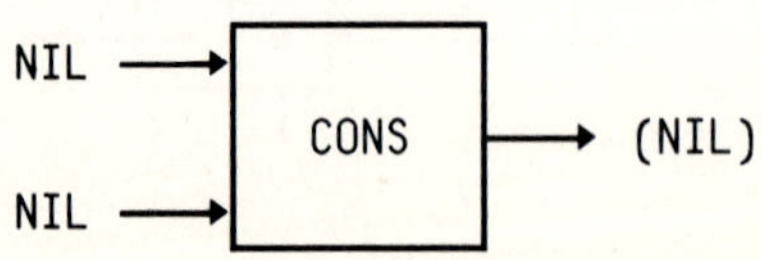

7.2. Building Nested Lists with CONS

Any time the first input to CONS is a nonempty list, the result will be a nested list, that is, a list with more than one level of cons cells. Examples:

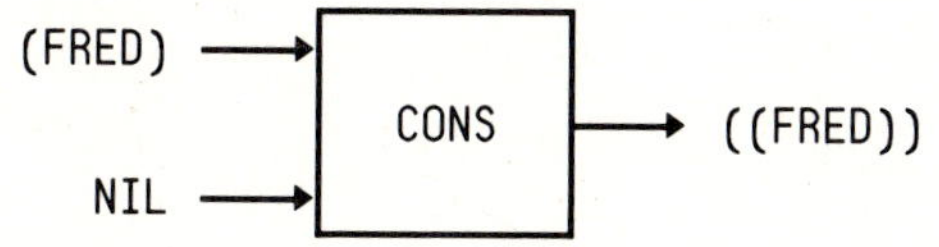

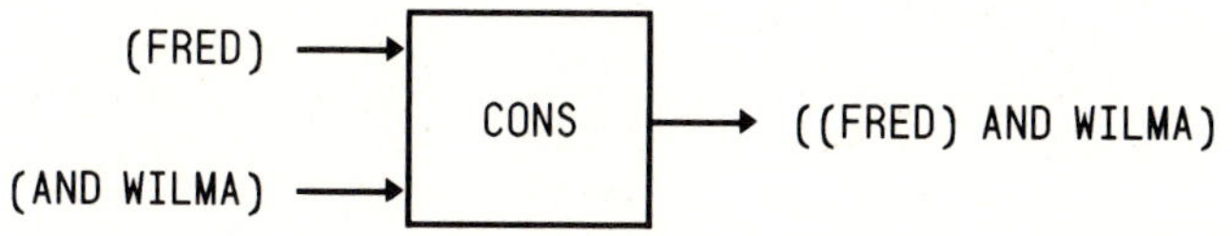

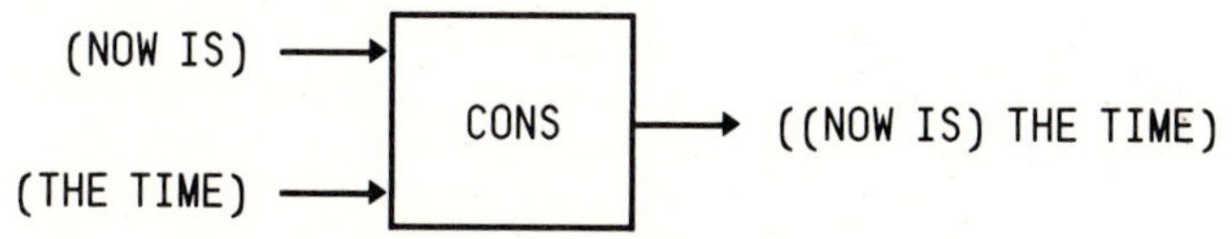

7.3. CONS Can Build Lists from Scratch

Suppose we wish to construct the list (FOO BAR BAZ) from scratch. We could start by adding the symbol BAZ onto the empty list. This gives us the list (BAZ).

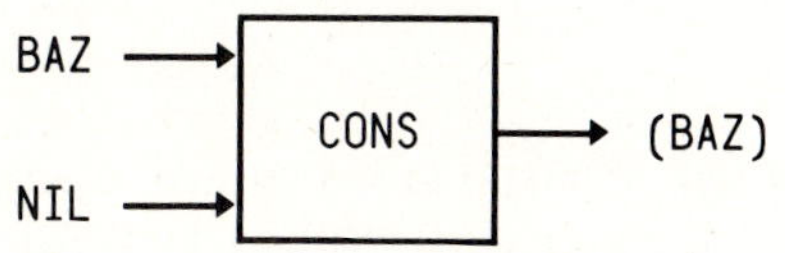

Then we can add BAR onto that:

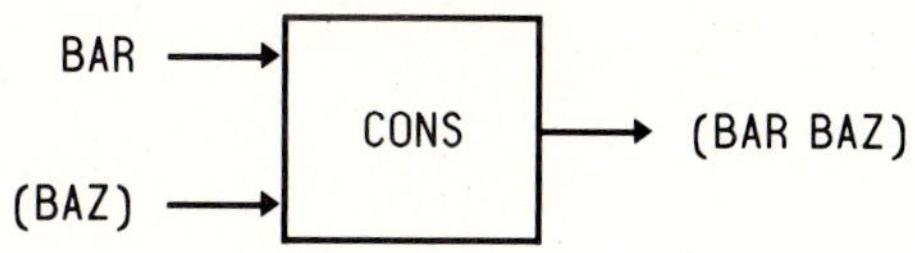

Finally we add the FOO:

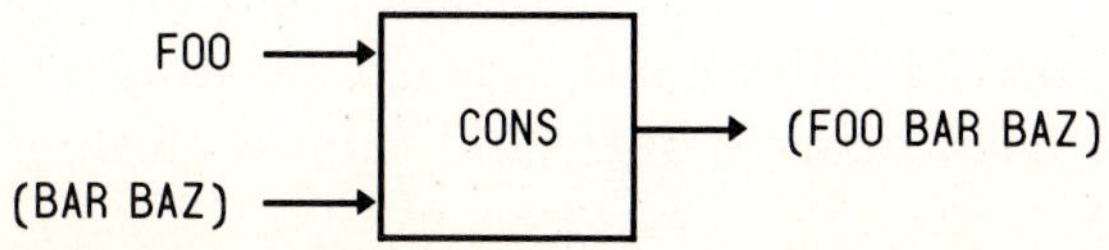

We have cascaded three CONS's together to build the list (FOO BAR BAZ) from scratch. Here is a diagram of the cascade:

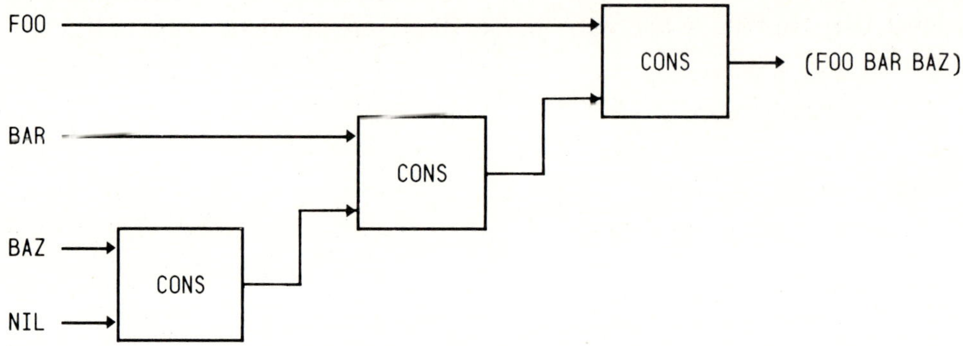

If you turn the diagram sideways, you will see that it is almost identical to the cons cell diagram for the list (FOO BAR BAZ) given in figure 2.1a. This should give you a clue as to why cons cells and the CONS function share the same name.

Exercise

Write a function that takes any two inputs and makes a list of them using CONS.

8. LIST

Creating a list from a bunch of elements is such a common operation that Lisp includes a special function to do just that. The LIST function takes any number of inputs and makes a list of them.

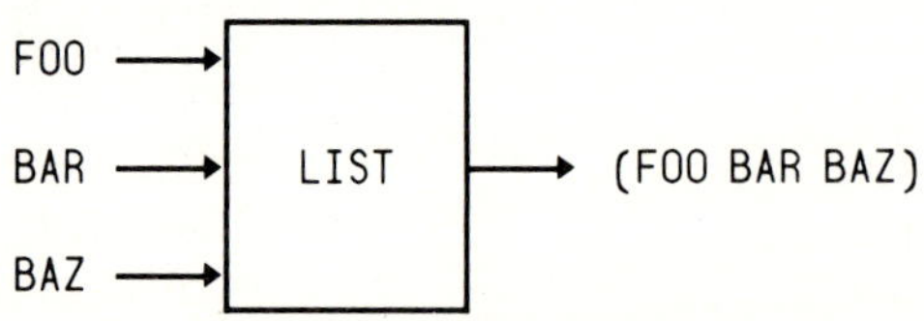

Recall that CONS appeared to add its first input onto the list that was its second input. LIST, on the other hand, starts by writing a brand-new left parenthesis, then each of its inputs, and then a closing right parenthesis. CONS required exactly two inputs, while LIST can take any number.

LIST actually works by building a new chain of cons cells, one cell for each input. The CAR halves of the cells point to the inputs LIST received. Figures 2.9a to 2.9c show how LIST would build the list (FOO BAR BAZ) from the inputs FOO, BAR, and BAZ.

FOO BAR BAZ

Figure 2.9a The inputs to LIST.

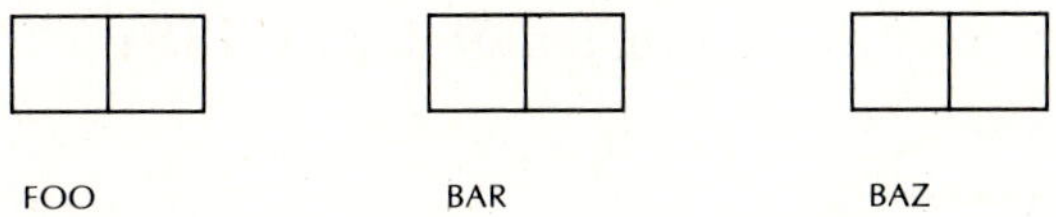

Figure 2.9b New cons cells allocated by LIST.

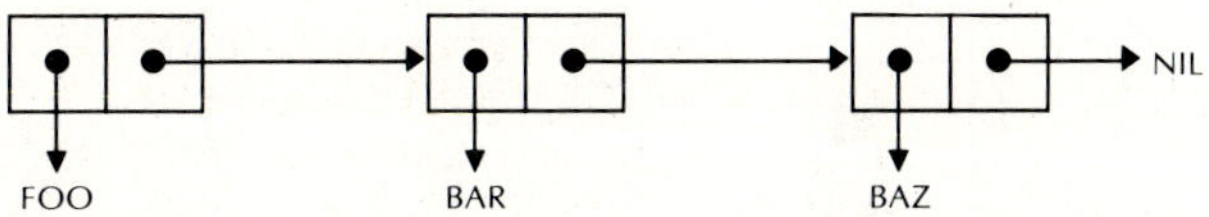

Figure 2.9c The result of LIST: the list (FOO BAR BAZ).

More examples of LIST:

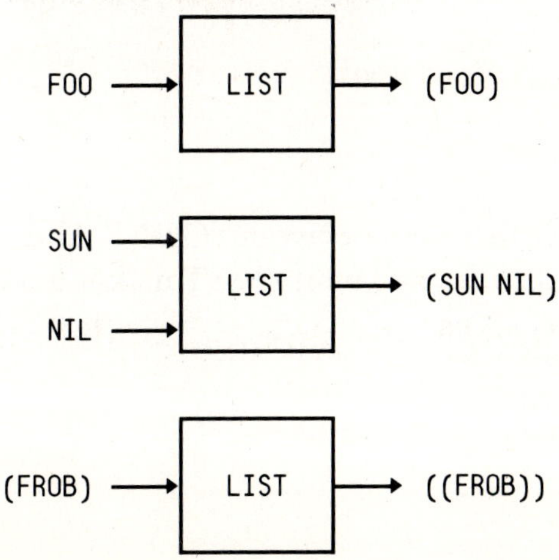

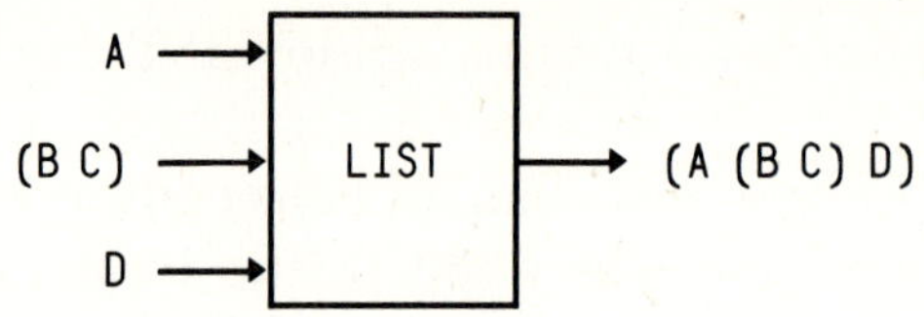

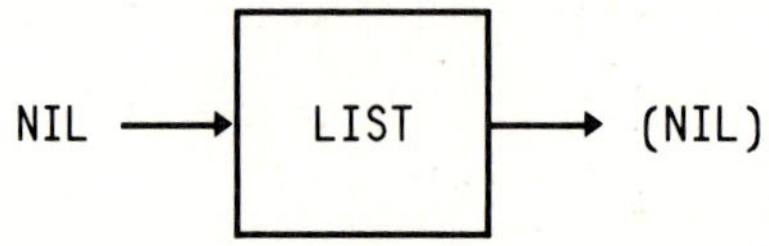

Here is a function called **BLURT** that takes two inputs and uses them to fill in the blanks in a sentence constructed with **LIST**:

Definition of BLURT:

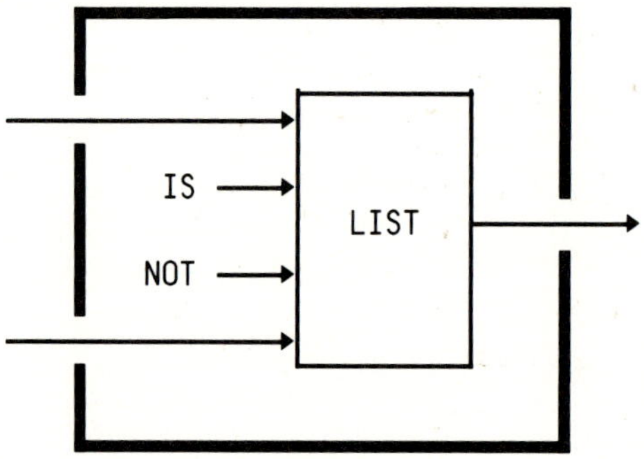

Example of **BLURT**:

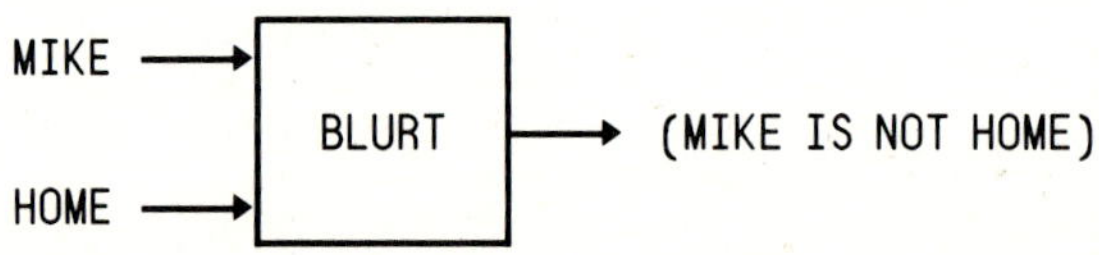

Let's look again at the difference between **CONS** and **LIST**. **CONS** adds an element to the front of a list, while **LIST** makes a new list out of however many inputs it receives.

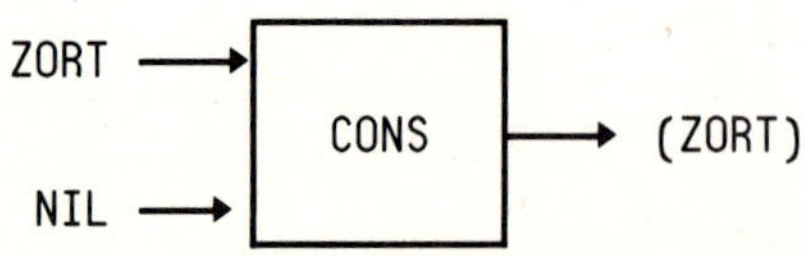

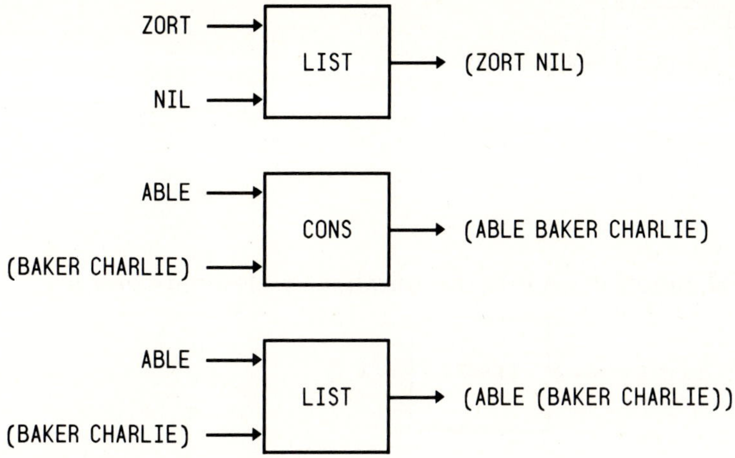

Exercise

Fill in the results of the following computations.

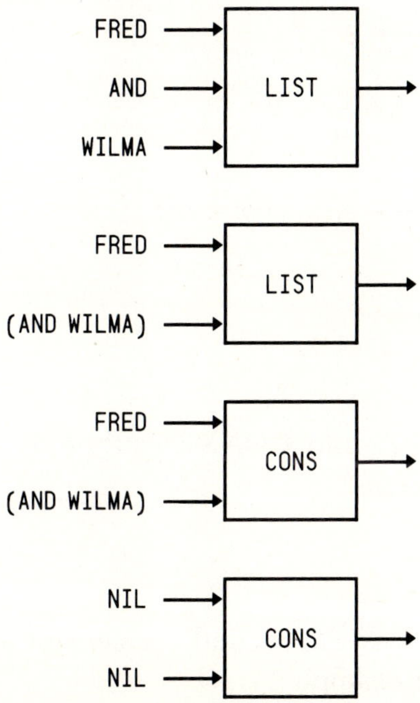

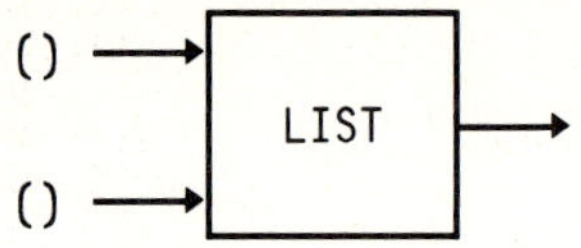

9. LENGTH

The LENGTH function counts the number of elements in a list.

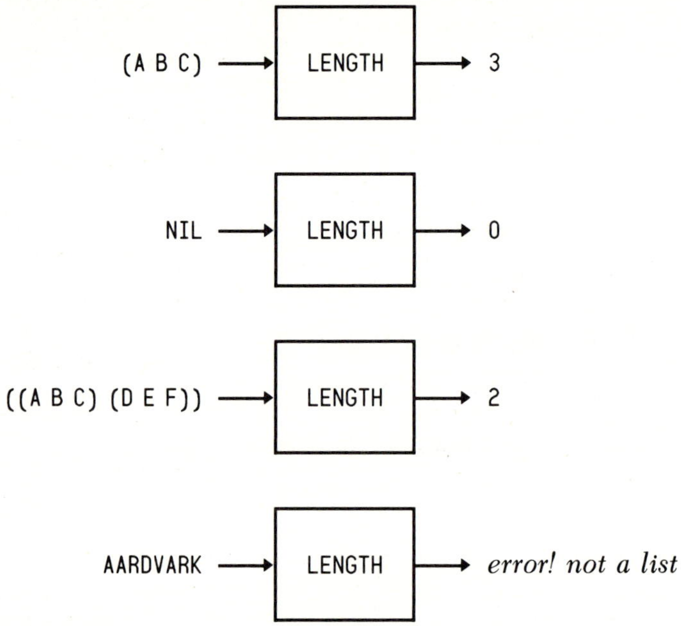

10. PROGRAMMING WITH LISTS

In this section we will put CAR, CDR, and CONS together to solve more complicated programming problems.

10.1. Extracting an Element from a List

Suppose we want a function that returns the second element of a list. Here is a typical list we can use as an example:

```
(FEE FIE FOE FUM)
```

How can we extract the second element of this list? If we use the CDR function, we will eliminate the first element:

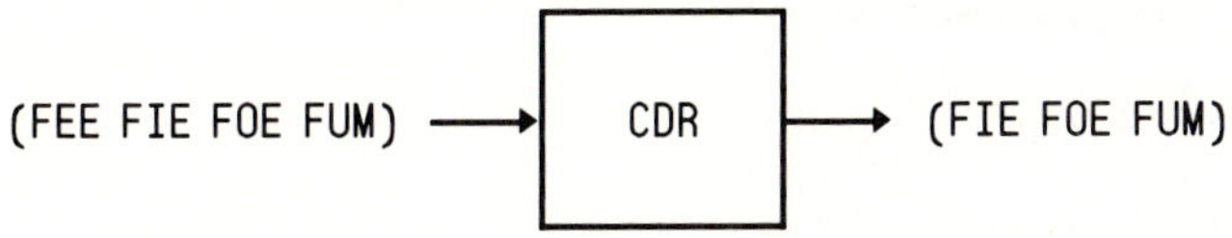

Notice that FIE, the second element of (FEE FIE FOE FUM), is the first element of the output of CDR. This leads us to use the CAR function on the output of CDR:

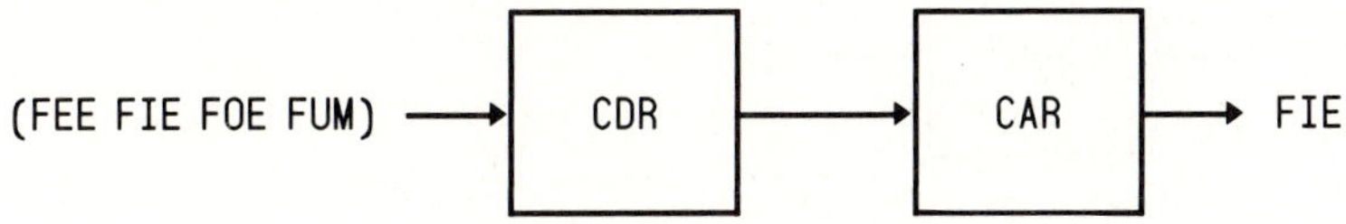

And so we define the CADR function (pronounced "kadder") to take the *CAR* of the *CDR* of a list:

Definition of CADR:

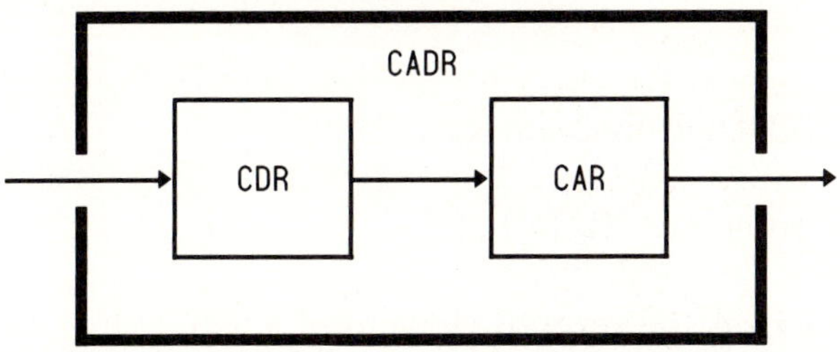

The function's name is CADR, but reading its definition from left to right you see "CDR" and then "CAR." Don't let that confuse you. First we take the CDR of the list, then we take the CAR of the result, so we get the CAR of the CDR of the list—the CADR!

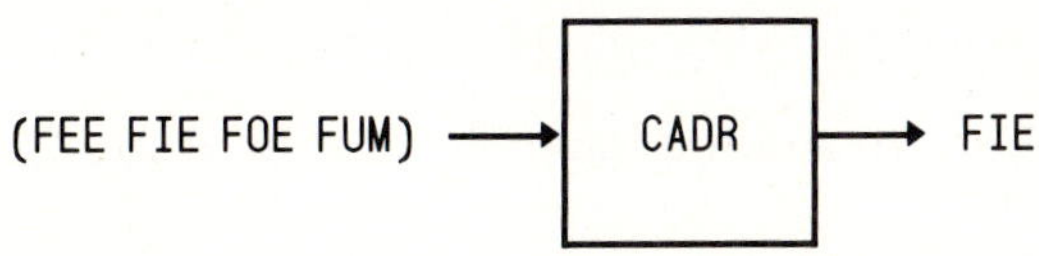

If CADR extracts the second element of a list, what element does the CADDR function extract? (CADDR is pronounced "ka-didder.") Note that CADDR takes the CAR of the CDR of the CDR of the list. That is, it removes the first two elements and returns the CAR of what remains. The answer, therefore, is that CADDR extracts the third element of a list.

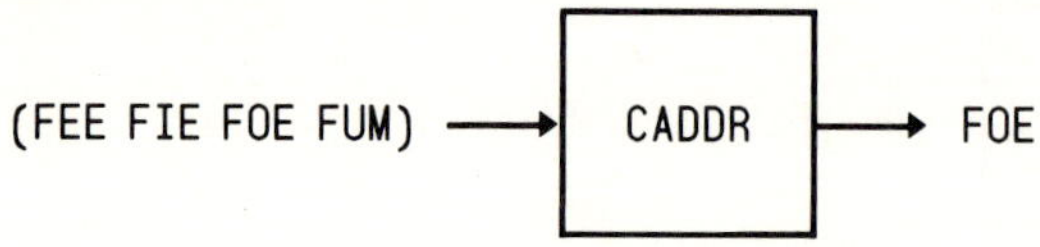

What happens when the CADDR function is given a two-element list as input?

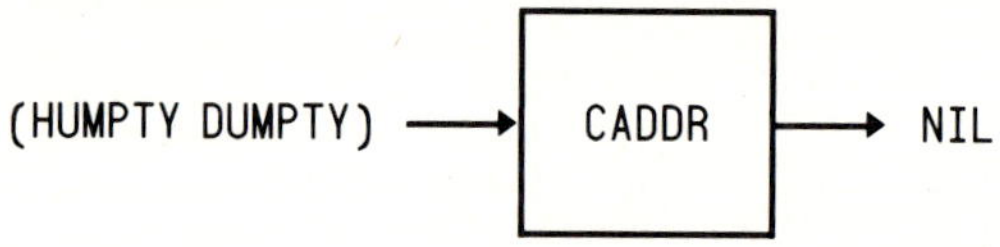

The CDR of (HUMPTY DUMPTY) is the list (DUMPTY). The CDR of that is NIL. The CAR of NIL is just NIL again, so CADDR returns NIL.

Exercises

1. What does the CADDDR function do?

2. How would you pronounce CADDDR?

3. What function extracts the seventh element of a list?

4. What does the CADDDDDDDDDDR function return when given the input (FRED)?

5. What does CAAR (the CAR of the CAR) do when given the input (FRED)?

6. Which of the functions we've studied takes the CADR of the CDR of a list?

10.2. Taking Nested Lists Apart

We can combine CAR and CDR in complex patterns to extract arbitrary substructures of a nested list. For example, if we wanted the second element of the second element of a list, we would take the CADR of the CADR, which is also called the CADADR (pronounced "ka-dadder"). Let's go through the process of taking the CADADR of the list ((ABC) (DEF) (GHI)) step by step.

Step	Result
start	`((A B C) (D E F) (G H I))`
`C...DR`	`((D E F) (G H I))`
`C..ADR`	`(D E F)`
`C.DADR`	`(E F)`
`CADADR`	`E`

Notice how we worked from right to left when processing the As and Ds in the function name. Given a function name and a list, you can always figure out what result the function will produce by reading the pattern of As and Ds in its name as in the preceding example.

Exercise

Using the list ((A B) (C D) (E F)), fill in the missing parts of this table.

Function	Result
`CAR`	`(A B)`
`CDDR`	____
`CADR`	____
`CDAR`	____
____	`B`
`CDDAR`	____
____	`A`
`CDADDR`	____
____	`F`

10.3. Replacing the First Element of a List

Suppose we want to replace the first element of a list with the symbol WHAT. The CDR function can be used to remove the first element; then we can use CONS to add the symbol WHAT. We'll call our function SAY-WHAT.

Definition of SAY-WHAT:

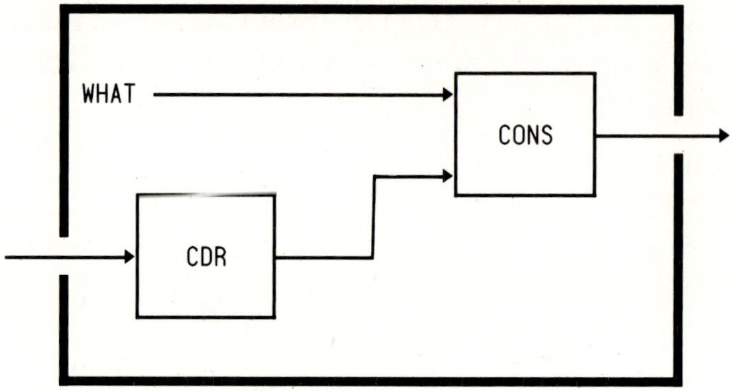

Example of SAY-WHAT:

11. NONLIST CONS STRUCTURES

Cons cells can form structures other than lists, though we will not make much use of them in this book. One such nonlist structure, called a **dotted pair,** results when a symbol is used as the second input to CONS.

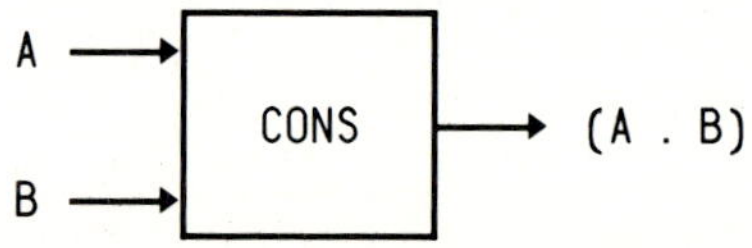

The result of the CONS of A and B is the dotted pair (A . B), shown in cons cell notation in figure 2.10a. This object is not a list because its last cons cell doesn't point to NIL. The true list (A B) is shown in figure 2.10b for comparison.

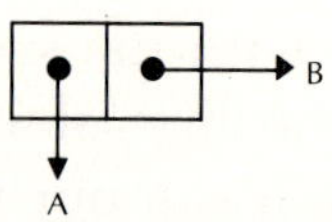

Figure 2.10a The dotted pair (A . B).

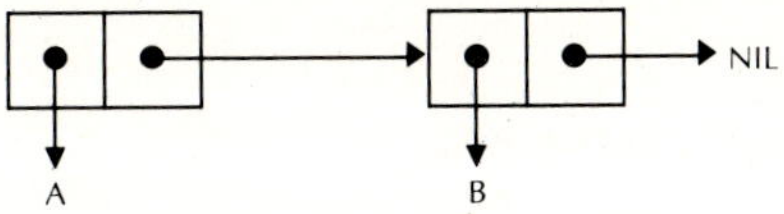

Figure 2.10b The list (A B).

Not all functions that work on lists will work on dotted pairs. CAR and CDR do, but LENGTH does not:

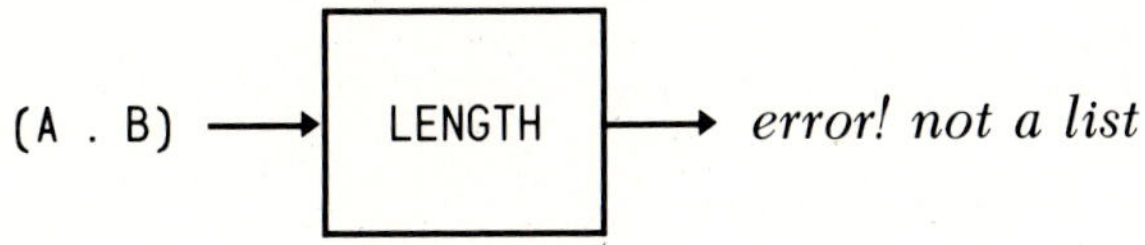

Stranger structures are possible. Figure 2.11 shows a **circular list,** which doesn't even *have* a last cons cell. If the computer tried to display this list in printed form, it would print:

(A B C A B C A B C A B C A B C A B C *etc.*

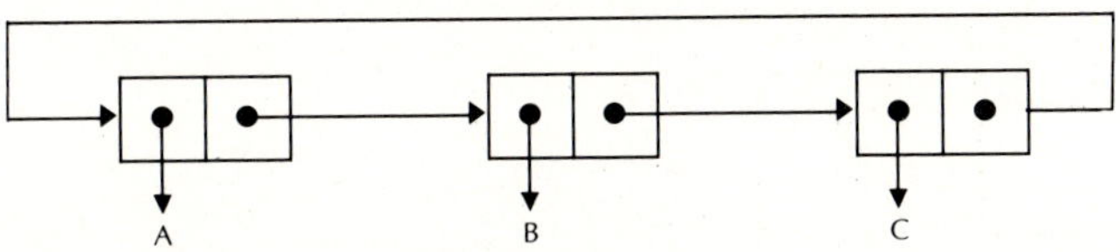

Figure 2.11 A list with no "last" cons cell.

An even more deviant structure appears in figure 2.12, where a cons cell points directly to itself. The printed representation of this structure is an infinite series of left parentheses!

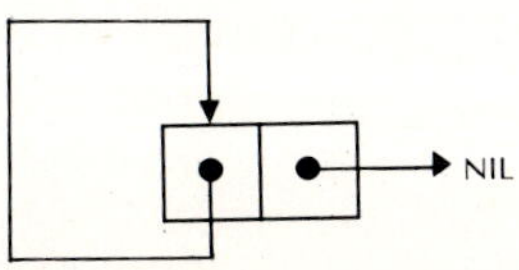

Figure 2.12 A cons cell that points directly to itself.

Chapter Exercises

1. What results are returned by the following?

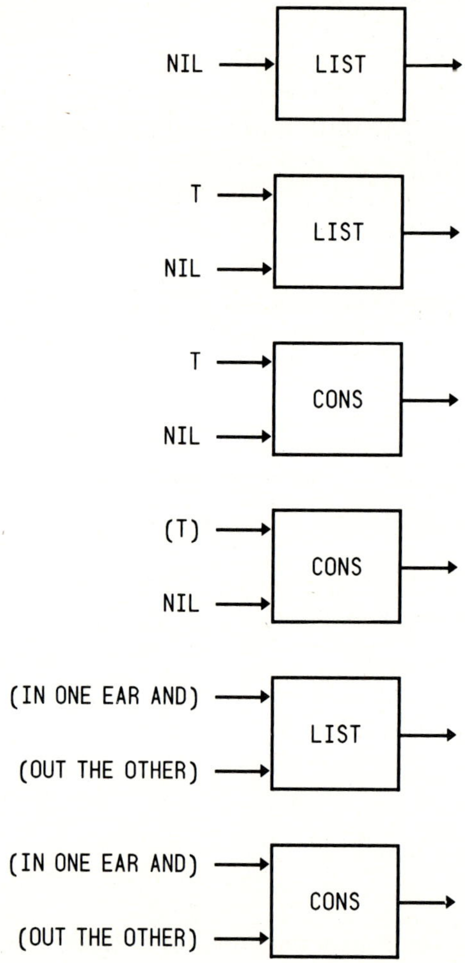

2. Draw the cons cell representations of the following lists:

```
((BREVITY IS) (THE SOUL) (OF WIT))
((ARE TWO LEVELS BETTER THAN ONE))
(A (B (C) D) E)
(((((FRED)))))
```

3. Write a function that takes four inputs and returns a two-element nested list. The first element should be a list of the first two inputs and the second element a list of the last two inputs.

4. Suppose we wanted to make a function called DUO-CONS that added two elements to the front of a list. Remember that the regular CONS function adds only one element to a list. DUO-CONS would be a function of three inputs. For example, if the inputs were the symbol PATRICK, the symbol SEYMOUR, and the list (MARVIN), DUO-CONS would return the list (PATRICK SEYMOUR MARVIN). Show how to write the DUO-CONS function.

5. TWO-DEEPER is a function that surrounds its input with two levels of parentheses. TWO-DEEPER of MOO is ((MOO)). TWO-DEEPER of (BOW WOW) is (((BOW WOW))). Show how to write TWO-DEEPER using LIST. Write another version using CONS.

6. What function returns the second element of the third element of a list?

12. SUMMARY

This chapter introduced the most versatile data type in Lisp: lists. Lists have both a printed and an internal representation. They may contain numbers, symbols, or other lists as elements. We can take lists apart using CAR and CDR ("first" and "rest") and put them together with CONS or LIST. The LENGTH function counts the number of elements in a list, which is the same as the number of cons cells in its top level. The symbol NIL has several interesting properties:

- NIL is a symbol and a list at the same time.
- NIL and ( ) are interchangeable.
- NIL is the name of the empty list.
- NIL means "no" or "false."
- In many Lisp dialects, the CAR and CDR of NIL are defined to be NIL.

Review Exercises

1. Why do cons cells and the CONS function share the same name?

2. What will this function do when given the input (A B C)?

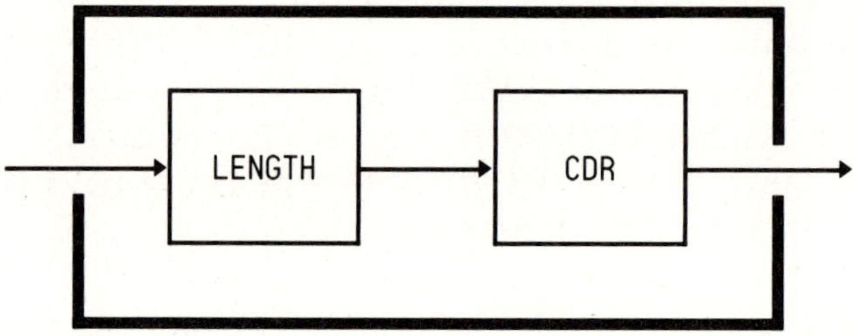

3. When does the internal representation of a list involve more cons cells than the list has elements?

4. Using just CAR and CDR, is it possible to write a function that returns the *last* element of a list of arbitrary length? Explain.

Functions Covered in This Chapter

List functions: CAR, CDR, CONS, LIST, LENGTH
Compositions of CAR and CDR: CADR, CADDR

Advanced Topics 2

1. SYMMETRY OF CONS AND CAR/CDR

There is an interesting symmetry between CONS and CAR/CDR. Given some list X, if we know the CAR of X and the CDR of X we can CONS them together to figure out what X is. For example, if the CAR of X is the symbol A and the CDR of X is the list (E I O U), we know that X must be the list (A E I O U).

The symmetry between CONS and CAR/CDR can be expressed formally as

X = CONS of (CAR of X) and (CDR of X)

However, there is one point where the symmetry breaks down. When X is NIL, the CAR and CDR of X are also NIL. If we reconstruct X by consing together its CAR and CDR portions—that is, CONS of NIL and NIL—we get the list (NIL), not the empty list NIL! This should not be taken to mean that NIL and (NIL) are identical, for we know that they are not. Instead it shows that NIL, an exceptional symbol for so many reasons, violates the CONS/CAR/CDR symmetry that holds for all other lists.

2. CDR AND CLOSURE

Why should the CDR of NIL be defined as NIL? Recall from the previous advanced topics section the definition of closure: a function is closed over a set if every input from that set produces an output that is in the set. Defining the CDR of NIL to be NIL makes the CDR function closed over lists.

If a function is closed over some set, we can apply the function to its own output repeatedly and the result will still be in the set. Thus CDR can always be applied to the output of CDR, since it is closed over lists. Example:

1. CDR of (FOO BAR) is (BAR).
2. CDR of (BAR) is NIL.
3. CDR of NIL is NIL.
4. CDR of NIL is NIL.

   etc. . . .

The range of CDR is **list**, but the range of CAR is **any**. CAR isn't closed over lists. The CAR of (A B C) is A, which is a symbol. The CAR of (1 2 3) is a number. The CAR of ((A)) is the list (A), but since the range of CAR also includes nonlists, CAR isn't closed over lists.

Exercise

Is CDDR closed over lists? Is CADR closed over lists? Explain your answers.

3. UNARY ARITHMETIC WITH LISTS

Lists can be used to do unary ("base one") arithmetic. In this system, numbers are represented by lists of tally symbols, like the marks a prisoner might make on the wall of a cell to record the passage of time: one mark per day. The number 1 is represented by one tally, the number 2 by two tallies, and so on. We can represent 0 by no tallies; we will not consider the case of negative numbers.

Let's use X as our tally symbol. We can write down unary numbers as lists of Xs:

0 is represented as NIL
1 is represented as (X)
2 is represented as (X X)
3 is represented as (X X X)

Having defined unary numbers in terms of lists, we may proceed to investigate what effects list manipulation functions have on them. The CDR function subtracts 1 in unary, just as SUB1 takes 1 away from an ordinary integer. Let's subtract 1 from 3:

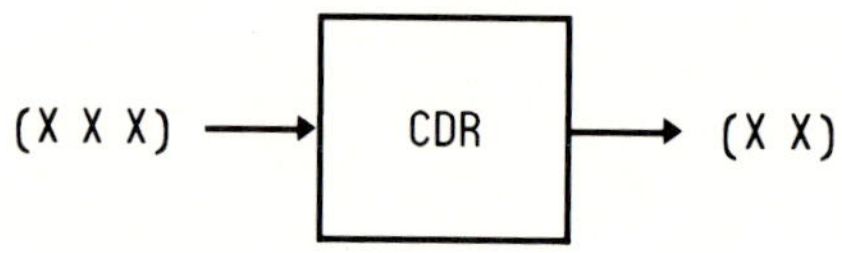

3 SUB1 is 2

Subtracting 1 from 1 yields 0:

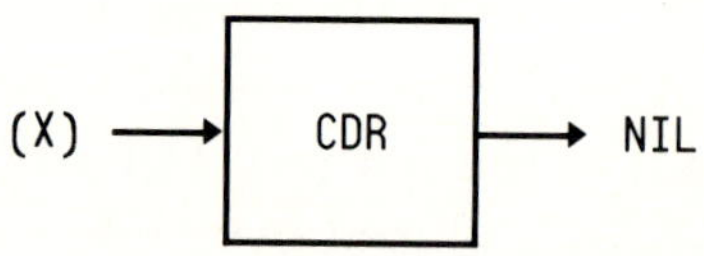

1 SUB1 is 0

But subtracting 1 from 0 yields 0, not −1. Remember that our unary number scheme was only defined for nonnegative integers.

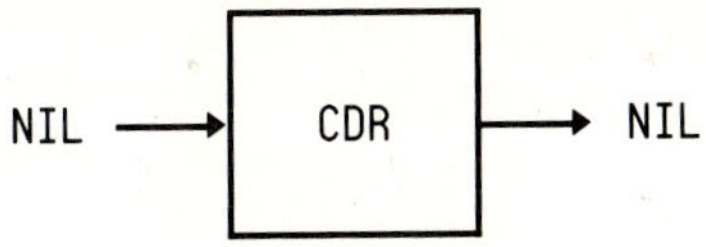

0 SUB1 is 0!

The LENGTH function converts unary numbers to regular integers. Here is an instance of LENGTH operating on the unary number (X X X X):

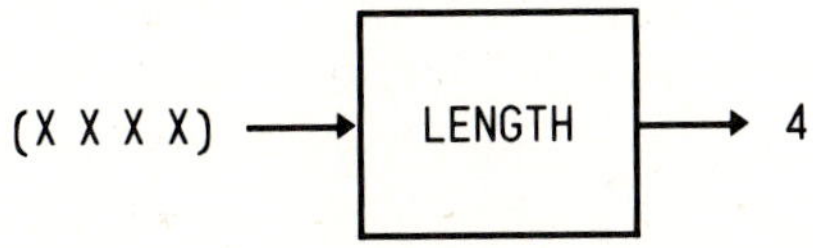

Not all primitive list functions translate into interesting unary arithmetic functions. The CAR function does not, for example. However, it is possible to write our own nonprimitive functions that perform useful unary operations.

Exercises

1. Write a function UNARY-ADD1 that increases a unary number by one.

2. What does the CDDR function do to unary numbers?

3. Write a UNARY-ZEROP predicate.

4. Write a UNARY-GREATERP predicate.

5. CAR can be viewed as a predicate on unary numbers. Instead of returning T or NIL, CAR returns X or NIL. Remember that X or any other non-NIL object is taken as *true* in Lisp. What question about a unary number does CAR answer?

3
EVAL Notation

1. INTRODUCTION

Before progressing further in our study of Lisp, we must switch to a more flexible notation—**EVAL notation.** Instead of using boxes to represent functions, we will use lists. Box notation was easy to read, but EVAL notation has several important advantages:

- Programming concepts that are too sophisticated to express in box notation can be expressed in EVAL notation.
- Eval notation is easier to type on a computer terminal than box notation.
- From a mathematical standpoint, representing functions as lists is an elegant thing to do, because we can use the same notation for functions as for data.
- In Lisp, functions *are* data. EVAL notation allows us to write functions that accept other functions as inputs. We'll explore this possibility further in chapter 7.
- When you have mastered EVAL notation, you will know most of what you need to begin conversing in Lisp with a computer.

2. THE EVAL FUNCTION

The EVAL function is the heart of any Lisp system. EVAL's job is to evaluate Lisp **expressions.** For our purposes, an expression is a function plus a set of inputs. If we give EVAL the expression (PLUS 2 2), EVAL will invoke the built-in function PLUS with inputs 2 and 2. PLUS will return 4, so EVAL will return 4. We say that the expression (PLUS 2 2) evaluates to 4.

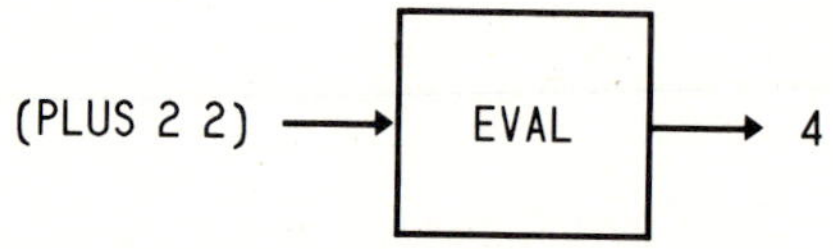

Here are some more examples of expressions and what they evaluate to:

(ADD1 6) evaluates to 7
(ODDP (ADD1 6)) evaluates to T
(TIMES 3 (PLUS 2 2)) evaluates to 12
(CONS T NIL) evaluates to the list (T)
(CONS T T) evaluates to the dotted pair (T . T)

3. EVALUATION RULES DEFINE THE BEHAVIOR OF EVAL

EVAL works by following a set of evaluation rules. One rule is that numbers always evaluate to themselves. Another rule is that the special symbols T and NIL evaluate to themselves.

23 evaluates to 23
T evaluates to T
NIL evaluates to NIL

There is also a rule for evaluating lists. Lists represent expressions. The first element of the list is the name of a function; the remaining elements specify **arguments** to that function. ("Argument" is another term for "input.") A function's arguments must be evaluated before the function can use them. For example, to evaluate the expression

```
(SUB1 (PLUS 3 7))
```

we first evaluate the argument to SUB1, which is (PLUS 3 7). To evaluate that expression, we first evaluate 3 and 7. So,

3 evaluates to 3
7 evaluates to 7
(PLUS 3 7) evaluates to 10

Now we can use the result as input to SUB1:

(SUB1 (PLUS 3 7)) evaluates to 9

Here's another example. To evaluate the expression

```
(CONS T (CONS 38 NIL))
```

we first evaluate the arguments to CONS:

T evaluates to T
(CONS 38 NIL) evaluates to (38) (Details not shown.)

Now we can invoke CONS with inputs T and (38):

(CONS T (CONS 38 NIL)) evaluates to (T 38)

Exercises

1. Write down the results of evaluating each of the following lists:

```
(DIFFERENCE 8 2)
(CONS NIL NIL)
(EQUAL 5 (ADD1 4))
(NOT (ODDP 4))
(LIST (PLUS 5 3) (DIFFERENCE 5 3) (TIMES 5 3))
(LENGTH (CONS T NIL))
```

2. Write an expression in EVAL notation to add 8 to 12 and divide the result by 2.

3. Write an expression in EVAL notation to make a list from the elements 1, 2, T, and the sum of 8 and 9.

4. You can square a number by multiplying it by itself. Write an expression in EVAL notation to add the square of 3 and the square of 4.

4. EVAL NOTATION CAN DO ANYTHING BOX NOTATION CAN DO

It should be obvious that any expression we write in box notation can also be written in EVAL notation. The expression

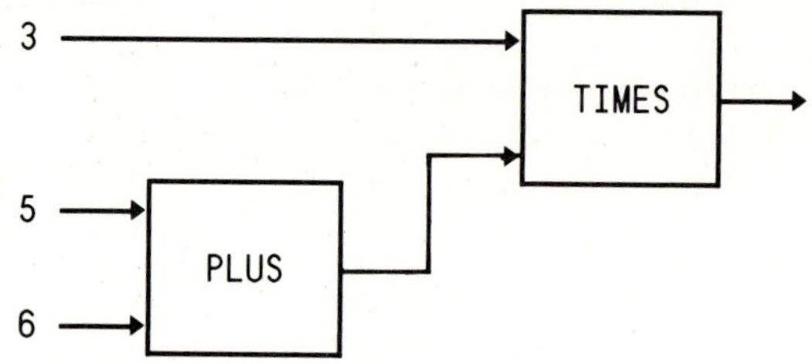

can be represented in EVAL notation as

```
(TIMES 3 (PLUS 5 6))
```

Conversely, the EVAL notation expression

```
(NOT (EQUAL 5 6))
```

is represented in box notation as

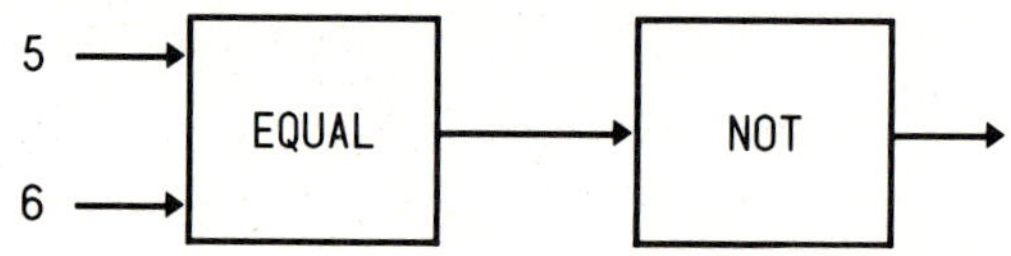

Not only can EVAL notation do everything box notation does, it can do much more. In succeeding chapters we will learn programming constructs made possible by EVAL that have no analog in box notation.

5. WHY WE NEED QUOTING

The expression

`(CONS T NIL)` evaluates to `(T)`

because the inputs to CONS, the special symbols T and NIL, evaluate to themselves. What happens when we evaluate (CONS FRED NIL)?

(CONS FRED NIL) evaluates to *error! FRED unbound variable*

EVAL treats symbols other than **T** and **NIL** as **variables,** and variables that have no value associated with them are called **unbound.** We'll learn how to **bind** variables shortly. Right now we need a way to use symbols as inputs to functions without having the symbols evaluated first. The solution is called **quoting.**

If we place a quote mark before something, **EVAL** will consume the quote and treat what remains as data, without evaluating it further. That is the evaluation rule for quoted marks. So

FRED evaluates to *error! FRED unbound variable,* but
'FRED evaluates to FRED, and
(CONS 'FRED NIL) evaluates to (FRED).

Now consider the expression

(CDR (WE HOLD THESE TRUTHS))

EVAL will first evaluate the argument to **CDR**:

(WE HOLD THESE TRUTHS) evaluates to *error! WE undefined function*

How do we give **CDR** the list (**WE HOLD THESE TRUTHS**) without having it evaluated first? By quoting it, of course! We quote lists for the same reason we quote symbols: to keep them from being evaluated when they should not be.

'(WE HOLD THESE TRUTHS) evaluates to (WE HOLD THESE TRUTHS)
(CDR '(WE HOLD THESE TRUTHS)) evaluates to (HOLD THESE TRUTHS)

Here are some more examples of the difference between quoting and not quoting a list:

(CADDR (MY AUNT MARY)) evaluates to *error! MY undefined function*
(CADDR '(MY AUNT MARY)) evaluates to MARY

(PLUS 1 2) evaluates to 3
'(PLUS 1 2) evaluates to the list (PLUS 1 2)

(ADD1 (PLUS 1 2)) evaluates to 4
(ADD1 '(PLUS 1 2)) evaluates to *error! wrong type input*

The error in the last example occurs because ADD1 is invoked with *the list* (PLUS 1 2) as input. Quoting prevented the list from being evaluated. ADD1 can't accept lists as inputs; it can only accept numbers.

6. THE PROBLEM OF MISQUOTING

It is easy for beginning Lisp programmers to get confused about quoting and either put quotes in the wrong place or leave them out where they are needed. The error messages Lisp gives are a good hint about what went wrong. An unbound variable or undefined function error usually indicates that a quote was left out:

`(LIST 'A 'B C)` evaluates to *error! C unbound variable*
`(LIST 'A 'B 'C)` evaluates to `(A B C)`

`(CONS 'A (B C))` evaluates to *error! B undefined function*
`(CONS 'A '(B C))` evaluates to `(A B C)`

On the other hand, wrong-type input errors or funny results may be an indication that a quote was put in where it doesn't belong.

`(PLUS 2 '(ADD1 2))` evaluates to *error! wrong type input*
`(PLUS 2 (ADD1 2))` evaluates to `5`

`(LIST 'BUY '(TIMES 27 34) 'BAGELS)` evaluates to `(BUY (TIMES 27 34) BAGELS)`
`(LIST 'BUY (TIMES 27 34) 'BAGELS)` evaluates to `(BUY 918 BAGELS)`

When we quote a list, the quote must go *outside* the list in order to prevent the list from being evaluated. If we put the quote inside the list, EVAL will try to evaluate the list and an error will result:

`('FOO 'BAR 'BAZ)` evaluates to *error! 'FOO undefined function*
`'(FOO BAR BAZ)` evaluates to `(FOO BAR BAZ)`

7. TWO WAYS TO MAKE LISTS

We have seen two ways to make lists using EVAL notation. We can write the list out directly, using a quote to prevent its evaluation, or we can use **LIST** or **CONS** to build the list up from individual elements. If we use the latter method, we must quote each argument to the function.

> `'(FOO BAR BAZ)` evaluates to `(FOO BAR BAZ)`
> `(LIST 'FOO 'BAR 'BAZ)` evaluates to `(FOO BAR BAZ)`
> `(CONS 'FOO '(BAR BAZ))` evaluates to `(FOO BAR BAZ)`

One advantage of building the list up from individual elements is that some of the elements can be *computed* rather than specified directly.

> `(LIST 33 'SQUARED 'IS (TIMES 33 33))` evaluates to
> `(33 SQUARED IS 1089)`

If we quote a list, nothing inside it will get evaluated:

> `'(33 SQUARED IS (TIMES 33 33))` evaluates to
> `(33 SQUARED IS (TIMES 33 33))`

We have seen several ways things can go wrong if quotes are not used properly when building a list:

> `(LIST FOO BAR BAZ)` evaluates to *error! FOO unbound variable*
> `(FOO BAR BAZ)` evaluates to *error! FOO undefined function*
> `('FOO 'BAR 'BAZ)` evaluates to *error! 'FOO undefined function*

Exercises

1. The following expressions evaluate without any errors. Write down the results.

```
(CONS 5 (LIST 6 7))
(CONS 5 '(LIST 6 7))
(LIST 3 'FROM 9 'GIVES (DIFFERENCE 9 3))
(PLUS (LENGTH '(1 FOO 2 MOO)) (CADDR '(1 FOO 2 MOO)))
(CDR '(CONS IS SHORT FOR CONSTRUCT))
```

2. The following expressions all result in errors. Write down the type of error that occurs, explain how the error arose (e.g., missing quote, quote in wrong place), and correct the expression by changing *only* the quotes.

```
(CADDDR (THE QUICK BROWN FOX))
```

```
(LIST 2 AND 2 IS 4)
(SUB1 '(LENGTH (LIST T T T T)))
(CONS 'PATRICK (SEYMOUR MARVIN))
(CONS 'PATRICK (LIST SEYMOUR MARVIN))
```

8. DEFINING FUNCTIONS IN EVAL NOTATION

In box notation we defined a function by showing what went on inside the box. Here, for example, is the definition of SUB2:

Definition of SUB2:

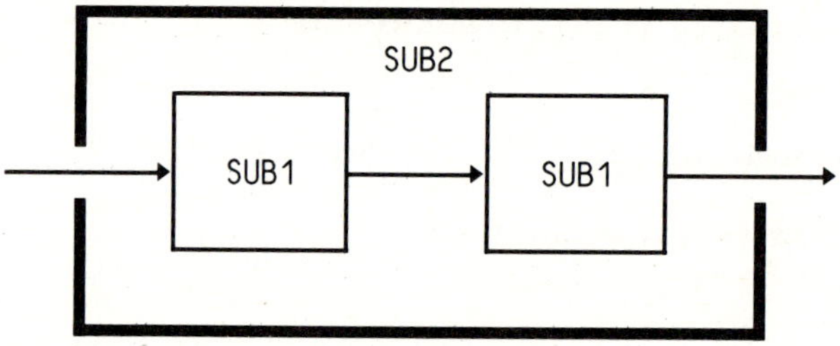

In EVAL notation we use lists to define functions. We refer to the function's arguments by giving them names. Let's use X as the name of SUB2's argument. The SUB2 function can be defined in EVAL notation as follows:

```
(DEFUN SUB2 (X) (SUB1 (SUB1 X)))
```

The right way to read this definition is: "DEFUN SUB2 of X: SUB1 of SUB1 of X." DEFUN is a **special form** that *de*fines *fun*ctions. A special form is a function whose arguments need not be quoted. Some dialects of Lisp use a different name for this special form, such as DE, DEF, or DEFINE, but the idea is the same.

The definition of SUB2 contains three parts: the function name, the argument list, and the function body. The function name is SUB2. The argument list is (X). The body is the expression (SUB1 (SUB1 X)).

Here are some more examples of function definitions:

```
(DEFUN HALF (N) (QUOTIENT N 2))
(DEFUN SQUARE (N) (TIMES N N))
(DEFUN ONEMOREP (X Y) (EQUAL X (ADD1 Y)))
```

```
(DEFUN GREET (X) (CONS 'HELLO X))
(DEFUN BLURT (X Y) (LIST X 'IS 'NOT Y))
```

The names a function uses for its arguments are independent of the names any other function uses. HALF and SQUARE both call their arguments N, but the N in HALF refers only to the input of the HALF function; it has no relation to the N in SQUARE. Any symbol except for T or NIL can serve as the name of an argument. X, Y, and N are commonly used, but BOZO or ARTICHOKE would also work.

Functions are more readable when their argument names mean something. A function that computed the total cost of a merchandise order might name its three arguments QUANTITY, PRICE, and HANDLING-CHARGE rather than X, Y and Z.

```
(DEFUN TOTAL-COST (QUANTITY PRICE HANDLING-CHARGE)
  (PLUS (TIMES QUANTITY PRICE) HANDLING-CHARGE))
```

Exercises

Use EVAL notation for all problems unless stated otherwise.

1. Define a function called CUBE that computes the cube of a number.

2. Define a function called AVERAGE that computes the average of two numbers. (The average of two numbers is half their sum.)

3. Define a predicate called LONGER-THAN that takes two lists as input and returns T if the first list is longer than the second.

4. Write a function ADDLENGTH that takes a list as input and returns a new list with the length of the input added onto the front of it. If the input is (MOO GOO GAI PAN), the output should be (4 MOO GOO GAI PAN). What is the result of (ADDLENGTH (ADDLENGTH '(A B C)))?

5. Study this function definition:

   ```
   (DEFUN CALL-UP (CALLER CALLEE)
     (LIST 'HELLO CALLEE 'THIS 'IS CALLER 'CALLING))
   ```

   How many arguments does this function require? What are the names of the arguments? What is the result of (CALL-UP 'FRED 'WANDA)?

6. Here is a variation on the CALL-UP function introduced in the previous problem:

```
(DEFUN CRANK-CALL (CALLER CALLEE)
  '(HELLO CALLEE THIS IS CALLER CALLING))
```

   What is the result of (CRANK-CALL 'WANDA 'FRED)? Why?

7. Define a function MILES-PER-GALLON that takes three inputs, called INITIAL-ODOMETER-READING, FINAL-ODOMETER-READING, and GALLONS-CONSUMED, and computes the number of miles traveled per gallon of gas.

8. The SQUARE function defined earlier takes one input, but it uses this input twice—its body is (TIMES N N). How would you draw a definition for SQUARE in box notation?

9. FOUR WAYS TO MISDEFINE A FUNCTION

Beginning users of EVAL notation sometimes have trouble writing syntactically correct function definitions. Let's take a close look at a proper definition for the function INTRO:

```
(DEFUN INTRO (X Y) (LIST X 'THIS 'IS Y))
```

`(INTRO 'STANLEY 'LIVINGSTONE)` evaluates to `(STANLEY THIS IS LIVINGSTONE)`

Notice that INTRO's argument list consists of two symbols, X and Y, with neither quotes nor parentheses around them, and the variables X and Y are not quoted or parenthesized in the body, either.

The first way to misdefine a function is to put something other than plain, unadorned symbols in the function's argument list. If we use quotes or extra levels of parentheses in the argument list, the function won't work.

```
(DEFUN INTRO ('X 'Y) (LIST X 'THIS 'IS Y))       bad argument list
(DEFUN INTRO ((X) (Y)) (LIST X 'THIS 'IS Y))     bad argument list
```

The second way to misdefine a function is to put parentheses around variables where they appear in the body. Only functions should have parentheses around them. Putting parentheses around a variable will cause an undefined function error:

```
(DEFUN INTRO (X Y) (LIST (X) 'THIS 'IS (Y)))
```

(INTRO 'STANLEY 'LIVINGSTONE) evaluates to *error! X undefined function*

The third way to misdefine a function is to quote a variable. Symbols *must* be left unquoted when they are used as variables. Here is an example of what happens when variables are quoted:

```
(DEFUN INTRO (X Y) (LIST 'X 'THIS 'IS 'Y))
```

(INTRO 'STANLEY 'LIVINGSTONE) evaluates to (X THIS IS Y)

The fourth way to misdefine a function is to *not* quote something that should be quoted. In the INTRO function, the symbols X and Y are variables but THIS and IS are not. If we don't quote THIS and IS, an unbound variable error results.

```
(DEFUN INTRO (X Y) (LIST X THIS IS Y))
```

(INTRO 'STANLEY 'LIVINGSTONE) evaluates to
error! THIS unbound variable

10. EXPLANATION OF VARIABLE BINDING

We've heard a lot about unbound variables; what about **bound** variables? Bound variables are just symbols that have a value associated with them. In Lisp, a function's variables become bound automatically when the function is invoked; they become unbound again when the function returns. Consider the SQUARE function, which uses a variable named N:

```
(DEFUN SQUARE (N) (TIMES N N))
```

Initially N is unbound. Suppose we evaluate (SQUARE 6). The number 6 must be associated with the symbol N somehow, so that evaluating the body (**TIMES N N**) produces the same result as (**TIMES** 6 6). That's what variable binding is for. When we invoke **SQUARE**, **N** becomes bound to 6. After the **SQUARE** function returns its result, **N** becomes unbound again.

```
N is unbound
    ┌──── (SQUARE 6)
    │
  N = 6     (TIMES N N) evaluates to 36
    │
    └──── SQUARE returns 36
N is unbound again
```

Let's try an example with two variables. Here is the definition of **ONEMOREP**:

```
(DEFUN ONEMOREP (X Y) (EQUAL X (ADD1 Y)))
```

The symbols **X** and **Y** are initially unbound. When we evaluate (**ONEMOREP** 7 6), the following happens:

```
X and Y are unbound
    ┌──── (ONEMOREP 7 6)
    │
  X = 7        (ADD 1 Y) evaluates to 7
  Y = 6     (EQUAL X (ADD1 Y)) evaluates to T
    │
    └──── ONEMOREP returns T
X and Y are unbound again
```

Exercises

1. Define an ADD50 function that adds 50 to its input. Then write down a binding diagram like the preceding ones to show what happens when we evaluate (ADD50 37).

2. Consider the following function, paying close attention to the quotes:

   ```
   (DEFUN SCRABBLE (WORD) (LIST WORD 'IS 'A 'WORD))
   ```

The symbol WORD is used two different ways in this function. What are they? What is the result of (SCRABBLE 'AARDVARK)? What is the result of (SCRABBLE 'WORD)?

3. Here's a real confuser:

```
(DEFUN STOOGE (LARRY MOE CURLY)
  (LIST LARRY (LIST 'MOE CURLY) CURLY 'LARRY))
```

What does the following evaluate to? It will help to write down what value each variable is bound to and, of course, mind the quotes!

```
(STOOGE 'MOE 'CURLY 'LARRY)
```

4. Why can't the special symbols T or NIL be used as variables in a function definition? (Consider the evaluation rule for T and NIL versus the rule for evaluating ordinary symbols.)

11. SUMMARY

In this chapter we learned EVAL notation, which allows expressions to be represented as lists. Lists are interpreted by the EVAL function according to a built-in set of evaluation rules. The evaluation rules we learned were:

- Numbers evaluate to themselves. So do T and NIL.
- When evaluating a list, the first element is the name of a function and the remaining elements specify its arguments. Arguments are evaluated before the function is invoked.
- A quoted list or symbol evaluates to itself, without the quote.
- A list of form (DEFUN function-name (argument-list) function-body) defines a function. DEFUN is a special form; its inputs do not have to be quoted. A function's argument list gives names for the function's inputs. The body is evaluated after the function's variables have been bound.
- Symbols other than T or NIL are treated as variables. A variable evaluates to the value it is bound to. Symbols that aren't bound cause unbound variable errors when they are evaluated, unless they are quoted.

Review Exercises

1. Name two advantages of EVAL notation over box notation.

2. Evaluate each of the following lists. If the list causes an error, tell what the error is. Otherwise, write the result of the evaluation.

```
(CONS 'GRAPES '(OF WRATH))
(LIST T 'IS 'NOT NIL)
(CAR '(LIST MOOSE GOOSE))
(CAR (LIST 'MOOSE 'GOOSE))
(CADR '(WE HOLD THESE TRUTHS))
(CONS 'HOME ('SWEET 'HOME))
```

3. Here is a mystery function:

```
(DEFUN MYSTERY (X) (LIST (CADR X) (CAR X)))
```

What result or error is produced by evaluating each of the following?

```
(MYSTERY '(DANCING BEAR))
(MYSTERY 'DANCING 'BEAR)
(MYSTERY '(ZOWIE))
(MYSTERY (LIST 'FIRST 'SECOND))
```

4. What is wrong with each of the following function definitions?

```
(DEFUN SPEAK (X Y) (LIST 'ALL 'X 'IS 'Y))
(DEFUN SPEAK (X) (Y) (LIST 'ALL X 'IS Y))
(DEFUN SPEAK ((X) (Y)) (LIST ALL 'X IS 'Y))
```

Functions Covered in This Chapter

The evaluator: EVAL
Special form: DEFUN

Meet the Computer

Congratulations! Having made it successfully through all the pencil-and-paper work, it's time for you to meet the computer. Unfortunately

I can't give you a formal introduction; there are too many types of computers for that to be practical. You might want to find the owner's manual or user's guide for the model you use and spend a few minutes glancing through it, or look in appendix B to see if the dialect of Lisp you use is covered there. A better approach would be to talk to someone familiar with your machine.

1. RUNNING LISP

If you're using a personal computer (which usually means a microcomputer), you need to learn how to turn it on, load the operating system, and start Lisp running. Someone familiar with your machine can teach you to do this; it only takes a minute or two.

If you're running Lisp on a timesharing system, you need to know your personal account number and password so you can sign on to the machine. You also need to know the commands for signing on, running Lisp, and signing off. The commands for my computer probably won't work for yours, but here is how I sign on and run Lisp on a DecSystem-20 computer running the TOPS-20 operating system.

```
↑C
Carnegie-Mellon University TOPS-F, TOPS-20 Monitor 5.1(4773)-2
@login dt50
Password: secret
    Job 30 on TTY270    10-Sep-82    06:16:51
@lisp
User-Friendly MacLisp version 2130 for DT50
*
```

2. TERMINAL KEYBOARD LAYOUT

A terminal keyboard is laid out quite similar to a typewriter's, with a few extra keys not found on a typewriter keyboard. Here is a list of some of the important keys on a computer terminal:

Shift Like the shift key on a typewriter, this key is held down to type capital letters or special characters.

Control	Frequently abbreviated CTRL, this key is another type of shift key used to send special "control characters" to the computer.
Return	Like the carriage return key on a typewriter, the Return key is used to end each line. The key tells the computer that you are finished typing, and it is now the computer's turn to type if it has something to say.
Delete	The Delete or Rubout key is used to erase the most recently typed character. On a TV-type terminal, the character will actually disappear from the screen.

Another important thing about terminal keyboards is that there are always separate keys for the letter "O" and the digit "0," and for the letter "l" and the digit "1". On conventional typewriters it's fine to type "O" for "0" or "l" for "1," but when you talk to a computer you must be sure to use the correct character for what you mean.

3. THE READ-EVAL-PRINT LOOP

A computer running Lisp behaves a lot like a pocket calculator. It reads expressions that you type on the terminal. It evaluates the expressions and prints the results. This process is called a **read-eval-print loop.**

Here is a sample dialog with a computer, in which I will define a function, use it, and have the computer print out its definition. Whenever the computer wants me to type something, it prints an asterisk, called a **prompt.** What I type appears in lowercase; what the computer types is in uppercase.

`*(square 4)`	*try to square 4*
`;SQUARE - UNDEFINED FUNCTION`	*but there's no SQUARE function*
`*(defun square (n) (times n n))`	*so I define one*
`SQUARE`	*computer accepts my definition*
`*(square 4)`	*try to square 4 again*
`16`	*computer prints the answer*
`*(square 5)`	*try squaring another number*
`25`	*yes, computers can multiply*

```
*(square 512)                     square a big number . . .
262144                            and get a really big result

*(grindef square)                 me: show me my SQUARE function
(DEFUN SQUARE (N) (TIMES N N))    computer: here it is
```

Remember that DEFUN is a special form that has other names in other dialects of Lisp. GRINDEF is a special form that prints out the definition of a function. (GRINDEF stands for "*grin*d out the *def*inition of.") It too has a different name in some dialects; frequently it is called PP (for "*p*retty *p*rint.") Because there are so many dialects of Lisp, I must leave it to you to discover the proper names to use on your system.

The rest of this book assumes that you have access to a computer and that its version of Lisp is similar to MacLisp or Common Lisp. See appendix C for information on how to make your computer's Lisp more compatible with the version used in the book.

4. TIPS FOR COMPUTER USERS

One important thing you will need to know is how to recover from errors. In my version of Lisp, whenever I get an error or want to discard the expression I'm typing and start over, I type Control-G. (That is, I hold down the CTRL key and hit "G".) Control-G, which the computer prints as "↑G", erases the error and any input I've typed and puts me back at the read-eval-print loop. Example:

```
*(add1 'foo)                      tried to add 1 to a symbol
;FOO - WRONG TYPE INPUT           computer gives an error message

(ADD1 FOO)
debug option (? for help): ↑G     type ↑G to get out of the error

*(add1 37)                        got a new prompt; try again
38

*(defun add87 ((x))               too many parens in argument list
   (plus x ↑G                     so hit ↑G to abort typein
```

```
*(defun add87 (x)                      this time I typed it correctly
   (plus x 87))
ADD87
```

If you define a function in Lisp and it doesn't work, you can redefine it and try again. You can redefine a function as often as you like; only the last definition is retained. The following example illustrates this and also shows that you can hit carriage return at any point in an expression with no ill effect. This is because expressions are lists; their spacing and indentation is arbitrary.

```
*(defun intro (x y)                      INTRO misdefined: no quotes
   (list x this is y))
INTRO

*(intro 'stanley 'livingstone)           testing the INTRO function
;THIS - UNBOUND VARIABLE                  the error is discovered

(LIST X THIS IS Y)
debug option (? for help): ↑G            use ↑G to abort

*(defun intro (x y)                      redefine INTRO correctly
   (list x 'this 'is y))
INTRO

*(intro 'stanley 'livingstone)           test it again . . .
(STANLEY THIS IS LIVINGSTONE)            now it works

*(grindef intro)                         show me the INTRO function
(DEFUN INTRO (X Y) LIST X 'THIS 'IS Y))  shows the newer version
```

It's a good idea to display each function as soon as you've typed it in. This makes it easy to detect typing errors and check parenthesization. Here's another important point: don't use names like CONS, PLUS, or LIST for your own functions; in Lisp these are the names of built-in functions. Redefining these functions may cause a "fatal" error, in which case you will have to reset the computer and start up Lisp again, and any functions you defined previously will be lost.

First Keyboard Exercise

Keyboard exercises are small programming assignments for you to work on at a computer terminal. Before attempting a keyboard exercise you should have a firm understanding of the material in the chapter and be able to work the exercises included there.

This first keyboard exercise consists of a collection of simple functions for you to write or debug. Feel free to experiment and improvise on your own.

1. Find out how to run Lisp on your computer, and start it up.

2. For each expression below, write down what you think it evaluates to or what kind of error it will cause. Then try it on the computer and see.

```
(PLUS 3 5)
(3 PLUS 5)
(PLUS 3 (5 6))
(PLUS 3 (TIMES 5 6))
'(MORNING NOON NIGHT)
('MORNING 'NOON 'NIGHT)
(LIST 'MORNING 'NOON 'NIGHT)
(CAR NIL)
(PLUS 3 FOO)
(PLUS 3 'FOO)
```

3. Here is an example of the function MYFUN, a strange function of two inputs.

   `(MYFUN 'ALPHA 'BETA)` evaluates to `((ALPHA) BETA)`

   Write MYFUN. Test your function to make certain it works correctly.

4. Write a predicate FIRSTP that returns T if its first argument (a symbol) is equal to the first element of its second argument (a list). That is, (FIRSTP 'FOO '(FOO BAR BAZ)) should return T. (FIRSTP 'BOING '(FOO BAR BAZ)) should return NIL.

5. Write a function MID-ADD1 that adds 1 to the middle element of a three-element list. For example, (MID-ADD1 '(TAKE 2 COOKIES))

should return the list (TAKE 3 COOKIES). Note: You are *not* allowed to make MID-ADD1 a function of three inputs. It has to take a single input that is a list of three elements.

6. Write a function F-TO-C that converts a temperature from Fahrenheit to Celsius. The formula for doing the conversion is: Celsius temperature = [5×(Fahrenheit temperature−32)]/9.

7. What is wrong with this function? What does (FOO 5) do?

```
(DEFUN FOO (X) (ADD1 (ZEROP X)))
```

8. Make up a function of your own to do anything you like. Try your function on three sets of input to be sure it does what it's supposed to.

Advanced Topics 3

1. A NOTE ON LAMBDA NOTATION

Lambda notation was created by Alonzo Church, a mathematician at Princeton University, as an unambiguous way of specifying functions, their inputs, and the computations they perform. In lambda notation, a function that added 3 to a number would be written $\lambda x.(3 + x)$. The λ is the Greek letter lambda.

John McCarthy, the originator of Lisp, adopted Church's notation for specifying functions. The Lisp equivalent of the unnamed function $\lambda x.(3+x)$ is the list

```
(LAMBDA (X) (PLUS 3 X))
```

A function $F(x,y) = 3x+y^2$ would be written $\lambda(x,y).(3x+y^2)$ in lambda notation. In Lisp it is written

```
(LAMBDA (X Y) (PLUS (TIMES 3 X) (TIMES Y Y)))
```

As you can see, the syntax of lambda expressions in Lisp is similar to that of Church's notation and even more similar to DEFUN. But unlike DEFUN, LAMBDA is not a function; it is a marker treated specially by EVAL. We'll learn more about lambda expressions in chapter 7.

Exercise

Write each of the following functions in Church's lambda notation: HALF, SQUARE, ONEMOREP.

2. FUNCTIONS OF NO ARGUMENTS

Suppose we wanted to write a function that multiplies 85 by 97. Notice that this function requires no inputs; it does its computation using only prespecified constants. Since the function doesn't take any inputs, when we write its definition it will have an *empty* argument list. The empty list, of course, is NIL. Let's define this function under the name TEST:

```
(DEFUN TEST () (TIMES 85 97))
```

After doing this, we see that

(TEST) evaluates to 8245
(TEST 1) evaluates to *error! too many arguments*
TEST evaluates to *error! TEST unbound variable*

3. DYNAMIC SCOPING AND THE REBINDING OF VARIABLES

In Lisp, variables become bound when a function is called and unbound again when it returns. If one function calls another and they use the same names for their inputs, the variables are **rebound** when the second function is called and are restored to their initial values when the second function returns. Some examples should make this clearer.

Let's define the functions DOUBLE and QUADRUPLE as

```
(DEFUN DOUBLE (X) (PLUS X X))

(DEFUN QUADRUPLE (X) (DOUBLE (DOUBLE X)))
```

Both DOUBLE and QUADRUPLE call their input X. Suppose we evaluate the expression (QUADRUPLE 5). Inside QUADRUPLE, X is bound to 5 and the expression (DOUBLE (DOUBLE X)) gets evaluated. What happens when we call DOUBLE with input 5? DOUBLE rebinds the symbol X to *its own* input, which is also 5; in doing so, the old 5 is set aside temporarily. The body of DOUBLE evaluates to 10. When DOUBLE returns, X's binding is restored to the first 5. Now we have evaluated (DOUBLE X), so we can use that result to evaluate (DOUBLE (DOUBLE X)). DOUBLE is called again with input 10, so it rebinds X to 10 and evaluates its body. After DOUBLE returns 20, X is 5 again, and QUADRUPLE returns 20 as its result. X is unbound by QUADRUPLE and left with no value at all.

```
X is unbound
   ┌──── (QUADRUPLE 5)
   │
 X = 5     (DOUBLE (DOUBLE X))
   │
   │    ┌──── DOUBLE of 5
   │    │
   │  X = 5     (PLUS X X)
   │    │
   │    └──── DOUBLE returns 10
   │
 X = 5  again
   │
   │    ┌──── DOUBLE of 10
   │    │
   │  X = 10    (PLUS X X)
   │    │
   │    └──── DOUBLE returns 20
   │
 X = 5  again
   │
   └──── QUADRUPLE returns 20
X is unbound again
```

What we see from this diagram is that a symbol can be rebound repeatedly by functions. When a function is called it is free to rebind any variables it needs to name its inputs; when it returns, the variables get their previous values back.

In our second example we will rebind two variables. To make things more interesting, we will rebind each to the other's value.

```
(DEFUN MAKE-PAIR ( X Y) (LIST 'A X 'AND 'A Y))
```

`(MAKE-PAIR 'WING 'PRAYER)` evaluates to `(A WING AND A PRAYER)`

```
(DEFUN SWITCH (X Y) (MAKE-PAIR Y X))
```

`(SWITCH 'TWO 'ONE)` evaluates to `(A ONE AND A TWO)`

SWITCH takes two inputs **X** and **Y** and supplies them in reverse order to **MAKE-PAIR**, which also calls its inputs **X** and **Y**. Here is the binding diagram:

```
X and Y are unbound
   ┌── (SWITCH 'TWO 'ONE)
   │
  X = TWO    (MAKE-PAIR Y X)
  Y = ONE
   │
   │     ┌── MAKE-PAIR of ONE and TWO
   │     │
   │    X = ONE    (LIST 'A X 'AND 'A Y)
   │    Y = TWO
   │     │
   │     └── MAKE-PAIR returns (A ONE AND A TWO)
   │
  X = TWO again
  Y = ONE again
   │
   └── SWITCH returns (A ONE AND A TWO)
X and Y are unbound again
```

The value a variable has at any given time depends solely on which function was the last to bind it. This is called **dynamic scoping.** In contrast, some other computer languages, such as Algol or Pascal, employ **lexical scoping.** In lexical scoping it is possible to tell, simply by looking at a function, where each variable binding will come from. In dynamic scoping we cannot do this if the function references any variables it hasn't bound itself. For example, we can define a function MULT that takes one input, X, and multiplies it by the value of another variable, Y.

```
(DEFUN MULT (X) (TIMES X Y))
```

Since Y is initially unbound, if we call MULT directly we'll get an error.

`(MULT 5)` evaluates to *error! Y unbound variable*

However, if we define other functions that bind Y, we can use MULT in the body of those functions with no trouble.

```
(DEFUN DOUBLE (Y) (MULT 2))
```

`(DOUBLE 5)` evaluates to `10`

```
(DEFUN SQUARE (Y) (MULT Y))
```

`(SQUARE 5)` evaluates to `25`

If we look at just the MULT function, we can't tell where Y will be bound because it is bound *outside of* MULT. Y's binding is determined dynamically—that is, on the spot—when we evaluate MULT, hence the term dynamic scoping.

```
X and Y are unbound
    ┌─── (DOUBLE 5)
    │
  Y = 5       (MULT 2)
    │
    │    ┌─── MULT of 2
    │    │
    │  X = 2    (TIMES X Y)
    │    │
    │    └─── MULT returns 10
    │
    │  X is unbound again
    │
    └─── DOUBLE returns 10
Y is unbound again
```

Exercise

Assume we have defined the following functions:

```
(DEFUN ALPHA (X Y) (DIFFERENCE (BRAVO X) (CHARLIE (ADD1 Y) Y)))

(DEFUN BRAVO (Y) (TIMES X Y))

(DEFUN CHARLIE (Y Z) (TIMES Y (SUB1 Z)))
```

Suppose we now evaluate (ALPHA 2 3). Trace the values of the variables X, Y, and Z as they are bound, rebound, and unbound. Use a diagram like the one preceding.

4. THE QUOTE SPECIAL FORM

QUOTE, like DEFUN, is a special form: its inputs do not get evaluated. The QUOTE special form simply returns its input. For example:

`(QUOTE FOO)` evaluates to `FOO`
`(QUOTE (HELLO WORLD))` evaluates to `(HELLO WORLD)`

Early versions of Lisp used QUOTE instead of an apostrophe to indicate that something shouldn't be evaluated. That is, where we would write

```
(CONS 'UP '(DOWN SIDEWAYS))
```

old-style Lisp programmers would write

```
(CONS (QUOTE UP) (QUOTE (DOWN SIDEWAYS)))
```

Modern Lisp systems use the apostrophe as shorthand for QUOTE. Internally, however, they convert the apostrophe to QUOTE. We can demonstrate that this happens by using multiple quotes. The first quote is stripped away by the evaluation process, but any extra quotes remain.

`'FOO` evaluates to `FOO`
`''FOO` evaluates to `'FOO` *also written* `(QUOTE FOO)`
`(LIST 'QUOTE 'FOO)` evaluates to `(QUOTE FOO)` *also written* `'FOO`
`(CAR ''FOO)` evaluates to `QUOTE`
`(CDR ''FOO)` evaluates to `(FOO)`
`(LENGTH ''FOO)` evaluates to `2`

Depending on the version of Lisp your computer runs, you may occasionally see QUOTE written out instead of in its shorthand form, the apostrophe.

5. EVAL AND APPLY

EVAL is a Lisp primitive function. Each use of EVAL gives one level of evaluation.

`'(PLUS 2 2)` evaluates to `(PLUS 2 2)`
`(EVAL '(PLUS 2 2))` evaluates to `4`

`'''BOING` evaluates to `''BOING`
`(EVAL '''BOING)` evaluates to `'BOING`
`(EVAL (EVAL '''BOING)` evaluates to `BOING`
`(EVAL (EVAL (EVAL '''BOING)))` evaluates to
error! BOING unbound variable

`'(LIST 'TIMES 9 6))` evaluates to `(LIST 'TIMES 9 6)`
`(EVAL '(LIST 'TIMES 9 6))` evaluates to `(TIMES 9 6)`
`(EVAL (EVAL '(LIST 'TIMES 9 6)))` evaluates to `54`

We won't use EVAL explicitly in any of the programs we write, but we make implicit use of it all the time. You can think of the computer as a physical manifestation of EVAL. When it runs Lisp, everything you type is evaluated.

APPLY is also a Lisp primitive function. APPLY takes a function name and a list of inputs and invokes the specified function with those inputs. The inputs are *not* evaluated first.

`(APPLY 'PLUS '(2 3))` evaluates to `5`
`(APPLY 'EQUAL '(12 17))` evaluates to `NIL`
`(APPLY 'CONS '(AS (YOU LIKE IT)))` evaluates to `(AS YOU LIKE IT)`

EVAL and APPLY are related to each other. A popular exercise in more advanced Lisp texts involves writing each function in terms of the other.

Exercise

What do each of the following expressions evaluate to?

```
(LIST 'CONS T NIL)
(EVAL (LIST 'CONS T NIL))
(EVAL (EVAL (LIST 'CONS T NIL)))
(APPLY 'CONS '(T NIL))
(EVAL NIL)
(LIST 'EVAL NIL)
(EVAL (LIST 'EVAL NIL))
```

Functions Covered in Advanced Topics

EVAL-related function: APPLY
Special form: QUOTE

4
Conditionals

1. Introduction

Decision making is a fundamental part of computing; all nontrivial programs must make decisions. In this chapter we will study a class of decision-making functions called **conditionals** that decide on an action based on the results of some predicates. Since we can write our own predicates, we can use conditionals to construct functions that make arbitrarily complex decisions.

2. THE IF SPECIAL FORM

IF is the simplest Lisp conditional. It is not found in all dialects of Lisp, but it is easy to add to any dialect that lacks it. Conditionals are always special forms—that is, their arguments do not get evaluated automatically. DEFUN and QUOTE are two other special forms that have already been discussed.

IF takes three arguments: a **condition,** a **true-part,** and a **false-part.** If the condition is true, IF evaluates the true-part. If the condition is false, it skips the true-part and evaluates the false-part instead. Here are some examples. From this point on in the book, instead of writing "evaluates to" for each example, I will show the actual result the computer prints. The examples will appear in lowercase; my computer always responds in uppercase.

```
*(if (oddp 1) 'odd 'even)
ODD

*(if (oddp 2 ) 'odd 'even)
EVEN

*(if t 'condition-was-true 'condition-was-false)
CONDITION-WAS-TRUE

*(if nil 'condition-was-true 'condition-was-false)
CONDITION-WAS-FALSE

*(if (symbolp 'foo) (times 5 5) (plus 5 5))
25

*(if (symbolp 1) (times 5 5) (plus 5 5))
10
```

Let's use **IF** to construct a function that takes the absolute value of a number. Absolute values are always nonnegative. For negative numbers the absolute value is the negation of the number; for positive numbers and zero the absolute value is the number itself. This leads to a simple definition for **ABS**, our absolute value function:

```
(DEFUN ABS (X)
  (IF (LESSP X 0) (MINUS X) X))
```

The condition part of the **IF** is the expression (LESSP X 0)). If the condition evaluates to true, the true-part, (MINUS X), will be evaluated. (MINUS X) returns the negation of X. If the condition evaluates to false, meaning X is zero or positive, the false-part of the **IF** will be evaluated. The false-part is just X, so the input to **ABS** will be returned unchanged in this case. Here is how you should be reading the definition of **ABS**: "DEFUN ABS of X: IF (LESSP X 0) then (MINUS X) else X." The words "then" and "else" don't actually appear in the function, but mentally inserting them can help to clarify the function in your mind.

```
*(abs -5)     true-part takes the negation
5

*(abs 5)      false-part returns the number unchanged
5
```

Here's another simple decision-making function. SYMBOL-TEST returns a message telling whether or not the input is a symbol.

```
(DEFUN SYMBOL-TEST (X)
  (IF (SYMBOLP X) (LIST 'YES X 'IS 'A 'SYMBOL)
      (LIST 'NO X 'IS 'NOT 'A 'SYMBOL)))
```

When you read this function definition to yourself, you should read the IF part as "If SYMBOLP of X then . . . else . . ." Examples of SYMBOL-TEST:

```
*(symbol-test 'rutabaga)      evaluate true-part
(YES RUTABAGA IS A SYMBOL)

*(symbol-test 12345)          evaluate false-part
(NO 12345 IS NOT A SYMBOL)
```

IF can be given two inputs instead of three, in which case it behaves as if its third input (the false-part) were the symbol NIL.

```
*(if t 'happy)
HAPPY

*(if nil 'happy)
NIL
```

Exercises

1. Write a function MAKE-EVEN that makes an odd number even by adding one to it. If the input to MAKE-EVEN is already even, it should be returned unchanged.

2. Write a function FURTHER that makes a positive number more positive by adding one to it and a negative number more negative by subtracting one from it. What does your function do if given the number 0?

3. Recall the primitive function NOT: it returns NIL for a true input and T for a false one. Suppose Lisp didn't have a NOT primitive. Show how to write NOT using just IF and constants (no other functions). Call your function MY-NOT.

4. Write a function ORDERED that takes two numbers as input and makes a list of them in ascending order. (ORDERED 3 4) should return the list (3 4). (ORDERED 4 3) should also return (3 4)—that is, the first and second inputs should appear in reverse order when the first is greater than the second.

3. THE COND SPECIAL FORM

COND is the classic Lisp conditional. Its input consists of any number of **condition-action clauses.** The general form of a COND expression is

```
(COND  (cond-1 action-1)
       (cond-2 action-2)
       (cond-3 action-3)
           .....
       (cond-n action-n))
```

Here is how COND works: it goes through the clauses one at a time. If the condition part of a clause evaluates to *true*, COND evaluates the action part and returns its value. If the condition evaluates to *false*, COND skips the action part and examines the next clause.

Let's use COND to write a function COMPARE that compares two numbers. If the numbers are equal, COMPARE will say "numbers are the same"; if the first number is less than the second, it will say "first is smaller"; if the first number is greater than the second, it will say "first is bigger." Each case is handled by a separate COND clause.

```
(DEFUN COMPARE (X Y)
  (COND ((EQUAL X Y) 'NUMBERS-ARE-THE-SAME)
        ((LESSP X Y) 'FIRST-IS-SMALLER)
        ((GREATERP X Y) 'FIRST-IS-BIGGER)))
```

Take a closer look at the COND. It is a four-element list, where the first element is the symbol COND and the remaining three elements are condition-action clauses. The first clause is a two-element list whose first element is the expression (EQUAL X Y). This is the condition part of the clause. The second element, the action part, is the quoted symbol 'NUMBERS-ARE-THE-SAME.

Here are some examples of the COMPARE function:

```
*(compare 3 5)
FIRST-IS-SMALLER

*(compare 7 2)
FIRST-IS-BIGGER

*(compare 4 4)
NUMBERS-ARE-THE-SAME
```

Exercise

For each of the following calls to COMPARE, write "1," "2," or "3" to indicate which clause of the COND will have a predicate that evaluates to true.

```
_______    (COMPARE 9 1)
_______    (COMPARE (PLUS 2 2) 5)
_______    (COMPARE 6 (TIMES 2 3))
```

COND and IF are similar functions. COND may appear more versatile since it accepts any number of clauses, but there is a way to do the same thing with nested IFs. This is discussed in more detail later in the chapter.

4. USING T AS A CONDITION

One of the standard tricks for using COND is to include a clause of form

```
(T action)
```

The condition part, T, is always true, so if COND ever reaches this clause it is guaranteed to evaluate the action part. We put this clause at the very end of the COND expression so that it will be reached only if all the condition parts of the preceding clauses fail. Example: The following function returns the name of a country given the name of its capital. If the function doesn't know about a particular capital, it returns the symbol UNKNOWN.

```
(DEFUN WHERE-IS (X)
  (COND ((EQUAL X 'PARIS) 'FRANCE)
        ((EQUAL X 'LONDON) 'ENGLAND)
        ((EQUAL X 'PEKING) 'CHINA)
        (T 'UNKNOWN)))
```

Note the last clause of the COND begins with T. If none of the preceding clauses have conditions that return true, the last clause will be reached and the function will return UNKNOWN.

```
*(where-is 'london)
ENGLAND

*(where-is 'peking)
CHINA

*(where-is 'hackensack)
UNKNOWN
```

Exercise

Use the T-as-condition trick to construct a version of the absolute value function, ABS, based on COND instead of IF.

5. TWO MORE EXAMPLES OF COND

Here is another function, called EMPHASIZE, that changes the first word of a phrase from "good" to "great," or from "bad" to "awful," and returns the modified phrase:

```
(DEFUN EMPHASIZE (X)
  (COND ((EQUAL (CAR X) 'GOOD) (CONS 'GREAT (CDR X)))
        ((EQUAL (CAR X) 'BAD) (CONS 'AWFUL (CDR X)))))
```

Let's take as an example the phrase (GOOD MYSTERY STORY). What happens inside EMPHASIZE? The variable X is bound to (GOOD MYSTERY STORY), and COND starts going through the condition-action clauses. The first one is:

```
((EQUAL (CAR X) 'GOOD) (CONS 'GREAT (CDR X)))
```

Since (CAR X) evaluates to GOOD, the condition part of this clause is true. The action part then constructs a new list from the symbol GREAT and the CDR of the input, and that is what the function returns:

```
*(emphasize '(good mystery story))
(GREAT MYSTERY STORY)
```

Now suppose we try to emphasize (MEDIOCRE MYSTERY STORY). The first clause compares MEDIOCRE to GOOD and returns NIL. The next compares MEDIOCRE to BAD and also returns NIL. Now COND has run out of clauses, so it returns NIL. Therefore, NIL is the result of the EMPHASIZE function:

```
*(emphasize '(mediocre mystery story))
NIL
```

What if we want EMPHASIZE to return the original input instead of NIL when it can't figure out how to emphasize it? We simply use the T-as-condition trick, demonstrated in the function EMPHASIZE2:

```
(DEFUN EMPHASIZE2 (X)
  (COND ((EQUAL (CAR X) 'GOOD) (CONS 'GREAT (CDR X)))
        ((EQUAL (CAR X) 'BAD) (CONS 'AWFUL (CDR X)))
        (T X)))
```

If the COND reaches the last clause, the condition T is guaranteed to evaluate to true and the input, X, is returned.

```
*(emphasize2 '(good day))
(GREAT DAY)

*(emphasize2 '(bad day))
(AWFUL DAY)

*(emphasize2 '(long day))
(LONG DAY)
```

Here is a function COMPUTE that takes three inputs. If the first input is the symbol SUM-OF, the function returns the sum of the second and third inputs. If it is the symbol PRODUCT-OF, the function returns the product of the second and third inputs. Otherwise it returns the list (THAT DOES NOT COMPUTE).

```
(DEFUN COMPUTE (OP X Y)
  (COND ((EQUAL OP 'SUM-OF) (PLUS X Y))
        ((EQUAL OP 'PRODUCT-OF) (TIMES X Y))
        (T '(THAT DOES NOT COMPUTE))))
```

Here are some examples of the COMPUTE function:

```
*(compute 'sum-of 3 7)
10

*(compute 'product-of 2 4)
8

*(compute 'zorch-of 3 1)
(THAT DOES NOT COMPUTE)
```

6. COND AND PARENTHESIS ERRORS

Parenthesis errors can play havoc with COND expressions. Most COND clauses begin with exactly two parentheses. The first marks the beginning of the clause, and the second marks the beginning of the condition part of the clause. For example, in the WHERE-IS function, the condition part of the first clause is the expression

```
(EQUAL X 'PARIS)
```

so the clause itself looks like

```
((EQUAL X 'PARIS) . . .)
```

If the condition part of a clause is just a symbol, not a call to a function, then the clause should begin with a single parenthesis. Notice that in WHERE-IS, the clause with T as the condition begins with only one parenthesis.

Here are two of the more common parenthesis errors made with COND. First, suppose we leave a parenthesis out of a COND clause. What would happen?

```
(COND (EQUAL X 'PARIS 'FRANCE)
      (. . .)
      (. . .)
      (T 'UNKNOWN))
```

The first clause of the COND starts with only one left parenthesis instead of two. As a result, the condition part of this clause is just the symbol EQUAL. When the condition part is evaluated, EQUAL will cause an unbound variable error.

On the other hand, consider what happens when too many parentheses are used:

```
(COND ((. . .) 'FRANCE)
      ((. . .) 'ENGLAND)
      ((. . .) 'CHINA)
      ((T 'UNKNOWN)))
```

If X is bound to, say, the symbol HACKENSACK, we will reach the fourth COND clause. Due to the presence of an extra pair of parentheses in this clause, the condition part is (T 'UNKNOWN) instead of simply the symbol T. T is not a function, so this condition part will generate an undefined function error.

Exercises

1. For each of the following COND expressions, tell whether the parenthesization is correct or incorrect. If incorrect, explain where the error lies.

```
(COND (SYMBOLP X) 'SYMBOL
      (T 'NOT-A-SYMBOL))

(COND ((SYMBOLP X) 'SYMBOL)
      (T 'NOT-A-SYMBOL))

(COND ((SYMBOLP X) ('SYMBOL))
      (T 'NOT-A-SYMBOL))

(COND ((SYMBOLP X) 'SYMBOL)
      ((T 'NOT-A-SYMBOL)))
```

2. Write EMPHASIZE3, which is like EMPHASIZE2 but adds the symbol VERY onto the list if it doesn't know how to emphasize it. For example, EMPHASIZE3 of (LONG DAY) should produce (VERY LONG DAY). What does EMPHASIZE3 of (VERY LONG DAY) produce?

3. Extend your EMPHASIZE3 function to also change "nice" to "exceptional" and "poor" to "abysmal." Call your new function EMPHASIZE4. Test it out on some examples you make up yourself.

4. Type in the following suspicious function definition:

```
(DEFUN MAKE-ODD (X)
  (COND (T X)
        ((NOT (ODDP X)) (ADD1 X))))
```

   What is wrong with this function? Try out the function on the numbers 3, 4, and −2. Rewrite it so it works correctly; then try it on those numbers again.

5. Write a function FIRSTZERO that takes a list of three numbers as input and returns a word (one of "first," "second," "third," or "none") indicating where the first zero appears in the list. Example: (FIRSTZERO '(3 0 4)) should return SECOND. What happens if you try to call FIRSTZERO with three separate numbers instead of a list of three numbers—for example, (FIRSTZERO 3 0 4)?

6. Write a function CYCLE that cyclically counts from 1 to 99. CYCLE called with an input of 1 should return 2, with an input of 2 should return 3, with an input of 3 should return 4, and so on. With an input of 99, CYCLE should return 1. That's the cyclical part. Do not try to solve this with 99 COND clauses!

7. Write a function HOWCOMPUTE that is the inverse of the COMPUTE function described previously. HOWCOMPUTE takes three numbers as input and figures out what operation would produce the third from the first two. (HOWCOMPUTE 3 4 7) should return SUM-OF. (HOWCOMPUTE 3 4 12) should return PRODUCT-OF. HOWCOMPUTE should return the list (BEATS ME) if it can't find a relationship between the first two inputs and the third. Suggest some ways to extend HOWCOMPUTE.

7. THE AND AND OR SPECIAL FORMS

Often we will need to construct complex predicates from simple ones. The AND and OR special forms make this possible. Suppose we want a predicate for small (no more than two-digit) positive odd numbers. We use AND to express this conjunction of simple conditions:

```
(DEFUN SMALL-POSITIVE-ODDP (X)
  (AND (LESSP X 100)
       (GREATER X 0)
       (ODDP X)))
```

Or suppose we want a function GTEST that takes two numbers as input and returns T either if the first is greater than the second or if one of them is zero. These conditions form a disjunctive set; only one need be true for GTEST to return T. OR is used for disjunctions.

```
(DEFUN GTEST (X Y)
  (OR (GREATERP X Y)
      (ZEROP X)
      (ZEROP Y)))
```

Like COND, AND and OR are special forms and can take any number of clauses as input. For AND and OR, however, the clauses are conditions, not condition-action pairs.

8. EVALUATING AND AND OR

AND and OR have slightly different meanings in Lisp than they do in logic or in English. The precise rule for evaluating AND is: evaluate the clauses one at a time; if a clause returns NIL, stop; otherwise go on to the next one. If all the clauses yield non-NIL results, AND returns the value of the last clause. Examples:

```
*(and nil t t)
NIL

*(and 'george nil 'harry)
NIL

*(and 'george 'fred 'harry)
HARRY

*(and 1 2 3 4 5)
5
```

The rule for evaluating OR is: evaluate the clauses one at a time; if a clause returns something other than NIL, stop and return that value; otherwise go on to the next clause, or return NIL if none are left.

```
*(or nil t t)
T

*(or 'george nil 'harry)
GEORGE

*(or 'george 'fred 'harry)
GEORGE

*(or nil 'fred 'harry)
FRED
```

Exercise

What results do the following expressions produce? Read the evaluation rules for AND and OR carefully before answering.

```
(AND 'FEE 'FIE 'FOE)
(OR 'FEE 'FIE 'FOE)
(OR NIL 'FOE NIL)
(AND 'FEE 'FIE NIL)
(AND (EQUAL 'ABC 'ABC) 'YES)
(OR (EQUAL 'ABC 'ABC) 'YES)
```

9. BUILDING COMPLEX PREDICATES

The HOW-ALIKE function compares two numbers several different ways to see in what way they are similar. It uses AND to construct complex predicates as part of a COND clause:

```
(DEFUN HOW-ALIKE (A B)
  (COND ((EQUAL A B) 'THE-SAME)
        ((AND (ODDP A) (ODDP B)) 'BOTH-ODD)
        ((AND (NOT (ODDP A)) (NOT (ODDP B))) 'BOTH-EVEN)
        ((AND (LESSP A 0) (LESSP B 0)) 'BOTH-NEGATIVE)
        (T 'NOT-ALIKE)))
```

Here are some examples of **HOW-ALIKE**:

```
*(how-alike 7 7)
THE-SAME

*(how-alike 3 5)
BOTH-ODD

*(how-alike 4 8)
BOTH-EVEN

*(how-alike -2 -3)
BOTH-NEGATIVE

*(how-alike 5 8)
NOT-ALIKE
```

The **SAME-SIGN** predicate uses a combination of AND and OR to test if its two inputs have the same sign:

```
(DEFUN SAME-SIGN (X Y)
  (OR (AND (ZEROP X) (ZEROP Y))
      (AND (LESSP X 0) (LESSP Y 0))
      (AND (GREATERP X 0) (GREATERP Y 0))))
```

SAME-SIGN returns T if any of the inputs to OR returns T. Each of these inputs is an AND expression; the first one tests whether X is zero and Y is zero, the second tests whether X is negative and Y is negative, and the third tests whether X is positive and Y is positive. Examples:

```
*(same-sign 0 0)
T

*(same-sign -3 -4)
T

*(same-sign 3 4)
T

*(same-sign -3 4)
NIL
```

Exercises

Write the following functions and test them on the computer to make sure they work.

1. A predicate called GEQ that returns T if its first input is greater than or equal to its second input.

2. A function that squares a number if it is odd and positive, doubles it if it is odd and negative, and otherwise divides the number by 2.

3. A predicate that returns T if the first input is either BOY or GIRL and the second input is CHILD, or if the first input is either MAN or WOMAN and the second input is ADULT.

4. A function that plays the Rock-Scissors-Paper game. In this game, each player picks one of Rock, Scissors, or Paper, and then both players tell what they picked. Rock "breaks" Scissors, so if you pick Rock and your opponent picks Scissors, you win. Scissors "cuts" Paper, and Paper "covers" Rock. If both players pick the same thing it's a tie. The function PLAY should take two inputs, each of which is either ROCK, SCISSORS, or PAPER, and return one of the symbols YOU-WIN, YOU-LOSE, or TIE. Assume you are the first player and your opponent is the second. Examples: (PLAY 'ROCK 'SCISSORS) should return YOU-WIN. (PLAY 'PAPER 'SCISSORS) should return YOU-LOSE.

10. WHY AND AND OR ARE CONDITIONALS

Why are AND and OR classed as conditionals instead of regular functions? The answer has to do with a conditional's ability to *not* evaluate a clause. If any clause of an AND returns NIL, or any clause of an OR returns non-NIL, none of the succeeding clauses get evaluated. One reason we may wish to halt evaluation is to avoid errors. For example, consider the POSNUMP predicate:

```
(DEFUN POSNUMP (X)
  (AND (NUMBER X) (GREATER X 0)))
```

POSNUMP returns T if its input is a number and is positive. The GREATERP function can be used to tell if a number is positive by comparing it to zero. However, if GREATERP is used on something other than a number, we will get a wrong-type input error, so it is important to make sure that the input to POSNUMP is a number *before* invoking GREATERP. If the input isn't a number we must not call GREATERP.

Here is an incorrect version of POSNUMP:

```
(DEFUN FAULTY-POSNUMP (X)
  (AND (GREATERP X 0) (NUMBERP X)))
```

If FAULTY-POSNUMP is called on the symbol FRED instead of a number, the first thing it does is check if FRED is greater than 0, which causes a wrong-type input error. However, if the regular POSNUMP function is called with input FRED, the NUMBERP predicate returns NIL, so AND returns NIL *without ever calling* GREATERP.

11. CONDITIONALS ARE INTERCHANGEABLE

Functions that use AND and OR can also be implemented using COND or IF, and vice versa. Recall the definition of POSNUMP:

```
(DEFUN POSNUMP (X)
  (AND (NUMBERP X) (GREATERP X 0)))
```

Here is a version of POSNUMP written with IF instead of AND:

```
(DEFUN POSNUMP-2 (X)
  (IF (NUMBERP X) (GREATERP X 0) NIL))
```

This version of POSNUMP tests for a number first, and if the condition succeeds, the true-part of the IF evaluates (GREATERP X 0). If the number tests fails, the false-part of the IF is NIL. Trace the evaluations of the function on paper with inputs like FRED, 7, and −2 to better understand how it works. Here is another version of POSNUMP, this time using COND:

```
(DEFUN POSNUMP-3 (X)
  (COND ((NUMBERP X) (GREATERP X 0))
        (T NIL)))
```

Let's look at another use of conditionals. This is the original version of WHERE-IS using COND:

```
(DEFUN WHERE-IS (X)
  (COND ((EQUAL X 'PARIS) 'FRANCE)
        ((EQUAL X 'LONDON) 'ENGLAND)
        ((EQUAL X 'PEKING) 'CHINA)
        (T 'UNKNOWN)))
```

This COND has four clauses. We can write WHERE-IS using IF instead of COND by putting three IFs together. Such a construct is called a **nested if.**

```
(DEFUN WHERE-IS-2 (X)
  (IF (EQUAL X 'PARIS) 'FRANCE
      (IF (EQUAL X 'LONDON) 'ENGLAND
          (IF (EQUAL X 'PEKING) 'CHINA
              'UNKNOWN))))
```

Suppose we call WHERE-IS-2 with the input PEKING. X is bound to PEKING. The body of WHERE-IS-2 is a single IF whose condition part tests if X is equal to PARIS. It is not, so the IF evaluates its false part. The false part is also an IF, and this IF's condition tests whether X is equal to LONDON. It is not, so the IF evaluates its own false part—yet another IF. This third IF tests if X is equal to PEKING, which it is, so its true part evaluates to CHINA. The third IF returns CHINA, which is now the value of the false-part of the second IF so it returns CHINA, which is now the value of the false-part of the first IF so it returns CHINA as well. The result of (WHERE-IS-2 'PEKING) is CHINA.

We can write another version of WHERE-IS using AND and OR. This version employs a simple two-level scheme rather than the more complex nesting required for IF.

```
(DEFUN WHERE-IS-3 (X)
  (OR (AND (EQUAL X 'PARIS) 'FRANCE)
      (AND (EQUAL X 'LONDON) 'ENGLAND)
      (AND (EQUAL X 'PEKING) 'CHINA)
      'UNKNOWN))
```

Let's evaluate (WHERE-IS-3 'LONDON). X is bound to LONDON, and OR starts going through its clauses looking for one that isn't

NIL. The first clause is an AND expression; AND evaluates (EQUAL X 'PARIS) and gets a NIL result, so AND gives up and returns NIL. OR moves on to its second clause. This is also an AND expression; (EQUAL X 'LONDON) returns T, so AND moves on to its next clause. 'ENGLAND evaluates to ENGLAND; AND has run out of clauses so it returns the value of the last one. Since OR has found a non-NIL clause, OR now returns ENGLAND.

Since IF, COND, AND, and OR are interchangeable conditionals, you may wonder why Lisp has more than one. It's a matter of convenience. IF is the easiest to use for simple functions like absolute value. AND or OR are good for writing complex predicates like SMALL-POSITIVE-ODDP. COND is easiest to use when we have many conditions to check, as in WHERE-IS and HOW-ALIKE. Choosing the right conditional for the job is part of the art of programming.

Exercises

1. Show how to write the expression (AND X1 X2 X3 X4) using nested IFs instead of AND.

2. Write a version of the COMPARE function using IF instead of COND. Also write a version using AND and OR.

3. Write versions of GTEST (page 105) using IF and COND.

4. Use COND to write a predicate BOILINGP that takes two inputs, TEMP and SCALE, and returns T if the temperature is above the boiling point of water on the specified scale. If the scale is FAHRENHEIT the boiling point is 212 degrees; if CELSIUS, the boiling point is 100 degrees. Also write versions using IF and AND/OR instead of COND.

5. The WHERE-IS function has four COND clauses, so WHERE-IS-2 needs three nested IFs. Suppose WHERE-IS had eight COND clauses. How many IFs would WHERE-IS-2 need? How many ORs would WHERE-IS-3 need? How many ANDs would it need?

SUMMARY

Conditionals allow the computer to make decisions that control its behavior. IF is a simple conditional; its syntax is (IF condition true-part false-part). COND, the most general conditional, takes a set of condition-action clauses as input and evaluates the condition parts one at a time until it find a true one. It then returns the value of the action part of that clause.

AND and OR are also conditionals. AND evaluates clauses one at a time until one of them returns NIL. If all the clauses evaluate to true, AND returns the value of the last one. OR evaluates clauses until a non-NIL value is found and returns that value. If all the clauses are NIL, OR returns NIL.

A useful programming trick when writing COND expressions is to place a list of form (T action) as the final clause of the COND. Since the condition part of this clause will always be true, the clause serves as a kind of catchall case that will be evaluated when the conditions of all the preceding clauses are false.

An important feature of conditionals is their ability to not evaluate all of their inputs. This lets us prevent errors by protecting a sensitive expression with predicates that can cause evaluation to stop. Conditionals can do this because they are special forms, not regular functions.

Review Exercises

1. Why are conditionals important?

2. What does IF do if given two inputs instead of three?

3. COND can accept any number of clauses, but IF takes at most three inputs. How is it then that any function involving COND can be rewritten to use IF instead?

4. What does COND return if given *no* clauses—that is, what does (COND) evaluate to?

Functions Covered in This Chapter

Conditionals: IF, COND, AND, OR
Functions on numbers: ABS, MINUS

Advanced Topics 4

1. BOOLEAN FUNCTIONS

Boolean functions are functions whose inputs and outputs are truth values, that is, T or NIL. We have already encountered boolean functions under the name **truth functions** in previous chapters. The term boolean comes from George Boole, an English mathematician. Boolean logic is used today to describe the behavior of most computer circuits.

Yet another name for boolean functions is **logical functions,** since they use the logical values *true* and *false*. Let's define a two-input LOGICAL-AND function:

```
(DEFUN LOGICAL-AND (X Y) (AND X Y T))
```

This function differs from the AND special form in several respects. First, as already noted, it must be given exactly two inputs. This is a minor point because we can always nest or cascade several of them to handle more inputs. More important, LOGICAL-AND returns only the logical values T or NIL, nothing else.

```
*(logical-and 'tweet 'woof)
T

*(and 'tweet 'woof)
WOOF
```

Most important of all is the fact that LOGICAL-AND is not a special form: it cannot control whether or not its inputs get evaluated. In the following example, the expression (ODDP 'FRED) causes an error for LOGICAL-AND but not for AND, because AND never evaluates the second clause.

```
*(and (numberp 'fred) (oddp 'fred))
NIL

*(logical-and (numberp 'fred) (oddp 'fred))
;FRED - WRONG TYPE INPUT
```

Boolean functions are simpler than conditionals. Boolean functions in Lisp correspond to boolean circuits in electronics; they are the primitive logical operations from which computer circuitry is built.

Exercises

1. Write versions of LOGICAL-AND using IF and COND instead of AND.

2. Write LOGICAL-OR. Make sure it returns only T or NIL for its result.

3. Is NOT a conditional? Is it a boolean function? Do you need to write a LOGICAL-NOT function?

2. TRUTH TABLES

Truth tables are a convenient way of describing boolean functions. To describe a function via a truth table, we simply consider in turn every possible combination of inputs and write down the result the function should produce. Here is the truth table for NOT:

X	(NOT X)
T	NIL
NIL	T

Here is the truth table for LOGICAL-AND. Since this function takes two inputs, each of which has two possible values, the table has $2^2=4$ lines.

X	Y	(LOGICAL-AND X Y)
T	T	T
T	NIL	NIL
NIL	T	NIL
NIL	NIL	NIL

Exercises

1. Construct a truth table for LOGICAL-OR.

2. Imagine a LOGICAL-IF function that works like IF does, except it always takes exactly three inputs and its outputs are limited to T or NIL. How many lines are in its truth table?

3. Write down the truth table for LOGICAL-IF.

3. DEMORGAN'S THEOREM

DeMorgan's Theorem concerns the interchangeability of AND and OR. If you have one of these functions plus NOT, you can always build the other. Here is DeMorgan's Theorem stated two different ways:

```
(AND X Y) = (NOT (OR (NOT X) (NOT Y)))

(OR X Y) = (NOT (AND (NOT X) (NOT Y)))
```

These equations look pretty tricky, so let me also state them in English. The first equation says that if X and Y are true, then neither X is false nor Y is false. The second equation says that if either X or Y is true, then X and Y can't both be false. The English version sounds obvious, but do you believe the equations? Let's test them out.

```
(DEFUN DEMORGAN-AND (X Y) (NOT (OR (NOT X) (NOT Y))))

(DEFUN DEMORGAN-OR (X Y) (NOT (AND (NOT X) (NOT Y))))

*(logical-and t t)
T
```

```
*(demorgan-and t t)
T

*(logical-and t nil)
NIL

*(demorgan-and t nil)
NIL

*(logical-or t nil)
T

*(demorgan-or t nil)
T

*(logical-or nil nil)
NIL

*(demorgan-or nil nil)
NIL
```

This is not a complete test of the equations; you are welcome to test out the remaining cases yourself.

DeMorgan's Theorem proved the interchangeability of the *logical* AND and OR functions. Does it hold for Lisp's *conditional* AND and OR functions as well? Not exactly. The use of double NOTs means that arbitrary inputs like FOO will be changed to the canonical true value T on output, so in this sense DeMorgan's Theorem doesn't hold.

```
*(and 'foo 'bar)
BAR

*(not (or (not 'foo) (not 'bar)))
T
```

However, DeMorgan's Theorem does preserve the conditional property of AND and OR. That is, clauses that (AND X Y) would evaluate would also be evaluated by (NOT (OR (NOT X) (NOT Y))), and clauses that AND would not evaluate would not be evaluated by the other expression. Example:

```
*(and (numberp 'fred) (greaterp 'fred 0))
NIL
```

```
*(not (or (not (numberp 'fred)) (not (greaterp 'fred 0))))
NIL
```

Exercises

1. Write down the DeMorgan equations for the three-input versions of AND and OR.

2. The NAND function (NAND is short for Not AND) is also commonly found in computer circuitry. Here is a definition of NAND. Write down its truth table.

   ```
   (DEFUN NAND (X Y) (NOT (AND X Y)))
   ```

3. NAND is called a **logically complete** function because we can construct all other boolean functions from various combinations of it. For example, here is a version of NOT called NOT2 constructed from NAND:

   ```
   (DEFUN NOT2 (X) (NAND X X))
   ```

   Construct versions of AND and OR by putting together NANDs. In each case you will have to use more than one NAND.

4. Consider the NOR function (short for Not OR). Construct versions of NOT, AND, NAND, and OR by putting NORs together.

5. Is AND logically complete the way NAND and NOR are?

5 Global Variables and Side Effects

1. INTRODUCTION

The variables in a function's argument list are called **local variables.** They are bound when the function is called and unbound again when it returns, hence their values are local to the function's body. All the variables we've seen so far have been local ones.

Global variables are not associated with any particular function; they remain bound all the time. In the first half of this chapter we will learn to use global variables.

The latter half of the chapter is devoted to the topic of **side effects.** The normal effect of a function is to compute and return a value, but some functions are useful for additional actions they perform, such as printing a message on the terminal or changing the value of a global variable. These actions are called the side effects of the function.

2. SETQ ASSIGNS A VALUE TO A VARIABLE

SETQ is a special form that assigns a value to a variable. If the variable is unbound, it will become globally bound. If the variable is bound, either locally or globally, SETQ changes the value it is bound to. Here is an example of SETQ creating a global variable and later changing its value.

`*vowels` `;VOWELS - UNBOUND VARIABLE`	*VOWELS is initially unbound*
`*(setq vowels '(a e i o u))` `(A E I O U)`	*SETQ gives VOWELS a global value*
`*vowels` `(A E I O U)`	*now VOWELS is globally bound*
`*(length vowels)` `5`	*we can use VOWELS in expressions*
`*(cdr vowels)` `(E I O U)`	
`*(cddr vowels)` `(I O U)`	
`*vowels` `(A E I O U)`	*VOWELS still has the same value*
`*(setq vowels '(a e i o u and sometimes y))` `(A E I O U AND SOMETIMES Y)`	*give VOWELS a new value*
`*vowels` `(A E I O U AND SOMETIMES Y)`	*now VOWELS has the new value*

The first input to SETQ is the name of a variable; SETQ does not evaluate this input. The second input to SETQ is the value to set the variable to; this input is evaluated. The value returned by SETQ is the value it set the variable to.

Global variables are useful for holding on to values so we don't have to retype them continually. Example:

```
*(setq long-list '(a b c d e f g h i))
(A B C D E F G H I)

*(setq first (car long-list))
A

*(setq rest (cdr long-list))
(B C D E F G H I)
```

```
*(cons first rest)
(A B C D E F G H I)

*(equal long-list (cons first rest))
T

*(list first rest)
(A (B C D E F G H I))
```

FIRST, REST, and LONG-LIST are all global variables.

3. BOUNDP AND MAKUNBOUND

The BOUNDP predicate takes the name of a variable as input and returns T if the variable is bound or NIL if it is unbound. BOUNDP is not available in all Lisp dialects.

```
*(boundp 'fred)
NIL

*fred
;FRED - UNBOUND VARIABLE

*(setq fred '(frederick wentworth thistlebottom iii))
(FREDERICK WENTWORTH THISTLEBOTTOM III)

*(boundp 'fred)
T

*fred
(FREDERICK WENTWORTH THISTELEBOTTOM III)
```

Lisp also allows us to take away the binding of a variable, to make it unbound again. The function for doing this is called MAKUNBOUND ("make unbound"). MAKUNBOUND is not used very often. Like BOUNDP, it is not available in all Lisp dialects.

```
*(setq bell '(ding dong))
(DING DONG)
```

```
*(boundp 'bell)
T

*bell
(DING DONG)

*(makunbound 'bell)
BELL

*(boundp 'bell)
NIL

*bell
;BELL - UNBOUND VARIABLE
```

4. PROGRAMMING WITH GLOBAL VARIABLES

One way for functions to communicate with one another is by passing data as arguments. We have used this method many times. Another way for functions to communicate is by keeping their data in a global variable. Suppose we want a function to keep a running total of how many glasses a lemonade stand sells. We can use a global variable to hold this information. Whenever another glass is sold, a function can update the total by changing the value of the global variable. Here is an updating function for the lemonade stand:

```
(DEFUN SOLD (GLASSES)
   (SETQ TOTAL (PLUS GLASSES TOTAL)))
```

To use our SOLD function we must give the global variable TOTAL an initial value, so the expression (PLUS TOTAL GLASSES) doesn't cause an unbound variable error the first time we sell a glass of lemonade. This is called **initializing** the variable. Naturally we'll start TOTAL off at 0. After TOTAL is initialized we can use SOLD to record each sale.

```
*(setq total 0)     initialize global variable TOTAL to 0
0
```

```
*total             TOTAL now has a global binding
0

*(sold 1)          sold one glass
1

*total             total sales = 1
1
```

Let's trace through the first call to SOLD. Initially the value of TOTAL is 0. We called SOLD with input 1, so GLASSES (a local variable) is bound to 1. The expression (PLUS GLASSES TOTAL) evaluates to 1, so SETQ makes this the new value of TOTAL. After SOLD returns, GLASSES becomes unbound again, but the value of TOTAL is still 1 because TOTAL is a global variable. Let's sell a few more glasses:

```
*(sold 1)          sold another glass
2

*(sold 3)          sold three more glasses
5

*total             total sales = 5 glasses
5

*(sold 1)          sold another glass
6

*(sold 2)          sold two more glasses
8

*total             total sales = 8 glasses
8
```

Exercise

Suppose we had forgotten to set TOTAL to zero before calling SOLD for the first time. What would happen? Suppose we initialized TOTAL to the symbol FOO instead of 0. When would the error become apparent?

5. SIDE EFFECTS

Ordinary functions like CAR or PLUS are useful only because of the values they return. Other functions are useful primarily because of their side effects. SETQ's side effect is that it changes the value of a variable. The side effect is much more important than the value SETQ returns.

The possibility of side effects allows a function to compute one thing and return something else. For example, we can modify our lemonade stand function to always return the symbol SALE-RECORDED. This will not interfere with the actual recording of the sale, which takes place in the global variable TOTAL.

```
*(defun sold (glasses)
   (setq total (plus glasses total))
   'sale-recorded)
SOLD

*total
8

*(sold 1)
SALE-RECORDED

*total
9
```

Notice that the SOLD function now has two expressions in its body. Only the value of the second expression is returned, but the first expression is important because of its side effect.

Another place where multiple expressions can occur is in the action part of a COND clause. As in function bodies, only the value of the last expression is returned. The additional expressions are useful only if they have side effects. Here is a set of functions for updating a bank balance as deposits and withdrawals are made. The functions communicate through a global variable called BALANCE.

```
(DEFUN BANK (TRANSACTION AMOUNT)
  (COND ((EQUAL TRANSACTION 'DEPOSIT) (MAKE-DEPOSIT AMOUNT))
        ((EQUAL TRANSACTION 'WITHDRAWAL) (MAKE-WITHDRAWAL AMOUNT))
        (T '(UNKNOWN TRANSACTION))))
```

```
(DEFUN MAKE-DEPOSIT (AMOUNT)
  (SETQ BALANCE (PLUS BALANCE AMOUNT))
  (LIST 'DEPOSITED AMOUNT 'NEW 'BALANCE 'IS BALANCE))

(DEFUN MAKE-WITHDRAWAL (AMOUNT)
  (COND ((LESSP BALANCE AMOUNT) '(INSUFFICIENT FUNDS))
        (T (SETQ BALANCE (DIFFERENCE BALANCE AMOUNT))
           (LIST 'WITHDREW AMOUNT 'NEW 'BALANCE 'IS BALANCE))))
```

After initializing BALANCE to be 250 dollars, we can test out our functions:

```
*(setq balance 250)
250

*(bank 'deposit 25)
(DEPOSITED 25 NEW BALANCE IS 275)

*(bank 'steal 200)
(UNKNOWN TRANSACTION)

*(bank 'withdraw 200)
(WITHDREW 200 NEW BALANCE IS 75)

*(bank 'withdraw 150)
(INSUFFICIENT FUNDS)

*balance
75
```

Exercises

1. The following function is a variant of our lemonade stand function, SOLD. What's wrong with the function? If we do (SOLD 3) and then (SOLD 5), what will the value of TOTAL be?

```
(DEFUN SOLD (GLASSES)
  (SETQ TOTAL 0)
  (SETQ TOTAL (PLUS GLASSES TOTAL)))
```

2. The following function has two expressions in its body. What would happen if the first expression were deleted?

```
(DEFUN SOLD (GLASSES)
  'SALE-RECORDED
  (SETQ TOTAL (PLUS GLASSES TOTAL)))
```

3. Write a function FLIP that takes no inputs but changes the value of the global variable SWITCH to ON if it is OFF, or to OFF if it is ON. FLIP should return the symbol CLICK; its side effect will be to change the value of SWITCH. Call the function by typing (FLIP).

4. Write a function of no arguments called EXCHANGE that exchanges the values of the global variables A and B. For example, if the value of A is WOOF and the value of B is TWEET, after typing (EXCHANGE) the value of A should be TWEET and the value of B should be WOOF. (Hint: You may want to use a third variable for temporary storage, though it is not strictly necessary to do so.)

6. SUMMARY

A variable is global to a function if it is not locally bound by that function. Local variables are bound when the function is called and become unbound when it returns, but global variables remain bound all the time. Global variables are useful for holding data between calls to functions.

The BOUNDP predicate returns T if a variable is bound. The MAKUNBOUND function removes the binding of a variable.

SETQ is a special form that changes the value of a variable, giving it a global binding it if is not bound already. This side effect is what makes SETQ useful.

When multiple expressions appear in a function body or COND clause, the value of the last expression is returned. The other expressions are useful only for their side effects.

Review Exercises

1. What is the difference between local and global binding of a variable?

2. What is a side effect?

3. Why must SETQ be a special form instead of a regular function?

4. Would side effects be possible without global variables?

Functions Covered in This Chapter

Special form: SETQ
Binding functions: BOUNDP, MAKUNBOUND

Keyboard Exercise

In this keyboard exercise we will construct a scheduling system for keeping track of a set of tasks and deciding which one to work on next. The scheduling policy we will use is called LIFO, or "*l*ast *i*n *f*irst *o*ut," meaning the last task to be assigned is the first to be worked on.

1. The scheduling system needs to keep track of the current list of tasks. We will use a variable called TASKS for this purpose and another variable, COUNT, to keep track of how many times the task list has been updated. Write a function called INITIALIZE to initialize the system by setting TASKS and COUNT to appropriate values. (Should TASKS and COUNT be local or global to INITIALIZE?) Your function should also return some appropriate message.

2. Write a function called ADD-TASK that adds a task to the front of the list of tasks. (ADD-TASK 'SWEEP-FLOOR) should return a message like (ADDED SWEEP-FLOOR TO LIST OF TASKS). ADD-TASK must also update the variables TASKS and COUNT.

3. Write a function called WHAT-NOW that returns a message telling what the current task is. The first task on the list is considered the current task. If there are no tasks on the list, WHAT-NOW should return the symbol REST-FOR-A-WHILE. WHAT-NOW doesn't require any inputs, so its argument list will be NIL. You call it by typing (WHAT-NOW).

4. Write a function HOW-MANY that returns a message telling how many tasks remain to be done.

5. Write a function TASK-DONE that removes the first task on the task list, increments COUNT, and returns the symbol CONGRATULATIONS. If the task list is empty when TASK-DONE is called, it should not increment COUNT. TASK-DONE doesn't need any arguments, because all its information resides in global variables.

6. Try out the following sequence on the computer:

```
(INITIALIZE)
(WHAT-NOW)
(ADD-TASK 'CLEAN-ROOM)
(WHAT-NOW)
(ADD-TASK 'WASH-CAR)
COUNT
(HOW-MANY)
(WHAT-NOW)
(TASK-DONE)
COUNT
(WHAT-NOW)
(TASK-DONE)
COUNT
(TASK-DONE)
COUNT
```

Advanced Topics 5

1. THE SET FUNCTION

SET is like SETQ except both its arguments are evaluated. Therefore SET is not a special form. Here are some examples of SET:

```
*(set 'extras '(lettuce cheese pickle onion ketchup))
(LETTUCE CHEESE PICKLE ONION KETCHUP)

*extras
(LETTUCE CHEESE PICKLE ONION KETCHUP)

*(set 'necessities '(meat bun))
(MEAT BUN)

*necessities
(MEAT BUN)

*(set foo 'bar)
;FOO - UNBOUND VARIABLE

*(set 'foo 'bar)
BAR
```

Using a combination of **SET** and **EVAL**, we can write a function that increments a global variable:

```
(DEFUN INCREMENT (VAR)
  (SET VAR (ADD1 (EVAL VAR)))
  (LIST 'ADDED 1 'TO VAR))
```

INCREMENT takes the *name* of a variable as input. It uses EVAL to get the value of the variable and SET to change the value. Example:

```
*(setq cnt 0)
0

*(increment 'cnt)
(ADDED 1 TO CNT)

*cnt
1

*(increment 'cnt)
(ADDED 1 TO CNT)

*cnt
2
```

SET can do everything SETQ does, and more. So why have two functions? SETQ is a little more convenient to use because you don't have to quote the first argument. SETQ is the usual way to assign a value to a variable; SET is used only for special applications, such as the preceding one.

2. REBINDING GLOBAL VARIABLES

If a variable that has a global binding appears in a function's argument list, that variable is rebound temporarily to serve as a local variable. In other words, the variables in a function's argument list are *always* locally rebound inside the function, whether they were previously bound locally, globally, or not at all. When the function returns, its local variables either become unbound or get their old bindings back if they had them. Example:

```
*(setq x 'global-value)
GLOBAL-VALUE

*X
GLOBAL-VALUE

*(defun rebind (x) (list 'value 'of 'x 'is x))
REBIND

*(rebind 'whoopie)
(VALUE OF X IS WHOOPIE)

*X
GLOBAL-VALUE
```

Inside function REBIND the variable X was bound to WHOOPIE, but after REBIND returned, X's value was restored to GLOBAL-VALUE.

Functions Covered in Advanced Topics

Assignment function: SET

6
List Data Structures

1. INTRODUCTION

This chapter presents additional functions for manipulating lists. Lists are naturally viewed as sequences, but in Lisp they also serve to represent such things as sets and tables. Built-in functions are provided to manipulate these data structures. The functions in this chapter have been grouped according to the type of data structure they support.

2. SOME USEFUL PREDICATES

LISTP is a predicate that returns T if its input is a list. LISTP returns NIL for nonlists.

```
*(listp 'stitch)
NIL

*(listp '(a stitch in time))
T

*(listp nil)
T
```

ATOM is a predicate that returns T if its input is **atomic.** The word atomic comes from the Greek *atomos,* meaning indivisible. Numbers and symbols are atomic because they cannot be broken down into smaller components. Lists are not atomic; we use CAR and CDR to take them apart.

```
*(atom 3)
T

*(atom 'stitch)
T

*(atom '(a stitch in time))
NIL

*(atom nil)
T
```

ATOM and LISTP both return T when given NIL as input, because NIL is both a symbol and a list. NIL is the *only* atom that is also a list.

CONSP returns T if its input is a list of at least one cons cell—that is, any list except NIL. One way to define CONSP is as (AND (LISTP X) (NOT (ATOM X))).

```
*(consp '(a stitch in time))
T

*(consp nil)
NIL
```

NULL is the predicate that returns T if its input is NIL. NULL and NOT are actually the same predicate. For stylistic reasons, programmers use NOT when writing conditional expressions and NULL when talking about lists.

```
*(not (oddp 7))
NIL

*(null (cdr '(foo)))
T

*(null (cdr '(foo bar)))
NIL
```

Exercise

Write an expression to set the global variable DOG to the list (RIN TIN TIN). Then write down the result of each of the following expressions:

```
(LISTP DOG)
(LISTP 'DOG)
(ATOM DOG)
(ATOM (CAR DOG))
(CONSP (CDR DOG))
(CONSP (CDDDR DOG))
(NULL (CDDDR DOG))
(ATOM (CDDR DOG))
(ATOM (CDR NIL))
```

3. GENERAL PURPOSE LIST FUNCTIONS

A few list functions—CAR, CDR, CONS, LIST, and LENGTH—were covered in chapter 2. Many more functions exist for manipulating lists. Here we will cover REVERSE, APPEND, NCONS, LAST, NTHCDR, NTH, and SUBST.

3.1. REVERSE

REVERSE returns the reversal of a list.

```
*(reverse '(one two three four five))
(FIVE FOUR THREE TWO ONE)

*(reverse '(l i v e))
(E V I L)

*(reverse 'live)
;INPUT NOT A LIST

*(reverse '((my oversight) (your blunder) (his negligence)))
((HIS NEGLIGENCE) (YOUR BLUNDER) (MY OVERSIGHT))
```

Notice that REVERSE reverses only the *top level* of a list. It does not reverse the individual elements of a list of lists. Another point about

REVERSE is that it only works on lists. **REVERSE** of the list (L I V E) gives the list (E V I L), but **REVERSE** of the symbol **LIVE** gives an error because **LIVE** is not a list.

REVERSE does not change the value of any variable:

```
*(setq vow '(to have and to hold))
(TO HAVE AND TO HOLD)

*(reverse vow)
(HOLD TO AND HAVE TO)

*vow
(TO HAVE AND TO HOLD)
```

3.2. APPEND

APPEND combines the elements of two lists into a bigger list. The technical term for this is **concatenation.**

```
*(append '(we hold) '(these truths))
(WE HOLD THESE TRUTHS)

*(list '(we hold) '(these truths))
((WE HOLD) (THESE TRUTHS))

*(append '((a apple) (b banana)) '((c cherry) (d dumptruck)))
((A APPLE) (B BANANA) (C CHERRY) (D DUMPTRUCK))
```

Let's examine the differences among **APPEND**, **LIST**, and **CONS**:

```
*(append '(a b c d) '(e f g h))
( A B C D E F G H)

*(list '(a b c d) '(e f g h))
((A B C D) (E F G H))

*(cons '(a b c d) '(e f g h))
((A B C D) E F G H)
```

Unlike the **LIST** and **CONS** functions, **APPEND** requires its inputs to always be lists.

```
*(append '(rice and) '(beans))
(RICE AND BEANS)
```

```
*(append '(rice and) 'beans)
;ARGUMENT MUST BE A PROPER LIST

*(append 'rice '(and beans))
;ARGUMENT MUST BE A PROPER LIST

*(cons 'rice '(and beans))
(RICE AND BEANS)
```

Appending NIL to another list is like adding zero to a number: it has no effect. This is not true for LIST or CONS.

```
*(append '(april showers) nil)
(APRIL SHOWERS)

*(append nil '(may flowers))
(MAY FLOWERS)

*(append nil nil)
NIL
```

APPEND can take any number of inputs:

```
*(append '(a b) '(c d) '(e f g))
(A B C D E F G)

*(append '(a b))
(A B)
```

3.3. NCONS

NCONS is a very simple function. (NCONS X) is equivalent to (CONS X NIL).

```
*(ncons 'foo)
(FOO)

*(cons 'foo nil)
(FOO)

*(ncons '(artichoke hearts))
((ARTICHOKE HEARTS))
```

(NCONS X) is also equivalent to (LIST X).

3.4. LAST

LAST returns the last cons cell of a list—that is, the list whose CAR is the list's last element and whose CDR is NIL. Example:

```
*(last '(all is forgiven))
(FORGIVEN)

*(last nil)
NIL
```

3.5. NTHCDR and NTH

The NTHCDR function takes a number *n* and a list as input and returns the *n*th CDR of the list. Examples:

```
*(nthcdr 0 '(a b c))
(A B C)

*(nthcdr 1 '(a b c))
(B C)

*(nthcdr 2 '(a b c))
(C)

*(nthcdr 3 '(a b c))
NIL
```

NTH is like NTHCDR, except it takes the CAR of the *n*th CDR of the list. Thus the first element of the list is numbered 0, the second element is numbered 1, and so on.

```
*(nth 0 '(a b c))
A

*(nth 1 '(a b c))
B

*(nth 2 '(a b c))
C

*(nth 3 '(a b c))
NIL
```

3.6. SUBST

The SUBST function substitutes one symbol for another everywhere it appears in a list. It takes three inputs whose order is as in the phrase "substitute x for y in z." Here is an example of substituting FRED for BILL in a certain list:

```
*(subst 'fred 'bill '(bill jones sent me an itemized bill for the tires))
(FRED JONES SENT ME AN ITEMIZED FRED FOR THE TIRES)
```

If the symbol to look for doesn't appear at all in the list, SUBST returns the original list unchanged.

```
*(subst 'bill 'fred '(keep off the grass))
(KEEP OFF THE GRASS)

*(subst 'on 'off '(keep off the grass))
(KEEP ON THE GRASS)
```

SUBST looks at the entire structure of the list, not just the top-level elements.

```
*(subst 'the 'a '((a hatter) (a hare) and (a dormouse)))
((THE HATTER) (THE HARE) AND (THE DORMOUSE))
```

Exercises

1. Write an expression to set the global variable LINE to the list (ROSES ARE RED). Then write down what each of the following expressions evaluates to:

```
(REVERSE LINE)
(CAR (LAST LINE))
(NTH 1 LINE)
(REVERSE (REVERSE LINE))
(APPEND LINE (NCONS (CAR LINE)))
(APPEND (LAST LINE) LINE)
(LIST (LAST LINE) LINE)
(CONS (LAST LINE) LINE)
(APPEND LINE '(VIOLETS ARE BLUE))
(SUBST 'CHERRIES 'ROSES LINE)
```

2. Use the LAST function to write a function called LAST-ELEMENT that returns the last element of a list instead of the last cons cell. Write a version of LAST-ELEMENT using REVERSE instead of LAST. Write another version using NTH.

3. The CONS function adds an element to the front of a list. Suppose we wanted a function TACK-ON that added an element to the *back* of a list—for example, (TACK-ON '(A B C) 'D) should return (A B C D). If we simply write (APPEND '(A B C) 'D) we will get an error, because the inputs to APPEND must be lists. Write a version of TACK-ON using APPEND. Write another version of TACK-ON using REVERSE.

4. Write a NEXT-TO-LAST function that returns the next to last element of a list. Do not use NTH or NTHCDR in your solution.

5. Write a function BUTLAST that returns a list with the last element removed. (BUTLAST '(ROSES ARE RED)) should return the list (ROSES ARE). (BUTLAST '(A B C D E)) should return (A B C D).

6. What primitive function does the following reduce to?

   ```
   (DEFUN MYSTERY (X) (CAR (LAST (REVERSE X))))
   ```

7. A palindrome is a sequence that reads the same forward and backward. The list (A B C D C B A) is a palindrome; (A B C A B C) is not. Write a predicate PALINDROMEP that returns T if its input is a palindrome. Write a function MAKE-PALINDROME that makes a palindrome out of a list—for example, given (YOU AND ME) as input it should return (YOU AND ME ME AND YOU).

8. Write a function called ROYAL-WE that changes every occurrence of the symbol I in a list to the symbol WE. Calling this function on the list (IF I LEARN LISP I WILL BE PLEASED) should return the list (IF WE LEARN LISP WE WILL BE PLEASED).

Note: The Easy Way to Do These Exercises

It is perfectly permissible for you to do all these exercises on the computer instead of on paper. If you're not sure what a particular expression does, by all means use the computer to check it out. That's what computers are for!

4. LISTS AS SETS

A set is an unordered collection of items. Each item appears at most once in the set. Some typical sets are the set of days of the week, the set of integers (an infinite set), and the set of people in Hackensack, New Jersey, who had spaghetti for dinner last Tuesday.

Sets are undoubtedly one of the most useful data structures that can be built from lists. The basic set operations are **union, intersection, set difference** (also called set subtraction), and testing if an item is a member of a set. The Lisp functions for all these operations are described in the following sections. Of these, only MEMBER is standard; the remaining ones may or may not appear in the dialect you use. See appendix C for their definitions, if necessary.

4.1. UNION

The UNION function takes the union of two sets. It returns a list of items that appear in *either* set, without duplicates.

```
*(union '(finger hand arm) '(toe finger foot leg))
(FINGER HAND ARM TOE FOOT LEG)

*(union '(fred john mary) '(sue mary fred))
(FRED JOHN MARY SUE)

*(union '(a s d f g) '(v w s r a))
(A S D F G V W R)
```

4.2. INTERSECTION

The INTERSECTION function takes the intersection of two sets. It returns a list of only those items that appear in *both* sets.

```
*(intersection '(fred john mary) '(sue mary fred))
(FRED MARY)
```

```
*(intersection '(a s d f g) '(v w s r a))
(A S)

*(intersection '(foo bar baz) '(xam gorp bletch))
NIL
```

4.3. SETDIFFERENCE

The SETDIFFERENCE function performs set subtraction. It returns what is left of the first set when the elements in the second set have been removed.

```
*(setdifference '(alpha bravo charlie delta) '(bravo charlie))
(ALPHA DELTA)

*(setdifference '(alpha bravo charlie delta) '(echo alpha foxtrot))
(BRAVO CHARLIE DELTA)

*(setdifference '(alpha bravo) '(bravo alpha))
NIL
```

4.4. MEMBER

The MEMBER predicate checks whether an item is a member of a list. If the item is found in the list, the sublist beginning with that item is returned. Otherwise NIL is returned. MEMBER never returns T; it is regarded as a predicate because the value it returns is non-NIL (hence true) if the item is in the list. Example:

```
*(setq ducks '(huey dewey louie))   DUCKS holds a set of ducks
(HUEY DEWEY LOUIE)

*(member 'huey ducks)               Is Huey a duck?
(HUEY DEWIE LOUIE)                  Non-NIL result: yes.

*(member 'dewey ducks)              Is Dewey a duck?
(DEWEY LOUIE)                       Non-NIL result: yes.

*(member 'louie ducks)              Is Louie a duck?
(LOUIE)                             Non-NIL result: yes.
```

```
*(member 'mickey ducks)         Is Mickey a duck?
NIL                             NIL: no.
```

Exercises

1. Suppose the global variable A is bound to the list (SOAP WATER). What will be the result of each of the following expressions?

```
(UNION A '(NO SOAP RADIO))
(INTERSECTION A (REVERSE A))
(SETDIFFERENCE A '(STOP FOR WATER))
(SETDIFFERENCE A A)
(MEMBER 'SOAP A)
(MEMBER 'WATER A)
(MEMBER 'WASHCLOTH A)
```

2. The **cardinality** of a set is the number of elements it contains. What Lisp primitive determines the cardinality of a set?

3. Write a function ADD-VOWELS that takes a set of letters as input and adds the vowels (A E I O U) to the set. For example, invoking ADD-VOWELS on the set (X A E Z) should produce the set (X A E Z I O U).

4. We can use MEMBER to write a predicate that returns true if a sentence contains the word "the." Example:

```
(DEFUN CONTAINS-THE-P (SENT) (MEMBER 'THE SENT))
```

Suppose we instead want a predicate CONTAINS-ARTICLE-P that returns true if a sentence contains any article—"the," "a," or "an." Write a version of this predicate using INTERSECTION. Write another version using MEMBER and OR. Could you solve this problem with AND instead of OR? Could you solve it with UNION instead of INTERSECTION?

5. A set X is a **subset** of a set Y if the first set is contained within the second. (For example, the set of even numbers is a subset of the set of integers.) Another way of stating this is, if X is a subset of Y, subtracting Y from X should leave the empty set. Write the SUBSETP predicate, which returns T if its first input is a subset of its second input.

6. Sets are said to be equal if they contain exactly the same elements. Order does not matter in a set, so the sets (RED BLUE GREEN) and (GREEN BLUE RED) are considered equal. However, the EQUAL predicate does not consider them equal, because it treats them as lists, not as sets. Write a SET-EQUAL predicate that returns T if two things are equal as sets. (Hint: If two sets are equal, then each is a subset of the other.)

7. A set X is a **proper subset** of a set Y if X is a subset of Y but not equal to Y. Thus (A C) is a proper subset of (A B C). (A B C) is a subset of (A B C), but not a proper subset of it. Write the PROPER-SUBSETP predicate, which returns T if its first input is a proper subset of its second input.

5. PROGRAMMING WITH SETS

Here is an example of how to solve a modest programming problem using sets. The problem is to write a function that adds a title to a name, turning "John Doe" into "Mr. John Doe" or "Jane Doe" into "Ms. Jane Doe." If a name already has a title, that title should be kept, but if it doesn't have one we will try to determine the gender of the first name so that the appropriate title can be assigned.

To solve a problem like this, we must break it down into smaller pieces whose solutions are more straightforward. Let's start with the question of whether a name has a title or not. Here's how we'd write a function to answer that question:

```
*(defun titledp (name)
    (member (car name) '(mr ms miss mrs)))
TITLEDP

*(titledp '(jane doe))        "Jane" is not in the set of titles
NIL

*(titledp '(ms jane doe))  "Ms." is in the set of titles
(MS MISS MRS)
```

The next step is to write functions to figure out whether a word is a male or female first name. We will use only a few instances of each type, to keep the example brief.

```
*(setq male-first-names '(john richard fred george))
(JOHN RICHARD FRED GEORGE)

*(defun malep (name) (member name male-first-names))
MALEP

*(setq female-first-names '(jane mary wanda barbara))
(JANE MARY WANDA BARBARA)

*(defun femalep (name) (member name female-first-names))
FEMALEP

*(malep 'richard)            "Richard" is a male name
(RICHARD FRED GEORGE)

*(malep 'barbara)            "Barbara" is not a male name
NIL

*(femalep 'barbara)          "Barbara" is a female name
(BARBARA)
```

Now we can write the **GIVE-TITLE** function that adds a title to a name. Of course, we will only add a title if the name doesn't already have one. If the first name isn't recognized as male or female, we'll play it safe and use "Mr. or Ms."

```
*(defun give-title (name)
  (cond ((titledp name) name)
        ((malep (car name)) (cons 'mr name))
        ((femalep (car name)) (cons 'ms name))
        (t (append '(mr or ms) name))))
GIVE-TITLE

*(give-title '(miss jane adams))  name already has a title
(MISS JANE ADAMS)

*(give-title '(john q public))    untitled male name
(MR JOHN Q PUBLIC)

*(give-title '(barbara smith))    untitled female name
(MS BARBARA SMITH)

*(give-title '(p j maloney))      no title; gender indeterminate
(MR OR MS P J MALONEY)
```

The important features in this example are (1) breaking the problem down into simple little functions, and (2) writing and testing the functions one at a time. Once we had the **TITLEDP**, **MALEP**, and **FEMALEP** predicates written, **GIVE-TITLE** ws easy to write.

Decomposing a problem into subproblems is an important skill. Experienced programmers can often see right away how a problem breaks down into logical subdivisions, but beginners must build up their intuition through practice.

Mini Keyboard Exercise

We are going to write a program that compares the descriptions of two objects and tells how many features they have in common. The descriptions will be represented as a list of features, with the symbol -VS- separating the first object from the second. Thus when given a list like

```
(LARGE RED SHINY CUBE -VS- SMALL SHINY RED FOUR-SIDED PYRAMID)
```

the program will respond with (2 COMMON FEATURES). We will compose this program from several small functions which you will write and test one at a time.

1. Write a function RIGHT-SIDE that returns all the features to the right of the -VS- symbol. RIGHT-SIDE of the example list should return (SMALL SHINY RED FOUR-SIDED PYRAMID). (Hint: Remember that the MEMBER function returns the entire sublist starting with the item you search for.) Test your function to make sure it works correctly.

2. Write a function LEFT-SIDE that returns all the features to the left of the -VS-. You can't use the MEMBER trick directly for this one, but you can use it if you do something to the list first.

3. Write a function COUNT-COMMON that returns the number of features the left and right sides of the input have in common.

4. Write the main function, COMPARE, that takes a list of features describing two objects, with a -VS- between them, and reports the number of features they have in common. COMPARE should return a list of form (*n* COMMON FEATURES).

5. Try the expression

```
(COMPARE '(SMALL RED METAL CUBE -VS- RED PLASTIC SMALL CUBE))
```

You should get (3 COMMON FEATURES) as the result.

6. LISTS AS TABLES

Tables are another structure we can build from lists. A table, or **association list** (**a-list** for short) is a list of lists. Each list is called an **entry**, and the first element of each entry is its **key**. A table of five English words and their French equivalents follows. The table contains five entries; the keys are the English words.

```
((ONE UN)
 (TWO DEUX)
 (THREE TROIS)
 (FOUR QUATRE)
 (FIVE CINQ))
```

6.1. ASSOC

The ASSOC function looks up an entry in a table, given its key. Here are some examples. Assume the table of English and French words is stored in the global variable WORDS.

```
*(assoc 'three words)
(THREE TROIS)

*(assoc 'four words)
(FOUR QUATRE)

*(assoc 'six words)
NIL
```

ASSOC goes through the table one entry at a time until it finds a key equal to the key it is searching for; then it returns that entry. If ASSOC can't find the key in the table, it returns NIL.

Notice that when ASSOC does find an entry with the given key, the value it returns is the entire entry. If we want only the French word and not the entire entry, we can take the CADR of the result of ASSOC. Example:

```
*(defun translate (x) (cadr (assoc x words)))
TRANSLATE

*(translate 'one)
UN

*(translate 'five)
CINQ

*(translate 'six)
NIL
```

6.2. SUBLIS

SUBLIS is like SUBST, except it can make many substitutions simultaneously. The first input to SUBLIS is a table whose entries are dotted pairs. (Dotted pairs were discussed in chapter 2.) The second input is the list in which the substitutions are to be made. Example:

```
*(sublis '((roses . violets) (red . blue))
         '(roses are red))
(VIOLETS ARE BLUE)

*(setq dotted-words '((one . un)
                      (two . deux)
                      (three . trois)
                      (four . quatre)
                      (five . cinq))
((ONE . UN)
 (TWO . DEUX)
 (THREE . TROIS)
 (FOUR . QUATRE)
 (FIVE . CINQ))

*(sublis dotted-words '(three one four one five))
(TROIS UN QUATRE UN CINQ)
```

7. PROGRAMMING WITH TABLES

Here is another example of the use of ASSOC. We will create a table of objects and their descriptions, where the descriptions are similar to those in the last keyboard exercise. We'll store the table in the global variable THINGS. The table looks like this:

```
((OBJECT1 LARGE GREEN SHINY CUBE)
 (OBJECT2 SMALL RED DULL METAL CUBE)
 (OBJECT3 RED SMALL DULL PLASTIC CUBE)
 (OBJECT4 SMALL DULL BLUE METAL CUBE)
 (OBJECT5 SMALL SHINY RED FOUR-SIDED PYRAMID)
 (OBJECT6 LARGE SHINY GREEN SPHERE))
```

We can write a function called DESCRIPTION to retrieve the description of an object:

```
*(defun description (x) (cdr (assoc x things)))
DESCRIPTION

*(description 'object3)
(RED SMALL DULL PLASTIC CUBE)
```

The differences between two objects are whatever properties appear in the description of the first but not the second or in the description of the second but not the first. The technical term for this is **symmetric set difference.**

```
*(defun differences (x y)
   (union (setdifference (description x) (description y))
          (setdifference (description y) (description x))))
DIFFERENCES

*(differences 'object2 'object3)
(METAL PLASTIC)
```

OBJECT2 is metal but OBJECT3 is plastic, so METAL and PLASTIC are properties not common to both. We can classify properties according to the type of quality they refer to. Here is a table:

```
((LARGE SIZE)
 (SMALL SIZE)
 (RED COLOR)
 (GREEN COLOR)
 (BLUE COLOR)
 (SHINY LUSTER)
 (DULL LUSTER)
 (METAL MATERIAL)
 (PLASTIC MATERIAL)
 (CUBE SHAPE)
 (SPHERE SHAPE)
 (PYRAMID SHAPE)
 (FOUR-SIDED SHAPE))
```

If we store this table in the global variable **QUALITY-TABLE**, we can write a function to give us the quality a given property refers to:

```
*(defun quality (x)
   (cadr (assoc x quality-table)))
QUALITY

*(quality 'red)
COLOR

*(quality 'large)
SIZE
```

Using **DIFFERENCES** and **QUALITY**, we can write a function to tell us one quality that is different between a pair of objects.

```
*(defun quality-difference (x y)
   (quality (car (differences x y))))
QUALITY-DIFFERENCE

*(quality-difference 'object2 'object3)
MATERIAL

*(quality-difference 'object1 'object6)
SHAPE

*(quality-difference 'object2 'object4)
COLOR
```

What if we wanted a list of all the quality differences instead of just the first one? We would need some way to go from a list of differences like (RED BLUE METAL PLASTIC) to a list of corresponding qualities (COLOR COLOR MATERIAL MATERIAL), and then we'd have to eliminate duplicate elements. We cannot use ASSOC to look up each property in the list; ASSOC only looks up a single thing:

```
*(assoc '(red metal shiny) quality-table)
NIL

*(assoc 'red quality-table)
(RED COLOR)
```

In order to translate each element of the difference list to its corresponding quality, we must use an **applicative operator** called APPLY-TO-ALL. Applicative operators are discussed in the next chapter.

Exercises

1. What Lisp primitive returns the number of entries in a table?
2. Make a table called BOOKS of five books and their authors. The first entry might be (WAR-AND-PEACE LEO-TOLSTOY).
3. Write a function WHO-WROTE that takes the name of a book as input and returns the book's author.
4. Suppose we do (SETQ BOOKS (REVERSE BOOKS)), which reverses the order in which the five books appear in the table. What will the WHO-WROTE function do now?
5. Suppose we wanted a WHAT-WROTE function that took an author's name as input and returned the title of one of his or her books. Could we create such a function using ASSOC and the current table? If not, how would the table have to be changed?
6. Here is a table of states and the cities they contain, stored in the global variable ATLAS:

```
((PENNSYLVANIA PITTSBURGH)
 (NEW-JERSEY NEWARK)
```

```
(PENNSYLVANIA READING)
(OHIO COLUMBUS)
(NEW-JERSEY PRINCETON)
(NEW-JERSEY TRENTON))
```

Suppose we wanted to find all the cities a given state contains. ASSOC returns only the *first* entry with a matching key, not all such entries, so for this table ASSOC cannot solve our problem. Redesign the table so that ASSOC can be used successfully.

Mini Keyboard Exercise

In this problem we will simulate the behavior of a very simple-minded creature, *Nerdus americanis* (also known as *Computerus hackerus*). This creature has only five states: Sleeping, Eating, Waiting-for-a-Terminal, Programming, and Debugging. Its behavior is cyclic—after it sleeps it always eats, after it eats it always waits for a terminal, and so on, until after debugging it goes back to sleep.

1. What type of data structure would be useful for representing the connection between a state and its successor? Write such a data structure for the five-state cycle given in the preceding exercise.

2. Write a function NEXT-STATE that takes the name of a state as input and uses the data structure you designed to determine the next state the creature will be in. (NEXT-STATE 'SLEEPING) should return EATING, for example.

3. What value does your function return for each of the following?

```
(NEXT-STATE 'PROGRAMMING)
(NEXT-STATE (NEXT-STATE 'DEBUGGING))
(NEXT-STATE 'PLAYING-GUITAR)
```

4. Write an INITIALIZE function to initialize the state of the nerd to SLEEPING. Where will you store the state of the nerd?

5. Write a function ADVANCE to advance the state of the nerd. For example, if the nerd is sleeping and you type (ADVANCE), the result should be (THE NERD IS NOW EATING). Typing (ADVANCE) again should yield (THE NERD IS NOW WAITING-FOR-A-TERMINAL).

8. SUMMARY

Lists are an important data type in their own right, but in Lisp they are even more important because they are used to implement other data structures such as sets and tables.

The key to solving nontrivial programming problems is learning how to divide the problem into smaller, more manageable pieces. This is done by writing and testing several simple functions, then combining them to produce a solution to the main problem.

Review Exercises

1. What is the difference between atomic and nonatomic datatypes?

2. How do LISTP and CONSP differ?

3. ROTATE-LEFT and ROTATE-RIGHT are functions that rotate the elements of a list. (ROTATE-LEFT '(A B C D E)) returns (B C D E A), while ROTATE-RIGHT returns (E A B C D). Write these functions.

4. Give an example of two sets X and Y such that (SETDIFFERENCE X Y) equals (SETDIFFERENCE Y X). Also give an example where the set differences are *not* equal.

5. Recall the unary arithmetic system developed in advanced topics 2. What list function performs unary addition?

6. Show how to transform the list (A B C D) into a table so that the ASSOC function using the table gives the same result as MEMBER using the list.

Functions Covered in This Chapter

Predicates: LISTP, ATOM, CONSP, NULL
List functions: REVERSE, APPEND, NCONS, LAST, NTHCDR, NTH, SUBST
Set functions: UNION, INTERSECTION, SETDIFFERENCE, MEMBER
Table functions: ASSOC, SUBLIS

Keyboard Exercise

In this keyboard exercise we will write some routines for moving Robbie the Robot around in a house. The map of the house appears in figure 6.1. Robbie can move in any of four directions: north, south, east, or west. The layout of the house is described in a table, with one element for each room:

```
((LIVING-ROOM . . . )
 (UPSTAIRS-BEDROOM . . . )
 (DINING-ROOM . . . )
 (KITCHEN . . . )
 (PANTRY . . . )
 (DOWNSTAIRS-BEDROOM . . . )
 (BACK-STAIRS . . . )
 (FRONT-STAIRS . . . )
 (LIBRARY . . . ))
```

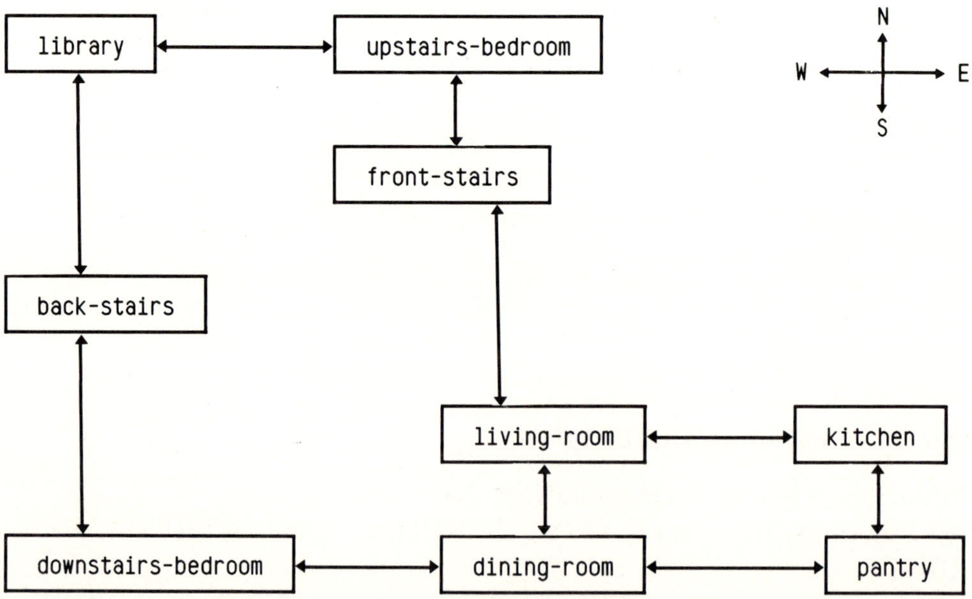

Figure 6.1 Map of the house.

The entry for each room is in turn a table listing the directions that Robbie can travel from that room and where he ends up for each direction. The entire table is shown in figure 6.2. The first element of the table is:

```
(LIVING-ROOM (NORTH FRONT-STAIRS)
             (SOUTH DINING-ROOM)
             (EAST KITCHEN))
```

If Robbie were in the living room, going north would take him to the front stairs, going south would take him to the dining room, and going east would take him to the kitchen. Since there is nothing listed for west, we assume that there is a wall there, so Robbie cannot travel west from the living room.

```
(SETQ ROOMS
   '((LIVING-ROOM        (NORTH FRONT-STAIRS)
                         (SOUTH DINING-ROOM)
                         (EAST KITCHEN))
     (UPSTAIRS-BEDROOM   (WEST LIBRARY)
                         (SOUTH FRONT-STAIRS))
     (DINING-ROOM        (NORTH LIVING-ROOM)
                         (EAST PANTRY)
                         (WEST DOWNSTAIRS-BEDROOM))
     (KITCHEN            (WEST LIVING-ROOM)
                         (SOUTH PANTRY))
     (PANTRY             (NORTH KITCHEN)
                         (WEST DINING-ROOM))
     (DOWNSTAIRS-BEDROOM (NORTH BACK-STAIRS)
                         (EAST DINING-ROOM))
     (BACK-STAIRS        (SOUTH DOWNSTAIRS-BEDROOM)
                         (NORTH LIBRARY))
     (FRONT-STAIRS       (NORTH UPSTAIRS-BEDROOM)
                         (SOUTH LIVING-ROOM))
     (LIBRARY            (EAST UPSTAIRS-BEDROOM)
                         (SOUTH BACK-STAIRS))))
```

Figure 6.2 Table of rooms and directions.

Instructions

1. If the table of rooms is already stored on the computer for you, load the file containing it. If not, you will have to type the table in as it appears in figure 6.2. Store the table in the global variable ROOMS.

2. Write a function CHOICES that takes the name of a room as input and returns the table of permissible directions Robbie may take from that room. For example, (CHOICES 'PANTRY) should return the list ((NORTH KITCHEN) (WEST DINING-ROOM)). Test your function to make sure it returns the correct result.

3. Write a function LOOK that takes two inputs, a direction and a room, and tells where Robbie would end up if he moved in that direction from that room. For example, (LOOK 'NORTH 'PANTRY) should return KITCHEN. (LOOK 'WEST 'PANTRY) should return DINING-ROOM. (LOOK 'SOUTH 'PANTRY) should return NIL. (Hint: The CHOICES function will be a useful building block.)

4. We will use the global variable LOC to hold Robbie's location. Type in an expression to set his location to be the pantry.

5. Write a function HOW-MANY-CHOICES that tells how many choices Robbie has for where to move to next. Your function should refer to the global variable LOC to find his location. If he is in the pantry, (HOW-MANY-CHOICES) should return 2.

6. Write a predicate UPSTAIRSP that returns T if its input is an upstairs location. (The library and the upstairs bedroom are the only two locations upstairs.) Write a predicate ONSTAIRSP that returns T if its input is either FRONT-STAIRS or BACK-STAIRS.

7. Where's Robbie? Write a function of no inputs called WHERE that tells where he is. If he is in the library, (WHERE) should say (ROBBIE IS UPSTAIRS IN THE LIBRARY). If he is in the kitchen, it should say (ROBBIE IS DOWNSTAIRS IN THE KITCHEN). If he is on the front stairs, it should say (ROBBIE IS ON THE FRONT-STAIRS).

8. Write a function MOVE that takes one input, a direction, and moves Robbie in that direction. MOVE should make use of the LOOK func-

tion you wrote previously. If Robbie can't move in the specified direction, an appropriate message should be returned. For example, if Robbie is in the pantry, (MOVE 'SOUTH) should return something like (OUCH! ROBBIE HIT A WALL). (MOVE 'NORTH) should change Robbie's location and return (ROBBIE IS DOWNSTAIRS IN THE KITCHEN).

9. Starting from the pantry, take Robbie to the library via the back stairs. Then take him to the kitchen, but do not lead him through the downstairs bedroom on the way.

Advanced Topics 6

1. EQ VS. EQUAL

Recall from chapter 2 that every piece of data in the computer's memory has a unique number associated with it called its **address.** The address indicates *where* in memory the data is stored. The EQ (pronounced "eek") predicate is used to compare the addresses of two objects.

Since a symbol is stored only once in memory, all references to that symbol refer to the same location. Thus we see that if symbols are EQUAL they will have the same address, so they will be EQ as well. This is not the case for lists. Two lists can be EQUAL without having the same address if they are composed of different cons cells.

Figure 6.3 shows two instances of the list (A B C) in cons cell notation. The address of each cons cells is written above it. The address of a list is the address of its first cons cell, so the address of the first list is #17503 and the address of the second list is #16045. The two lists are EQUAL but they are not EQ, since they do not have the same address.

Numbers have different internal representations in different Lisp systems. In some dialects each number has a unique address, so EQ and EQUAL are equivalent for numbers. In other dialects two numbers are never guaranteed to be EQ, even if they are EQUAL.

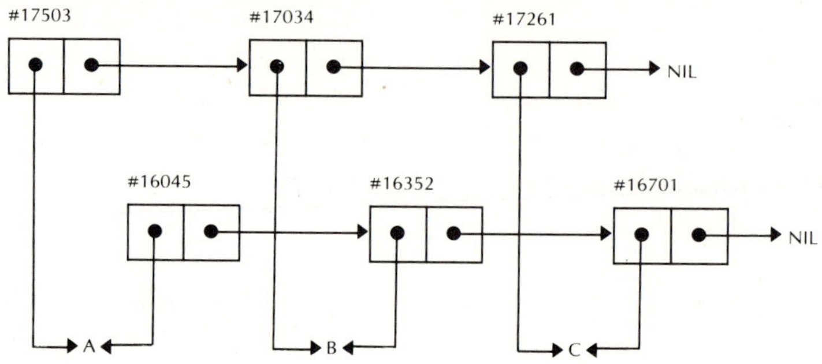

Figure 6.3 Two instances of the list (A B C). The address of each cons cell appears above it.

The EQ function is faster than the EQUAL function because EQ only has to compare an address against another address, while EQUAL first has to test if its inputs are lists, and if so it must compare each element of one against the corresponding element of the other. Due to its greater efficiency, programmers often use EQ instead of EQUAL when symbols are being compared. EQ is not usually used to compare lists; it should never be used to compare numbers.

The MEMBER and ASSOC functions also involve an equality test. These functions use EQUAL rather than EQ so that numbers and lists can be compared as reliably as symbols. Lisp also provides analogous functions that use EQ; in Common Lisp they are called MEMQ and ASSQ, but they may have different names in other dialects. Efficiency-conscious programmers will use MEMQ rather than MEMBER to search a set of symbols. If the set contains numbers or lists, however, MEMBER must be used. Similarly, ASSQ is used instead of ASSOC when a table's keys are exclusively symbols.

2. SHARED STRUCTURE

Two lists are said to share structure if they have cons cells in common. Lists that are typed in from the terminal will never share structure (hence they will never be EQ to each other), but using CAR, CDR, and CONS it is possible to create lists that do share structure. For example, we can make X and Y share some structure by doing the following:

```
*(setq x '(a b c))
(A B C)

*(setq y (cons 'd (cdr x)))
(D B C)
```

The value of X is (A B C) and the value of Y is (D B C). The lists share the same cons cell structure for (B C), as indicated in figure 6.4. The sharing comes about because we built Y from (CDR X). If we had simply said (SETQ Y '(D B C)), no structure would be shared.

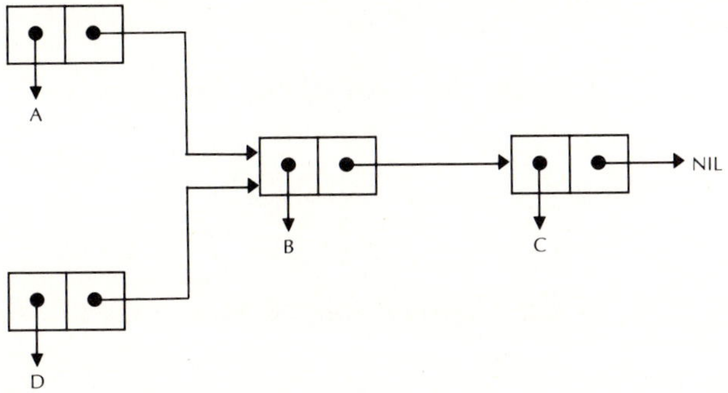

Figure 6.4 Two lists (A B C) and (D B C) that share structure for (B C).

3. DESTRUCTIVE OPERATIONS

None of the functions we've seen so far can change the value of a cons cell after it is allocated. Functions like REVERSE and SUBST, which appear to change a list, actually create new lists. REVERSE, for example, creates a list that is the reverse of its input.

Destructive operations are those that do change the contents of a cons cell. These operations are "dangerous" because they may create circular structure that cannot be printed, and their effect on shared structure may be hard to predict. But destructive operations are a powerful and efficient tool when used wisely. They are especially useful for modifying complex list structures without rebuilding them.

3.1. RPLACA, RPLACD, and DISPLACE

RPLACA ("re-plak-a") and RPLACD ("re-plak-dee") are destructive operations that *replace* the CAR or CDR part of a cons cell, respectively. Both functions return the entire cell after the change has been made. Examples:

```
*(setq x '(hi there))
(HI THERE)

*(setq y x)                    now X and Y point to the same structure
(HI THERE)                       see figure 6.5a

*(rplaca x 'look)              change the CAR of the first cons cell
(LOOK THERE)

*x                             X has changed; see figure 6.5b
(LOOK THERE)

*y                             Y has changed too, because structure was
(LOOK THERE)                     shared

*(cdr y)                       (CDR Y) gives the second cons cell
(THERE)

*(rplacd (cdr y) '(bob))       change CDR of second cell from NIL to a
(THERE BOB)                      pointer to the list (BOB)

*x                             X and Y have both changed; see figure 6.5c
(LOOK THERE BOB)
```

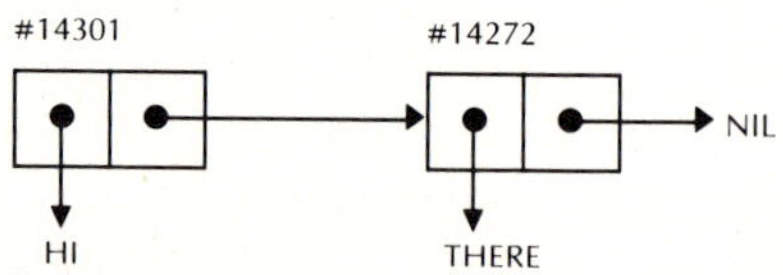

Figure 6.5a The variables X and Y both point to this structure.

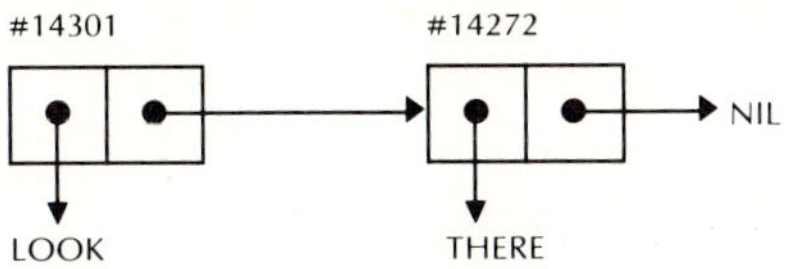

Figure 6.5b The structure of 6.5a after RPLACA has replaced the CAR of the first cons cell.

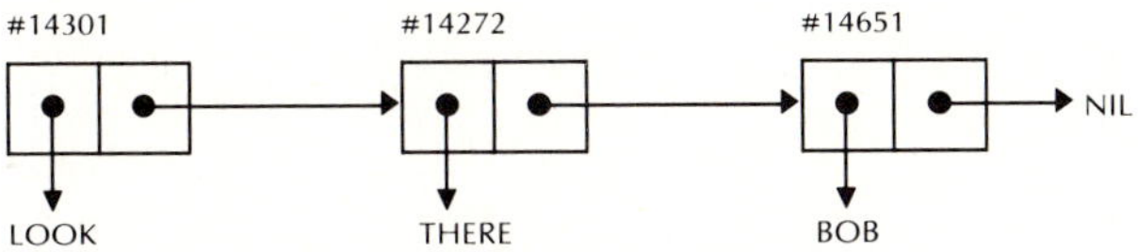

Figure 6.5c The structure of 6.5b after RPLACD has replaced the CDR of the second cons cell with a pointer to a new cons cell.

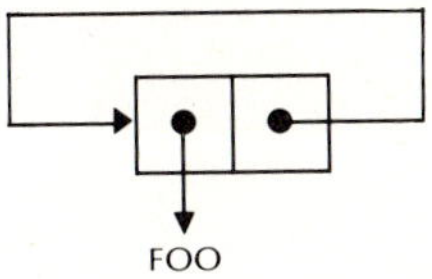

Figure 6.6 A circular list structure created with RPLACD.

We can use RPLACD to create the circular structure shown in figure 6.6:

```
*(setq circ (list 'foo))
(FOO)

*(rplacd circ circ)
(FOO FOO FOO FOO FOO FOO FOO FOO FOO FOO FOO FOO . . . etc.
```

The DISPLACE function is a combination of RPLACA and RPLACD. It replaces both halves of one cons cell with the values in the halves of another. We could write DISPLACE as:

```
(DEFUN DISPLACE (X Y)
  (RPLACA X (CAR Y))
  (RPLACD X (CDR Y)))
```

```
*(setq x '(a b c))
(A B C)

*(setq y '(fee fie foe))          X and Y are as in figure 6.7a
(FEE FIE FOE)

*(displace (cdr x) (cdr y))       now X and Y share structure; see
(FIE FOE)                           figure 6.7b

*x
(A FIE FOE)

*y
(FEE FIE FOE)
```

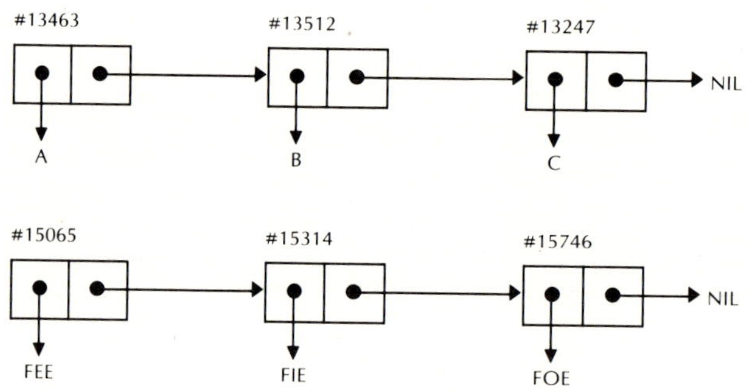

Figure 6.7a The lists (A B C) and (FEE FIE FOE). No shared structure.

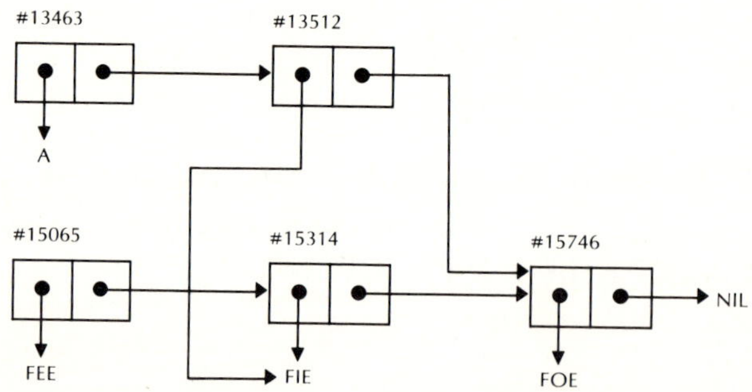

Figure 6.7b After DISPLACE returns, X points to the list (A FIE FOE) while Y points to (FEE FIE FOE). The two lists share structure.

3.2. NCONC

NCONC (pronounced "en-konk," derived from "concatenate") is a destructive version of APPEND. While APPEND creates a new list for its result, NCONC physically changes the last cons cell of its first input to point to its second input. Example:

```
*(setq x '(a b c))
(A B C)

*(setq y '(d e f))
(D E F)

*(append x y)            APPEND does not change X or Y, but the
(A B C D E F)              result does share structure with Y

*x                       X is unchanged
(A B C)

*(setq z (nconc x y))    NCONC changes the list structure of X
(A B C D E F)

*x                       X has changed
(A B C D E F)

*y                       Y has not
(D E F)
```

4. PROGRAMMING WITH DESTRUCTIVE OPERATIONS

One place where destructive operations are especially useful is in making small changes to complex list structures. Suppose we have the following table stored in the global variable THINGS:

```
((OBJECT1 LARGE GREEN SHINY CUBE)
 (OBJECT2 SMALL RED DULL METAL CUBE)
 (OBJECT3 RED SMALL DULL PLASTIC CUBE))
```

How might we change the symbol OBJECT1 to FROB? The expression (ASSOC 'OBJECT1 THINGS) will return the list (OBJECT1

LARGE GREEN SHINY CUBE). We can use RPLACA on this list to physically change it; since RPLACA is a destructive operation, the value of THINGS will be changed as well. Let's go ahead and write a general function for renaming objects:

```
(DEFUN RENAME (OBJ NEWNAME)
  (RPLACA (ASSOC OBJ THINGS) NEWNAME))

*(rename 'object1 'frob)
(FROB LARGE GREEN SHINY CUBE)

*things
((FROB LARGE GREEN SHINY CUBE)
 (OBJECT2 SMALL RED DULL METAL CUBE)
 (OBJECT3 RED SMALL DULL PLASTIC CUBE))
```

We can use NCONC, another destructive operation, to add a new property to an object already in THINGS.

```
(DEFUN ADD (OBJ PROP)
  (NCONC (ASSOC OBJ THINGS) (LIST PROP)))

*(assoc 'object2 things)
(OBJECT2 SMALL RED DULL METAL CUBE)

*(add 'object2 'sharp-edged)
(OBJECT2 SMALL RED DULL METAL CUBE SHARP-EDGED)

*things
((FROB LARGE GREEN SHINY CUBE)
 (OBJECT2 SMALL RED DULL METAL CUBE SHARP-EDGED)
 (OBJECT3 RED SMALL DULL PLASTIC CUBE))
```

Exercises

1. If two things are EQ, are they necessarily EQUAL?

2. What values are returned by each of the following?

```
(RPLACA '(FOO BAR) 'BAZ)
(RPLACD '(BEEP) 'MEEP)
(NCONC '(A B C) (CDR '(A B C)))
```

3. Write a destructive function CHOP that shortens any non-NIL list to a list of one element. (CHOP '(FEE FIE FOE FUM)) should return (FEE).

4. Write a function NTACK that *destructively* tacks a symbol onto a list. (NTACK '(FEE FIE FOE) 'FUM) should return (FEE FIE FOE FUM).

5. Draw the cons cell structure that results from the following sequence of operations:

```
(SETQ X '(A B C))
(RPLACD (LAST X) X)
```

6. Draw the cons cell structure that results from the following sequence of operations:

```
(SETQ X (LIST NIL))
(SETQ Y (LIST X X))
(DISPLACE X Y)
```

Functions Covered in Advanced Topics

Functions based on address equality: EQ, MEMQ, ASSQ
Destructive operations: RPLACA, RPLACD, DISPLACE, NCONC

7 Applicative Operators

1. INTRODUCTION

An **applicative operator** is a function that takes another function as input. The applicative operators covered in this chapter take a function and a list as input and apply the function to the elements of the list. Applicative operators are a powerful form of **control structure.** Another control structure we learned about was the conditional. Conditionals control behavior by linking conditions to actions. Applicative operators control behavior by specifying how a function is to be applied to a data structure.

Of the operators covered in this chapter, only APPLY-TO-ALL is found in all versions of Lisp. Its usual name is MAPCAR. The remaining operators exist in Common Lisp and certain other dialects, sometimes under different names. One of the best features of Lisp is that new functions and operators can be added to any of its dialects. Consult appendix B for more information.

2. THE APPLY-TO-ALL OPERATOR

APPLY-TO-ALL applies a function to each element of a list and returns a list of the results. Suppose we have written a function to square a single number. By itself, this function cannot square a list of numbers:

```
*(defun square (x) (times x x))
SQUARE

*(square 3)
9

*(square '(1 2 3 4 5))
;(1 2 3 4 5) NON-NUMERIC ARGUMENT TO TIMES
```

But with APPLY-TO-ALL we can apply SQUARE to each element of the list individually:

```
*(apply-to-all 'square '(1 2 3 4 5))
(1 4 9 16 25)

*(apply-to-all 'square '(3 8 -3 5 2 10))
(9 64 9 25 4 100)

*(apply-to-all 'square '())
NIL
```

If APPLY-TO-ALL is used on a list of length *n*, the resulting list also has *n* elements. If APPLY-TO-ALL is used on the empty list, the result is the empty list.

2.1. Manipulating Tables with APPLY-TO-ALL

Suppose we set the global variable WORDS to the following table:

```
((ONE UN)
 (TWO DEUX)
 (THREE TROIS)
 (FOUR QUATRE)
 (FIVE CINQ))
```

With APPLY-TO-ALL, we can perform several useful manipulations on this table. We can extract the English words by taking the CAR of each table element:

```
*(apply-to-all 'car words)
(ONE TWO THREE FOUR FIVE)
```

We can extract the French words by taking the CADR of each element:

```
*(apply-to-all 'cadr words)
(UN DEUX TROIS QUATRE CINQ)
```

We can create a French–English dictionary from the English–French one by reversing each table element:

```
*(apply-to-all 'reverse words)
((UN ONE)
 (DEUX TWO)
 (TROIS THREE)
 (QUATRE FOUR)
 (CINQ FIVE))
```

And given a function TRANSLATE, defined thus:

```
(DEFUN TRANSLATE (X) (CADR (ASSOC X WORDS)))
```

we can translate a string of English digits into a string of French ones:

```
*(apply-to-all 'translate '(three one four one five))
(TROIS UN QUATRE UN CINQ)
```

As you can see, APPLY-TO-ALL offers an elegant tool for manipulating tables, as well as other list structures. There are many useful applicative operators. Only a few are built into Lisp; the rest are written by programmers as they need them.

Exercises

1. Write an expression to add one to each element of the list (1 3 5 7 9).

2. Let the global variable DAILY-PLANET contain the following table:

```
((OLSEN JAMES 123-76-4535 CUB-REPORTER)
 (KENT CLARK 089-52-6787 REPORTER)
 (LANE LOIS 951-26-1438 REPORTER)
 (WHITE PERRY 355-16-7439 EDITOR))
```

Each table entry consists of a last name, a first name, a social security number, and a job title. Use APPLY-TO-ALL on this table to extract a list of social security numbers.

3. Write an expression to invoke the ZEROP predicate on each element of the list (2 0 3 4 0 −5 −6). The answer you get should be a list of Ts and NILs.

4. Suppose we want to solve a problem similar to the preceding one, but instead of testing whether an element is zero, we want to test whether it is greater than zero. We can't use GREATERP directly for this because GREATERP is a function of two inputs; APPLY-TO-ALL will only give it one input. Show how first writing a one-input function called GREATER-THAN-ZEROP would help.

3. LAMBDA EXPRESSIONS

There are two ways to specify the function to be used by an applicative operator. The first way is to define the function with DEFUN and then specify it by name, which is how we passed the SQUARE function to APPLY-TO-ALL in an earlier example. The second way is to supply the *definition* of the function directly. This is done by writing a list called a **lambda expression.** Example:

```
*(apply-to-all '(lambda (x) (times x x)) '(1 2 3 4 5))
(1 4 9 16 25)
```

The lambda expression

```
(LAMBDA (X) (TIMES X X))
```

looks similar to a DEFUN, except that the function name is missing and the word LAMBDA appears in place of DEFUN. Lambda expressions are actually unnamed functions. LAMBDA is not a special form that has to be evaluated like DEFUN. Rather it is a marker that says "this list represents a function."

Lambda is especially useful for synthesizing one-input functions from related functions of two inputs. For example, suppose we wanted to multiply every element of a list by 10. We might be tempted to write something like

```
(APPLY-TO-ALL 'TIMES '(1 2 3 4 5))
```

but where is the 10 to appear? Another problem is that TIMES is a function of two inputs, but APPLY-TO-ALL is only going to give it one. The correct way to solve this problem is to write a lambda expression of *one* input that multiplies its input by 10 and then use that lambda expression with APPLY-TO-ALL.

```
*(apply-to-all '(lambda (x) (times x 10)) '(1 2 3 4 5))
(10 20 30 40 50)
```

Here is another example of the use of APPLY-TO-ALL along with a lambda expression. We will turn each element of a list of names into a list of form (HI THERE *name*).

```
*(apply-to-all '(lambda (x) (list 'hi 'there x))
               '(joe fred wanda))
((HI THERE JOE) (HI THERE FRED) (HI THERE WANDA))
```

Exercises

1. Write a lambda expression to subtract seven from a number.

2. Write a lambda expression that returns T if its input is T or NIL, but NIL for any other input.

3. Write a function that takes a list such as (UP DOWN UP UP) and "flips" each element, returning (DOWN UP DOWN DOWN). Your function should include a lambda expression that knows how to flip an individual element plus an applicative operator to do this to every element of the list.

4. THE FIND-IF OPERATOR

FIND-IF is another applicative operator. If you give FIND-IF a predicate and a list as input, it will find the first element of the list for which the predicate returns *true*. FIND-IF returns that element. Example:

```
*(find-if 'oddp '(2 4 6 7 8 9))
7

*(find-if '(lambda (x) (not (oddp x))) '(2 4 6 7 8 9))
2
```

If no elements satisfy the predicate, FIND-IF returns NIL.

```
*(find-if 'oddp '(2 4 6 8))
NIL
```

4.1. Writing ASSOC with FIND-IF

If ASSOC were not a primitive function, we could write it ourselves using FIND-IF. After all, what the ASSOC function does is simply search for some element of a table whose key is equal to the key we are looking for. Here is MY-ASSOC, a version of ASSOC written with FIND-IF:

```
(DEFUN MY-ASSOC (SEARCH-KEY TBL)
   (FIND-IF '(LAMBDA (ENTRY) (EQUAL (CAR ENTRY) SEARCH-KEY))
            TBL))
```

In this example, the lambda expression that MY-ASSOC supplies to FIND-IF takes a table entry as input. FIND-IF will call the lambda expression on successive elements of the table until the lambda expression returns T. It will return T only when the CAR of the entry matches the key we are searching for.

Notice that although the lambda expression takes only one input, the expression inside it refers to *two* variables: ENTRY and SEARCH-KEY. ENTRY is local to the lambda expression. SEARCH-KEY is local to MY-ASSOC, but it appears as a *global* variable to the lambda expression. SEARCH-KEY will always be bound when the lambda expression is evaluated because the lambda expression is contained within MY-ASSOC, which binds SEARCH-KEY.

Exercises

1. Write a function that takes two inputs, X and K, and returns the first number in the list X that is greater than K. Your function should include a lambda expression that references K as a global variable.

2. Write a function that returns the first element of a list that is not a list.

Mini Keyboard Exercise

In this exercise we will write a program to transpose a song from one key to another. In order to manipulate notes more efficiently, we will translate them into numbers. Here is the correspondence between notes and numbers for a one-octave scale:

```
C        =  1        F-SHARP   =  7
C-SHARP  =  2        G         =  8
D        =  3        G-SHARP   =  9
D-SHARP  =  4        A         =  10
E        =  5        A-SHARP   =  11
F        =  6        B         =  12
```

1. Write a table to represent this information. Store it in a global variable called NOTE-TABLE.

2. Write a function called NUMBERS that takes a list of notes as input and returns the corresponding list of numbers. (NUMBERS '(E D C D E E E)) should return (5 3 1 3 5 5 5). This list represents the first seven notes of "Mary Had a Little Lamb."

3. Write a function called NOTES that takes a list of numbers as input and returns the corresponding list of notes. (NOTES '(5 3 1 3 5 5 5)) should return (E D C D E E E). (Hint: Since NOTE-TABLE is keyed by note, ASSOC can't look up numbers in it. Write your own table-searching function to search NOTE-TABLE by number instead of by note.)

4. Notice that NOTES and NUMBERS are mutual inverses, that is,

   ```
   X = (NOTES (NUMBERS X))     for X a list of notes
   X = (NUMBERS (NOTES X))     for X a list of numbers
   ```

   What can be said about (NOTES (NOTES X)) and (NUMBERS (NUMBERS X))?

5. To transpose a piece of music up by *n* half steps, we begin by adding the value *n* to each note in the piece. Write a function called RAISE that takes a number *n* and a list of numbers as input and raises each number in the list by the value *n*. (RAISE 5 '(5 3 1 3 5 5 5)) should return (10 8 6 8 10 10 10), which is "Mary Had a Little Lamb" transposed 5 half steps from the key of C to the key of F.

6. Sometimes when we raise the value of a note, we may raise it right into another octave. For instance, if we raise the triad C-E-G represented by the list (1 5 8) into the key of F by adding 5 to each note, we get (6 10 13), or F-A-C. Here the C note, represented by the number 13, is an octave above the regular C represented by 1. Write a function called NORMALIZE that takes a list of numbers as input and "normalizes" them to make them be between 1 and 12. A number greater than 12 should have 12 subtracted from it; a number less than 1 should have 12 added to it. (NORMALIZE '(6 10 13)) should return (6 10 1).

7. Write a function TRANSPOSE that takes a number *n* and a song as input, and returns that song after it has been transposed by *n* half steps. (TRANSPOSE 5 '(E D C D E E E)) should return (A G F G A A A). Your solution should assume the availability of the NUMBERS, NOTES, RAISE, and NORMALIZE functions. Try transposing "Mary Had a Little Lamb" up by 11 half steps. What happens if you transpose it by 12 half steps? How about −1 half steps?

5. SUBSET

While FIND-IF returns the first item that satisfies a predicate, SUBSET returns a list of all the items that satisfy it. For example, if we choose

ODDP as the predicate, SUBSET will pick out all the odd numbers from a list:

```
*(subset 'oddp '(1 2 3 4 5 6 7))
(1 3 5 7)

*(subset 'oddp '(1 3 5 7 9 10))
(1 3 5 7 9)

*(subset 'oddp '(2 4 6 8 10))
NIL
```

Here are some additional examples of SUBSET:

```
*(subset '(lambda (x) (greaterp x 0)) '(1 -2 4 5 -7 -9 13))
(1 4 5 13)

*(subset 'numberp '(3 apples 4 pears and 2 little plums))
(3 4 2)

*(subset 'symbolp '(3 apples 4 pears and 2 little plums))
(APPLES PEARS AND LITTLE PLUMS)
```

COUNT-ZEROS is a function that counts how many zeros appear in a list of numbers. It does this by taking the subset of the list elements that are zero and then taking the length of the result.

```
*(subset 'zerop '(34 0 0 95 0))
(0 0 0)

*(defun count-zeros (x) (length (subset 'zerop x)))
COUNT-ZEROS

*(count-zeros '(34 0 0 95 0))
3

*(count-zeros '(1 0 63 0 38)
2

*(count-zeros '(0 0 0 0 0))
5

*(count-zeros '(1 2 3 4 5))
0
```

Exercises

1. Write a function to pick out those numbers in a list that are greater than one and less than five.

2. Write a function that counts how many times the word "the" appears in a sentence.

3. Write a function that picks from a list of lists those of exactly length two.

4. Here is a version of SETDIFFERENCE written with SUBSET:

```
(DEFUN MY-SETDIFF (X Y)
  (SUBSET '(LAMBDA (X1) (NOT (MEMBER X1 Y)))
          X))
```

   Show how the INTERSECTION and UNION functions can also be written using SUBSET.

6. EVERY

EVERY returns T if every element of a list satisfies a given predicate. Otherwise, it returns NIL. Examples:

```
*(every 'numberp '(1 2 3 4 5))
T

*(every 'numberp '(1 2 A B C 5))
NIL

*(every '(lambda (x) (greaterp x 0)) '(1 2 3 4 5))
T

*(every '(lambda (x) (greaterp x 0)) '(1 2 3 -4 5))
NIL
```

If EVERY is called with NIL as its second argument, it simply returns T, since the empty list has no elements that could fail to satisfy a predicate.

```
*(every 'oddp nil)
T

*(every '(lambda (x) (not (oddp x))) nil)
T
```

Exercises

1. Write a function ALL-ODD that returns T if every element of a list of numbers is odd.

2. Write a function NONE-ODD that returns T if every element of a list of numbers is not odd.

3. Write a function NOT-ALL-ODD that returns T if not every element of a list of numbers is odd.

4. Write a function NOT-NONE-ODD that returns T if it is not the case that a list of numbers contains no odd elements.

5. Are all four of the preceding functions distinct from one another, or are some of them the same? Can you think of better names for the last two?

Mini Keyboard Exercise

In this keyboard exercise we will do some card tricks with applicative operators. A card will be represented by a list of form (*rank suit*)—for example, (ACE SPADES) or (2 CLUBS). A hand will be represented by a list of cards.

1. Write the functions RANK and SUIT that return the rank and suit of a card, respectively. (RANK '(2 CLUBS)) should return 2, while (SUIT '(2 CLUBS)) should return CLUBS.

2. Set the global variable MY-HAND to the following hand of cards:

```
((3 HEARTS)
 (5 CLUBS)
 (2 DIAMONDS)
 (4 DIAMONDS)
 (ACE SPADES))
```

3. Write a function COUNT-SUIT that takes two inputs—a suit and a hand of cards—and returns the number of cards belonging to that suit. (COUNT-SUIT 'DIAMONDS MY-HAND) should return 2.

4. Set the global variable COLORS to the following table:

```
((CLUBS BLACK)
 (DIAMONDS RED)
 (HEARTS RED)
 (SPADES BLACK))
```

5. Write a function COLOR-OF that uses the table COLORS to retrieve the color of a card. (COLOR-OF '(2 CLUBS)) should return BLACK. (COLOR-OF '(6 HEARTS)) should return RED.

6. Write a function FIRST-RED that returns the first card of a hand that is of a red suit or NIL if none are.

7. Write a predicate ALL-BLACK that takes a hand of cards as input and returns T if all cards in the hand are black cards.

8. Write a function WHAT-RANKS that takes two inputs—a suit and a hand—and returns the ranks of all cards belonging to that suit. (WHAT-RANKS 'DIAMONDS MY-HAND) should return the list (2 4). (WHAT-RANKS 'SPADES MY-HAND) should return the list (ACE). (Hint: First extract all the cards of the specified suit. Then use another operator to get the ranks of those cards.)

7. THE REDUCE OPERATOR

REDUCE is an applicative operator that reduces the elements of a list into a single result. REDUCE takes a function and a list as input, but unlike the other operators we've seen, REDUCE must be given a function of *two* inputs. Example: To add up a list of numbers with REDUCE, we use PLUS as the reducing function.

```
*(reduce 'plus '(1 2 3))
6

*(reduce 'plus '(10 9 8 7 6))
40

*(reduce 'plus '(5))
5

*(reduce 'plus nil)
0
```

Similarly, to multiply a bunch of numbers together, we use **TIMES** as the reducing function:

```
*(reduce 'times '(2 4 5))
40

*(reduce 'times '(3 4 0 7))
0

*(reduce 'times '(8))
8
```

We can also apply reduction to lists of lists. To turn a table into a one-level list, we use **APPEND** as the reducing function:

```
*(reduce 'append '((one un) (two deux) (three trois)))
(ONE UN TWO DEUX THREE TROIS)
```

Exercises

1. Suppose we had a list of sets ((A B C) (C D A) (F B D) (G)) that we wanted to collapse into one big set. If we used APPEND for our reducing function the result wouldn't be a true set, because some elements would appear more than once. What should we do instead?

2. Write a function that, given a list of lists, returns the total length of all the lists. (This problem can be solved two different ways.)

3. (REDUCE 'PLUS NIL) returns 0, but (REDUCE 'TIMES NIL) returns 1. Why do you think this is?

8. SUMMARY

Applicative operators are functions that apply other functions to data structures. There are many possible applicative operators, only a few of which are built into Lisp. Advanced Lisp programmers make up their own operators whenever they need new ones.

APPLY-TO-ALL applies a function to every element of a list and returns a list of the results. FIND-IF searches a list and returns the first element that satisfies a predicate. SUBSET returns all the elements that satisfy a predicate. EVERY returns T only if every element of a list satisfies a predicate. REDUCE uses a reducing function to reduce a list to a single value.

APPLY-TO-ALL is called MAPCAR in almost all Lisp implementations. I prefer the name APPLY-TO-ALL because it is more suggestive of what the operator does. The remaining operators in this chapter are not found in all dialects of Lisp. They sometimes appear under different names.

Review Exercises

1. What is an applicative operator?

2. Why are lambda expressions useful? Is it possible to do without them?

3. Show how to write FIND-IF given SUBSET.

4. Show how to write EVERY given SUBSET.

Functions Covered in This Chapter

Applicative operators: APPLY-TO-ALL, FIND-IF, SUBSET, EVERY, REDUCE

Keyboard Exercise

In this keyboard exercise we will develop a system for representing knowledge about a collection of toy blocks. A typical configuration of blocks is shown in figure 7.1. Assertions about objects in the blocks world are represented as triples of form

```
(block    attribute    value)
```

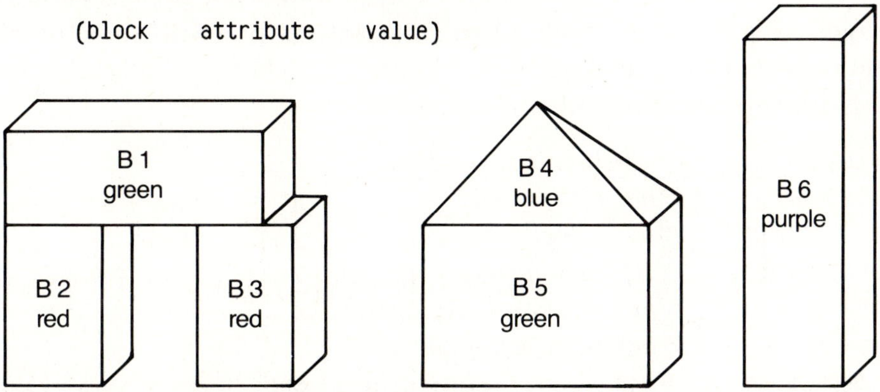

Figure 7.1 A typical configuration of blocks.

Here are some assertions about block B2:

```
(B2 SHAPE BRICK)
(B2 COLOR RED)
(B2 SIZE SMALL)
(B2 SUPPORTS B1)
(B2 LEFT-OF B3)
```

A collection (i.e., a list) of assertions is called a **database.** Given a database describing the blocks in the figure, we can write functions to answer questions such as "What color is block B2?" or "What blocks support block B1?" To answer these questions, we will use a function called a **pattern matcher** to search the database for us. For example, to find out the color of block B2, we use the pattern (B2 COLOR ?).

```
*(fetch '(b2 color ?))
((B2 COLOR RED))
```

To find which blocks support B1, we use the pattern (? SUPPORTS B1):

```
*(fetch '(? supports b1))
((B2 SUPPORTS B1) (B3 SUPPORTS B1))
```

The FETCH function returns those assertions from the database that match a given pattern. It should be apparent from the preceding examples that a pattern is a triple, like an assertion, but with some of its elements replaced by question marks. Figure 7.2 shows a collection of patterns with their English interpretations.

Pattern	English Interpretation
`(B1 COLOR ?)`	*What color is B1?*
`(? COLOR RED)`	*Which blocks are red?*
`(B1 COLOR RED)`	*Is B1 known to be red?*
`(B1 ? B2)`	*What relation is B1 to B2?*
`(B1 ? ?)`	*What is known about B1?*
`(? SUPPORTS ?)`	*What support relationships exist?*
`(? ? B1)`	*What blocks are related to B1?*
`(? ? ?)`	*What assertions are in the database?*

Figure 7.2 Some patterns and their interpretations.

A question mark in a pattern means any value can match in that position. Thus the pattern (B2 COLOR ?) can match assertions like (B2 COLOR RED), (B2 COLOR GREEN), (B2 COLOR BLUE), and so on. It cannot match the assertion (B1 COLOR RED) because the first element of the pattern is the symbol B2 while the first element of the assertion is B1.

Instructions

1. If the blocks database is already stored on the computer for you, load the file containing it. If not, you will have to type it in as it appears in figure 7.3. Save the database in the global variable DATABASE.

```
(SETQ DATABASE
      '((B1 SHAPE BRICK)
        (B1 COLOR GREEN)
        (B1 SIZE SMALL)
        (B1 SUPPORTED-BY B2)
        (B1 SUPPORTED-BY B3)
        (B2 SHAPE BRICK)
        (B2 COLOR RED)
        (B2 SIZE SMALL)
        (B2 SUPPORTS B1)
        (B2 LEFT-OF B3)
        (B3 SHAPE BRICK)
        (B3 COLOR RED)
        (B3 SIZE SMALL)
        (B3 SUPPORTS B1)
        (B3 RIGHT-OF B2)
        (B4 SHAPE PYRAMID)
        (B4 COLOR BLUE)
        (B4 SIZE LARGE)
        (B4 SUPPORTED-BY B5)
        (B5 SHAPE CUBE)
        (B5 COLOR GREEN)
        (B5 SIZE LARGE)
        (B5 SUPPORTS B4)
        (B6 SHAPE BRICK)
        (B6 COLOR PURPLE)
        (B6 SIZE LARGE)))
```

Figure 7.3 The blocks database.

2. Write a function MATCH-ELEMENT that takes two symbols as input. If the two are equal, or if the second is a question mark, MATCH-ELEMENT should return T. Otherwise it should return NIL. Thus (MATCH-ELEMENT 'RED 'RED) and (MATCH-ELEMENT 'RED '?) should return T, but (MATCH-ELEMENT 'RED 'BLUE) should return NIL. Make sure your function works correctly before proceeding further.

3. Write a function MATCH-TRIPLE that takes an assertion and a pattern as input and returns T if the assertion matches the pattern. Both inputs will be three-element lists. (MATCH-TRIPLE '(B2 COLOR RED) '(B2 COLOR ?)) should return T. (MATCH-TRIPLE '(B2 COLOR RED) '(B1 COLOR GREEN)) should return NIL. (Hint: Use MATCH-ELEMENT as a building block.)

4. Write the function FETCH that takes a pattern as input and returns all assertions in the database that match the pattern. Remember that DATABASE is a global variable. (FETCH '(B2 COLOR ?)) should return ((B2 COLOR RED)), and (FETCH '(? SUPPORTS B1)) should return ((B2 SUPPORTS B1) (B3 SUPPORTS B1)).

5. Use FETCH with patterns you construct yourself to answer the following questions. What shape is block B4? Which blocks are bricks? What relation is block B2 to block B3? List the color of every block. What facts are known about block B4?

6. Write a function that takes a block name as input and returns a *pattern* asking the color of the block. For example, given the input B3, your function should return the list (B3 COLOR ?).

7. Write a function SUPPORTERS that takes one input—a block—and returns a list of the blocks that support it. (SUPPORTERS 'B1) should return the list (B2 B3). Your function should work by constructing a pattern containing the block's name, using that pattern as input to FETCH, and then extracting the block names from the resulting list of assertions.

8. Write a predicate SUPP-CUBE that takes a block as input and returns a non-NIL value if that block is supported by a cube. (SUPP-CUBE 'B4) should return a true value; (SUPP-CUBE 'B1) should not because B1 is supported by bricks but not by cubes. (Hint: Use the result of the SUPPORTERS function as a starting point.)

9. We are going to write a DESCRIPTION function that returns the description of a block. (DESCRIPTION 'B2) will return (SHAPE BRICK COLOR RED SIZE SMALL SUPPORTS B1 LEFT-OF B3). We will do this in steps:

a. Write a function DESC1 that takes a block as input and returns all assertions dealing with that block. (DESC1 'B6) should return ((B6 SHAPE BRICK) (B6 COLOR PURPLE) (B6 SIZE LARGE)).

b. Write a function DESC2 of one input that calls DESC1 and strips the block name off each element of the result. (DESC2 'B6) should return the list ((SHAPE BRICK) (COLOR PURPLE) (SIZE LARGE)).

c. Write the DESCRIPTION function. It should take one input, invoke DESC2, and merge the resulting list of lists into a single list. (DESCRIPTION 'B6) should return (SHAPE BRICK COLOR PURPLE SIZE LARGE).

d. What is the description of block B1? Of block B4?

10. Block B1 is made of wood, but block B2 is made of plastic. How would you add this information to the database?

Advanced Topics 7

1. IDENTITY VALUES

The REDUCE operator exhibits some interesting behavior when we reduce the empty list. (REDUCE 'PLUS NIL) returns 0, while (REDUCE 'TIMES NIL) returns 1. To appreciate why this should be so, we must understand the concept of an **identity value.**

Zero is the identity value for addition, because adding zero to any number yields the number itself. One is the identity value for multiplication; multiplying any number by one gives the number itself. Here is how identity values are related to reduction. Suppose X and Y are lists of numbers. We know from the associative property of addition that the sum of the numbers in X plus the sum of the numbers in Y equals the sum of the numbers in (APPEND X Y). Now, if Y is the empty list, (APPEND X Y) is just X, so the sum of the numbers in X plus whatever the sum of the numbers in Y is must equal the sum of the numbers in X itself. This means the sum of the numbers in Y (the empty list) is the identity value for addition, which is zero.

Similarly, we know from mathematics that the product of the numbers in X times the product of the numbers in Y equals the product of the numbers in (APPEND X Y). If Y is the empty list, (APPEND X Y) is just X, so the product of the numbers in X times the product of the numbers in Y must equal just the product of the numbers in X. This tells us that the product of the numbers in Y (the empty list) is the identity value for multiplication, which is one.

The result of reducing an empty list will always be the identity value for the reducing function, *provided* the function has one. If the function does not have one, an error results.

Exercises

1. Does APPEND have an identity value? Does CONS? Does UNION?

2. INTERSECTION has an identity value in set theory but not in Lisp. Why?

3. The identity value for DIFFERENCE is 0, but this is only a *right* identity because while N minus 0 equals N, it is not the case that 0 minus N equals N. DIFFERENCE has no left identity. What kind of identity does QUOTIENT have?

4. What are the identity values for AND and OR? Are they left identities, right identities, or both? (Ignore the fact that AND and OR are conditionals rather than normal functions. Assume they are given exactly two inputs, and concentrate on the values they return.)

5. Prove that if a function has a left identity and a right identity, the two identities must be the same.

6. EQUAL does not have an identity value in the general case, but when restricted to the domain {T, NIL} it does have one. What is it?

2. LEFT VS. RIGHT REDUCTION

When we reduce a list we can choose either left or right nesting of operations. (LEFT-REDUCE 'PLUS '(1 2 3 4 5)) would compute ((((1+2)+3)+4)+5), while (RIGHT-REDUCE 'PLUS '(1 2 3 4 5)) computes (1+(2+(3+(4+5)))). Either way the result is 15, because PLUS is an **associative** function. Associativity means that (A+B)+C always equals A+(B+C). We use just plain REDUCE instead of LEFT-REDUCE or RIGHT-REDUCE when direction of nesting doesn't matter.

```
*(left-reduce 'plus '(1 2 3 4 5))
15

*(right-reduce 'plus '(1 2 3 4 5))
15

*(reduce 'plus '(1 2 3 4 5))
15
```

For nonassociative functions the direction of nesting is important. DIFFERENCE is one such function.

```
*(left-reduce 'difference '(1 2 3 4 5))
-13

*(right-reduce 'difference '(1 2 3 4 5))
3
```

With LEFT-REDUCE we compute ((((1−2)−3)−4)−5), which is −13, while with RIGHT-REDUCE we compute (1−(2−(3−(4−5)))), which is 3. LIST is also a nonassociative function:

```
*(left-reduce 'list '(a b c d e f))
(((((A B) C) D) E) F)

*(right-reduce 'list '(a b c d e f))
(A (B (C (D (E F)))))
```

With LIST, the nesting of parentheses in the result directly reflects the order of operations chosen by the reduce operator. With LEFT-REDUCE we get left nesting; with RIGHT-REDUCE, right nesting.

Exercises

1. Let the variable XL be bound to the list (((((A B) C) D) E) F) and the variable XR be bound to the list (A (B (C (D (E F))))). How many successive CARs of XL do we need to get a symbol as a result? What is this result? How many successive CADRs of XL does it take to reach a symbol? What symbol do we reach with successive CADRs? Compare your answers with the corresponding answers for XR.

2. Does (LEFT-REDUCE 'APPEND X) equal (RIGHT-REDUCE 'APPEND X)? Why?

3. Does using LEFT-REDUCE on a list X yield the same result as RIGHT-REDUCE on (REVERSE X)? Give an example where it does and an example where it does not.

4. A list of truth values (Ts or NILs) is said to have **odd parity** if it has an odd number of Ts. Use reduction to construct an ODD-PARITY predicate that returns T if its input has odd parity. Does it matter whether you use left or right reduction? Why?

3. OPERATING ON MULTIPLE LISTS

In the beginning of this chapter we used APPLY-TO-ALL to apply a one-input function to the elements of a list. APPLY-TO-ALL is not restricted to one-input functions. Given a function of n inputs, APPLY-TO-ALL will map it over n lists. For example, given a list of people and a list of jobs, we can use APPLY-TO-ALL with a two-input function to pair each person with a job:

```
*(apply-to-all '(lambda (x y) (list x 'gets y))
               '(fred wilma george diane)
               '(job1 job2 job3 job4))
((FRED GETS JOB1)
 (WILMA GETS JOB2)
 (GEORGE GETS JOB3)
 (DIANE GETS JOB4))
```

APPLY-TO-ALL goes through the two lists in parallel, taking one element from each at each step. If one list is shorter than the other, APPLY-TO-ALL stops when it reaches the end of the shorter list.

Another example of operating on multiple lists is the problem of adding two lists of numbers pairwise:

```
*(apply-to-all 'plus '(1 2 3 4 5) '(60 70 80 90 100))
(61 72 83 94 105)

*(apply-to-all 'plus '(1 2 3) '(10 20 30 40 50))
(11 22 33)
```

EVERY can also operate on multiple lists, given a predicate that accepts multiple inputs. Example:

```
*(every 'greaterp '(11 22 33 44) '(10 20 30 40))
T
```

Since 11 is greater than 10, 22 greater than 20, 33 greater than 30, and 44 greater than 40, EVERY returns T.

Exercise

Recall the English–French dictionary we stored in the global variable WORDS earlier in the chapter. Given this dictionary plus the list (UNO DOS TRES QUATRO CINCO), write an expression to return a trilingual dictionary. The first entry of the dictionary should be (ONE UN UNO).

4. THE MAP FUNCTIONS

The original Lisp applicative operators were called **mapping functions.** (This is a technical term derived from mathematics.) MAPCAR is the most famous applicative. We know it as APPLY-TO-ALL. MacLisp and other Lisp dialects provide a variant of MAPCAR called MAPC that returns the original input list rather than a list of results. Example:

```
*(mapcar 'ncons '(a b c d))
((A) (B) (C) (D))

*(mapc 'ncons '(a b c d))
(A B C D)
```

MAPC doesn't appear very useful at first, because it throws the results away. However, if the function that is the first input to MAPC has some side effect, such as setting a global variable or printing something on the terminal, then MAPC can be useful because it is more efficient than MAPCAR.

A similarly related pair of functions is MAPLIST and MAP. MAPLIST applies a function to each sublist of a list and returns a list of the results.

```
*(maplist '(lambda (x) (cons 'eat x)) '(wholesome organic peanut butter))
((EAT WHOLESOME ORGANIC PEANUT BUTTER)
 (EAT ORGANIC PEANUT BUTTER)
 (EAT PEANUT BUTTER)
 (EAT BUTTER))

*(maplist 'reverse '(a b c d e))
((E D C B A) (E D C B) (E D C) (E D) (E))
```

MAP works similarly to MAPLIST but returns the original input rather than the list of results. MAP is to MAPLIST what MAPC is to MAPCAR.

Finally, the functions MAPCAN and MAPCON are destructive functions that are similar to MAPCAR and MAPLIST, respectively, except that they NCONC successive results together rather than making a list of them. If a function returns a NIL result it will make no contribution to the result list, since (NCONC X NIL) equals X, just as (APPEND X NIL) does. If a function returns a list, that list is destructively added to the result list. If the function returns anything else, an error occurs.

MAPCAN is often used to take subsets of a list. For example, we can extract the odd elements from a list of numbers as follows:

```
(DEFUN EXTRACT-ODD (L)
  (MAPCAN '(LAMBDA (X) (AND (ODDP X) (NCONS X))) L))
```

MAPCAN will apply the lambda expression (LAMBDA (X) (AND (ODDP X) (NCONS X))) to each element of L. If an element is odd, the lambda expression makes a list of it, and this list is NCONC'ed into the result list. If the element is even the lambda expression returns NIL, so nothing is added to the result list. Example:

```
*(mapcan '(lambda (x) (and (oddp x) (ncons x)))
        '(1 2 3 4 5 6 7))
(1 3 5 7)

*(mapcar '(lambda (x) (and (oddp x) (ncons x)))
        '(1 2 3 4 5 6 7))
((1) NIL (3) NIL (5) NIL (7))
```

Exercise

MAPCAN is useful, but sometimes we need a function that is nondestructive. The MAPAPPEND operator is similar to MAPCAN, but it combines results with APPEND instead of NCONC. Show how to construct a MAPAPPEND operator using REDUCE and APPLY-TO-ALL.

Functions Covered in Advanced Topics

Reduction operators: LEFT-REDUCE, RIGHT-REDUCE
MAP functions: MAPCAR, MAPC, MAPLIST, MAP, MAPCAN, MAPCON

8 Recursion

1. INTRODUCTION

Recursion is one of the most beautiful ideas in computer science. The main topic of this chapter is recursive control structures—conditionals and applicative operators are two other control structures we've studied—but we will also take a look at recursive *data structures* in the advanced topics section. The insight necessary to solve recursive problems must be developed through many examples and much practice. We begin with a fairy tale.

2. MARTIN AND THE DRAGON

Long, long ago, before the time of computers, there were alchemists who were curious about mathematics. Since these alchemists lacked computers, they used dragons to do their work for them, but the dragons were lazy and bad-tempered; the worst ones would sooner burn a man to a crisp than do a single bit of work for him. This is the story of how Martin, an alchemist's apprentice, discovered recursion by outsmarting a lazy dragon.

One day the alchemist for whom Martin worked gave him a list of numbers and told him to go down to the dungeon and ask the dragon if any of them were odd. Martin had never been to the dungeon before. He took a candle down with him and in the far corner found an old dragon, none too friendly looking. Timidly he stepped forward. He did not want to be burned to a crisp.

"What do YOU want?" grumped the dragon as it eyed Martin suspiciously.

"I have a list of numbers," said Martin, "and I want to know if any of them are odd. Here it is." Martin wrote the list in the dirt with his finger:

```
(3142 5798 6550 8914)
```

The dragon was in a disagreeable mood that day. In fact, being a dragon, it always was. "Sorry, kid," the dragon said. "I might be willing to tell you if the *first* number in that list is odd, but that's the best I could possibly do. Anything else would be too complicated; probably not worth my trouble."

"But I need to know if *any* number in the list is odd, not just the first number," Martin explained.

"Tough toadstools, kid. I'll only look at the first number of the list. But I'll look at as many lists as you like if you give them to me one at a time."

Martin thought for a while. There had to be a way around the dragon's orneriness. "How about this first list then?" he asked, pointing to the one he had drawn on the ground:

```
(3142 5798 6550 8914)
```

"The first number in that list is not odd," said the dragon.

Then Martin had an idea. He covered the first part of the list with his hand and drew a new left parenthesis, leaving

```
(5798 6550 8914)
```

and said, "How about this list?"

"The first number in that list is not odd," the dragon replied.

Martin covered some more of the list. "How about this list then?"

```
(6550 8914)
```

"The first number in that list isn't odd either," said the dragon. It looked a little bored, but at least it was cooperating.

"And this one?" asked Martin.

```
(8914)
```

"Not odd."

"And this one?"

```
()
```

"That's the empty list," the dragon snorted. "There can't be an odd number in there, because there's *nothing* in there."

"Well," said Martin, "I now know that not one of the numbers in the list the alchemist gave me is odd. They're *all* even."

"I NEVER said that!" bellowed the dragon. "I only told you about the *first* number in each list you showed me."

"That's true, Dragon. Shall I write down all of the lists you looked at?"

"If you wish," the dragon replied. Martin wrote in the dirt:

```
(3142 5798 6550 8914)
     (5798 6550 8914)
          (6550 8914)
               (8914)
                   ()
```

Now take the first number of each list," Martin said. "What do you get?"

"3142, 5798, 6550, 8914, and nothing for the last one."

"Don't you see?" Martin asked. "By telling me that the first element of each of those lists wasn't odd, you told me that *none* of the elements in my original list was odd."

"That's pretty tricky," the dragon said testily. "It looks like you've discovered recursion. But don't ask me what that means—you'll have to figure it out for yourself." And with that it closed its eyes and refused to utter another word.

3. A LISP VERSION OF MARTIN'S ALGORITHM

Here is a Lisp function called ANYODDP that returns T if any element of a list of numbers is odd. It returns NIL if none of them are.

```
(DEFUN ANYODDP (X)
  (COND ((NULL X) NIL)
        ((ODDP (CAR X)) T)
        (T (ANYODDP (CDR X)))))
```

If the list of numbers is NIL, **ANYODDP** returns NIL, since, as the dragon noted, there can't be an odd number in a list that contains nothing. If the list is not empty (second **COND** clause) and the first element is odd, then **ANYODDP** returns T. Otherwise, **ANYODDP** invokes *itself* on the tail of the list to search for odd elements. That is the recursive part of the function.

To see better how **ANYODDP** works, we will use a special form called **TRACE**. **TRACE** is a way to get Lisp to announce every invocation of a function and every value returned by that function. An example will make clear what this means.

```
*(defun anyoddp (x)
   (cond ((null x) nil)
         ((oddp (car x)) t)
         (t (anyoddp (cdr x)))))
ANYODDP

*(trace anyoddp)
(ANYODDP)

*(anyoddp '(3142 5798 6550 8914))
Enter ANYODDP:
!    X = (3142 5798 6550 8914)
!    Enter ANYODDP:
!    !    X = (5978 6550 8914)
!    !    Enter ANYODDP:
!    !    !    X = (6550 8914)
!    !    !    Enter ANYODDP:
!    !    !    !    X = (8914)
!    !    !    !    Enter ANYODDP:
!    !    !    !    !    X = NIL
!    !    !    !    ANYODDP = NIL
!    !    !    ANYODDP = NIL
!    !    ANYODDP = NIL
!    ANYODDP = NIL
ANYODDP = NIL
NIL
```

```
*(anyoddp '(2 4 5 6 8))
Enter ANYODDP:
!     X = (2 4 5 6 8)
!     Enter ANYODDP:
!     !     X = (4 5 6 8)
!     !     Enter ANYODDP:
!     !     !     X = (5 6 8)
!     !     ANYODDP = T
!     ANYODDP = T
ANYODDP = T
T
```

Note that in the second example of ANYODDP the function did not recurse all the way down to NIL. Since the CAR of (5 6 8) is odd, ANYODDP returned T at that point.

4. MARTIN VISITS THE DRAGON AGAIN

"Hello, Dragon!" Martin called as he made his way down the rickety dungeon staircase.

"Hmmmph! You again. I'm on to your recursive tricks." The dragon did not sound glad to see him.

"The boss wants me to find out what five factorial is," Martin said. "What's *factorial* mean, anyway?"

At this the dragon put on a most offended air and said, "I'm not going to tell you. Look it up in a book."

"All right," said Martin. "Just tell me what five factorial is and I'll leave you alone."

"You don't know what factorial means, but you want *me* to tell you what factorial of five is? All right, buster, I'll tell you, not that it will do you any good. Factorial of five is five times factorial of four. Good-bye."

"But what's factorial of four?" asked Martin, not at all pleased with the dragon's evasiveness.

"Factorial of four? Why, it's four times factorial of three, of course."

"And I suppose you're going to tell me that factorial of three is three times factorial of two," Martin said.

"What a bright boy you are!" said the dragon. "Now go away."

"Not yet," Martin replied. "Factorial of two is two times factorial of one. Factorial of one is one times factorial of zero. Now what?"

"Factorial of zero is one," said the dragon. "That's really all you ever need to remember about factorials."

"Hmmm," said Martin. "There's something recursive about the factorial function. Perhaps I should write down the steps I've gone through." Here is what he wrote:

```
Factorial(5) = 5 × Factorial(4)
Factorial(4) = 4 × Factorial(3)
Factorial(3) = 3 × Factorial(2)
Factorial(2) = 2 × Factorial(1)
Factorial(1) = 1 × Factorial(0)
```

and

```
Factorial(0) = 1
```

"Well," said the dragon, "you've recursed all the way down to zero. You can't go any farther in that direction. Why don't you try working your way back up—" When it realized what it was saying, the dragon stopped in midsentence. Dragons aren't supposed to be helpful.

Martin started to write again:

```
Factorial(1) = 1 × Factorial(0) = 1
Factorial(2) = 2 × Factorial(1) = 2
Factorial(3) = 3 × Factorial(2) = 6
Factorial(4) = 4 × Factorial(3) = 24
Factorial(5) = 5 × Factorial(4) = 120
```

"Hey!" Martin yelped. "Factorial of 5 is 120. That's the answer! Thanks!"

"*I* didn't tell you the answer," the dragon said testily. "*I* only told you that factorial of zero is one. You did the rest yourself. Recursively, I might add."

"That's true," said Martin. "Now if I only knew what 'recursively' really meant."

5. A LISP VERSION OF THE FACTORIAL FUNCTION

The dragon's words gave a very precise definition of factorial. Here is a function called FACT that computes factorials recursively:

```
(DEFUN FACT (N)
  (COND ((ZEROP N) 1)
        (T (TIMES N (FACT (SUB1 N))))))
```

And here is how Lisp would solve Martin's problem:

```
*(defun fact (n)
   (cond ((zerop n) 1)
         (t (times n (fact (sub1 n))))))
FACT

*(trace fact)
(FACT)

*(fact 5)
Enter FACT:
!     N = 5
!     Enter FACT:
!     !     N = 4
!     !     Enter FACT:
!     !     !     N = 3
!     !     !     Enter FACT:
!     !     !     !     N = 2
!     !     !     !     Enter FACT:
!     !     !     !     !     N = 1
!     !     !     !     !     Enter FACT:
!     !     !     !     !     !     N = 0
!     !     !     !     !     FACT = 1
!     !     !     !     FACT = 1
!     !     !     FACT = 2
!     !     FACT = 6
!     FACT = 24
FACT = 120
120
```

6. THE DRAGON'S DREAM

The next time Martin returned to the dungeon, he found the dragon rubbing its eyes, as if it had just awakened from a long sleep, which in fact it had.

"I had a most curious dream," the dragon said. "It was a recursive dream, in fact. Would you like to hear about it?"

Martin was so surprised to find the dragon in a friendly mood he forgot all about the alchemist's latest problem. "Yes, please do tell me about your dream," he said.

"Very well," began the dragon. "Last night I was looking at a long loaf of bread, and I wondered how many slices it would make. To answer my question I actually went and cut one slice from the loaf. But now what? I had one slice, one slightly shorter loaf of bread, and no answer. I kept puzzling and puzzling over the problem until finally I fell asleep."

"And that's when you had the dream?" Martin asked.

"Yes, a very curious one. I dreamed about another dragon, who had a loaf of bread just like mine except his was a slice shorter. And he too wanted to know how many slices his bread would make, but he had the same problem I did. He cut off a slice, like me, and stared at the remaining loaf, like me, and then he fell asleep like me as well."

"So neither one of you found the answer," Martin said disappointedly. "You don't know how long your loaf is, and you don't know how long his is either, except that it's one slice shorter than yours."

"But I'm not done yet," the dragon said. "When the dragon in *my* dream fell asleep, *he* had a dream as well. He dreamed about—of all things—a dragon whose loaf of bread was one slice shorter than *his own* loaf. And this dragon also wanted to find out how many slices his loaf would make, and he tried to find out by cutting a slice, but that didn't tell him the answer, so he fell asleep thinking about it."

"Dreams within dreams!" Martin exclaimed. "You're making my head swim. Did that last dragon have a dream as well?"

"Yes, and he wasn't the last either. Each dragon dreamed of a dragon with a loaf one slice shorter than his own. I was piling up a pretty deep stack of dreams there."

"How did you manage to wake up then?" Martin asked.

"Well," the dragon said, "eventually one of the dragons dreamed of a dragon whose loaf was so small it wasn't there at all. You might call it 'the empty loaf.' That dragon could see his loaf contained no slices, so the answer to his question was zero and he didn't fall asleep.

"When the dragon who dreamed of that dragon woke up, he knew that since his own loaf was one slice longer, it must be exactly one slice long. So he awoke knowing the answer to his question.

"Now, when the dragon who dreamed of *that* dragon woke up, *he* knew that his loaf had to be two slices long, since it was one slice longer than that of the dragon he dreamed about. And when the dragon who dreamed of *him* woke up . . ."

"I get it!" Martin said. "He added one to the length of the loaf of the dragon he dreamed about, and that answered his own question. And when *you* finally woke up, you had the answer to yours. How many slices did your loaf make?"

"Twenty-seven," said the dragon. "It was a very long dream."

7. A LISP FUNCTION FOR COUNTING SLICES OF BREAD

If we represent a slice of bread by a symbol, then a loaf can be represented as a list of symbols. The problem of finding how many slices a loaf contains is thus the problem of finding how many elements a list contains. This is of course what LENGTH does, but if we didn't have LENGTH we could still count the slices recursively.

```
(DEFUN COUNT-SLICES (L)
  (COND ((NULL L) 0)
        (T (ADD1 (COUNT-SLICES (CDR L))))))
```

If the input is the empty list then its length is zero, so COUNT-SLICES simply returns 0. Otherwise COUNT-SLICES invokes itself recursively to get the length of the CDR of the list and then adds one to the result. Here is a trace of the COUNT-SLICES function:

```
*(trace count-slices)
(COUNT-SLICES)
```

```
*(count-slices '(x x x x x))
Enter COUNT-SLICES:
!    L = (X X X X X)
!    Enter COUNT-SLICES:
!    !    L = (X X X X)
!    !    Enter COUNT-SLICES:
!    !    !    L = (X X X)
!    !    !    Enter COUNT-SLICES:
!    !    !    !    L = (X X)
!    !    !    !    Enter COUNT-SLICES:
!    !    !    !    !    L = (X)
!    !    !    !    !    Enter COUNT-SLICES:
!    !    !    !    !    !    L = NIL
!    !    !    !    !    COUNT-SLICES = 0
!    !    !    !    COUNT-SLICES = 1
!    !    !    COUNT-SLICES = 2
!    !    COUNT-SLICES = 3
!    COUNT-SLICES = 4
COUNT-SLICES = 5
5
```

8. THE THREE RULES OF RECURSION

The dragon, beneath its feigned distaste for Martin's questions, thoroughly enjoyed teaching him about recursion. One day it broke down and actually taught him what recursion means. The dragon told Martin to approach every recursive problem as if it were a journey. If he followed three rules for solving problems recursively, he would always complete the journey successfully. The dragon explained the rules this way:

1. Find out how to take just one step.
2. Break each journey down into one step plus a smaller journey.
3. Know when to stop.

Let's see how each of these rules applies to the Lisp functions we wrote. The first rule, "Find out how to take just one step," asks us to break off from the problem one tiny piece that we instantly know how to solve. In ANYODDP we only check whether the CAR of a list is an odd number; if so we return true. In the factorial function we perform a single multiplication, multiplying the input N by factorial of N−1. In COUNT-SLICES the step is the ADD1 function: for each slice we cut off the loaf, we added one to whatever the length of the resulting loaf turned out to be.

The second rule, "Break each journey down into one step plus a smaller journey," means find a way for the function to call (i.e., invoke) itself recursively on the slightly smaller problem that results from breaking a tiny piece off. The ANYODDP function calls itself on the CDR of the list, a shorter list than the original, to see if there are any odd numbers there. The factorial function recursively computes factorial of N−1, a slightly simpler problem than factorial of N, and then uses the result to get factorial of N. In COUNT-SLICES we use a recursive call to count the number of slices in the CDR of a loaf and then add one to the result to get the size of the whole loaf.

The third rule, "Know when to stop," warns us that any recursive function must check to see if the journey has been completed before recursing further. Usually this is done in the first COND clause. In ANYODDP the first clause checks if the input is the empty list, and if so the function stops and returns NIL, since the empty list cannot contain an odd number. The factorial function, FACT, stops when the input gets down to zero. Zero factorial is one, and, as the dragon said, that's all you ever need to remember about factorial; the rest is computed recursively. In COUNT-SLICES the first COND clause checks for NIL, "the empty loaf." COUNT-SLICES returns zero if NIL is the input. Again, this is based on the realization that the empty loaf contains no slices, so we do not have to recurse any further.

Figure 8.1 shows how these three rules were applied in ANYODDP, FACT, and COUNT-SLICES. Now that you know the rules, you can write your own recursive functions.

Function	Stop when input is:	Return	Step to take	Rest of problem
ANYODDP	NIL	NIL	(ODDP (CAR X))⇒T	(ANYODDP (CDR X))
FACT	0	1	N × Factorial(N−1)	(FACT (SUB1 N))
COUNT-SLICES	NIL	0	ADD1	(COUNT-SLICES (CDR L))

Figure 8.1 The three rules of recursion applied to ANYODDP, FACT, and COUNT-SLICES.

First Recursion Exercise

We are going to write a function called LAUGH that takes a number as input and returns a list of that many HAs. (LAUGH 3) should return the list (HA HA HA). (LAUGH 0) should return a list with no HAs in it, or, as the dragon might put it, "the empty laugh."

Here is a skeleton for the LAUGH function:

```
(DEFUN LAUGH (N)
  (COND (α β)
        (T (CONS 'HA γ))))
```

Under what condition should the LAUGH function stop recursing? Replace the symbol α in the skeleton with that condition. What value should LAUGH return for that case? Replace symbol β in the skeleton with that value. Given that a single step for this problem is to add a HA onto the result of a subproblem, fill in that subproblem by replacing the symbol γ.

Type your LAUGH function into the computer. Then type (TRACE LAUGH) to trace it and (LAUGH 5) to test it. Do you get the result you want? What happens for (LAUGH 0)? What happens for (LAUGH −1)?

Second Recursion Exercise

In this exercise we are going to write a function ADD-UP to add up all the numbers in a list. You already know how to solve this problem applicatively with REDUCE; now you'll learn to solve it recursively. Before writing ADD-UP we must answer three questions posed by our three rules of recursion.

1. Do we know how to take a single step? Look at the second COND clause in the definition of COUNT-SLICES or FACT. Does this give you any ideas on what the single step should be for ADD-UP?

2. How should ADD-UP call itself recursively to solve the rest of the problem? Look at COUNT-SLICES or FACT again if you need inspiration.

3. When do we stop? Is there any list for which we immediately *know* what the sum of its elements is? What is that list? What value should the function return if it gets that list as input?

Write down the complete definition of ADD-UP. Type it into the computer. Type (TRACE ADD-UP) to trace it and then try adding up a list of numbers.

Note: If your function looks like it's going to be running forever, break out of it and get back to the read-eval-print loop. Exactly how this is done depends on the particular version of Lisp you use. Ask your local Lisp expert if you don't know how to do it.

More Exercises

1. Write ALLODDP, a recursive function that returns T if all the numbers in a list are odd.

2. Write a recursive version of MEMBER. Call it REC-MEMBER so you don't redefine the built-in MEMBER function.

3. Write a recursive version of ASSOC. Call it REC-ASSOC.

4. Write a recursive version of NTH. Call it REC-NTH.

5. For x, a nonnegative integer, and y, a positive integer, $x+y$ equals $x+1+(y-1)$. If y is zero, then $x+y$ equals x. Use these equations to build a recursive version of PLUS called REC-PLUS out of ADD1, SUB1, COND, and ZEROP.

9. MARTIN DISCOVERS INFINITE RECURSION

On his next trip to the dungeon Martin brought with him a parchment scroll. "Look, Dragon," he called. "Someone else must know about recursion. I found this scroll in the alchemist's library."

The dragon peered suspiciously while Martin unrolled the scroll and placed a candlestick at each end to hold it flat. "This scroll makes no sense," the dragon said. "For one thing, it's got far too many parentheses."

"The punctuation *is* a little strange," Martin agreed, "but I think I've figured out the message. It's an algorithm for computing Fibonacci numbers."

"I already know how to compute Fibonacci numbers," said the dragon.

"How?"

"Oh, I wouldn't *dream* of spoiling the fun by telling you."

"I didn't think you would," Martin shot back. "But the scroll says that Fib of n equals Fib of n−1 plus Fib of n−2. That's a *recursive* definition, and I know how to work with recursion."

"What else does the scroll say?" the dragon asked.

"Why, nothing. Should it say more?"

The dragon suddenly assumed a most ingratiating tone. "Dear boy, would you do a poor old dragon, no doubt soon to be replaced by a parchment scroll, one last favor? Compute a Fibonacci number for me. I promise only to ask you for a small one."

"Well, I'm supposed to be upstairs now, cleaning the cauldrons," Martin began, but seeing the hurt look on the dragon's face, he added "but I guess I have time for a *small* one."

"You won't regret it," said the dragon. "Tell me: what is Fib of four?"

Martin traced his translation of the Fibonacci algorithm in the dust:

```
Fib(n) = Fib(n-1) + Fib(n-2)
```

Then he began to compute Fib of four:

```
Fib(4)  = Fib(3)  + Fib(2)
Fib(3)  = Fib(2)  + Fib(1)
Fib(2)  = Fib(1)  + Fib(0)
Fib(1)  = Fib(0)  + Fib(-1)
Fib(0)  = Fib(-1) + Fib(-2)
Fib(-1) = Fib(-2) + Fib(-3)
Fib(-2) = Fib(-3) + Fib(-4)
Fib(-3) = Fib(-4) + Fib(-5)
```

"Finished?" the dragon asked innocently.

"No," Martin replied. "Something is wrong. The numbers are becoming more and more negative."

"Will you be finished soon, then? It's almost time for lunch."

"It looks like I won't ever be finished," Martin said. "This recursion keeps going on forever."

"Aha! You see? An *infinite* recursion!" the dragon said smugly. "I noticed it at once."

"Then why didn't you say something?" Martin demanded.

The dragon rolled its eyes skyward for a moment. "How will you *ever* learn anything if you rely on a dragon to do your thinking for you?" it answered.

"But how did you spot the problem so *quickly?*"

"Elementary, my boy. The scroll told you only how to take a single step and how to break the journey down to a smaller one. It said nothing at all about when you get to stop. Ergo"—the dragon grinned—"you don't."

10. INFINITE RECURSION IN LISP

Lisp functions can be made to recurse infinitely by ignoring the dragon's third rule of recursion, which is to know when to stop. Here is the Lisp implementation of Martin's algorithm:

```
*(defun fib (n)
   (plus (fib (difference n 1)) (fib (difference n 2))))
FIB

*(trace fib)
(FIB)
```

```
*(fib 4)
Enter FIB:
!     N = 4
!     Enter FIB:
!     !     N = 3
!     !     Enter FIB:
!     !     !     N = 2
!     !     !     Enter FIB:
!     !     !     !     N = 1
!     !     !     !     Enter FIB:
!     !     !     !     !     N = 0
!     !     !     !     !     Enter FIB:
!     !     !     !     !     !     N = -1
!     !     !     !     !     !     Enter FIB:
!     !     !     !     !     !     !     N = -2
!     !     !     !     !     !     !     Enter FIB:
!     !     !     !     !     !     !     !     N = -3
```
ad infinitum

Exercises

1. The missing part of Martin's Fibonacci algorithm is the rule for Fib(1) and Fib(0). Both of these are defined to be 1. Using this information, write a correct version of the FIB function. (FIB 4) should return 5. (FIB 5) should return 8.

2. Consider the following version of ANY-7-P, a recursive function that searches a list for the number seven:

```
(DEFUN ANY-7-P (X)
  (COND ((EQUAL (CAR X) 7) T)
        (T (ANY-7-P (CDR X)))))
```

   Give a sample input for which this function will work correctly. Give one for which the function will recurse infinitely.

3. Review the definition of the factorial function, FACT, given previously. What sort of input could you give it to cause an infinite recursion?

4. Write the very shortest infinite recursion function you can.

5. Consider the circular list shown in figure 8.2. What is the CAR of this list? What is the CDR? What will the COUNT-SLICES function do when given this list as input?

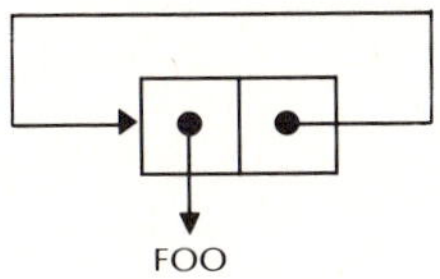

Figure 8.2 A circular list.

11. BUILDING LISTS WITH RECURSION

Recursive functions are very good at building list structures. Here is a function COUNTDOWN that generates a list of integers from N down to 1.

```
(DEFUN COUNTDOWN (N)
  (COND ((ZEROP N) NIL)
        (T (CONS N (COUNTDOWN (SUB1 N))))))
```

COUNTDOWN uses CONS and a recursive call to itself to build the list up from NIL. Example:

```
*(countdown 5)
(5 4 3 2 1)

*(countdown 0)
NIL

*(trace countdown)
(COUNTDOWN)
```

```
*(countdown 3)
Enter COUNTDOWN:
!     N = 3
!     Enter COUNTDOWN:
!     !     N = 2
!     !     Enter COUNTDOWN:
!     !     !     N = 1
!     !     !     ENTER COUNTDOWN:
!     !     !     !     N = 0
!     !     !     COUNTDOWN = NIL
!     !     COUNTDOWN = (1)
!     COUNTDOWN = (2 1)
COUNTDOWN = (3 2 1)
(3 2 1)
```

Counting up is a little harder because there is no built-in function to add an element to the end of a list the way CONS adds elements to the front. One way to solve this problem is with APPEND. Figure 8.3 shows how COUNTUP constructs the list (1 2 3 4 5) with APPEND as each recursive call returns.

```
(DEFUN COUNTUP (N)
  (COND ((ZEROP N) NIL)
        (T (APPEND (COUNTUP (SUB1 N)) (LIST N)))))

*(countup 5)
(1 2 3 4 5)

*(countup 0)
NIL
```

Value of N	First input to APPEND	Second input to APPEND	Result of COUNTUP
0	—	—	NIL
1	NIL	(1)	(1)
2	(1)	(2)	(1 2)
3	(1 2)	(3)	(1 2 3)
4	(1 2 3)	(4)	(1 2 3 4)
5	(1 2 3 4)	(5)	(1 2 3 4 5)

Figure 8.3 COUNTUP counting up from 1 to 5.

COUNTDOWN built lists with CONS, and COUNTUP built them with APPEND. Here is a recursive function called BURY that builds nested lists with LIST. BURY buries an item under N levels of parentheses:

```
(DEFUN BURY (ITEM N)
  (COND ((ZEROP N) ITEM)
        (T (LIST (BURY ITEM (SUB1 N))))))
```

BURY takes two inputs and recurses on the second one. It passes the first input, ITEM, unchanged.

```
*(bury 'fred 2)
((FRED))

*(bury 'fred 5)
(((((FRED)))))

*(bury 'fred 1)
(FRED)

*(bury 'fred 0)
FRED
```

Exercises

1. Five factorial is 1×2×3×4×5. How could you use COUNTUP or COUNTDOWN plus an applicative operator to write an applicative version of FACT?

2. Write MAKE-LOAF, a function that returns a loaf of size N. (MAKE-LOAF 4) should return (X X X X).

3. Write PAIRINGS, a function that pairs the elements of two lists. (PAIRINGS '(A B C) '(1 2 3)) should return ((A 1) (B 2) (C 3)). You may assume that the two lists will be of equal length.

4. Write SUBLISTS, a function that returns all sublists of a list. (SUBLISTS '(FEE FIE FOE)) should return ((FEE FIE FOE) (FIE FOE) (FOE)).

5. Write REC-REVERSE, a recursive version of REVERSE.

12. TWO-PART RECURSIONS

Sometimes a recursive approach to a problem involves a two-part solution, that is, a solution consisting of two functions. The first function invokes the second with an extra argument to start it going; the second function recurses and does the actual work. Let's write a two-part version of COUNTUP. We'll call the main function IOTA and the subfunction IOTA1. (IOTA is the name for COUNTUP in *APL*, another popular programming language.)

```
(DEFUN IOTA (N) (IOTA1 N 1))

(DEFUN IOTA1 (N CNT)
  (COND ((GREATERP CNT N) NIL)
        (T (CONS CNT (IOTA1 N (ADD1 CNT))))))
```

This is how we will do our counting: IOTA will give IOTA1 a second input, which IOTA1 calls CNT, that starts at 1 and goes *up* with each recursive call. Each call to IOTA1 will pass the value of N unchanged, so IOTA1 knows when to stop, but the value of CNT will go up by 1. When CNT is greater than N, IOTA1 stops and returns NIL.

```
*(trace iota1)
(IOTA1)

*(iota 5)
Enter IOTA1:
!     N = 5
!     CNT = 1
!     Enter IOTA1:
!     !     N = 5
!     !     CNT = 2
!     !     Enter IOTA1:
!     !     !     N = 5
!     !     !     CNT = 3
!     !     !     Enter IOTA1:
!     !     !     !     N = 5
!     !     !     !     CNT = 4
!     !     !     !     Enter IOTA1:
```

```
!    !    !    !    !    N = 5
!    !    !    !    !    CNT = 5
!    !    !    !    !    Enter IOTA1:
!    !    !    !    !    !    N = 5
!    !    !    !    !    !    CNT = 6
!    !    !    !    !    IOTA1 = NIL
!    !    !    !    IOTA1 =(5)
!    !    !    IOTA1 = (4 5)
!    !    IOTA1 = (3 4 5)
!    IOTA1 = (2 3 4 5)
IOTA1 = (1 2 3 4 5)
(1 2 3 4 5)

*(untrace iota1)
(IOTA1)

*(iota 3)
(1 2 3)
```

Note the use of the UNTRACE special form in the preceding example to turn off tracing of IOTA1. Figure 8.4 shows how IOTA1 constructs the list (1 2 3 4 5) as the recursive calls return.

Value of N	Value of CNT	Second input to CONS	Result of IOTA1
5	6	—	NIL
5	5	NIL	(5)
5	4	(5)	(4 5)
5	3	(4 5)	(3 4 5)
5	2	(3 4 5)	(2 3 4 5)
5	1	(2 3 4 5)	(1 2 3 4 5)

Figure 8.4 IOTA1 counting up from 1 to 5.

The trick of defining a subfunction to help implement a function is widely used in recursive programming. The main function provides initial values for the extra inputs required by the recursive subfunction. From now on, whenever you are asked to write a function, you should feel free to define your own subfunctions if you need them.

Exercises

1. The simplest way to write REC-REVERSE, a recursive version of REVERSE, is with CONS and a subfunction of two inputs. Write this version of REC-REVERSE.

2. Write LARGEST, a recursive function that returns the largest member of a list of nonnegative integers. (LARGEST '(3 5 2 4)) should return 5. (LARGEST NIL) should return 0.

3. Write a recursive function HUGE that raises a number to its own power. (HUGE 2) should return 2^2, (HUGE 3) should return 3^3, (HUGE 4) should return 4^4, and so forth. Do not use REDUCE.

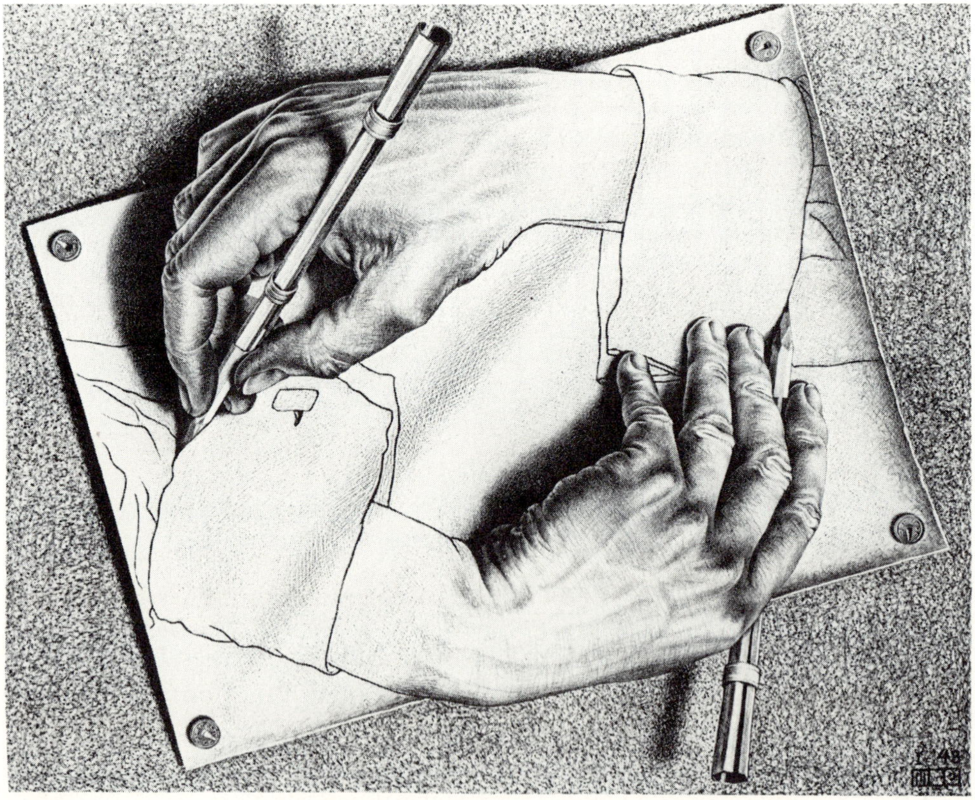

Figure 8.5 M.C. Escher's "Drawing Hands."

13. RECURSION IN ART AND LITERATURE

Recursion can be found not only in computer programs but also in stories and in paintings. The book *One Thousand and One Arabian Nights* contains stories within stories within stories, giving it a recursive flavor. Some of the most imaginative representations of recursion in art are the works of the Dutch artist M.C. Escher, whose lithograph "Drawing Hands" appears in figure 8.5. Douglas Hofstadter discusses the role of recursion in music, art, and mathematics in his book *Godel, Escher, Bach: An Eternal Golden Braid*. The dragon stories in this chapter were inspired by characters in Hofstadter's book.

14. SUMMARY

Recursion is a very powerful control structure and one of the most important ideas in computer science. A function is said to be recursive if it calls itself. In order to write a recursive function we must solve three problems posed by the three rules of recursion:

1. Find out how to take just one step.
2. Break each journey down into one step plus a smaller journey.
3. Know when to stop.

Review Exercises

1. What distinguishes a recursive function from a nonrecursive one?

2. Write REC-LAST, a recursive version of LAST.

3. Write EVERY-OTHER, a recursive function that returns every other element of a list (i.e., the first, third, fifth, etc.). (EVERY-OTHER '(A B C D E F G)) should return (A C E G). (EVERY-OTHER '(I CAME I SAW I CONQUERED)) should return (I I I).

4. Write LEFT-HALF, a recursive function in two parts that returns the first $n/2$ elements of a list of length n. You may assume that n will be even. (LEFT-HALF '(A B C D E F)) should return (A B C). (LEFT-

HALF '(1 2 3 4 5 6 7 8)) should return (1 2 3 4). You may use LENGTH but not REVERSE in your definition.

5. Here is another definition of the factorial function:

```
Factorial(0) = 1
Factorial(N) = Factorial(N+1) / (N+1)
```

Verify that these equations are true. Is the definition recursive? Write a Lisp function that implements it. For which inputs will the function return the correct answer? For which inputs will it fail to return the correct answer? Which of the three rules of recursion does the definition violate?

Functions Covered in This Chapter

Special forms for tracing: TRACE, UNTRACE

Keyboard Exercise

In this exercise we will extract different sorts of information from a genealogical database. The database gives information for five generations of a family, as shown in figure 8.6. Such diagrams are usually called family trees, but this family's genealogical history is not a simple tree structure. Marie has married her first cousin Nigel. Wanda has had one child with Vincent and another with Ivan. Zelda and Robert, the parents of Yvette, have two great grandparents in common.

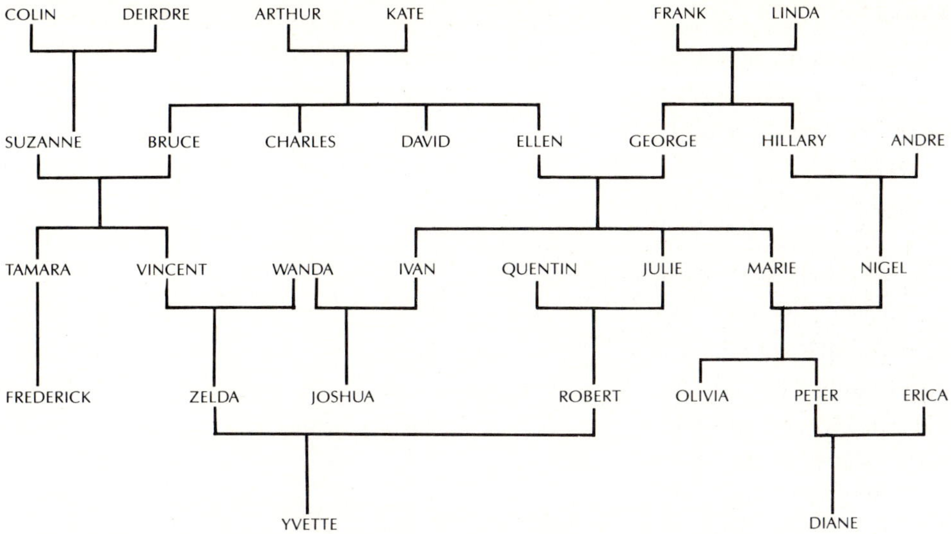

Figure 8.6 Genealogy information for five generations of a family.

Each person in the database is represented by an entry of form

(*name father mother*)

When someone's father or mother is unknown, a value of NIL is used.

Instructions

The functions you write in this keyboard exercise need not be recursive, except where indicated.

1. If the genealogy database is already stored on the computer for you, load the file containing it. If not, type it in as it appears in figure 8.7. Save the database in the global variable FAMILY.

2. Write the functions FATHER, MOTHER, PARENTS, and CHILDREN that return a person's father, mother, a list of his or her known parents, and a list of his or her children, respectively. (FATHER 'SUZANNE) should return COLIN. (PARENTS 'SUZANNE) should return (COLIN DEIRDRE). (PARENTS 'FREDERICK) should return (TAMARA), since Frederick's father is unknown. (CHILDREN 'ARTHUR) should return the set (BRUCE

```
(SETQ FAMILY
      '((COLIN NIL NIL)
        (DEIRDRE NIL NIL)
        (ARTHUR NIL NIL)
        (KATE NIL NIL)
        (FRANK NIL NIL)
        (LINDA NIL NIL)
        (SUZANNE COLIN DEIRDRE)
        (BRUCE ARTHUR KATE)
        (CHARLES ARTHUR KATE)
        (DAVID ARTHUR KATE)
        (ELLEN ARTHUR KATE)
        (GEORGE FRANK LINDA)
        (HILLARY FRANK LINDA)
        (ANDRE NIL NIL)
        (TAMARA BRUCE SUZANNE)
        (VINCENT BRUCE SUZANNE)
        (WANDA NIL NIL)
        (IVAN GEORGE ELLEN)
        (JULIE GEORGE ELLEN)
        (MARIE GEORGE ELLEN)
        (NIGEL ANDRE HILLARY)
        (FREDERICK NIL TAMARA)
        (ZELDA VINCENT WANDA)
        (JOSHUA IVAN WANDA)
        (QUENTIN NIL NIL)
        (ROBERT QUENTIN JULIE)
        (OLIVIA NIGEL MARIE)
        (PETER NIGEL MARIE)
        (ERICA NIL NIL)
        (YVETTE ROBERT ZELDA)
        (DIANE PETER ERICA)))
```

Figure 8.7 The genealogy database.

CHARLES DAVID ELLEN). If any of these functions is given NIL as input, it should return NIL. This feature will be useful later when we write some recursive functions.

3. Write SIBLINGS, a function that returns a list of a person's siblings, including genetic half-siblings. (SIBLINGS 'BRUCE) should return (CHARLES DAVID ELLEN), (SIBLINGS 'ZELDA) should return (JOSHUA).

4. Write MAPUNION, an applicative operator that takes a function and a list as input, applies the function to every element of the list, and computes the union of all the results. Example: (MAPUNION 'CDR '((1 A B C) (2 E C J) (3 F A B C D))) should return the set (A B C E J F D). (Hint: MAPUNION can be defined as a combination of two applicative operators you already know.)

5. Write GRANDPARENTS, a function that returns the set of a person's grandparents. Use MAPUNION in your solution.

6. Write COUSINS, a function that returns the set of a person's genetically related first cousins (i.e., the children of any of their parents' siblings). (COUSINS 'JULIE) should return the set (TAMARA VINCENT NIGEL). Use MAPUNION in your solution.

7. Write a two-input *recursive* predicate DESCENDED-FROM that returns a true value if the first person is descended from the second. (DESCENDED-FROM 'TAMARA 'ARTHUR) should return T. (DESCENDED-FROM 'TAMARA 'LINDA) should return NIL. (Hint: You are descended from someone if he is one of your parents or if either your father or mother is descended from him. This is a recursive definition.)

8. Write a *recursive* function ANCESTORS that returns a person's set of ancestors. (ANCESTORS 'MARIE) should return the set (ELLEN ARTHUR KATE GEORGE FRANK LINDA). The exact order in which these names appear is unimportant, but there should be no duplicates. Hint: A person's ancestors are his parents plus his parents' ancestors. This is a recursive definition.)

9. Write a *recursive* function GENERATION-GAP that returns the number of generations separating a person and one of his or her

ancestors. (GENERATION-GAP 'SUZANNE 'COLIN) should return 1. (GENERATION-GAP 'FREDERICK 'COLIN) should return 3. (GENERATION-GAP 'FREDERICK 'LINDA) should return NIL, because Linda is not an ancestor of Frederick.

10. Use the functions you have written to answer the following questions:
    a. Is Robert descended from Deirdre?

    b. Who are Yvette's ancestors?

    c. What is the generation gap between Olivia and Frank?

    d. Who are Peter's cousins?

    e. Who are Olivia's grandparents?

Advanced Topics 8

1. STRUCTURAL RECURSION

Structural recursion refers to a style of programming where the structure of a function's recursive calls mirrors the cons cell structure of its input. Our first example of structural recursion is the **REMOVE** function, which removes all top-level appearances of a symbol from a list. This function makes a copy from new cons cells of the top level structure of its input. It deletes symbols by *not* including them in the new structure it builds.

```
(DEFUN REMOVE (X L)
  (COND ((NULL L) NIL)
        ((EQUAL X (CAR L)) (REMOVE X (CDR L)))
        (T (CONS (CAR L) (REMOVE X (CDR L))))))

*(remove 'a '(d a b a j c))
(D B J C)

*(trace remove)
(REMOVE)
```

```
*(remove 'a '(d a b a j c))
Enter REMOVE:
!     X = A
!     L = (D A B A J C)
!     Enter REMOVE:
!     !     X = A
!     !     L = (A B A J C)
!     !     Enter REMOVE:
!     !     !     X = A
!     !     !     L = (B A J C)
!     !     !     Enter REMOVE:
!     !     !     !     X = A
!     !     !     !     L = (A J C)
!     !     !     !     Enter REMOVE:
!     !     !     !     !     X = A
!     !     !     !     !     L = (J C)
!     !     !     !     !     Enter REMOVE:
!     !     !     !     !     !     X = A
!     !     !     !     !     !     L = (C)
!     !     !     !     !     !     ENTER REMOVE:
!     !     !     !     !     !     !     X = A
!     !     !     !     !     !     !     L = NIL
!     !     !     !     !     !     REMOVE = NIL
!     !     !     !     !     REMOVE = (C)
!     !     !     !     REMOVE = (J C)
!     !     !     REMOVE = (J C)
!     !     REMOVE = (B J C)
!     REMOVE = (B J C)
REMOVE = (D B J C)
(D B J C)
```

A more interesting application of structural recursion is in searching nested lists. Consider the problem of determining whether a particular symbol appears at any level of a list. We can't use MEMBER because MEMBER only checks the top level. That is, as far as MEMBER is concerned, the symbol D is a member of the list (A B C D E) but not the list ((A) B (C D) E), because in the latter list it does not appear at the top level.

Searching for a symbol *anywhere* in a list appears at first to be a complex problem, since lists may be of any length and may nest arbitrarily deeply, but it helps to recall that lists are constructed of cons cells, and each cons cell has just two halves, the CAR and the CDR. If we forget about the length and nesting of the list and concentrate on recursing on the cons cell structure, the following solution suggests itself:

```
(DEFUN APPEARS-IN (X L)
  (COND ((NULL L) NIL)
        ((ATOM L) (EQUAL X L))
        (T (OR (APPEARS-IN X (CAR L))
               (APPEARS-IN X (CDR L))))))
```

```
*(trace appears-in)
(APPEARS-IN)

*(appears-in 'd '((a) b (c d) e))
Enter APPEARS-IN:
!     X = D
!     L = ((A) B (C D) E)
!     Enter APPEARS-IN·
!     !     X = D
!     !     L = (A)
!     !     Enter APPEARS-IN:
!     !     !     X = D
!     !     !     L = A
!     !     APPEARS-IN = NIL
!     !     Enter APPEARS-IN:
!     !     !     X = D
!     !     !     L = NIL
!     !     APPEARS-IN = NIL
!     APPEARS-IN = NIL
!     Enter APPEARS-IN:
!     !     X = D
!     !     L = (B (C D) E)
!     !     Enter APPEARS-IN:
!     !     !     X = D
!     !     !     L = B
```

```
!    !    APPEARS-IN = NIL
!    !    Enter APPEARS-IN:
!    !    !    X = D
!    !    !    L = ((C D) E)
!    !    !    Enter APPEARS-IN:
!    !    !    !    X = D
!    !    !    !    L = (C D)
!    !    !    !    Enter APPEARS-IN:
!    !    !    !    !    X = D
!    !    !    !    !    L = C
!    !    !    !    APPEARS-IN = NIL
!    !    !    !    Enter APPEARS-IN:
!    !    !    !    !    X = D
!    !    !    !    !    L = (D)
!    !    !    !    !    Enter APPEARS-IN:
!    !    !    !    !    !    X = D
!    !    !    !    !    !    L = D
!    !    !    !    !    APPEARS-IN = T
!    !    !    !    APPEARS-IN = T
!    !    !    APPEARS-IN = T
!    !    APPEARS-IN = T
!    APPEARS-IN = T
APPEARS-IN = T
T
```

The trace of this function shows that it does not recurse all the way down and then pop all the way back up again in a straight line. Each call to **APPEARS-IN** will either return, if the input is an atom, or else result in one or possibly *two* recursive calls, one after the other. The first call recurses on the CAR of the list while the second recurses on the CDR. The nesting of recursive calls is related to the cons cell structure of the list.

Exercises

1. Write a function COUNT-SYMBOLS that counts the number of symbols that appear in an arbitrary list structure. (COUNT-SYMBOLS '(A B A)) should return 3. (COUNT-SYMBOLS '(A (B ((C) D) C))) should return 5.

2. Write REMOVE-ALL, a version of REMOVE that removes all appearances of a symbol at all levels of a list. (REMOVE-ALL 'G '(G (A (T A G) G Q) R G S)) should return ((A (T A) Q) R S).

3. Write REC-SUBST, a recursive version of SUBST. (REC-SUBST 'O 'A '(B A (N A N) A)) should return (B O (N O N) O).

4. Write MAXDEPTH, a function that returns the depth of the most deeply nested atom of a list. (MAXDEPTH NIL) should return 0. (MAXDEPTH '(A)) should return 1. (MAXDEPTH '(A ((B)) C D)) should return 3. You may want to define a MAX function first.

5. Write COUNT-CONS, a function that returns the number of cons cells in an arbitrary piece of data. (COUNT-CONS '(FOO)) should return 1. (COUNT-CONS '(FOO BAR)) should return 2. (COUNT-CONS '((FOO))) should also return 2, since the list ((FOO)) requires two cons cells. (COUNT-CONS 'FRED) should return 0.

6. Write FLATTEN, a function that returns all the elements of an arbitrarily nested list in a single-level list. (FLATTEN '((A B (R)) A C (A D ((A (B)) R) A))) should return (A B R A C A D A B R A).

2. TAIL RECURSION

Tail-recursive functions are a special kind of recursive function where all the work is done *before* the recursive call; the value returned by the call is passed to the level above with no further changes. ANYODDP is a tail-recursive function. COUNT-SLICES is not, because the ADD1 step is done *after* the recursive call (COUNT-SLICES (CDR L)) returns. Compare COUNT-SLICES with the following two-part version, which *is* tail recursive:

```
(DEFUN TR-COUNT-SLICES (LOAF) (TR-CS1 0 LOAF))

(DEFUN TR-CS1 (N LOAF)
  (COND ((NULL LOAF) N)
        (T (TR-CS1 (ADD1 N) (CDR LOAF)))))
```

```
*(trace tr-cs1)
(TR-CS1)

*(tr-count-slices '(x x x x))
ENTER TR-CS1:
!     N = 0
!     LOAF = (X X X X)
!     Enter TR-CS1:
!     !     N = 1
!     !     LOAF = (X X X)
!     !     Enter TR-CS1:
!     !     !     N = 2
!     !     !     LOAF = (X X)
!     !     !     Enter TR-CS1:
!     !     !     !     N = 3
!     !     !     !     LOAF = (X)
!     !     !     !     Enter TR-CS1:
!     !     !     !     !     N = 4
!     !     !     !     !     LOAF = NIL
!     !     !     !     TR-CS1 = 4
!     !     !     TR-CS1 = 4
!     !     TR-CS1 = 4
!     TR-CS1 = 4
TR-CS1 = 4
4
```

Notice how, in the tail-recursive version, the result 4 is computed as the calls stack up and is then returned unchanged by each level. Tail-recursive functions have particularly efficient implementations in some versions of Lisp, which is what makes them important. Here is a two-part, tail-recursive definition of **REVERSE**:

```
(DEFUN TR-REVERSE (X) (TR-REV1 X NIL))

(DEFUN TR-REV1 (X Y)
  (COND ((NULL X) Y)
        (T (TR-REV1 (CDR X) (CONS (CAR X) Y)))))

*(trace tr-rev1)
(TR-REV1)
```

```
*(tr-reverse '(a b c d e))
Enter TR-REV1:
!     X = (A B C D E)
!     Y = NIL
!     Enter TR-REV1:
!     !     X = (B C D E)
!     !     Y = (A)
!     !     Enter TR-REV1:
!     !     !     X = (C D E)
!     !     !     Y = ( B A)
!     !     !     Enter TR-REV1:
!     !     !     !     X = (D E)
!     !     !     !     Y = (C B A)
!     !     !     !     Enter TR-REV1:
!     !     !     !     !     X = (E)
!     !     !     !     !     Y = (D C B A)
!     !     !     !     !     Enter TR-REV1:
!     !     !     !     !     !     X = NIL
!     !     !     !     !     !     Y = (E D C B A)
!     !     !     !     !     TR-REV1 = (E D C B A)
!     !     !     !     TR-REV1 = (E D C B A)
!     !     !     TR-REV1 = (E D C B A)
!     !     TR-REV1 = (E D C B A)
!     TR-REV1 = (E D C B A)
TR-REV1 = (E D C B A)
(E D C B A)
```

Not all recursive functions have tail-recursive versions. Any function that recurses more than once per call, such as **APPEARS-IN**, cannot be tail recursive, since after the first recursive call returns there is another one waiting to be done.

Exercises

1. Write a tail-recursive version of COUNTUP.

2. Write a tail-recursive version of FACT.

3. Write tail-recursive versions of UNION, INTERSECTION, and SET-DIFFERENCE. Your functions need not return results in the same order as the built-in functions.

4. Write a tail-recursive version of NTH. Do not use a subfunction.

3. RECURSIVE DATA STRUCTURES

This chapter has been devoted to writing functions with recursive definitions. Data structures may also have recursive definitions. Consider the following definition of an **S-expression** ("symbolic expression"):

S-expression Either an atom or a cons cell whose CAR and CDR parts are S-expressions.

The term S-expression is used inside its own definition. That is what makes the definition recursive. S-expressions are instances of a very common recursive data structure called a **tree.** Trees have important applications in all areas of computer science. Here is another example of a tree, this time representing an arithmetic expression:

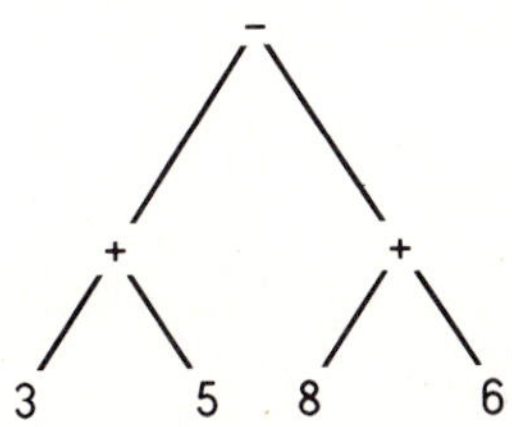

The bottom nodes of the tree are called **terminal nodes** because they have no branches descending from them. The remaining nodes are called **nonterminal nodes.** A tree can be defined recursively just as S-expressions were:

tree Either a terminal node or a nonterminal node whose branches are trees.

Trees are naturally represented by lists. The preceding tree corresponds to the following list:

```
((3 + 5) - (8 + 6))
```

Let's look at another arithmetic expression tree. In this tree, the "%" symbol signifies division, and the "*" signifies multiplication.

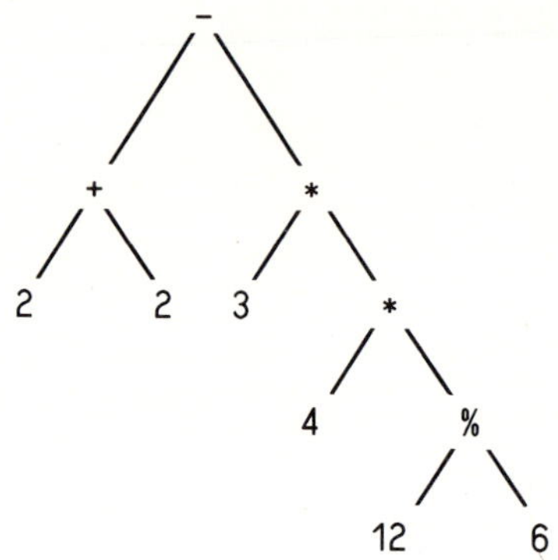

This tree illustrates the fact that the two branches of a nonterminal node need not be of the same length. The list representation of this tree is ((2 + 2) − (3 * (4 * (12 % 6)))). We can define arithmetic expressions recursively:

Arithmetic expression Either a number or a three-element list whose first and third elements are arithmetic expressions and whose middle element is one of +, −, *, or %.

Exercises

1. Write ARITH-EVAL, a function that evaluates arithmetic expressions. (ARITH-EVAL '(2 + (3 * 4))) should return 14.

2. Write a predicate LEGALP that returns T if its input is a legal arithmetic expression. Examples: (LEGALP 4) and (LEGALP '((2 * 2) − 3)) should return T. (LEGALP NIL) and (LEGALP '(A B C D)) should return NIL.

3. Here are the first few members of an infinite sequence of sentences:

   John hit the ball.

He said that John hit the ball.

He said that he said that John hit the ball.

He said that he said that he said that John hit the ball.

Write a recursive definition of the elements of this set.

4. Of the positive integers greater than one, some are **primes** while others are not. Primes are numbers that are divisible only by themselves and by 1. A nonprime, which is known as a **composite** number, can always be factored into primes. Here is a factorization tree for the number 60 that was obtained by successive divisions by primes:

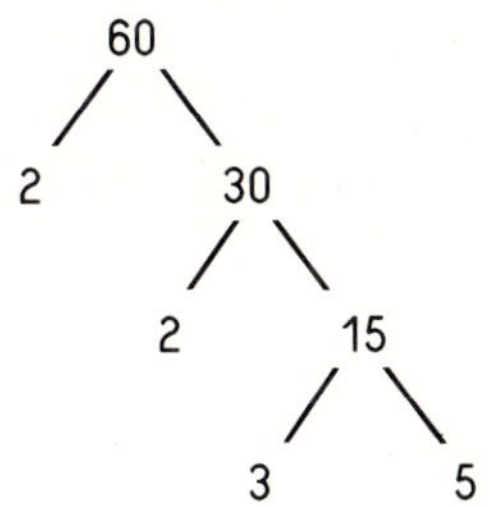

The number 60 has factors 2, 2, 3, and 5, which means $60 = 2\times2\times3\times5$. Write a recursive definition for positive integers greater than one in terms of prime numbers.

5. The trees for arithmetic expressions are called **binary trees,** because each nonterminal node has exactly two branches. Any list can be viewed as a binary tree. Draw a binary tree representing the cons cell structure of the list (A B (C D) E). What are the terminal nodes of the tree? What are the nonterminal nodes?

6. More general types of trees are possible in which different nodes have different numbers of branches. Pick some concept or object and describe it in terms of a general tree structure.

9
Elementary Input/Output

1. INTRODUCTION

Input/output, or "i/o," is a broad topic in computer programming that includes not only a program's interactions with the terminal but also with magnetic disks and tapes, color graphic displays, graphic input devices, sound synthesizers, and other specialized kinds of hardware. Input/output is one of the areas of greatest disagreement among Lisp dialects. There are no absolute standards for even the simplest kinds of terminal i/o; where more sophisticated functions are required the dialects diverge greatly.

We will concentrate on terminal i/o using the MSG ("message") special form for output and the READ function for input. READ is one of the few i/o functions found in all Lisp dialects. MSG is nonstandard, but it is easier to use than the more commonly provided output primitives. Some of these are discussed in the advanced topics section.

2. CHARACTER STRINGS

In order to get the computer to print informative messages on the terminal, we must first learn about **character strings.** Character strings (or **strings** for short) are a type of sequence; they are similar to both lists and atoms, but they have a different set of primitive operations.

A character string is written as a sequence of characters enclosed in quotation marks. Notice in the examples that follow that strings are not converted to all uppercase, the way symbols are. Like numbers, strings evaluate to themselves. The STRINGP predicate returns T if its input is a string.

```
*"strings are things"
"strings are things"

*(setq a "This object is a string")
"This object is a string"

*(stringp a)
T

*a
"this object is a string"

*(setq b 'this-object-is-a-symbol)
THIS-OBJECT-IS-A-SYMBOL

*(stringp b)
NIL
```

Not all versions of Lisp provide strings but most modern ones do.

3. THE MSG SPECIAL FORM

The MSG (pronounced "message") special form always returns T, but as a side effect it causes things to be printed on the terminal. The inputs to MSG are evaluated and printed one at a time, but there are two special rules. First, strings are printed without the enclosing quotes. Second, if one of the inputs to MSG is the symbol T, when MSG gets to that input it will move the terminal's cursor to a new line; it will not print the T.

Here are some examples of the use of MSG. Notice how the presence of Ts in the input control the way the message is broken into lines. Also, a T is the last thing printed in each example, because it is the *value* returned by MSG.

```
*(msg "Alas, poor Yorick" "I knew him well")
Alas, poor YorickI knew him wellT
```

```
*(msg "Alas, poor Yorick" t "I knew him well" t)
Alas, poor Yorick
I knew him well
T

*(msg "Alas" " poor Yorick" t t "I knew him " "well" t)
Alas poor Yorick

I knew him well
T
```

Here is an example of using MSG to write out the value of a variable as part of a message. The variable is PERSON:

```
*(defun greet (person)
   (msg "Hi there, " person "!" t)
   (msg "How are you today?" t))
GREET

*(greet 'fred)
Hi there, FRED!
How are you today?
T
```

Here are some examples of using expressions in calls to MSG. The first such expression is (PLUS 2 2):

```
*(msg "2 plus 2 equals " (plus 2 2) t "How about that?" t)
2 plus 2 equals 4
How about that?
T

*(defun square-talk (x)
   (msg x " squared is " (times x x) t))
SQUARE-TALK

*(square-talk 10)
10 squared is 100
T

*(apply-to-all 'square-talk '(1 2 3 4 5))
1 squared is 1
2 squared is 4
```

```
3 squared is 9
4 squared is 16
5 squared is 25
(T T T T T)
```

Exercises

1. Write a function called MARY that prints the poem "Mary Had a Little Lamb" on the terminal.

2. Write a recursive function DRAW-LINE that draws a line of a specified length by doing (MSG "*") the correct number of times. (DRAW-LINE 10) should produce

```
**********
```

3. Write a recursive function DRAW-BOX that draws a box of specified dimensions. (DRAW-BOX 10 4) should produce

```
**********
**********
**********
**********
```

4. Write a recursive function NINETY-NINE-BOTTLES that sings the well-known song "Ninety-Nine Bottles of Beer on the Wall." The first verse of this song is

```
99 bottles of beer on the wall,
99 bottles of beer!
Take one down,
Pass it around,
98 bottles of beer on the wall.
```

NINETY-NINE-BOTTLES should take a number N as input and start counting from N down to zero. (This is so you can run it on 5 bottles instead of all 99.) Your function should also leave a blank line between each verse, and say something appropriate when it runs out of beer.

5. Part of any tic-tac-toe playing program is a function to display the board. Write a function PRINT-BOARD that takes a list of nine ele-

ments as input. Each element will be either an X, an O, or NIL. PRINT-BOARD should display the corresponding tic-tac-toe board. Example: (PRINT-BOARD '(X O O NIL X NIL O NIL X)) should print:

```
 x | o | o
-----------
   | x |
-----------
 o |   | x
```

4. THE READ FUNCTION

READ is a function that reads one Lisp object (e.g., a number, a symbol, or a list) from the terminal and returns that object as its value. By placing calls to READ inside a function, we can make the computer read data from the terminal under program control. Here are some examples. What the user types in response to READ is underlined.

```
*(defun my-square ()
    (msg "Please type in a number? ")
    (setq x (read))
    (msg "The number " x " squared is " (times x x) t))
MY-SQUARE

*(my-square)
Please type in a number? 7
The number 7 squared is 49
T

*(my-square)
Please type in a number? -4
The number -4 squared is 16
T

*(defun square-loop ()
    (my-square)
    (msg t "Would you like to square another number? Type YES or
NO . . .")
    (setq a (read))
    (if (equal a 'yes (square-loop) 'goodbye))
SQUARE-LOOP
```

```
*(square-loop)
Please type in a number? 2
The number 2 squared is 4

Would you like to square another number? Type YES or NO . . . yes
Please type in a number? 12
The number 12 squared is 144

Would you like to square another number? Type YES or NO . . . no
GOODBYE
```

Exercises

1. Write a function to compute an hourly worker's gross pay given an hourly wage in dollars and the number of hours he or she worked. Your function should prompt for each input it needs by printing a message in English. It should display its answer in English as well—for example, "The worker earned 250 dollars."

2. The COOKIE-MONSTER function keeps reading data from the terminal until it reads the symbol COOKIE. Write COOKIE-MONSTER. Here is a sample interaction:

```
*(cookie-monster)
Give me cookie!!!
Cookie? rock
No want ROCK . . .

Give me cookie!!!
Cookie? hairbrush
No want HAIRBRUSH . . .

Give me cookie!!!
Cookie? cookie
Thank you! . . . Munch munch munch . . . BURP
T
```

5. SUMMARY

MSG is a special form that takes an arbitrary number of inputs. MSG evaluates and prints its inputs one at a time. Strings are printed without the enclosing quotes, and the input T causes MSG to move to a new line. MSG prints things as a *side effect*; the value it returns is always T.

The READ function reads one Lisp object from the terminal and returns that object.

Input/output is handled differently by each Lisp dialect. MSG is not a standard function, but is easier to use than the more commonly provided primitives. Not all dialects support strings; even fewer support MSG. More information about MSG is given in appendix C. You should look in the user's manual for your particular Lisp dialect to see how i/o is done.

Review Exercises

1. How are strings different from symbols?

2. What is printed by each of the following:

```
(MSG "a" "b")
(MSG "a" " " "b")
(MSG "a" T "b")
```

3. What is the difference between (MSG "X") and (MSG X)?

4. Does the READ function involve side effects? What are they?

Functions Covered in This Chapter

String predicate: STRINGP
Input function: READ
Output special form: MSG

Keyboard Exercise

In this exercise we will write a program for producing a graph of an arbitrary function. The program will prompt for a function name F and then plot Y = F(X) for a specified range of X values. Here is an example of how the program works:

```
*(make-graph)
Function to graph? square
Starting x value? -7
Ending x value? 7
Plotting symbol? ****
                                                 ****
                                    ****
                         ****
                ****
         ****
    ****
 ****
****
 ****
    ****
         ****
                ****
                         ****
                                    ****
                                                 ****

T
```

Instructions

1. Write a recursive function SPACE that takes a number N as input and moves the cursor to the right by printing N spaces, one at a time. SPACE should print "error!" and return NIL if N is negative.

2. Write a function PLOT-ONE-POINT that takes two inputs, SYM and Y-VAL, prints symbol SYM in column Y-VAL, and then moves to a new line. The leftmost column is numbered zero.

3. Write a function PLOT-POINTS that takes a symbol and a list of y-values as input and plots them. (PLOT-POINTS '+O+ '(4 6 8 10 8 6 4)) should print

```
+O+
   +O+
      +O+
         +O+
      +O+
   +O+
+O+
```

4. Write a function GENERATE that takes two numbers M and N as input and returns a list of the integers from M to N. (GENERATE –3 3) should return (–3 –2 –1 0 1 2 3).

5. Write the MAKE-GRAPH function. MAKE-GRAPH should prompt for the values of FUNC, START, END, and SYM, and then graph the function. Note: You can pass FUNC as an input to APPLY-TO-ALL to generate the list of y-values for the function. What will the second input to APPLY-TO-ALL be?

6. Define the SQUARE function and graph it over the range −7 to 7. Use your first name as a plotting symbol.

Advanced Topics 9

1. THE LISP 1.5 OUTPUT PRIMITIVES

The primitive i/o functions TERPRI, PRIN1, PRINC, and PRINT were defined in Lisp 1.5 (the ancestor of all modern Lisp systems) and are still found in many dialects today. TERPRI stands for *ter*minate *pri*nt. It moves the cursor to a new line. PRIN1 and PRINC take a Lisp object as input and print it on the terminal. PRIN1 prints the object in a form that could be read back in with **READ**; **PRINC** prints it more simply. The difference between **PRIN1** and **PRINC** shows up in the case of strings. **PRIN1** prints the string enclosed by quotes, while **PRINC** does not. **PRIN1** and **PRINC** both return T.

```
*(setq a "Wherefore art thou, Romeo?")
"Wherefore art thou, Romeo?"

*(prin1 a)
"Wherefore art thou, Romeo?"T

*(princ a)
Wherefore art thou, Romeo?T
```

PRIN1 and **PRINC** will also print symbols differently if the symbols contain unusual characters such as embedded blanks or lowercase letters. The notation for representing symbols with unusual characters in their names differs across Lisp systems. We will not go into it here.

The primitive function **PRINT** is a combination of **TERPRI**, **PRIN1**, and **PRINC**. **PRINT** could be defined as follows:

```
(defun print (x)
  (terpri)
  (prin1 x)
  (princ " "))
PRINT

*(apply-to-all 'print '(0 1 2 3 4))
0
1
2
3
4 (T T T T T)
```

2. DEFINING MSG IN TERMS OF PRIMITIVES

The MSG special form is defined in terms of the **TERPRI** and **PRINC** primitives. Remember that MSG does not automatically evaluate its inputs. Suppose MSG called a subfunction MSG1 on each of its unevaluated inputs to print it. MSG1 would be defined as follows:

```
(DEFUN MSG1 (X)
  (COND ((EQUAL X T) (TERPRI))
        (T (PRINC (EVAL X)))))
```

Why is it important that MSG not evaluate its inputs? Otherwise it would not be able to tell the difference between the input T and an input that *evaluated* to T. We want (MSG T) to move to a new line, but (MSG (EQUAL 2 2)) should print the symbol T.

3. PRINTING IN DOT NOTATION

Dot notation is a variant of cons cell notation. In dot notation each cons cell is displayed as a left parenthesis, the CAR part, a dot, the CDR part, and a right parenthesis. The CAR and CDR parts, if lists, are themselves displayed in dot notation, making this a recursive definition. For example, the list (A) is represented by a single cons cell whose CAR is the symbol A and whose CDR is NIL. In dot notation this list is written (A . NIL). Here are some more examples of dot notation:

List Notation	Dot Notation
NIL	NIL
A	A
(A)	(A . NIL)
(A B)	(A . (B . NIL))
(A B C)	(A . (B . (C . NIL)))
(A (B) C)	(A . ((B . NIL) . (C . NIL)))

Exercises

1. Write a function DOT-PRIN1 that takes a list as input and prints it in dot notation. DOT-PRIN1 will print parentheses by (MSG "(") and (MSG ")"), and dots by (MSG " . "), and will call itself recursively to print lists within lists. DOT-PRIN1 should return T as its result.

2. Try (DOT-PRIN1 '(A (B) C)) and see if your output matches the result in the preceding table.

3. Try (DOT-PRIN1 '((((A))))).

4. Lisp can also *read* lists in dot notation. Try (DOT-PRIN1 '(A . (B . C))).

5. If you type in the quoted list '(A . NIL), Lisp types back (A). What happens when you type '(A . B)?

6. Consider the two circular structures shown in figure 9.1: What will DOT-PRIN1 print if given the first structure as input? What will it print given the second structure?

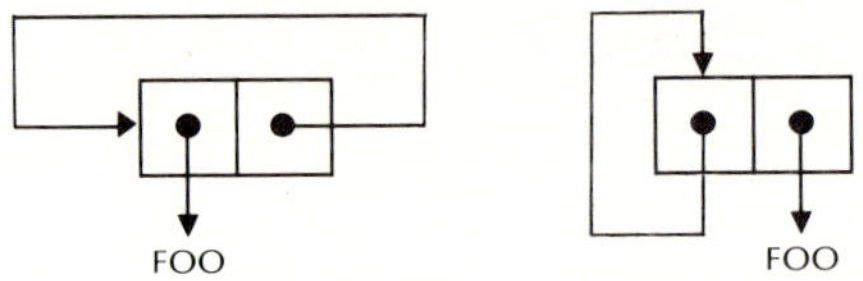

Figure 9.1 Two circular list structures.

4. HYBRID NOTATION

Lisp normally prints things in list notation. As we have seen, some cons cell structures, such as (A . B), cannot be written without dots. Lisp's policy is to print dots only when necessary; its output is thus a hybrid of pure list and pure dot notations, called **hybrid notation**. Examples:

Dot Notation	Hybrid Notation
`(A . NIL)`	`(A)`
`(A . B)`	`(A . B)`
`(A . (B . NIL))`	`(A B)`
`(A . (B . C))`	`(A B . C)`
`((A . NIL) . (B . (C . D)))`	`((A) B C . D)`

Exercise

Write HYBRID-PRIN1, a function that prints lists using hybrid notation. Here is how the function should decide whether to print a dot or not. If the CDR part of the cons cell is a list, HYBRID-PRIN1 continues to print in list notation. If the CDR part is NIL, HYBRID-PRIN1 should print a right parenthesis. If the CDR part is something else—for example, a symbol—HYBRID-PRIN1 should print a dot, the symbol, and a right parenthesis. You will probably find it useful to define a subfunction to print CDRs of lists, as these always begin with a space while CARs always begin with a left parenthesis. Test your function on the examples in the preceding table.

5. FILE I/O

A **file** is a collection of information stored in the computer's memory. Files are usually stored on magnetic disk or tape. Although Lisps differ somewhat in their approach to file i/o, the basic concepts are common to all Lisp systems and in fact to all programming languages. In this section I will give some brief examples of file i/o in one particular Lisp dialect—MacLisp.

Suppose we have a disk file named **MYDATA.LSP** with the following items in it:

```
THIS-IS-A-FILE-OF-STUFF
23
9
(A B C D E)
5
78
```

To read this file we must first tell the computer to open it for input. The **OPEN** function takes the name of a file and a mode (either IN or OUT) as input and opens the file in the specified mode. The value returned by **OPEN** is a special kind of data object called a **file object**. We must save this file object in a variable for later use. We'll use the variable **FVAR** for this purpose.

```
*(setq fvar (open 'mydata 'in))     Open file MYDATA.LSP for input
#FILE-IN-|PS:<DT50>MYDATA.LSP.1|-71732

*fvar                               Value of FVAR is a file object
#FILE-IN-|PS:<DT50>MYDATA.LSP.1|-71732
```

Now we can read from the file referenced by the file object by passing the object as an argument to **READ**. Each call to **READ** returns one piece of data from the file:

```
*(read fvar)
THIS-IS-A-FILE-OF-STUFF

*(read fvar)
23
```

```
*(read fvar)
9

*(read fvar)
(A B C D E)
```

When we are done reading from the file we must close it with the CLOSE function.

```
*(close fvar)                      Close file MYDATA.LSP
T
```

To write a file we use a similar sequence of operations. First we open the file for output. Then we use PRIN1, PRINC, PRINT, and TERPRI to write things to the file by passing the file object as a second argument to the function. When we are done, we close the file. Here is an example:

```
*(setq fvar (open 'test 'out))     Open file TEST.LSP for output
#FILE-OUT-|PS:<DT50>TEST.LSP.1|-71764

*(print 'hello fvar)               Write some data to the file
T

*(print 12345 fvar)
T

*(print '(bye for now) fvar)
T

*(close fvar)                      Close the file
T
```

Now the file TEST.LSP contains the following lines:

```
HELLO
12345
(BYE FOR NOW)
```

Functions Covered in Advanced Topics

Lisp 1.5 output primitives: TERPRI, PRIN1, PRINC, PRINT
File i/o functions: OPEN, CLOSE

10
Iteration

1. INTRODUCTION

The word "iterate" means to repeat, or to do something over and over. Iteration is one of the most primitive control structures. It is simpler than recursion or applicative operators; only conditionals are simpler still. Virtually all programming languages include a way to write iterative programs; most allow recursion as well; only a few provide applicatives. In Lisp, iteration in its most primitive form is available through a special form called PROG (for "program").

Modern Lisp dialects include more powerful special forms that make PROG all but obsolete. Two such forms, LET and DO, will be discussed in addition to PROG.

2. THE PROG SPECIAL FORM

The syntax of a PROG expression is:

```
(PROG (prog-vars)
      form1
      form2
      form3
      ....)
```

The first input to PROG is a list of local variables (called **prog variables**) that are to be bound to NIL when the PROG is entered and become unbound when it returns. Prog variables are similar to lambda variables in that both are bound locally; lambda variables are bound to a function's inputs, while prog variables are bound to NIL. The value of either type may be changed with SETQ.

The remaining inputs form the **body** of the PROG. They are called **forms**. If a form is a symbol it is called a **tag**; tags are not evaluated, but they are used with the GO special form to achieve iteration. (This will be explained a little later.) Forms that are not symbols are evaluated, one at a time. When PROG gets to the end of the body, it returns NIL. Example:

```
*(defun boing (x)
   (prog (y)
         (setq y (list x x x x))
         (msg y t)
         (msg "The length of Y is " (length y) t)))
BOING

*(boing 'hi)
(HI HI HI HI)
The length of Y is 4
NIL

*y
;Y - UNBOUND VARIABLE
```

In this example, X is a lambda variable while Y is a prog variable. Both of these are local variables that become unbound when the function returns. There are no tags in the preceding program. PROG evaluated each form and returned NIL when it finished the last one.

2.1. The GO Special Form

The GO special form tells PROG to go to a tag and begin evaluating expressions from that point on. We can use GO to create loops:

```
*(defun launch nil
   (prog (cnt)
         (setq cnt 10)
    keep-counting
         (msg cnt "...")
         (setq cnt (sub1 cnt))
         (if (greaterp cnt 0) (go keep-counting))
         (msg "Blast off!" t)))
LAUNCH

*(launch)
10...9...8...7...6...5...4...3...2...1...Blast off!
NIL
```

This PROG has one prog variable, called CNT. It also has a tag, called KEEP-COUNTING. The first expression in the PROG is a SETQ that initializes CNT to 10. Then comes the tag, KEEP-COUNTING. The forms after the tag constitute a loop that will be executed repeatedly until CNT is zero. The first time through the loop, the MSG expression prints "10 . . ." on the terminal and the expression after that reduces the value of CNT to 9. When we reach the IF, since CNT is greater than 0, the expression (GO KEEP-COUNTING) is evaluated, and PROG goes back to that tag and resumes evaluating expressions. Now the MSG expression prints "9 . . ." on the terminal, the SETQ reduces CNT to 8, the IF sends the PROG back to KEEP-COUNTING again, and so on until CNT reaches 0. When CNT is 0 the IF does not evaluate the expression (GO KEEP-COUNTING), so PROG proceeds to the next expression in the natural way, and the message "Blast off!" is printed.

2.2. The RETURN Function

PROG normally returns NIL, but with the RETURN function we can make it return whatever we want, wherever we want. Here is a function INTSUM that uses iteration to compute and return the sum of the first N integers—for example, (INTSUM 5) returns $5+4+3+2+1 = 15$.

```
*(defun intsum (n)
   (prog (sum)
         (setq sum 0)
     loop
         (setq sum (plus n sum))
         (setq n (sub1 n))
         (if (greaterp n 0) (go loop))
         (return sum)))
INTSUM

*(intsum 5)
15

*(intsum 10)
55
```

Do you see how INTSUM works? The lambda variable N is being counted down. However, at each step, N is also added to the value of the prog variable SUM. At the end, when N reaches zero, we will have accumulated in SUM the sum of the first N integers.

Local variables declared in a PROG are always initialized to NIL. Since we want the variable SUM to keep a numeric total, it should be initialized to zero instead. The first line of the PROG does this. Consider the following variant of INTSUM:

```
*(defun faulty-intsum (n)
   (prog (sum)
     loop
         (setq sum 0)
         (setq sum (plus n sum))
         (setq n (sub1 n))
         (if (greaterp n 0) (go loop))
         (return sum)))
FAULTY-INTSUM

*(faulty-intsum 5)
1
```

The fault in FAULTY-INTSUM is that the expression (SETQ SUM 0) appears *within* the loop instead of before it. Instead of initializing SUM to zero once upon entering the PROG, we set SUM to zero every time through the loop. Thus only the last non-zero value of N is retained in SUM when the PROG returns, so FAULTY-INTSUM always returns 1.

RETURN only works inside of PROG, but it need not appear at the very end of the PROG. Here is an example of a PROG with two RETURNs in it. This function returns the symbol EVEN if a list is of even length, and the symbol ODD otherwise.

```
*(defun test-length (x)
   (prog ()
     loop
         (if (null x) (return 'even))
         (setq x (cdr x))
         (if (null x) (return 'odd))
         (setq x (cdr x))
         (go loop)))
TEST-LENGTH

*(test-length '(a b c))
ODD

*(test-length '(a b c d))
EVEN
```

2.3. Programming with PROG

Using PROG it's very easy to write iterative loops to do all kinds of things. Here is an iterative version of the ADDUP function that adds up a list of numbers:

```
*(defun it-addup (x)
   (prog (sum)
         (setq sum 0)
     loop
         (if (null x) (return sum))
         (setq sum (plus sum (car x)))
         (setq x (cdr x))
         (go loop)))
IT-ADDUP
```

```
*(it-addup '(2 1 4 7))
14

*(it-addup nil)
0
```

And here is an iterative version of the INTERSECTION function:

```
*(defun it-intersection (x y)
   (prog (result)
     loop
         (if (null x) (return result))
         (if (member (car x) y)
             (setq result (cons (car x) result)))
         (setq x (cdr x))
         (go loop)))
IT-INTERSECTION

*(it-intersection '(a x c j f) '(a b c d e f))
(F C A)
```

IT-INTERSECTION peels off elements of X one at a time. If the first element of X is also a member of Y, it is added onto RESULT. Then X is set to (CDR X), removing the first element, and the process repeats by going back to the tag named LOOP. When X is finally empty, the value of RESULT is the intersection of the original value of X with Y. Notice that the elements of RESULT appear in the reverse of the order in which they appear in X.

There are two kinds of errors one can make in a PROG. One is to forget to use RETURN when you want to return a value other than NIL. Example:

```
*(defun wrong-way ()
   (prog (x)
         (setq x '(a b c d))
         (cdr x)))
WRONG-WAY

*(wrong-way)
NIL
```

```
*(defun right-way ()
   (prog (x)
         (setq x '(a b c d))
         (return (cdr x))))
RIGHT-WAY

*(right-way)
(B C D)
```

The other type of error is to use GO with a tag that does not appear in the PROG. If PROG doesn't understand where to go, it stops and gives an error message. Also, if you use GO outside of a PROG, an error results.

Exercises

1. Write an iterative version of the COUNT-SLICES function.

2. Write an iterative version of NTH. Call it IT-NTH.

3. Write the very shortest infinite loop you can, using PROG.

4. The MAKE-LOAF function creates a loaf of N slices, given the input N. (MAKE-LOAF 4) returns (X X X X). Here is an iterative version of MAKE-LOAF that contains errors:

   ```
   (DEFUN MAKE-LOAF (N)
     (PROG (CNT LOAF)
       LOOP
           (IF (EQUAL CNT N) (RETURN LOAF))
           (SETQ LOAF (CONS 'X LOAF))
           (SETQ CNT (ADD1 CNT))))
   ```

   First, what are the errors? Second, write a correct iterative version of this function.

5. Write an iterative function called ISOLATED-PRINT that prints each element of a list on a line by itself. Then write recursive and applicative versions of the same function. Which is the shortest? Which was easiest to write?

6. Write an iterative version of MEMBER. Call it IT-MEMBER.

7. What is wrong with this definition for an iterative ASSOC function?

```
(DEFUN IT-ASSOC (X L)
  (PROG ()
   LOOP
       (COND ((NULL L) NIL)
             ((EQUAL X (CAAR L)) (CAR L)))
       (SETQ L (CDR L))
       (GO LOOP)))
```

8. Write an iterative version of UNION. Call it IT-UNION. Your function need not return its result in the same order as the built-in UNION function.

9. Write an iterative version of REVERSE. Call it IT-REVERSE.

10. Why did the IT-INTERSECTION function return elements in reverse order from the order they appeared in its first input? How can you correct this?

3. THE LET SPECIAL FORM

One of the nice things about PROG apart from its facility for iteration is its ability to declare new local variables. LET is a special form that takes this one step further: with LET we can not only declare local variables but also specify their initial values. LET does not accept tags or the use of GO or RETURN. It is not an iteration function, just an elegant way to bind local variables.

The syntax of a LET expression is:

```
(LET ((var1 val1) (var2 val2) ...)
     form1
     form2
     form3
     ....)
```

LET binds each local variable to the specified value and then evaluates the forms in its body. The value of the last form is the value returned by LET. Example:

```
*(let ((alpha 1) (beta 2) (gamma '(hi there)))
     (list alpha beta gamma))
(1 2 (HI THERE))
```

LET is particularly useful for holding on to the result of a computation when we need to use it more than once. Consider the following inefficient definition of the function TEST:

```
(DEFUN TEST (X)
  (AND (EQUAL (CAR X) (CAR (REVERSE X)))
       (EQUAL (CADR X) (CADR (REVERSE X)))))
```

This definition is inefficient because (REVERSE X) is computed twice. A more elegant solution is to bind a local variable Y to the value of (REVERSE X) so we only have to compute it once.

```
(DEFUN TEST (X)
  (LET ((Y (REVERSE X)))
    (AND (EQUAL (CAR X) (CAR Y))
         (EQUAL (CADR X) (CADR Y)))))
```

Another way to avoid evaluating (REVERSE X) twice is to use SETQ to store the result in a variable.

```
(DEFUN TEST (X)
  (SETQ Y (REVERSE X))
  (AND (EQUAL (CAR X) (CAR Y))
       (EQUAL (CADR X) (CADR Y))))
```

This solution is less elegant because Y is a global variable that is left bound after the function returns. There's no good reason to leave Y lying around. We could fix this by making Y a prog variable:

```
(DEFUN TEST (X)
  (PROG (Y)
        (SETQ Y (REVERSE X))
        (RETURN (AND (EQUAL (CAR X) (CAR Y))
                     (EQUAL (CADR X) (CADR Y))))))
```

Since Y is a prog variable it won't be left around after TEST returns. But this solution is still less elegant than using LET, because PROG is a more complicated special form, and we can do the job just as well with the simpler LET function. Also, with LET we don't have to use RETURN, while with PROG we do.

4. THE DO SPECIAL FORM

DO is a cross between LET and PROG. DO provides the flexible binding syntax of LET plus the facility for iteration of PROG. DO goes a step further and provides a built-in loop as well: DO cycles through the expressions in its body until it is told to stop. The syntax of a DO expression is:

```
(DO ((var1 init1 upd1)
     (var2 init2 upd2)
     ...)
    (condition action-1 ... action-n)
  form1
  form2
  form3
  ....)
```

First, each variable in the DO's variable list is assigned its initial value. Then the *condition* is evaluated. If it is true, DO evaluates the termination actions and returns the value of the last one. Otherwise DO evaluates the forms in its body in order; the body may contain tags and GOs that change this order. The body may also contain RETURNs that force the DO to return immediately rather than iterate further. When DO reaches the end of the body, instead of returning NIL the way PROG does, it begins the next iteration of the loop. First each variable in the variable list is *updated* to the value of its *upd* expression. (The *upd* expression may be omitted, in which case the variable is left unchanged.) Then the condition is tried again. If it is true DO evaluates the termination actions; otherwise it resumes evaluating the body.

Here is an implementation of COUNT-SLICES using DO:

```
(DEFUN COUNT-SLICES (L)
  (DO ((CNT 0 (ADD1 CNT))
       (LOAF L (CDR LOAF)))
      ((NULL LOAF) CNT)))
```

This DO has an empty body—all the computation is done by expressions in the variable list. Suppose we evaluate (COUNT-SLICES '(X X)). When we enter the DO, CNT is initialized to 0 and LOAF is initialized to (X X). Since LOAF is not NIL, DO does not return. The body is empty, so DO goes to update its variables. CNT is set to the value of (ADD1 CNT), which is 1. LOAF is set to (CDR LOAF), which is (X). Now DO tries the test again. LOAF is still not NIL, so we iterate once more. CNT is set to 2. LOAF is set to NIL. This time the test is true. The return-expression is CNT, so DO returns 2.

Here is a version of LAUNCH written with DO. This time the body of the DO is not empty; it contains the expression (MSG CNT "...").

```
(DEFUN LAUNCH ()
  (DO ((CNT 10 (SUB1 CNT)))
      ((ZEROP CNT) (MSG "Blast off!" T))
    (MSG CNT "...")))
```

Exercise

Write versions of ADDUP, MAKE-LOAF, and FACT using DO.

5. HOW TO WRITE ELEGANT LISP PROGRAMS

Elegance is a subjective quality and thus hard to formalize, but experienced Lisp programmers do agree on some general principles of programming style. First, functions should be short. It is much better to solve a problem by writing many little functions than by writing one big one, because little functions are easier to read, test, and debug.

Second, use local instead of global variables whenever possible. One reason for doing so has to do with the way Lisp functions are translated into the computer's language of ones and zeros. This process is called **compilation**. We won't cover compilation in this book, since beginning Lispers seldom need it, but for large programs compilation is important because it can make a program run anywhere from ten to a hundred times faster. Lisp functions that use only local variables will run faster, when compiled, than those that use global variables. A good reason for even beginning Lispers to prefer local variables is that they become unbound again when a function returns, so the function will not be untidy and leave data lying around.

The third principle of elegant programming style is to not abuse PROG. It is possible to write PROG expressions with five tags, twelve GOs, eight RETURNs, and a body that is forty-seven lines long. Don't do it! All the PROGs in this chapter had just a single tag and a single GO, forming a simple loop. Don't allow your PROGs to grow any more complex than that. If you feel you absolutely must write a forty-seven-line PROG to get the job done, break your function down into several smaller ones instead.

Some Lisp programmers feel that PROG shouldn't be used at all. Of this group, some simply prefer recursive or applicative solutions to iterative ones. Others feel iterative solutions are perfectly acceptable, but suggest that iteration should be done with DO (using no additional tags or RETURNs) instead of with PROG, because DO makes the iteration implicit and provides a powerful variable-binding mechanism as well. That is an excellent piece of advice.

6. SUMMARY

PROG's principal use is to provide a simple control structure called iteration. The body of a PROG consists of expressions and tags. The GO function may be used to go to a particular tag in the body. The RETURN function causes the PROG to return with a specified value. GO, tags, and RETURN may only be used inside of PROG. If RETURN is not used, the PROG returns NIL when it runs out of expressions to evaluate. If the PROG is in an infinite loop it will never return a value.

LET provides a way to bind local variables to values other than NIL. LET is more elegant than PROG for binding variables; it does not support the use of GO, tags, or RETURN. One good use for LET is to bind the value of an expression to a local variable so we can use it more than once without having to recompute it.

DO is an iteration special form that combines features of PROG and LET. PROG is a standard part of Lisp, but LET and DO are found only in the more modern Lisp dialects.

Review Exercises

1. How do the variable lists of PROG, LET, and DO differ?

2. How does PROG tell the difference between a tag and an expression?

3. Here is an inefficient function definition:

```
(DEFUN FOO (X L)
  (LIST (CADDR (ASSOC X L))
        (CAR (ASSOC X L))
        (CADR (ASSOC X L))))
```

   Write a more efficient version using LET.

4. Here is an iterative version of the ANYODDP function:

```
(DEFUN ANYODDP (X)
  (PROG (Y)
        (SETQ Y X)
    LOOP
        (IF (NULL Y) (RETURN NIL))
        (IF (ODDP (CAR Y)) (RETURN T))
        (SETQ Y (CDR Y))
        (GO LOOP)))
```

   Write an equivalent version using DO.

5. One way to compute Fib(5) is to start with Fib(0) and Fib(1), which we know to be 1, and add them together, giving Fib(2). Then add Fib(1) and Fib(2) to get Fib(3). Add Fib(2) and Fib(3) to get Fib(4). Add Fib(3) and Fib(4) to get Fib(5). This is an iterative method involving no recursion; we merely have to keep around the last two

values of Fib to compute the next one. Write an iterative version of FIB using PROG and this technique.

Functions Covered in This Chapter

Special forms for iteration: PROG, DO
Related special forms and functions: GO, RETURN
Special form for binding variables: LET

Keyboard Exercise

In this keyboard exercise we will explore some properties of single- and double-stranded DNA, or deoxyribonucleic acid. DNA, and the related molecule RNA, make up the genetic material found in viruses and every type of cell, from bacteria to people. A strand of DNA is very much like a chain; the links in the chain are of four types, corresponding to the four bases adenine, thymine, guanine, and cytosine. We will represent a strand of DNA by a list of bases. The list (A G G T C A T T G) corresponds to a strand that is nine bases long, the first base being adenine and the next two guanine. Here is a schematic diagram of the strand:

```
-------------------------------------------------
 !    !    !    !    !    !    !    !    !
 A    G    G    T    C    A    T    T    G
```

Each of the four bases has a complement with which it can form a pair. Adenine pairs with thymine, while guanine pairs with cytosine. Two single strands of DNA can combine to form double-stranded DNA (whose shape is the famous "double helix") when each of their corresponding bases are complementary. The strand (A G G T C A T T G) and the strand (T C C A G T A A C) are complementary, for example. Double-stranded DNA looks like this:

```
-----------------------------------------------
 !    !    !    !    !    !    !    !    !
 A    G    G    T    C    A    T    T    G
 .    .    .    .    .    .    .    .    .
 .    .    .    .    .    .    .    .    .
 T    C    C    A    G    T    A    A    C
 !    !    !    !    !    !    !    !    !
-----------------------------------------------
```

Instructions

Write iterative solutions to all exercises. You may use either PROG or DO.

1. Write a function COMPLEMENT-BASE that takes a base as input and returns the matching complementary base. (COMPLEMENT-BASE 'A) should return T; (COMPLEMENT-BASE 'T) should return A; and so forth.

2. Write a function COMPLEMENT-STRAND that returns the complementary strand of a sequence of single-stranded DNA. (COMPLEMENT-STRAND '(A G G T)) should return (T C C A).

3. Write a function MAKE-DOUBLE that takes a single strand of DNA as input and returns a double-stranded version. We will represent double-stranded DNA by making a list of each base and its complement. (MAKE-DOUBLE '(G G A C T)) should return ((G C) (G C) (A T) (C G) (T A)).

4. One of the important clues to DNA's double-stranded nature was the observation that in naturally occurring DNA, whether from people, animals, or plants, the observed percentage of adenine is always very close to that of thymine, while the observed percentage of guanine is very close to that of cytosine. Write a function COUNT-BASES that counts the number of bases of each type in a DNA strand and returns the result as a table. Your function should work for both single- and double-stranded DNA. Example: (COUNT-BASES '((G C) (A T) (T A) (T A) (C G))) should return ((A 3) (T 3) (G 2) (C 2)), while (COUNT-BASES '(A G T A C T C T)) should return ((A 2) (T 3) (G 1) (C 2)). In the latter case the percentages are

not equal because we are working with only a single strand. What answer do you get if you apply COUNT-BASES to the corresponding double-stranded sequence?

5. Write a predicate PREFIXP that returns T if one strand of DNA is a prefix of another. In order to be a prefix, the elements of the first strand must exactly match the corresponding elements of the second. Example: (G T C) is a prefix of (G T C A T), but not of (A G G T C).

6. Write a predicate APPEARSP that returns T if one DNA strand appears anywhere within another. For example, (C A T) appears in (T C A T G) but not in (T C C G T A). Hint: If X appears in Y, then X is either a prefix of Y or of (CDR Y) or of (CDR (CDR Y)) or . . .

7. Write a predicate COVERP that returns T if its first input, repeated some number of times, matches all of its second input. Example: (A G C) covers (A G C A G C A G C) but not (A G C T T G). You may assume that neither strand will be NIL.

8. Write a function PREFIX that returns the leftmost N bases of a DNA strand. (PREFIX 4 '(C G A T T A G)) should return (C G A T). Do not confuse the function PREFIX with the predicate PREFIXP.

9. Biologists have found that portions of some naturally occurring DNA strands consist of many repetitions of a short sequence of bases. Write a function KERNEL that returns the shortest prefix of a DNA strand that can be repeated to cover the strand. (KERNEL '(A G C A G C A G C)) should return (A G C). (KERNEL '(A A A A A)) should return (A). (KERNEL '(A G G T C)) should return (A G G T C), since in this case only a single repetition of the entire strand will cover the strand. (Hint: To find the kernel, look at prefixes of increasing length until you find one that can be repeated to cover the strand.)

10. Write a function DRAW-DNA that takes a single-stranded DNA sequence as input and draws it along with its complementary strand, as in the double-stranded diagram given on page 257.

Advanced Topics 10

1. PROG1, PROG2, AND PROGN

PROG1, PROG2, and PROGN are three very simple functions that are related to PROG only superficially. They all take an arbitrary number of expressions as input and evaluate the expressions one at a time. PROG1 returns the value of the first expression; PROG2 returns the value of the second; PROGN returns the value of the last. Example:

```
*(prog1 (setq x 'foo)
        (setq x 'bar)
        (setq x 'baz)
        (msg "X is " x t))
X is BAZ
FOO

*(prog2 (setq x 'foo)
        (setq x 'bar)
        (setq x 'baz)
        (msg "X is " x t))
X is BAZ
BAR

*(progn (setq x 'foo)
        (setq x 'bar)
        (setq x 'baz)
        (msg "X is " x t))
X is BAZ
T
```

These forms are of little use today. They were important in earlier versions of Lisp, when the body of a function could contain at most one expression and the action part of a COND clause at most one action.

2. DEFINING SPECIAL FORMS

We can add our own special forms to Lisp. The exact way this is done differs across dialects. In MacLisp, a special form that does not evaluate its inputs is called a **FEXPR.** (Regular functions that do evaluate their inputs are called **EXPRs.**) A FEXPR is a function of one input. The variable in its argument list is bound to a list of the function's *unevaluated* arguments. Example:

```
*(defun garble fexpr (x)
   (cons 'say (reverse x)))
GARBLE

*(garble how now brown cow)
(SAY COW BROWN NOW HOW)
```

Notice that when we called the GARBLE function, we did not have to quote any of its inputs. That is the effect of making GARBLE a FEXPR.

The QUOTE special form is also defined as a FEXPR. We can define it ourselves; let's call our version MY-QUOTE:

```
*(defun my-quote fexpr (x) (car x))
MY-QUOTE

*(my-quote hello)
HELLO

*(my-quote (this is a test))
(THIS IS A TEST)
```

3. DEFINING MACROS

A **macro** is similar to a FEXPR in that its arguments are not evaluated. One difference is that a macro returns an *expression* that Lisp then proceeds to evaluate. A second difference is that the variable in a macro's argument list is bound to the entire macro form: not just the list of arguments, but the macro's name as well. An example will help to make this clear. Let's write a macro called DECREMENT. Writing (DECREMENT CNT) will be the same as writing (SETQ CNT (SUB1 CNT)).

```
*(defun decrement macro (x)
   (let ((name (cadr x)))
     (list 'setq name (list 'sub1 name))))
DECREMENT

*(setq cnt 5)
5

*(decrement cnt)
4

*cnt
4
```

When (DECREMENT CNT) is evaluated, the symbol X is bound to that expression. The body of the macro then binds NAME to the symbol CNT and constructs the expression (SETQ CNT (SUB1 CNT)). This is the value returned by DECREMENT, but because DECREMENT is a macro Lisp evaluates the expression it returns, producing 4 as the result.

Exercise

Show how to write SETQ as a macro based on SET.

4. FUNCTIONS WITH ARBITRARY NUMBERS OF INPUTS

Lisp provides another form for functions to take. A **LEXPR** is like an ordinary function except in place of an argument list, it has a single symbol. The symbol is bound to the *number* of arguments the LEXPR was called with, and the function ARG is used to access these arguments. The arguments to a LEXPR are always evaluated.

Here is a version of PLUS defined as a LEXPR:

```
*(defun poly-plus nargs
   (prog (i sum)
         (setq i 1)
         (setq sum 0)
     loop
         (if (greaterp i nargs) (return sum))
         (setq sum (plus sum (arg i)))
         (setq i (add1 i))
         (go loop)))
POLY-PLUS

*(poly-plus 8 3 5 6 9)
31
```

In this example, NARGS is bound to 5 because POLY-PLUS was called with five arguments. (NARGS stands for *n*umber of *arg*ument*s*.) The expression (ARG 1) evaluates to 8, (ARG 2) evaluates to 3, and so forth. In many versions of Lisp, functions such as PLUS, APPEND, and UNION are defined as LEXPRs so they can take any number of inputs.

Here is how PROG2 could be defined as a LEXPR:

```
(DEFUN PROG2 NARGS
  (IF (LESSP NARGS 2) NIL (ARG 2)))
```

Exercise

Show how to define PROG1, PROGN, and LIST as LEXPRs.

Functions Covered in Advanced Topics

PROG-like functions: PROG1, PROG2, PROGN
LEXPR-related function: ARG

11
Property Lists

1. INTRODUCTION

In Lisp, every symbol has an associated **property list.** We can give the symbol FRED a property called SEX with value MALE, a property called AGE with value 23, and a property called SIBLINGS with value (GEORGE WANDA). The property list of FRED would then look like this:

```
(SIBLINGS (GEORGE WANDA) AGE 23 SEX MALE)
```

In general, the format of a property list is

(*prop-1 value-1 prop-2 value-2* . . .)

Property names must be symbols, but property values can be any type of data.

2. ESTABLISHING PROPERTIES

We can use the PUTPROP function to give a symbol a property. The syntax we will use for PUTPROP is:

(PUTPROP *symbol propvalue propname*)

This is the syntax used in MacLisp; other dialects may order the arguments differently, or they may use the name PUT instead of

PUTPROP, but the effect is the same. Using PUTPROP we can establish the properties of FRED:

```
*(putprop 'fred 'male 'sex)
MALE

*(putprop 'fred 23 'age)
23

*(putprop 'fred '(george wanda) 'siblings)
(GEORGE WANDA)
```

Another way to establish a property is to use a special form called DEFPROP. The syntax of DEFPROP is the same as PUTPROP, but DEFPROP does not evaluate any of its arguments. We could have used DEFPROP instead of PUTPROP to set up FRED's property list. Here's how:

```
*(defprop fred male sex)
FRED

*(defprop fred 23 age)
FRED

*(defprop fred (george wanda) siblings)
FRED
```

3. RETRIEVING PROPERTIES

The GET function retrieves a particular property of a symbol. GET is the name MacLisp uses; in certain other dialects this function is called GETPROP. Let's try retrieving some properties of FRED:

```
*(get 'fred 'sex)
MALE

*(get 'fred 'age)
23

*(get 'fred 'siblings)
(GEORGE WANDA)
```

```
*(get 'fred 'favorite-color)
NIL
```

If a symbol does not have a particular property, GET returns NIL. Since FRED doesn't have a FAVORITE-COLOR property, (GET 'FRED 'FAVORITE-COLOR) returns NIL.

The PLIST function returns a symbol's entire property list.

```
*(plist 'fred)
(SIBLINGS (GEORGE WANDA) AGE 23 SEX MALE)
```

Different Lisp dialects have different names for PLIST. In some, such as UCI Lisp, a symbol's property list is obtained by taking the CDR of the symbol. Other dialects give an error if you do this.

4. MODIFYING PROPERTIES

We can replace the value of a property by specifying a new value with PUTPROP. This is a lot like assigning a new value to a variable with SETQ.

```
*(get 'fred 'age)
23

*(putprop 'fred 24 'age)
24

*(get 'fred 'age)
24

*(plist 'fred)
(SIBLINGS (GEORGE WANDA) AGE 24 SEX MALE)
```

We can remove a property entirely using a function called REMPROP. The value returned by REMPROP is the CDR of the property list from the point after the name of the removed property. Both the property name and its associated value are removed from the list.

```
*(plist 'fred)
(SIBLINGS (GEORGE WANDA) AGE 24 SEX MALE)
```

```
*(remprop 'fred 'age)
(24 SEX MALE)

*(plist 'fred)
(SIBLINGS (GEORGE WANDA) SEX MALE)
```

5. PROGRAMMING WITH PROPERTY LISTS

Suppose we are building a database about the characters in a story, and one of the facts we want to record is meetings between the characters. We can store a list of names under the **MET** property of each individual. A name should not appear on the list more than once—that is, the list should be a set. The easiest way to do this is to write a function called **ADDPROP** to add an element to a set stored under a property name. Here is the definition of **ADDPROP**:

```
(DEFUN ADDPROP (SYM ELEM PROP)
  (OR (MEMBER ELEM (GET SYM PROP))
      (PUTPROP SYM
               (CONS ELEM (GET SYM PROP))
               PROP)))
```

The **MEMBER** check prevents us from adding a name to the list more than once. Using **ADDPROP** we can easily write a function to record meetings:

```
(DEFUN RECORD-MEETING (X Y)
  (ADDPROP X Y 'MET)
  (ADDPROP Y X 'MET)
  T)
```

This function makes use of the fact that "met" is a symmetric relation—if **X** has met **Y** then **Y** has also met **X**.

```
*(plist 'little-red)
NIL

*(record-meeting 'little-red 'wolfie)
T
```

```
*(plist 'little-red)
(MET (WOLFIE))

*(plist 'wolfie)
(MET (LITTLE-RED))

*(record-meeting 'wolfie 'grandma)
T

*(plist 'wolfie)
(MET (GRANDMA LITTLE-RED))
```

Exercises

1. Write a function called SUBPROP that deletes an element from a set stored under a property name. For example, if the symbol A has the list (B C D E) as the value of its FOO property, doing (SUBPROP 'A 'D 'FOO) should leave (B C E) as the value of A's FOO property.

2. Write a function called FORGET-MEETING that forgets that two specified persons ever met each other.

3. If A doesn't have a FOO property, (GET 'A 'FOO) will return NIL. On the other hand, if A does have a FOO property but the value of that property is NIL, (GET 'A 'FOO) will still return NIL. Thus we can't use GET as a reliable test of whether a symbol has a given property or not. Write a predicate HASPROP that returns a true value if a symbol has a particular property, independent of the value of that property.

4. Using PLIST, write your own version of the GET function.

5. Write a function called REMPROPS that removes all of a symbol's properties.

Functions Covered in This Chapter

Property list functions: PUTPROP, GET, PLIST, REMPROP
Special form: DEFPROP

Keyboard Exercise

A cryptogram is a type of puzzle that requires the solver to decode a message. The code is known as a substitution cipher because it consists of substituting one letter for another throughout the message. For example, if we substitute J for F, T for A, and W for L, the word "fall" would be encoded as JTWW. Here is an actual cryptogram for you to solve:

```
(ZJ ZE KLJJLS JF SLAPZI EZVLIJ PIB KL JUFWXUJ P HFFV JUPI
 JF ENLPO PIB SLAFML PVV BFWKJ)
```

The purpose of this keyboard exercise, however, is not to solve cryptograms but to write a program to help you solve them. Suppose the preceding cryptogram has been stored in the global variable C1. Here is an example of how our cryptogram-solving program will start out:

```
*(solve c1)
--------------------
ZJ ZE KLJJLS JF SLAPZI EZVLIJ PIB KL JUFWXUJ P HFFV JUPI JF ENLPO

PIB SLAFML PVV BFWKJ

--------------------
Substitute which letter?
```

When tackling a new cryptogram it helps to look at the shortest words first. In English there are only two one-letter words: "I" and "a," so the tenth word of the cryptogram, P, must be one of those. Suppose we guess that P deciphers to A. Beneath each P in the text we write an A.

```
Substitute which letter? p
What does P decipher to? a
--------------------
ZJ ZE KLJJLS JF SLAPZI EZVLIJ PIB KL JUFWXUJ P HFFV JUPI JF ENLPO
                   A          A              A        A        A
```

```
PIB SLAFML PVV BFWKJ
A          A
--------------------
Substitute which letter?
```

Next we might look at all the two-letter words and guess that Z deciphers to I. Beneath each Z in the message we write an I.

```
Substitute which letter? z
What does Z decipher to? i
--------------------
ZJ ZE KLJJLS JF SLAPZI EZVLIJ PIB KL JUFWXUJ P HFFV JUPI JF ENLPO
I  I               AI   I     A              A        A        A

PIB SLAFML PVV BFWKJ
A          A
--------------------
Substitute which letter?
```

An important constraint on cryptograms that helps to make them solvable is that no letter can decipher to more than one thing, and no two letters can decipher to the same letter. Our program must check to ensure that this constraint is obeyed by any solution we generate.

```
Substitute which letter? z
Z has already been deciphered as I!
--------------------
ZJ ZE KLJJLS JF SLAPZI EZVLIJ PIB KL JUFWXUJ P HFFV JUPI JF ENLPO
I  I               AI   I     A              A        A        A

PIB SLAFML PVV BFWKJ
A          A
----------------------
Substitute which letter? k
What does K decipher to? a
But P already deciphers to A!
---------------------
ZJ ZE KLJJLS JF SLAPZI EZVLIJ PIB KL JUFWXUJ P HFFV JUPI JF ENLPO
I  I               AI   I     A              A        A        A
```

```
PIB SLAFML PVV BFWKJ
A          A
--------------------
Substitute which letter?
```

At some point we may want to take back a substitution. Suppose that after deciphering P and Z we decide that P shouldn't really decipher to A after all. The program must allow for this:

```
Substitute which letter? undo
Undo which letter? p
---------------------
ZJ ZE KLJJLS JF SLAPZI EZVLIJ PIB KL JUFWXUJ P HFFV JUPI JF ENLPO
I  I                I   I
PIB SLAFML PVV BFWKJ
--------------------
Substitute which letter?
```

The process continues until we have solved the cryptogram.

Instructions

1. Set the global variable ALPHABET equal to the list

   ```
   (A B C D E F G H I J K L M N O P Q R S T U V W X Y Z)
   ```

   Set the global variable C1 equal to the list

   ```
   (ZJ ZE KLJJLS JF SLAPZI EZVLIJ PIB KL JUFWXUJ P HFFV JUPI
    JF ENLPO PIB SLAFML PVV BFWKJ)
   ```

2. Find the Lisp function in your dialect that takes a symbol as input and returns the list of letters in its name. In most dialects this function is called EXPLODE. (EXPLODE 'FALL) returns (F A L L). If your dialect does not have an EXPLODE function, write one using whatever primitives are provided.

3. Write a function WORDS-TO-LIST that takes a list of words as input and returns a list of the letters in their names, with NIL between each word. (WORDS-TO-LIST '(ZJ ZE KLJJLS)) should return

```
(Z J NIL Z E NIL K L J J L S)
```

4. Since cryptograms can be arbitrarily long, we need to group the text into lines that will fit on a computer screen. Write a function GROUP-TEXT that groups a list of letters and NILs, such as is produced by WORDS-TO-LIST, into a list of lists, representing lines. Each list except for the last should contain at least 60 atoms and should end in NIL. (When grouping the text into lines, we don't want to split the letters of a single word across lines. Therefore we must break a line only at the first NIL encountered past the sixtieth atom.) (GROUP-TEXT (WORDS-TO-LIST C1)) should return

```
((Z J NIL Z E NIL K L J J L S NIL J F NIL S L A P Z I
  NIL E Z V L I J NIL P I B NIL K L NIL J U F W X U J NIL
  P NIL H F F V NIL J U P I NIL J F NIL E N L P O NIL)
 (P I B NIL S L A F M L NIL P V V NIL B F W K J))
```

This list contains two elements, corresponding to the fact that the cryptogram is broken into two lines.

5. Each letter in the alphabet has a corresponding letter that it deciphers to (e.g., P deciphers to A). As we solve the cryptogram we will store this information on the property list of the letter. For example, P will have a DECIPHERS property with value A, and A will have an ENCIPHERS property with value P. We will use the DECIPHERS property to print out the deciphered cryptogram. We need the ENCIPHERS property to check for two letters being deciphered to the same thing. For example, if P is deciphered to A and then we tried to decipher J to A, a look at the ENCIPHERS property of A would reveal that A had already been assigned to P. Similarly, if P is deciphered to A and then we tried deciphering P to E, a look at the DECIPHERS property of P would tell us that P had already been deciphered to A.

   Write a function MAKE-SUBSTITUTION that takes two letters as input and gives them DECIPHERS and ENCIPHERS properties so that the first letter deciphers to the second and the second letter enciphers to the first. This function does *not* need to check if either letter already has a DECIPHERS or ENCIPHERS property.

6. Write a function UNDO-SUBSTITUTION that takes one letter as input. It should remove the DECIPHERS property of that letter and the ENCIPHERS property of the letter if deciphered to.

7. Write a function CLEAR of no arguments that removes the ENCIPHERS and DECIPHERS properties of the symbols A through Z. CLEAR will be used to initialize our SOLVE function before starting on a new cryptogram.

8. Write a function SHOW-LINE that displays one line of cryptogram text, with the deciphered text displayed beneath it. Remember that a line is a list of letters and NILs. The NILs should print as spaces. When displaying the deciphered text below the original text, letters that do not have a DECIPHERS property yet should print as spaces. For example: if only P has a DECIPHERS property, and the value of that property is A, then

```
(SHOW-LINE '(P I B NIL S L A F M L NIL P V V NIL B F W K J))
```

should print out

```
PIB SLAFML PVV BFWKJ
A          A
```

(blank line)

9. Write a function SHOW-TEXT that takes a list of lines as input and displays the lines as in the examples at the beginning of this exercise.

10. Write a function SUB-LETTER that takes a letter as input. If that letter has been deciphered already, SUB-LETTER should print an error message that tells what the letter has been deciphered to. Otherwise SUB-LETTER should ask "WHAT does (*letter*) decipher to?" and read in a symbol. If that symbol is a letter and has not been enciphered, then SUB-LETTER should call MAKE-SUBSTITUTION to record the substitution. Otherwise, if the symbol read is not a letter or if it has already been enciphered as something else, an appropriate error message should be printed.

11. Write a function UNDO-LETTER that asks "Undo which letter?" and reads in a symbol. If that symbol is a letter that has been

deciphered, UNDO-LETTER should call UNDO-SUBSTITUTION on the letter. Otherwise an appropriate error message should be printed.

12. Write the main function, SOLVE, that takes a cryptogram as input. SOLVE should perform the following loop. First it should display the cryptogram. Then it should ask "Substitute which letter?" and read in a symbol. If the input is a letter, it should call SUB-LETTER; if the input is the symbol UNDO, it should call UNDO-LETTER; if the input is the symbol END, it should return T; otherwise it should issue an error message. Then it should go back to the beginning of the loop.

13. P deciphers to A, and Z deciphers to I. Solve the cryptogram.

Advanced Topics 11

1. PROPERTY LISTS AND FUNCTION DEFINITIONS

In many Lisp dialects, property lists are used to store function definitions. In MacLisp, for example, if we define a function (either an EXPR or LEXPR) with DEFUN, the lambda expression corresponding to that function is stored as the value of the function name's EXPR property:

```
*(defun sub2 (x) (sub1 (sub1 x)))
SUB2

*(plist 'sub2)
(EXPR (LAMBDA (X) (SUB1 (SUB1 X))))

*(get 'sub2 'expr)
(LAMBDA (X) (SUB1 (SUB1 X)))
```

Built-in functions in MacLisp have a SUBR or LSUBR property instead of an EXPR property. The value of the SUBR or LSUBR property is an address for the sequence of computer language instructions that implements the function.

```
*(plist 'cons)
(SUBR #406211)

*(plist 'list)
(LSUBR #425171)
```

Similarly, special forms are stored under the **FEXPR** property and built-in special forms under the **FSUBR** property.

```
*(plist 'and)
(FSUBR #432626)
```

Not all Lisp dialects use this convention. Franz Lisp, for example, stores a symbol's function definition in a special place called a **function cell** that is accessible via the built-in functions PUTD and GETD. These are analogous to PUTPROP and GET for property lists.

2. SPECIAL USES FOR PROPERTY LISTS

Two other special uses of property lists are worth mentioning. In some Lisp dialects, every symbol has a **PNAME** property that points to the symbol's name. PNAME is short for "Print NAME." Names are stored in the computer's memory as sequences of characters. Lisp uses the PNAME property to give every symbol (which is, as far as the computer is concerned, just an address) a name.

Symbols have printnames in all Lisp implementations, but the more modern dialects reserve a special cell in the internal structure of a symbol for storing its printname and thus do not have to put the printname on the symbol's property list.

The other special use of property lists is for storing variable bindings. In some Lisp implementations, (GET 'X 'VALUE) returns the current value of the variable X. More modern implementations store a symbol's value in a special place called a **value cell,** not on the property list.

Appendix A Recommended Further Reading

This appendix lists some of the most important and accessible works on Lisp and artificial intelligence. An extensive Lisp bibliography appears in *LISP* by Patrick Henry Winston and Berthold K. P. Horn.

Lisp Programming

Allen, John. 1978. *Anatomy of LISP.* New York: McGraw-Hill.

Bobrow, Daniel G., and Raphael, Bertram. 1974. "New Programming Languages for Artificial Intelligence Research." *ACM Computing Surveys* 6 (3): 155–174.

Byte Magazine. 1979. 4 (8). August issue devoted to Lisp.

Charniak, Eugene; Reisbeck, Christopher; and McDermott, Drew. 1979. *Artificial Intelligence Programming.* Hillsdale, NJ: Lawrence Erlbaum Associates.

Sandewall, Erik. 1978. "Programming in the Interactive Environment: The LISP Experience." *ACM Computing Surveys* 10 (1):35–71.

Schank, Roger C., and Riesbeck, Christopher K. (eds.). 1981. *Inside Computer Understanding: Five Programs Plus Miniatures.* Hillsdale, NJ: Lawrence Erlbaum Associates.

Shapiro, Stuart C. 1979. *Techniques of Artificial Intelligence.* New York: Van Nostrand.

Winston, Patrick Henry. 1977. *Artificial Intelligence.* Reading, MA: Addison-Wesley.

———, and Horn, Berthold K. P. 1981. *LISP.* Reading, MA: Addison-Wesley.

Artificial Intelligence

Barr, Avron; Cohen, Paul R.; and Feigenbaum, Edward A. (eds.). 1981–1982. *The Handbook of Artificial Intelligence*, vols. 1–3. Los Altos, CA: William Kaufmann.

Boden, Margaret. 1977. *Artificial Intelligence and Natural Man.* New York: Basic Books.

Feigenbaum, Edward A., and Feldman, Julian (eds.). 1963. *Computers and Thought.* New York: McGraw-Hill.

Hofstadter, Douglas. 1979. *Godel, Escher, Bach: An Eternal Golden Braid.* New York: Basic Books.

McCorduck, Pamela. 1979. *Machines Who Think.* San Francisco: W. H. Freeman.

Minsky, Marvin (ed.). 1968. *Semantic Information Processing.* Cambridge, MA: The MIT Press.

Nilsson, Nils J. 1971. *Problem Solving Methods in Artificial Intelligence.* New York: McGraw-Hill.

———. 1980. *Principles of Artificial Intelligence.* Palo Alto, CA: Tioga Publishing Company.

Raphael, Bertram. 1976. *The Thinking Computer: Mind Inside Matter.* San Francisco: W. H. Freeman.

Rich, Elaine. 1983. *Artificial Intelligence.* New York: McGraw-Hill.

Schank, Roger C., and Abelson, Robert P. 1977. *Scripts, Plans, Goals, and Understanding.* Hillsdale, NJ: Lawrence Erlbaum Associates.

Schank, Roger C., and Colby, Kenneth. 1973. *Computer Models of Thought and Language.* San Francisco: W. H. Freeman.

Weizenbaum, Joseph. 1976. *Computer Power and Human Reason.* San Francisco: W. H. Freeman.

Winograd, Terry. 1972. *Understanding Natural Language.* New York: Academic Press.

Winston, Patrick Henry. 1975. *The Psychology of Computer Vision.* Reading, MA: Addison-Wesley.

———. 1977. *Artificial Intelligence.* Reading, MA: Addison-Wesley.

Information on Particular Lisp Dialects

Blair, Fred W. 1979. "LISP/370 Concepts and Facilities." Report RC 7771. Yorktown Heights, NY: IBM Research Center.

Foderaro, John K. 1979. "The FRANZ LISP Manual." Berkeley, CA: University of California.

Greenblatt, Richard; Knight, Tom; Holloway, John; and Moon, David. 1979. *The Lisp Machine.* Cambridge, MA: MIT Artificial Intelligence Laboratory.

Griss, M. L., and Morrison, B. 1981. "The Portable Standard LISP Users Manual." Utah Symbolic Computation Group Technical Report TR-10. Salt Lake City: University of Utah Department of Computer Science.

Meehan, James. 1979. *New UCI LISP Manual.* Hillsdale, NJ: Lawrence Erlbaum Associates.

Moon, David. 1974, rev. 1978. *MacLisp Reference Manual.* Cambridge, MA: MIT Artificial Intelligence Laboratory.

Norman, Eric. 1978. "LISP Reference Manual for the UNIVAC 1108." Madison: University of Wisconsin Computing Center.

Steel, Guy L., Jr. 1982. "Common LISP Reference Manual." Spice Project Internal Report. Pittsburgh: Carnegie-Mellon University. To be published by Digital Press.

Teitelman, Warren. 1974, rev. 1978. *INTERLISP Reference Manual.* Palo Alto, CA: Xerox Palo Alto Research Center, and Cambridge, MA: Bolt, Beranek, and Newman.

Touretzky, David S. 1982. *A Summary of MacLisp Functions and Flags,* 4th ed. Pittsburgh: Carnegie-Mellon University Computer Science Department.

Urmi, Jaak, 1976. "INTERLISP/370 Reference Manual." Linkoeping, Sweden: Linkoeping University Department of Mathematics.

Weinreb, Daniel, and Moon, David. 1981. *Lisp Machine Manual,* 3rd ed. Cambridge, MA: MIT Artificial Intelligence Laboratory.

Works of Historical Interest

Berkeley, E. C., and Bobrow, Daniel G. (eds.). 1966. *The Programming Language LISP: Its Operation and Applications,* 2nd ed. Cambridge, MA: The MIT Press.

Church, Alonzo. 1941. "The Calculi of Lambda Conversion." *Annals of Mathematical Studies,* number 6, Princeton, NJ: Princeton University Press.

McCarthy, John. 1960. "Recursive Functions of Symbolic Expressions and Their Computation by Machine, Part I." *Communications of the Association for Computing Machinery* 3(4):184–195.

———. 1961. "A Basis for a Mathematical Theory of Computation." *Proceedings of the Western Joint Computer Conference,* 19: 225–238.

———. 1981. "History of LISP." In *History of Programming Languages,* edited by Richard L. Wexelblat, pp. 173–197. New York: Academic Press.

———; Abrahams, P. W.; Edwards, D. J.; Hart, T. P.; and Levin, M. I. 1962. *LISP 1.5 Programmer's Manual.* Cambridge, MA: The MIT Press.

Appendix B
Dialects of Lisp

The incompatibilities between Lisp dialects are substantial. Not only do different dialects provide different sets of primitive functions, they also provide different sets of datatypes: for example, some have strings and some do not; some have file objects while others use integer "channel numbers"; and so on. Even the most basic issues, such as what should be the result of taking the CAR or CDR of NIL, have no universally agreed-upon answer. Needless to say, there are myriad minor incompatibilities as well, such as functions having different names in different dialects (GET in MacLisp is called GETPROP in Interlisp) and functions with the same name having different meanings (such as NTH, which numbers elements starting from 0 in MacLisp but from 1 in UCI Lisp), or different argument orders.

The best (and often the only) guide to any Lisp implementation is its reference manual. Unfortunately, the reference manual is frequently too technical and too detailed to be of much benefit to a beginning Lisper. Therefore this appendix offers a quickie introduction to the most widely used dialects of Lisp. Each section shows how to define EXPRs, LEXPRs, FEXPRs, and macros in either a particular dialect or a family of related dialects, and how to print out the definition of a function. A detailed discussion of the differences between each dialect and the slightly enhanced version of MacLisp used in this book would be impractical, but see appendix C for some hints on how to make your dialect more compatible with mine.

1. MACLISP, COMMON LISP, AND LISP MACHINE LISP

In MacLisp, all functions are defined with DEFUN.

```
(DEFUN ADD2 (X) (ADD1 (ADD1 X)))

(DEFUN TEST NARGS (LIST 'CALLED 'WITH NARGS 'INPUTS))

(DEFUN INCREMENT FEXPR (X) (SET (CAR X) (ADD1 (EVAL (CAR X)))))

(DEFUN DECREMENT MACRO (X)
    (LIST 'SET (LIST 'QUOTE (CADR X)) (LIST 'SUB1 (CADR X))))
```

To print out a function definition we use GRINDEF—for example:

```
(GRINDEF ADD2)
```

Lisp Machine Lisp uses the same syntax as MacLisp. So does Common Lisp, except that FEXPRs are not provided.

2. FRANZ LISP

In Franz Lisp everything must be in lowercase. Franz Lisp accepts the same defun syntax as MacLisp but also offers an alternative syntax using a special form called def.

```
(def add2 (lambda (x) (add1 (add1 x))))

(def test (lexpr (nargs) (list 'called 'with nargs 'inputs)))

(def increment (nlambda (x) (set (car x) (add1 (eval (car x))))))

(def decrement
  (macro (x)
    (list 'set (list 'quote (cadr x)) (list 'sub1 (cadr x)))))
```

To print out a function definition in Franz Lisp we use pp, which stands for "*p*retty *p*rint":

```
(pp add2)
```

3. UCI LISP AND TLC-LISP

UCI Lisp uses DE to define an EXPR or LEXPR, DF to define a FEXPR, and DM to define a macro.

```
(DE ADD2 (X) (ADD1 (ADD1 X)))

(DE TEST NARGS (LIST 'CALLED 'WITH NARGS 'INPUTS))

(DF INCREMENT (X) (SET (CAR X) (ADD1 (EVAL (CAR X)))))

(DM DECREMENT (X)
    (LIST 'SET (LIST 'QUOTE (CADR X)) (LIST 'SUB1 (CADR X))))
```

UCI Lisp uses PP to print the definition of a function.

TLC-LISP uses a similar syntax to UCI Lisp for defining and displaying functions, although in most other respects this dialect is an offshoot of MacLisp. There is one area where TLC-LISP is unique: LEXPRs are supported, but not directly. Instead, users are advised to use the &REST keyword. Keywords in argument lists are available in most modern Lisp dialects, but they are beyond the scope of this book. The TLC-LISP equivalent of the TEST function is:

```
(DE TEST (&REST ARGLIST)
  (LIST 'CALLED 'WITH (LENGTH ARGLIST) 'INPUTS))
```

4. INTERLISP

Interlisp uses DEFINEQ to define EXPRs, LEXPRs, and FEXPRs.

```
(DEFINEQ
   (ADD2 (LAMBDA (X) (ADD1 (ADD1 X)))))

(DEFINEQ
    (TEST (LAMBDA NARGS (LIST 'CALLED 'WITH NARGS 'INPUTS))))

(DEFINEQ
    (INCREMENT (NLAMBDA X (SET (CAR X) (ADD1 (EVAL (CAR X)))))))
```

Interlisp does not have macros in the same sense as the other dialects. Interlisp macros are used only when programs are to be compiled. Compilation is beyond the scope of this text, but I'll include an example of an Interlisp macro just for the sake of completeness. Note that in Interlisp the order of the last two arguments to PUTPROP is the reverse of that used in the text.

```
(PUTPROP 'DECREMENT 'MACRO
  '(LAMBDA (X) (LIST 'SETQ X (LIST 'SUB1 X))))
```

Interlisp uses PP to print the definition of a function.

5. P-LISP

Functions are defined in P-LISP using DEFINE.

```
(DEFINE (ADD2 (LAMBDA (X) (ADD1 (ADD1 X)))))

(DEFINE
  (INCREMENT (FLAMBDA (X) (SET (CAR X) (ADD1 (EVAL (CAR X)))))))
```

As of this writing, P-LISP does not provide LEXPRs or macros. P-LISP uses the special form PPRINT to print the definition of a function.

Appendix C
Extensions to Lisp

While the dialect of Lisp used in this book is essentially MacLisp, I have enhanced the language in a few places to make up for some of its deficiencies. Readers familiar with other dialects may recognize a few imports from UCI Lisp and Common Lisp. The purpose of this appendix is to make it possible to tailor whatever dialect you are using so that it is reasonably compatible with the text. This is accomplished by supplying definitions for most of the extensions to Lisp 1.5 (the basic dialect from which all others are descended) that appear in the book.

The first section of the appendix gives simplified definitions. They are "simplified" in that, for example, set functions such as UNION and INTERSECTION accept only two inputs, and applicatives such as APPLY-TO-ALL operate on only a single list. The second part of the appendix is a MacLisp file that implements the extensions in all their glory, and in a manner that is at the same time efficient and capable of producing good error messages. This file will work verbatim on any TOPS-10 or TOPS-20 MacLisp system, and it can easily be adapted to Franz Lisp. Translations for other Lisp dialects, such as Interlisp and UCI Lisp, are possible but will require slightly more work.

1. SIMPLIFIED DEFINITIONS

The definitions that follow are iterative rather than recursive so that they can operate on long lists without danger of stack overflow. Also, they do not depend on CAR and CDR of NIL being NIL, since this is not true in all implementations.

1.1. Type Predicates

If your Lisp doesn't have SYMBOLP, you can fake it using ATOM and NUMBERP:

```
(DEFUN SYMBOLP (X) (AND (ATOM X) (NOT (NUMBERP X))))
```

Most Lisps provide a way to tell if something is a list or not. If your Lisp includes a CONSP predicate (or PAIRP, as it's called in MacLisp), you can define LISTP as follows:

```
(DEFUN LISTP (X) (OR (NULL X) (CONSP X)))
```

If your Lisp provides only a LISTP predicate, you can define CONSP as:

```
(DEFUN CONSP (X) (AND X (LISTP X)))
```

If your Lisp provides neither LISTP nor CONSP, you can probably get by by pretending that ATOM is the opposite of CONSP, although this is not strictly true. Then your definitions for LISTP and CONSP will be:

```
(DEFUN CONSP (X) (NOT (ATOM X)))

(DEFUN LISTP (X) (OR (NULL X) (CONSP X)))
```

STRINGP is the hardest predicate to define. If your Lisp doesn't have strings, you'll have to use symbols instead. It is possible to make lowercase letters and special characters part of a symbol name by using either "slashification" or special delimiters. The slashification technique, which was used in the earliest Lisp systems, involves prefacing every special character by a slash (/). Other Lisps provide a delimiter character, such as |, that works like quotation marks do for strings, but the object enclosed in |'s is still a symbol and will not evaluate to itself the way a string does. Here is an example of the different techniques:

`"Hi MOM"`	*a string—evaluates to itself*
`H/i/ MOM`	*a symbol: the lowercase i and the space are each preceded by a slash*
`|Hi MOM|`	*a symbol: its name is enclosed in special delimiters*

If you don't have strings and are faking them using symbols, here is a version of STRINGP that will at least work well enough to let you write a MSG function:

```
(DEFUN STRINGP (X) (AND (SYMBOLP X) (NOT (BOUNDP X))))
```

On the other hand, if your Lisp implements strings as symbols bound to themselves but does not include a STRINGP predicate, try this:

```
(DEFUN STRINGP (X)
   (AND (SYMBOLP X) (BOUNDP X) (EQ X (EVAL X))))
```

1.2. Functions on Lists

NCONS, LAST, NTH, and NTHCDR are all easy to define if your Lisp doesn't have them. Caution: Some Lisps, such as UCI Lisp, do have NTH and NTHCDR but use a different argument order and number the elements starting from 1 instead of 0.

```
(DEFUN NCONS (X) (CONS X NIL))

(DEFUN LAST (L)
  (PROG ()
        (OR L (RETURN NIL))
    LOOP
        (OR (CDR L) (RETURN L))
        (SETQ L (CDR L))
        (GO LOOP)))
```

```
(DEFUN NTHCDR (N X)
  (PROG ()
    LOOP
        (AND (ZEROP N) (RETURN X))
        (SETQ X (CDR X))
        (SETQ N (SUB1 N))
        (GO LOOP)))

(DEFUN NTH (N X) (CAR (NTHCDR N X)))
```

1.3 Functions on Sets

MEMBER is the only set function that is found in all Lisps. Here are definitions for the other set functions. These versions are EXPRs rather than LEXPRs, but unlike some of the simpler ones that appear in the text, they preserve the order of elements as given in the input.

```
(DEFUN INTERSECTION (X Y)
  (PROG (RESULT)
    LOOP
        (AND (NULL X) (RETURN (REVERSE RESULT)))
        (AND (MEMBER (CAR X) Y)
             (SETQ RESULT (CONS (CAR X) RESULT)))
        (SETQ X (CDR X))
        (GO LOOP)))

(DEFUN UNION (X Y)
  (APPEND X (SETDIFFERENCE Y X)))

(DEFUN SETDIFFERENCE (X Y)
  (PROG (RESULT)
    LOOP
        (AND (NULL X) (RETURN (REVERSE RESULT)))
        (OR (MEMBER (CAR X) Y)
            (SETQ RESULT (CONS (CAR X) RESULT)))
        (SETQ X (CDR X))
        (GO LOOP)))
```

1.4. IF and MSG

IF and MSG are easy to implement as FEXPRs. In the following definitions, the variable name *X* is used instead of X to avoid a problem caused by dynamic binding. Namely, a function inside an IF or MSG form that references X as a global variable would not work if X were rebound by the special form.

```
(DEFUN IF FEXPR (*X*)
  (COND ((EVAL (CAR *X*)) (EVAL (CADR *X*)))
        (T (AND (CDDR *X*) (EVAL (CADDR *X*))))))

(DEFUN MSG FEXPR (*X*)
  (PROG ()
   LOOP
        (AND (NULL *X*) (RETURN T))
        (COND ((EQ (CAR *X*) T) (TERPRI))
              ((STRINGP (CAR *X*)) (PRINC (CAR *X*)))
              (T (PRINC (EVAL (CAR *X*)))))
        (SETQ *X* (CDR *X*))
        (GO LOOP)))
```

If you need macro versions of IF and MSG, try these. The definitions assume that macros are called with the entire form as argument—for example, (IF A B C) calls the IF macro on the list (IF A B C), not (A B C) as is the case with FEXPRs.

```
(DEFUN IF MACRO (*X*)
  (LIST 'COND (LIST (CADR *X*) (CADDR *X*))
              (LIST T (AND (CDDDR *X*) (CADDDR *X*)))))
```

```
(DEFUN MSG MACRO (*X*)
  (PROG (FORM)
        (SETQ *X* (CDR *X*))
    LOOP
        (COND ((NULL *X*)
               (RETURN (CONS 'PROGN (REVERSE FORM))))
              ((EQ (CAR *X*) T)
               (SETQ FORM (CONS '(TERPRI) FORM)))
              ((STRINGP (CAR *X*))
               (SETQ FORM (CONS (LIST 'PRINC
                                      (LIST 'QUOTE (CAR *X*)))
                                FORM)))
              (T (SETQ FORM (CONS (LIST 'PRINC (CAR *X*)) FORM))))
        (SETQ *X* (CDR *X*))
        (GO LOOP)))
```

1.5. Applicative Operators

Most Lisps provide an APPLY-TO-ALL operator under the name MAPCAR. The other operators used in this book are found only in the more modern dialects, sometimes under different names than those used here. I am aware of no dialect in common use that provides a REDUCE operator.

```
(DEFUN APPLY-TO-ALL (FN L)
  (PROG (RESULT)
    LOOP
        (COND ((NULL L) (RETURN (REVERSE RESULT)))
              (T (SETQ RESULT
                       (CONS (APPLY FN (NCONS (CAR L))) RESULT))
                 (SETQ L (CDR L))
                 (GO LOOP)))))

(DEFUN FIND-IF (FN L)
  (PROG ()
    LOOP
        (COND ((NULL L) (RETURN NIL))
              ((APPLY FN (NCONS (CAR L))) (RETURN (CAR L)))
              (T (SETQ L (CDR L)) (GO LOOP)))))
```

```
(DEFUN SUBSET (FN L)
  (PROG (RESULT)
    LOOP
        (COND ((NULL L) (RETURN (REVERSE RESULT)))
              ((APPLY FN (NCONS (CAR L)))
               (SETQ RESULT (CONS (CAR L) RESULT))))
        (SETQ L (CDR L))
        (GO LOOP)))

(DEFUN EVERY (FN L)
  (PROG ()
    LOOP
        (COND ((NULL L) (RETURN T))
              ((NOT (APPLY FN (NCONS (CAR L)))) (RETURN NIL))
              (T (SETQ L (CDR L)) (GO LOOP)))))
```

REDUCE and it derivatives are the hardest operators to implement; much of the difficulty comes from the need to return an identity value when reducing an empty list. We fudge the solution here by simply retrieving the **IDENTITY** property of the reducing function.

```
(DEFUN REDUCE (FN L) (LEFT-REDUCE FN L))

(DEFUN LEFT-REDUCE (FN L)
  (PROG (RESULT)
        (OR L (RETURN (FIND-IDENTITY FN)))
        (SETQ RESULT (CAR L))
        (SETQ L (CDR L))
    LOOP
        (OR L (RETURN RESULT))
        (SETQ RESULT (APPLY FN (LIST RESULT (CAR L))))
        (SETQ L (CDR L))
        (GO LOOP)))
```

```
(DEFUN RIGHT-REDUCE (FN L)
  (PROG (RESULT)
        (OR L (RETURN (FIND-IDENTITY FN)))
        (SETQ RESULT (CAR (LAST L)))
        (SETQ L (CDR (REVERSE L)))
    LOOP
        (OR L (RETURN RESULT))
        (SETQ RESULT (APPLY FN (LIST (CAR L) RESULT)))
        (SETQ L (CDR L))
        (GO LOOP)))

(DEFUN FIND-IDENTITY (FN)
  (COND ((SYMBOLP FN) (GET FN 'IDENTITY))
        (T NIL)))
```

If your Lisp implements functions such as PLUS and TIMES as LEXPRs rather than EXPRs, you should be able to get identity values by typing, for example, (PLUS). Inside LEFT- or RIGHT-REDUCE the variable FN is bound to the name of the reducing function. Writing (FN) won't work in most Lisp dialects, but we can call the reducing function with no arguments via the expression (APPLY FN NIL). Of course, we should only do this if the reducing function is a LEXPR.

```
(DEFUN FIND-IDENTITY (FN)
  (COND ((LEXPR? FN) (APPLY FN NIL))
        ((SYMBOLP FN) (GET FN 'IDENTITY))
        (T NIL)))
```

LEXPR? is a predicate that returns true if its input is a LEXPR. In many Lisps, compiled LEXPRs are stored as the value of a symbol's LSUBR property. Interpreted LEXPRs are stored on the EXPR property, but the argument list of the lambda expression is a symbol (such as NARGS) rather than a list. The input to LEXPR? might be a lambda expression itself rather than a symbol, so we must check for that case as well.

```
(DEFUN LEXPR? (FN)
  (COND ((NULL FN) NIL)
        ((SYMBOLP FN) (OR (GET FN 'LSUBR)
                          (LEXPR? (GET FN 'EXPR))))
        ((LISTP FN) (AND (EQ (CAR FN) 'LAMBDA)
                         (CDR FN)
                         (SYMBOLP (CADR FN))))
        (T NIL)))
```

See "The MacLisp Extensions" for more sophisticated definitions of the reduction operators.

2. THE MACLISP EXTENSIONS

```
;;;This file is for use with TOPS-10 or TOPS-20 MacLisp systems.
;;; It works best when compiled.
;;;
;;; Note: internal functions are prefixed by $.

(DECLARE (FIXSW T))          ;use integer arithmetic for everything
(EVAL-WHEN (COMPILE LOAD)
  (SETQ BASE 10.)
  (SETQ IBASE 10.)
  (SSTATUS LINMODE T))

;;; Set up a prompting top-level read-eval-print loop. $PROMPT
;;; automatically sets the line length to 79 if MacLisp fails to
;;; supply a reasonable value for it.

(DEFUN $PROMPT NIL
  (AND (ZEROP (LINEL TYO)) (LINEL TYO 79.))
  (TERPRI)
  (PRINC '*))

(SETQ *-READ-EVAL-PRINT '$PROMPT)

;;; Some simple type predicates:
(DEFUN CONSP (X) (PAIRP X))
```

```
(DEFUN LISTP (X) (OR (NULL X) (PAIRP X)))

(DEFUN STRINGP (X)
  (AND (SYMBOLP X) (GET X '+INTERNAL-STRING-MARKER)))

;;; IF defined as a FEXPR -- will not work if called from compiled code, but
;;; in the interpreter this version gives better error messages than a
;;; comparable macro definition and also leaves the eval stack cleaner.
(DEFUN IF FEXPR (*X*)
  (COND ((OR (NULL (CDR *X*)) (CDDDR *X*))
         (ERROR '| - WRONG NUMBER OF ARGUMENTS|
                (LIST (CONS 'IF *X*) '(2. . 3.))
                'WRNG-NO-ARGS))
        ((EVAL (CAR *X*)) (EVAL (CADR *X*)))
        (T (EVAL (CADDR *X*)))))

;;; Simple I/O function, modeled after UCI Lisp.
(DEFUN MSG FEXPR (*Z*)
  (MAPC '(LAMBDA (*X*)
           (COND ((EQ *X* T) (TERPRI))
                 (T (PRINC (EVAL *X*)))))
        *Z*)
  T)

;;; These two internal functions are used by the functions that follow.
(DEFUN $LISTCHECK (X Y)
  (OR (LISTP X)
      (ERROR (IMPLODE (APPEND (EXPLODEC '|NOT A PROPER LIST - |)
                              (EXPLODEC Y)))
             X
             'WRNG-TYPE-ARG)))

(DEFUN $ARGCHECK (NARGS NAME)
  (OR (GREATERP NARGS 1.)
      (ERROR '|TOO FEW ARGUMENTS SUPPLIED|
             (LIST (CONS NAME (AND (GREATERP NARGS 0.) '(DUMMY)))
                   '(2. . 512.))
             'WRNG-NO-ARGS)))
```

```
;;; Functions on sets.
(DEFUN UNION NARGS
  (DO ((RESULT NIL)
       (L (MAPC '(LAMBDA (X) ($LISTCHECK X 'UNION))
                (LISTIFY NARGS))
          (PROGN (MAPC '(LAMBDA (X)
                          (OR (MEMBER X RESULT) (PUSH X RESULT)))
                       (CAR L))
                 (CDR L))))
     ((NULL L) (NREVERSE RESULT))))

(DEFUN INTERSECTION NARGS
  (AND (ZEROP NARGS)
       (ERROR '|HAS NO IDENTITY VALUE|
              'INTERSECTION
              'WRNG-TYPE-ARG))
  (DO ((RESULT (PROGN ($LISTCHECK (ARG 1.) 'INTERSECTION)
                      (ARG 1.))
               (MAPCAN '(LAMBDA (Z)
                          (AND (MEMBER Z (CAR CHECKLIST))
                               (NCONS Z)))
                       RESULT))
       (CHECKLIST (MAPC 'LAMBDA (X)
                          ($LISTCHECK X 'INTERSECTION))
                        (LISTIFY (DIFFERENCE 1. NARGS)))
                  (CDR CHECKLIST)))
      ((NULL CHECKLIST) RESULT)))
```

```
(DEFUN SETDIFFERENCE NARGS
  (PROG (INITIAL-SET SUBTRAHEND-SETS BIG-SUBTRAHEND)
    (AND (ZEROP NARGS) (RETURN NIL))
    (SETQ INITIAL-SET (ARG 1.))
    ($LISTCHECK INITIAL-SET 'SETDIFFERENCE)
    (SETQ SUBTRAHEND-SETS (LISTIFY (DIFFERENCE 1. NARGS)))
    (MAPC '(LAMBDA (X) ($LISTCHECK X 'SETDIFFERENCE))
          SUBTRAHEND-SETS)
    (SETQ BIG-SUBTRAHEND (APPLY 'UNION SUBTRAHEND-SETS))
    (RETURN (MAPCAN '(LAMBDA (Z)
                      (AND (NOT (MEMBER Z BIG-SUBTRAHEND))
                           (NCONS Z)))
                    INITIAL-SET))))

;;; Applicative operators defined here.
(DEFUN APPLY-TO-ALL NARGS
  (DO ((FN (PROGN ($ARGCHECK NARGS 'APPLY-TO-ALL) (ARG 1.)))
       (L (MAPC '(LAMBDA (X) ($LISTCHECK X 'APPLY-TO-ALL))
                (LISTIFY (DIFFERENCE 1. NARGS)))
          (MAPCAR 'CDR L))
       (RESULT NIL (CONS (APPLY FN (MAPCAR 'CAR L)) RESULT)))
    ((MEMQ NIL L) (NREVERSE RESULT))))

(DEFUN FIND-IF (FN X)
  ($LISTCHECK X 'FIND-IF)
  (DO ((L X (CDR L)))
    ((NULL L) NIL)
    (AND (FUNCALL FN (CAR L)) (RETURN (CAR L)))))

(DEFUN SUBSET (FN L)
  ($LISTCHECK L'SUBSET)
  (MAPCAN '(LAMBDA (X) (AND (APPLY FN (LIST X)) (NCONS X))) L))

(DEFUN EVERY NARGS
  (DO ((RESULT T (APPLY FN (MAPCAR 'CAR L)))
       (FN (PROGN ($ARGCHECK NARGS 'EVERY) (ARG 1.)))
       (L (MAPC '(LAMBDA (X) ($LISTCHECK X 'EVERY))
                (LISTIFY (DIFFERENCE 1. NARGS)))
          (MAPCAR 'CDR L)))
    ((OR (NULL RESULT) (MEMQ NIL L)) RESULT)))
```

```
;;; $LEXPR? is called by the reduce functions to test if a function is
;;; a lexpr. Note: if a symbol has multiple function properties, MacLisp
;;; uses the first one on the property list, so the FIRST definition must be
;;; a lexpr for this predicate to succeed. For LSUBR property: return T.
;;; For EXPR property: check if CADR of the lambda expression is a symbol
;;; and non-NIL. For functions passed as lambda expressions instead of as
;;; symbols, check the CADR directly.
(DEFUN $LEXPR? (FN)
  (COND ((SYMBOLP FN)
         (DO ((PROPS (PLIST FN) (CDR PROPS)))
           ((NULL PROPS) NIL)
           (COND ((MEMQ (CAR PROPS)
                        '(EXPR FEXPR MACRO SUBR LSUBR FSUBR))
                  (RETURN (OR (EQ (CAR PROPS) 'LSUBR)
                              (AND (EQ (CAR PROPS) 'EXPR)
                                   (LISTP (CADR PROPS))
                                   (SYMBOLP (CADADR PROPS))
                                   (CADADR PROPS))))))))
        ((LISTP FN)
         (AND (EQ (CAR FN) 'LAMBDA) (SYMBOLP (CADR FN)) (CADR FN)))
        (T NIL)))

;;; Reduce functions. REDUCE is defined here to work exactly as
;;; LEFT-REDUCE does. Technically, REDUCE is supposed to be ambiguous.
;;;
;;; Reduction works as follows. L is the list to be reduced.
;;; 1. If L holds two or more items, we do the obvious iteration.
;;; 2. If L holds one item and FN is a lexpr, we call FN with one input to
;;;    allow it to do type checking if it wishes.
;;; 3. If L holds one item and FN is not a lexpr, we return the item.
;;; 4. If L is empty and FN is a lexpr, we call FN with no inputs to get
;;;    its identity value.
;;; 5. If L is empty and FN is not a lexpr but is a symbol, and the symbol
;;;    has an IDENTITY property, we return the value of this property.
;;; 6. Otherwise we give a "no identity value" error.
```

```
(DEFUN REDUCE (FN L)
  ($LISTCHECK L 'REDUCE)
  (COND ((CDR L)
         (DO ((RESULT (CAR L) (FUNCALL FN RESULT (CAR X)))
              (X (CDR L) (CDR X)))
           ((NULL X) RESULT)))
        (($LEXPR? FN) (APPLY FN L))
        (L (CAR L))
        ((AND (SYMBOLP FN) (MEMQ 'IDENTITY (PLIST FN)))
         (GET FN 'IDENTITY))
        (T (ERROR '|- FUNCTION SUPPLIED HAS NO IDENTITY VALUE|
                  'REDUCE
                  'WRNG-TYPE-ARG))))

(DEFUN LEFT-REDUCE (FN L)
  ($LISTCHECK L 'LEFT-REDUCE)
  (COND ((CDR L)
         (DO ((RESULT (CAR L) (FUNCALL FN RESULT (CAR X)))
              (X (CDR L) (CDR X)))
           ((NULL X) RESULT)))
        (($LEXPR? FN) (APPLY FN L))
        (L (CAR L))
        ((AND (SYMBOLP FN) (MEMQ 'IDENTITY (PLIST FN)))
         (GET FN 'IDENTITY))
         (T (ERROR '|- FUNCTION SUPPLIED HAS NO IDENTITY VALUE|
                   'LEFT-REDUCE
                   'WRNG-TYPE-ARG))))
```

```
(DEFUN RIGHT-REDUCE (FN L)
  ($LISTCHECK L 'RIGHT-REDUCE)
  (COND ((CDR L)
         (DO ((RESULT (CAR (LAST L)) (FUNCALL FN (CAR X) RESULT))
              (X (CDR (REVERSE L)) (CDR X)))
           ((NULL X) RESULT)))
        (($LEXPR? FN) (APPLY FN L))
        (L (CAR L))
        ((AND (SYMBOLP FN) (MEMQ 'IDENTITY (PLIST FN)))
         (GET FN 'IDENTITY))
        (T (ERROR '|- FUNCTION SUPPLIED HAS NO IDENTITY VALUE|
                  'RIGHT-REDUCE
                  'WRNG-TYPE-ARG))))
```

Appendix **D**

Answers to Exercises

Introduction

pages 7–8

1. Computers route your phone calls, figure your gas bill, print the address labels on much of your mail, control the electronic cash register in the cafeteria where you eat lunch, and, even as you read this, maintain the date and time in the digital watch on your wrist.

2. People buy home computers for many different reasons. If you *did* buy one, I hope it runs Lisp. (Lisp is available for any machine that runs Unix or CP/M. It is also available for Apple machines.)

3. Many reasons could account for the failure of the prediction:

   - The economist's theory could be wrong, or incomplete.
   - The theory could be right, but the computer program that expresses the theory could contain an error.
   - The program could be correct but the computer it ran on could have malfunctioned in such a way that the results it produced looked plausible but were wrong. (This is rare but not unheard of.)
   - The economist's understanding of, or description of, the current state of the economy could be in error. Garbage in, garbage out.
   - The description of the economy could be correct, but it could have been entered into the computer incorrectly (e.g., a zero was left off one of the critical numbers).

- Important but unforseen events, such as war breaking out unexpectedly, may have occurred after the prediction was made.

4. Until a truly intelligent computer is demonstrated, there will be no firm answer to this question. One popular argument in favor of the possibility of thinking computers, based on an approach called *reductionism,* goes as follows. The mind is a function of the brain. The brain is composed of nerve cells, called neurons. Neurons are physical objects that operate according to the laws of chemistry and physics. These laws can be represented as equations understandable by a computer. Therefore, if we write a computer program to solve the equations for the behavior of neurons and feed the program a description of all the neurons found in a human brain (including connections to other neurons), we will have a simulation of a human mind.

   This argument is not without its flaws, as the opposing side is quick to point out. For example, no one has shown that mental phenomena—what occurs in the mind—correspond completely to physical phenomena—what occurs in the brain. (Those who believe the two classes of phenomena are distinct are called *dualists.* Descartes was one.) Another objection is that the human brain is so incredibly complex, involving billions of neurons and trillions of connections, that it may be impossible to describe one in sufficient detail to construct an accurate simulation.

   Naturally the reductionists have answers to these objections. I leave it as an exercise for you to come up with some of your own. For more information on artificial intelligence and the celebrated mind/body problem, see the list of recommended readings in appendix A.

Chapter 1

pages 11–12

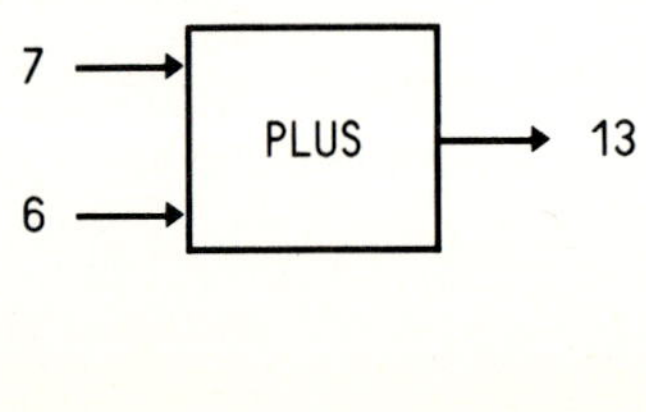

3
4
TIMES
12

16
8
QUOTIENT
2

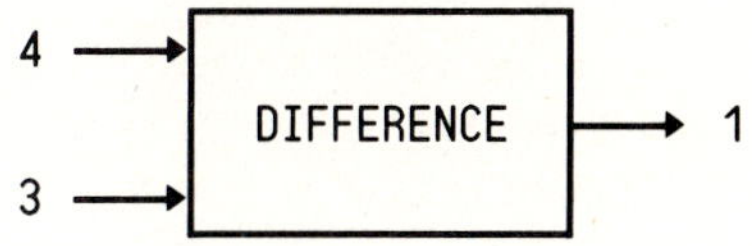
4
3
DIFFERENCE
1

8
3
REMAINDER
2

5
ADD1
6

2
SUB1
1

pages 12–13

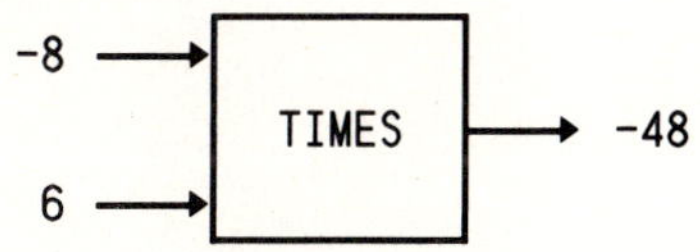
-8
6
TIMES
-48

17
3
QUOTIENT
5

8
0
PLUS
8

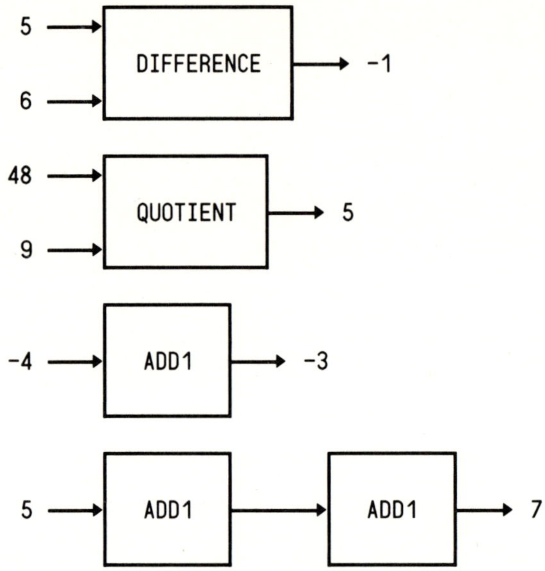

page 14

Symbols: **AARDVARK**, **PLUMBING**, **1-2-3-GO**, **TIMES**, **ZEROP**, **ZERO**, **SEVENTEEN**.
Numbers: 87, 1492, 314159265358979, 0, −12.

pages 17–18

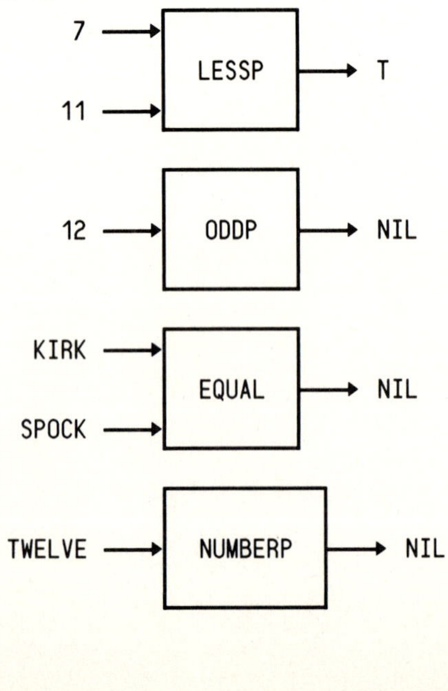

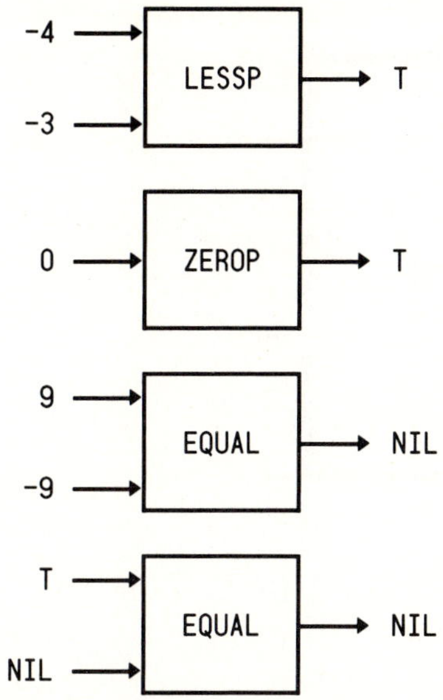

pages 21–22

1. Definition of ADD2:

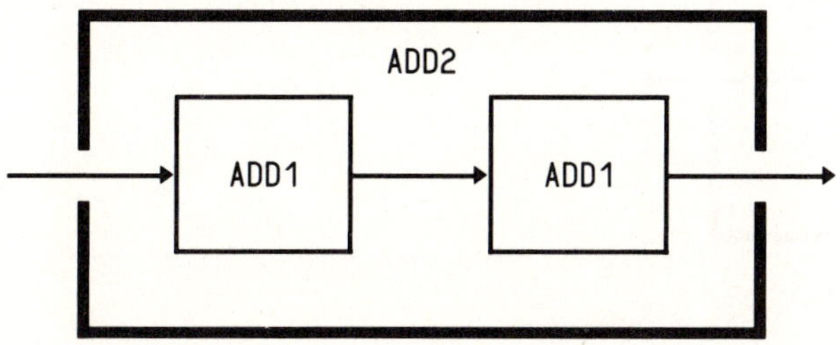

Definition of TWOMOREP:

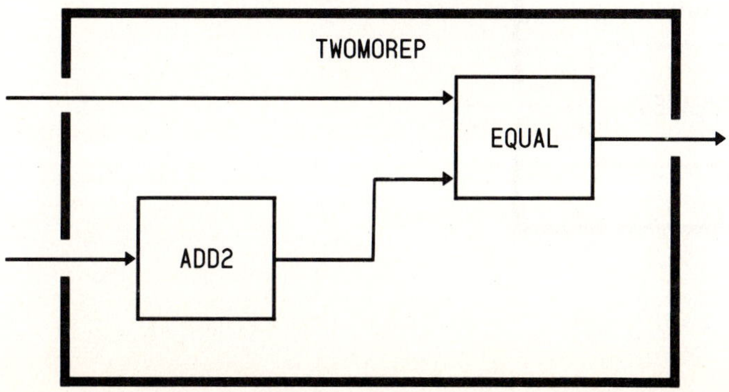

2. Definition of TWOMOREP:

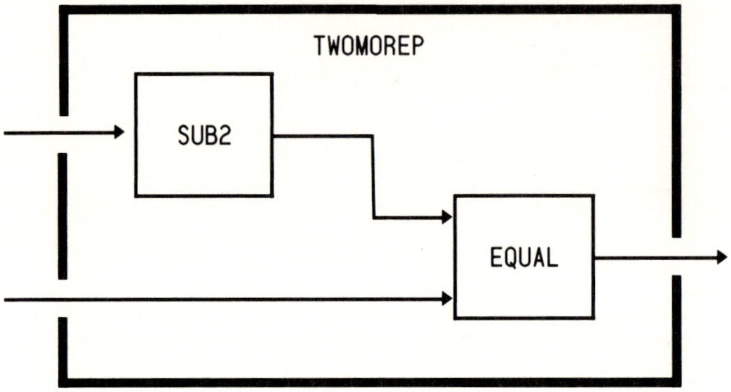

3. If we changed the constant to -1 we'd have MINUS, a function that returns the negation of a number.

4. Definition of ADD50:

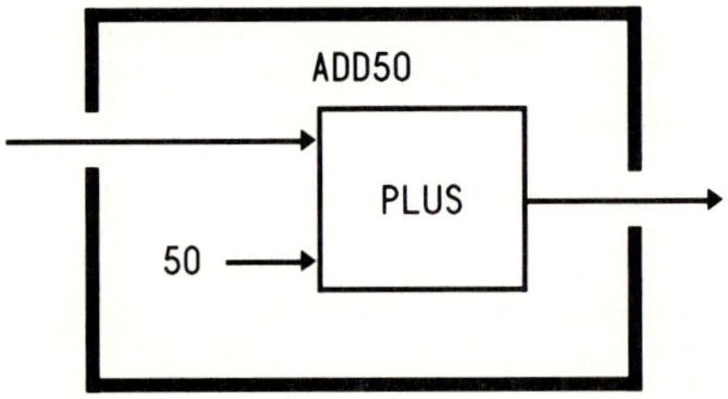

5. The POSITIVEP predicate can be written two ways:

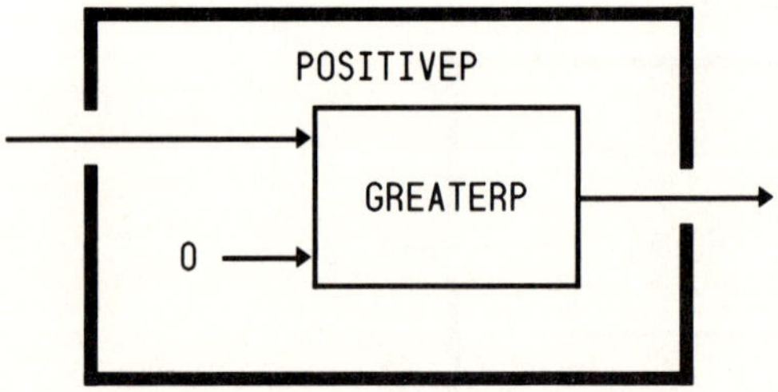

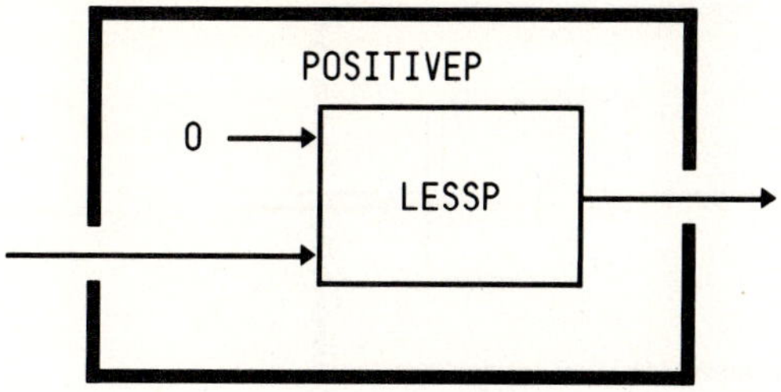

6. Definition of FREDP:

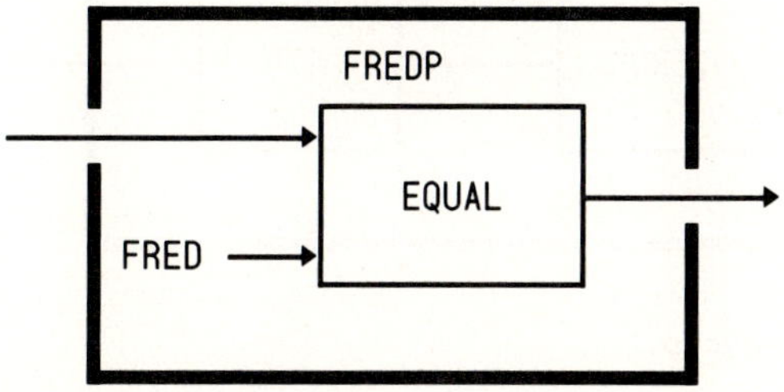

page 23

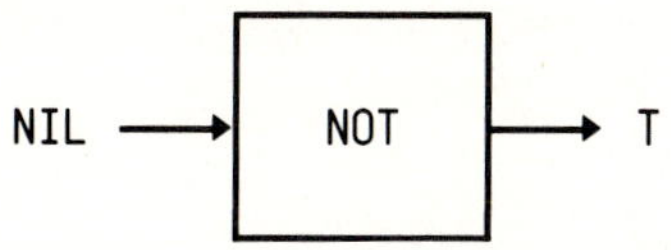

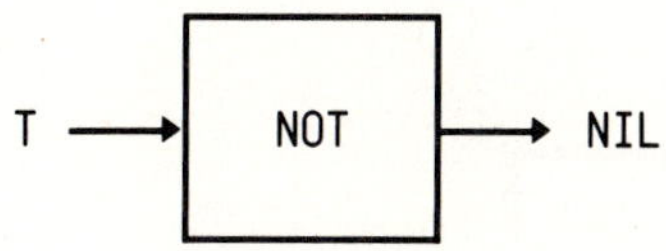

pages 24–25

1. The NOT-ONEP predicate can be written in several ways. Here are two of them:

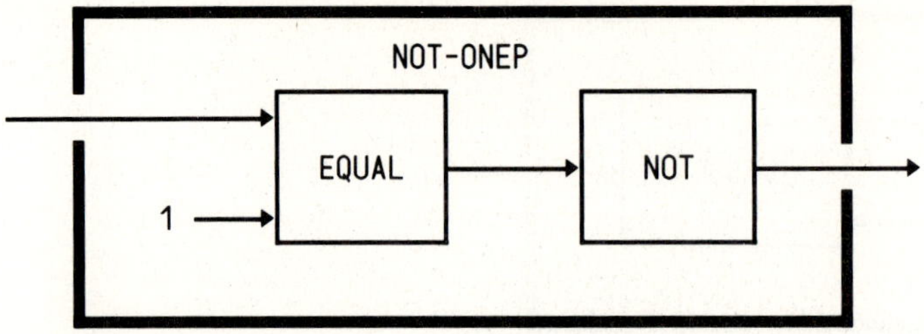

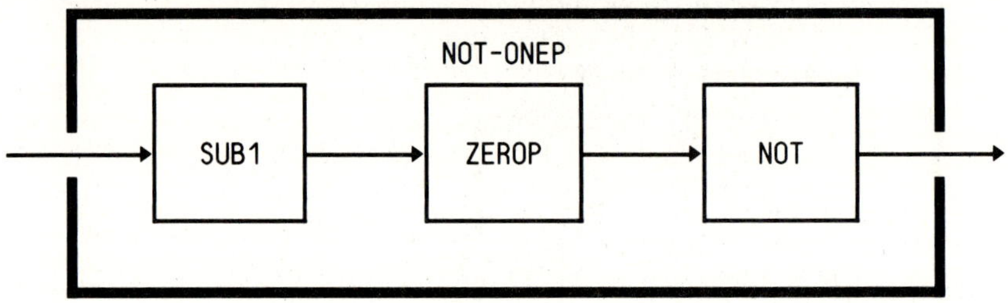

2. Definition of EVENP:

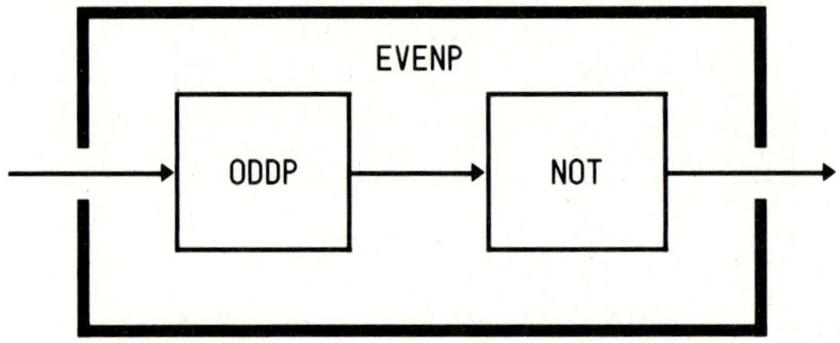

3. Definition of LESS-THAN-OR-EQUAL:

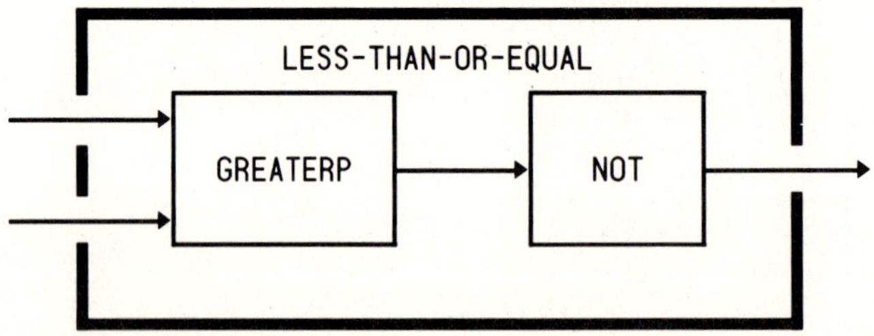

4. Only when the input is negative 2.

5. For the input NIL, it returns NIL. For the input T, it returns T. For the input RUTABAGA, it returns T, *not* RUTABAGA. Thus data does not flow through the function unchanged except for the special cases

T and NIL. What does remain unchanged is the truth or falsity of the data—for example, for any *true* input, the result will be *true*.

6. The definition of XOR is the same as that of NOT-EQUAL.

page 27

1.

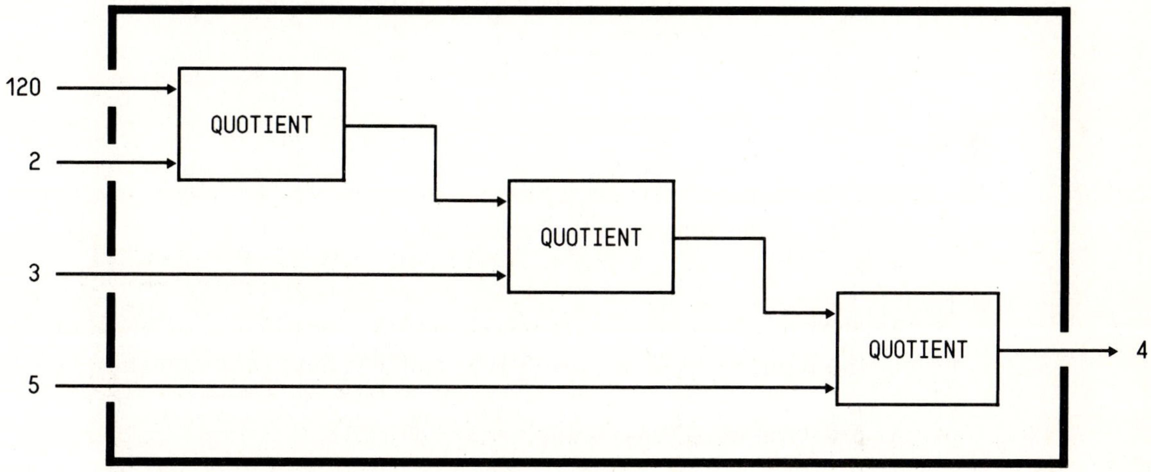

2. ZEROP will produce T or NIL as a result, but the input to ADD1 must be a number.

3. EQUAL must be given two inputs, not one.

page 28

1. Not all functions are predicates. PLUS is a function but it is not a predicate since it does not return T or NIL. All predicates *are* functions, however.

2. EQUAL and NOT.

3. SYMBOL and NUMBER are both symbols. An example of a number is 37.

4.

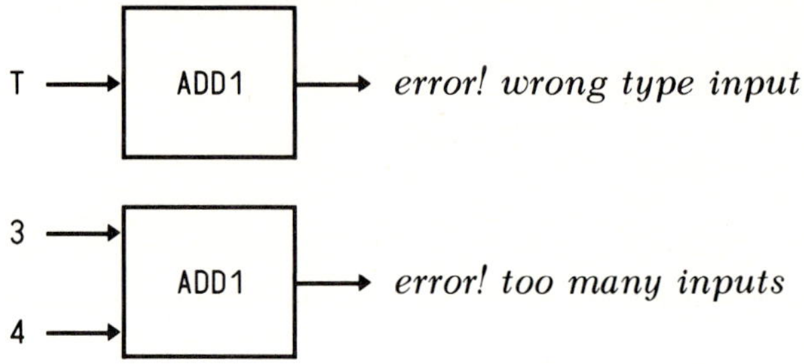

pages 33–34

1. The domain and range of Minus is **number.** Minus is closed over numbers. Some smaller sets over which Minus is closed are {−1,1} and {−3, −2, −1, 0, 1, 2, 3}.

2. NOT is not closed over the domain {FOO, NIL} because when NIL is the input to NOT the result is T, and T is not in the domain.

3. The type of EQUAL is `any × any → {T, NIL}`

   The type of TRI-PLUS is `number × number × number → number`

4. QUOTIENT isn't related to the other arithmetic primitives in a simple way, although it has a kind of partial inverse relation with TIMES. One number can be divided by another using successive subtractions, but we'd need a primitive to subtract repeatedly and a way to know when to stop.

5. Not all predicates are truth functions. ODDP, for example, is a predicate that does not accept T or NIL as an input. Therefore it is not a truth function.

6. There are four distinct one-input truth functions: one that always returns T, one that always returns NIL, one that returns T for T and NIL for NIL, and the NOT predicate that returns NIL for T and T for NIL. There are sixteen distinct two-input truth functions.

Chapter 2

pages 36–37

Ill-formed	Well-formed
`)A B(`	`((A) (B))`
`(A B (C`	`(A (B (C)))`
`A B ) (C D)`	
`(A (B (C))`	

page 37

6 elements: `(OPEN THE POD BAY DOORS HAL)`

3 elements: `((OPEN) (THE POD BAY DOORS) HAL)`

4 elements: `((1 2 3) (4 5 6) (7 8 9) (10 11 12))`

4 elements: `((ALL) FOR ONE (AND (TWO (FOR ME))))`

5 elements:
```
((Q SPADES)
 (7 HEARTS)
 (6 CLUBS)
 (5 DIAMONDS)
 (2 DIAMONDS))
```

6 elements:
```
((PENNSYLVANIA (THE KEYSTONE STATE))
 (NEW-JERSEY (THE GARDEN STATE))
 (MASSACHUSETTS (THE BAY STATE))
 (FLORIDA (THE SUNSHINE STATE))
 (NEW-YORK (THE EMPIRE STATE))
 (INDIANA (THE HOOSIER STATE)))
```

page 38

List	Matching List
()	NIL
(())	(NIL)
((()))	((NIL))
(() ())	(NIL NIL)
(() (()))	(NIL (NIL))

page 42

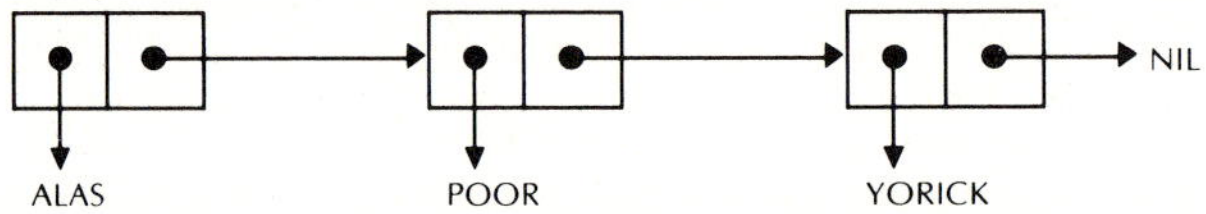

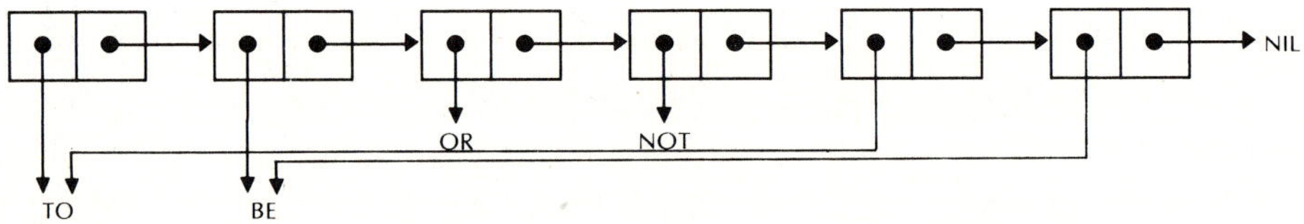

pages 45–46

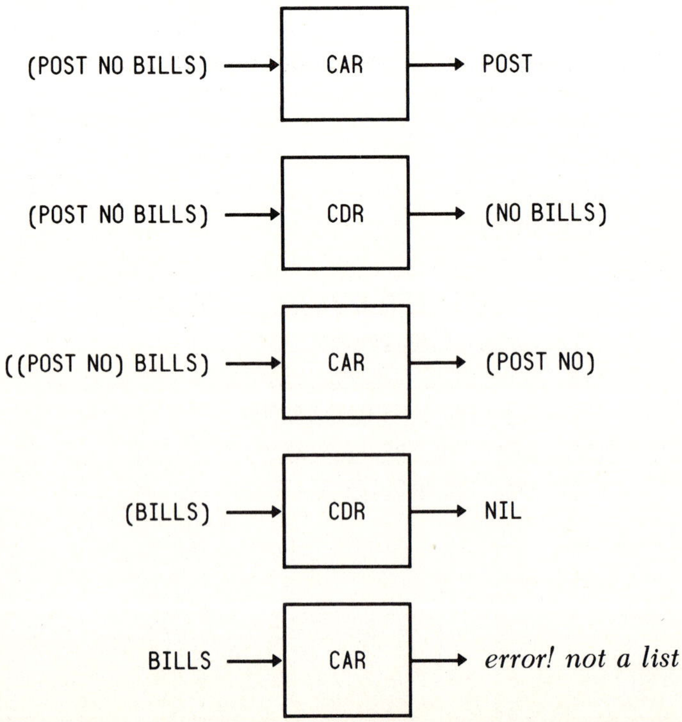

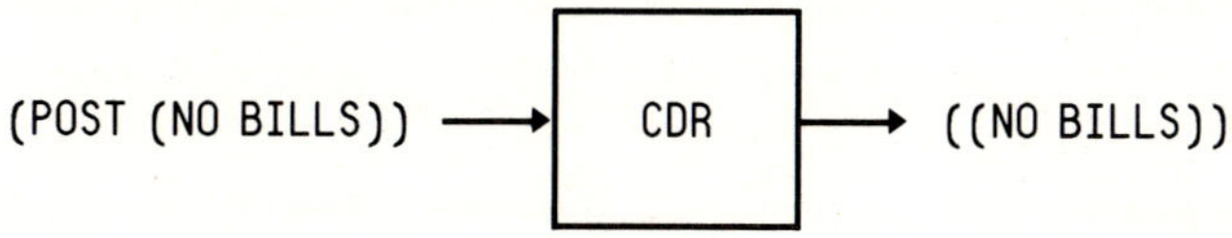

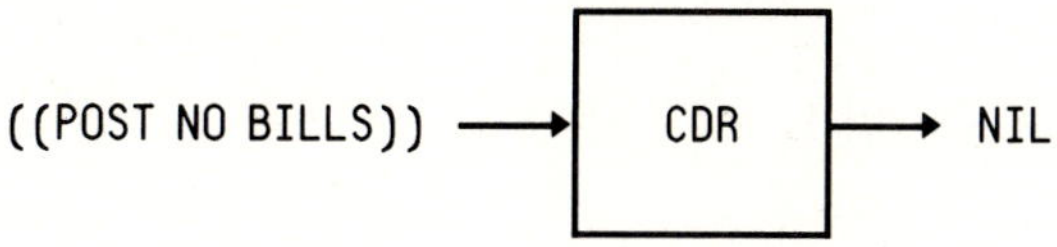

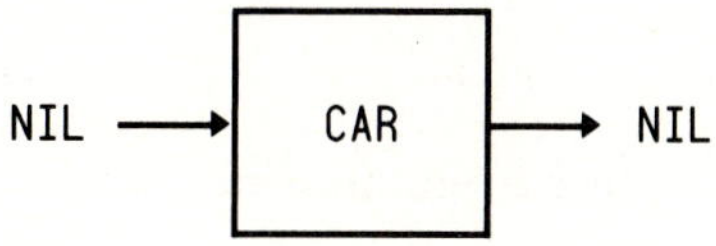

page 50

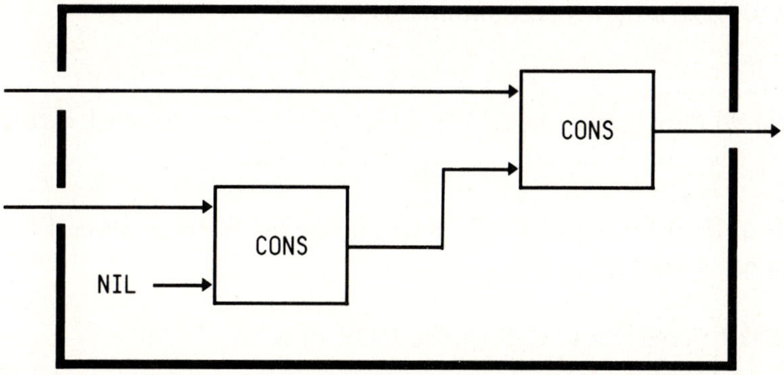

pages 53–54

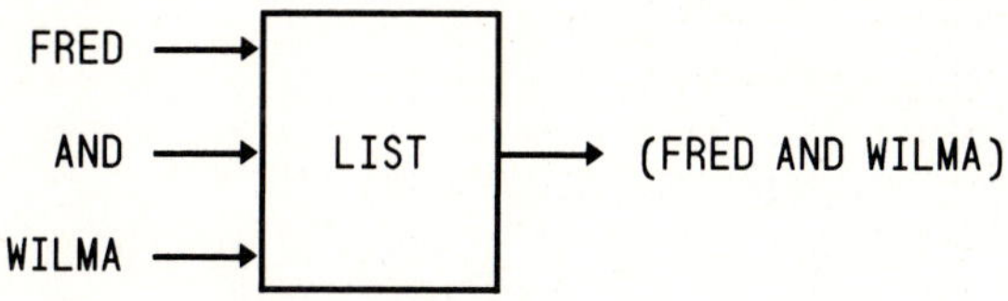

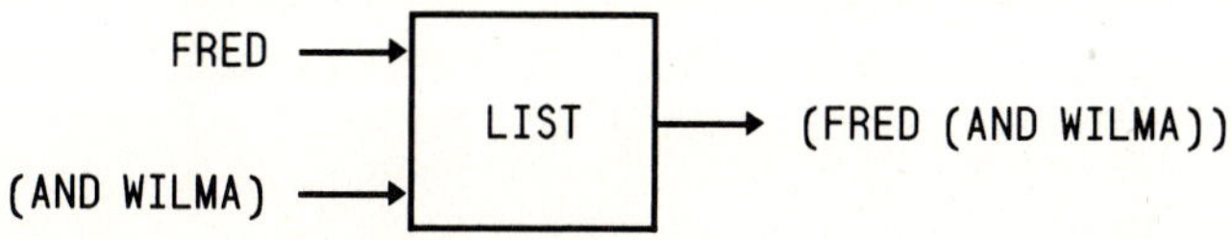

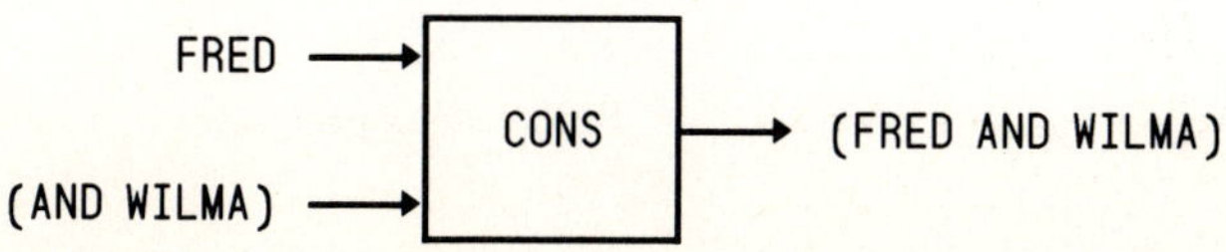

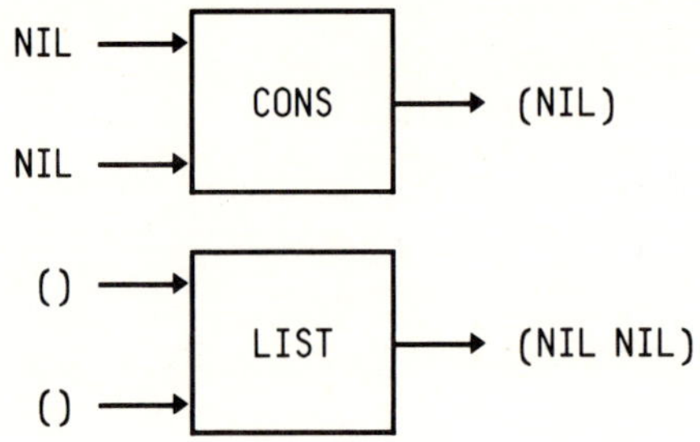

page 56

1. CADDDR extracts the fourth element of a list.

2. "Ka-dih-dih-der"

3. CADDDDDDR, which contains six Ds.

4. The first thing the function does is take the CDR of (FRED), which is NIL. All the following CDRs and the CAR at the end return NIL when their input is NIL, so the result is NIL.

5. CAR of (FRED) is FRED. CAR of that gives an error, since FRED is a symbol, not a list.

6. CADDR takes the CADR of the CDR of a list.

page 57

Function	Result
CAR	(A B)
CDDR	((E F))
CADR	(C D)
CDAR	(B)
CADAR	B
CDDAR	NIL
CAAR	A
CDADDR	(F)
CADADDR	F

pages 60–61

1.

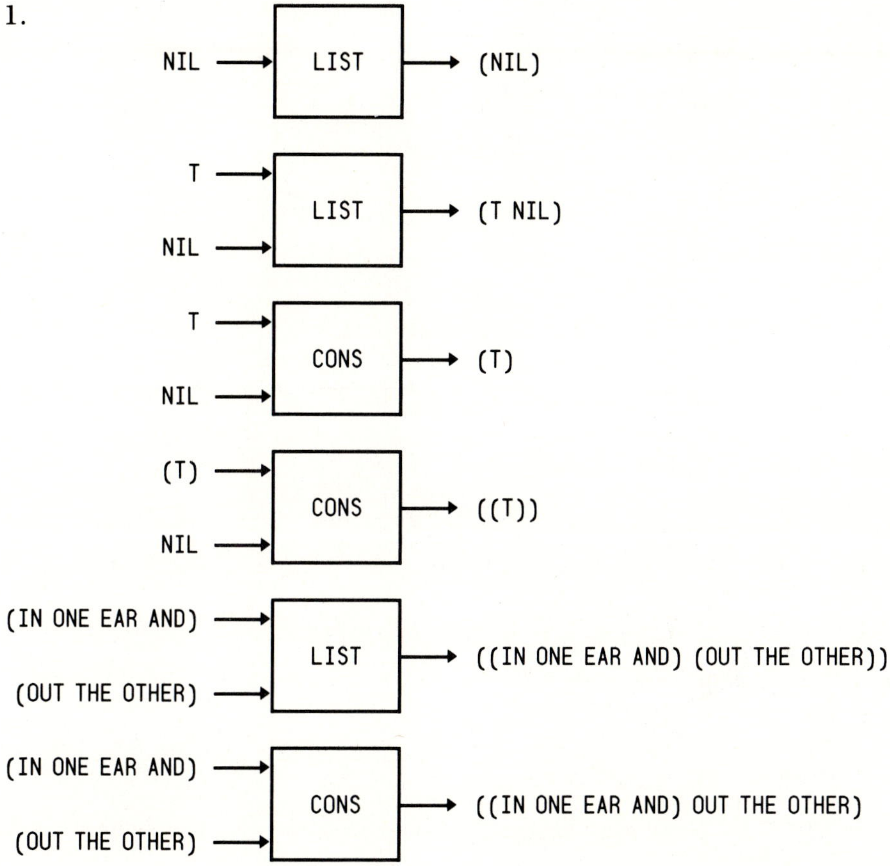

2.

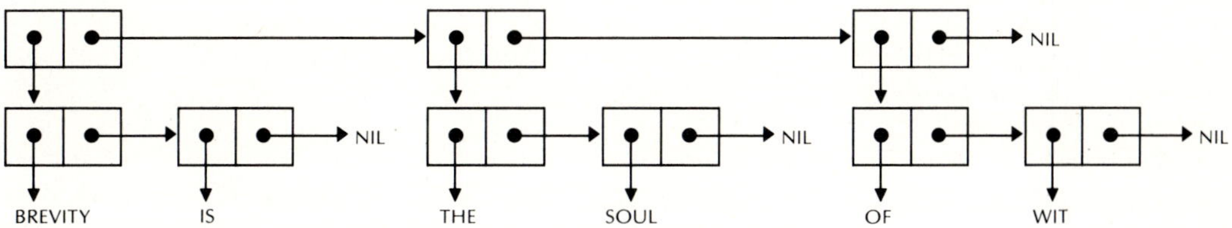

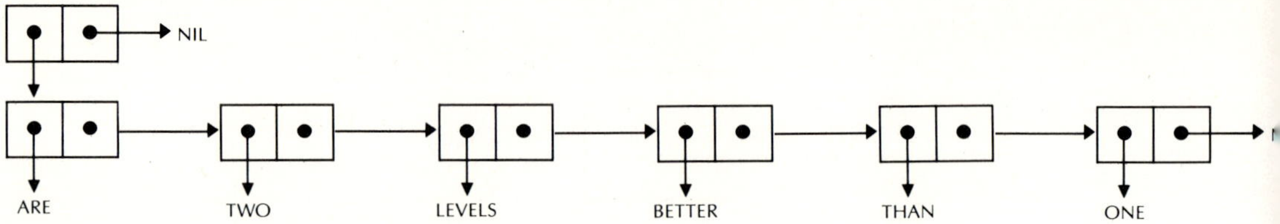
NIL
ARE
TWO
LEVELS
BETTER
THAN
ONE

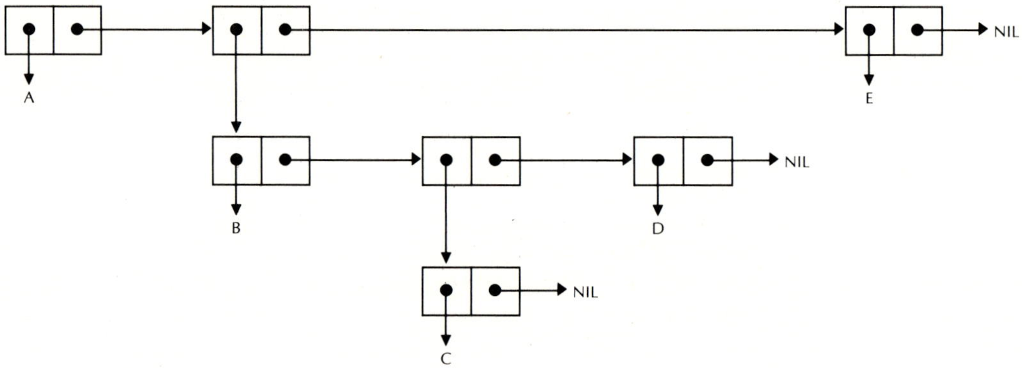
NIL
A
E
NIL
B
D
NIL
C

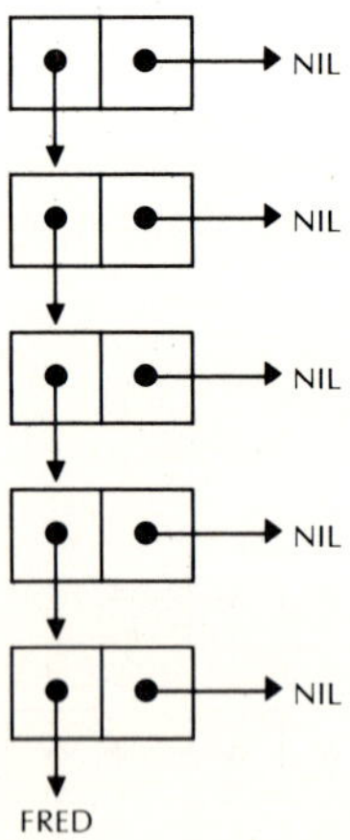
NIL
NIL
NIL
NIL
NIL
FRED

3.

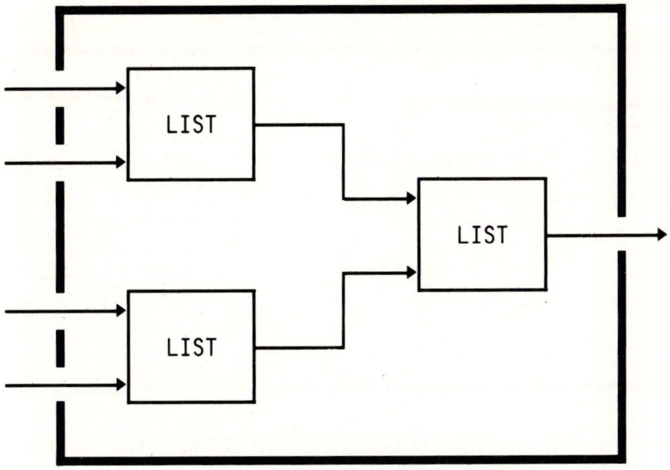

4. Definition of DUO-CONS:

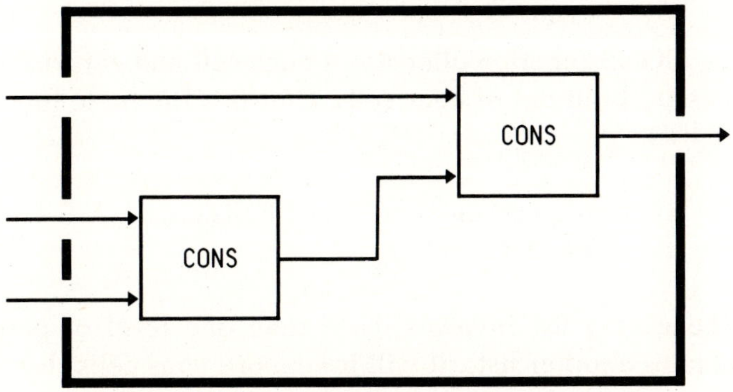

5. Here are two definitions for TWO-DEEPER:

Definition of TWO-DEEPER:

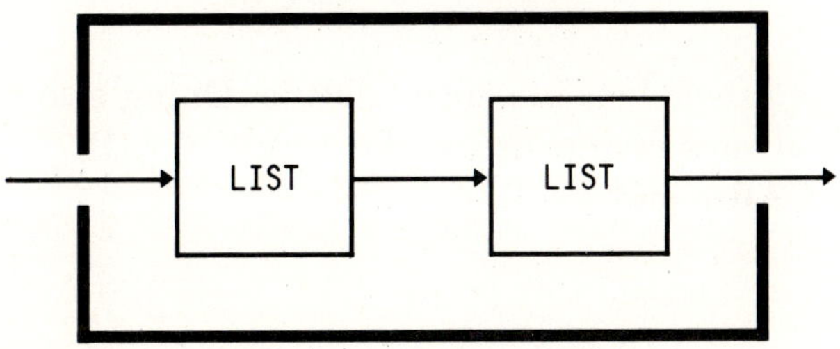

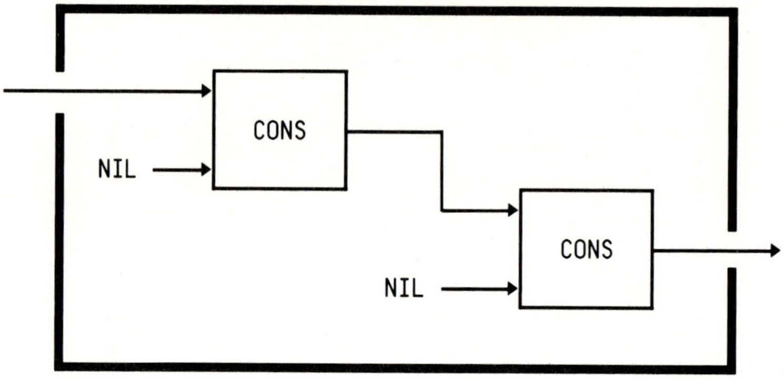

6. The function's name is CADADDR. It takes the CADR of the CADDR of the list.

page 62

1. The CONS function allocates a cons cell and returns a pointer to it. Lists are built out of cons cells. CONS is the basic function for building lists.

2. The function gives an error. The LENGTH of (A B C) is 3; you can't take the CDR of a number.

3. Whenever a list involves more than one level of parentheses (i.e., contains another list), it will have more cons cells than elements.

4. No, you can't return the last element of a list of arbitrary length because you can't know in advance how many CDRs to do.

page 64

CDDR is closed over lists because CDR is. Doing two CDRs in succession will still always give a list as the result. CADR is not closed over lists because CAR is not.

page 65

1. Definition of UNARY-ADD1:

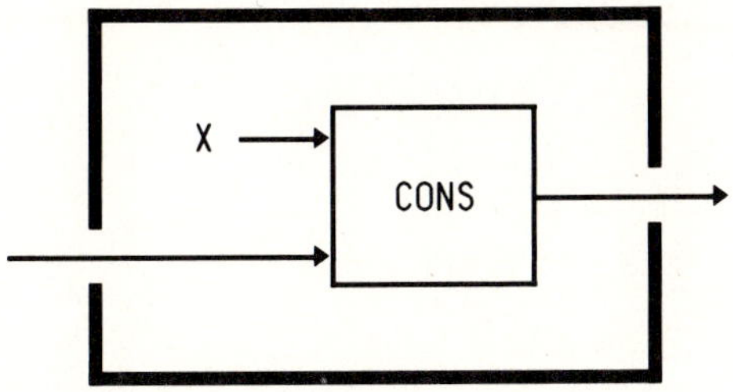

2. CDDR is the unary equivalent of SUB2—it subtracts two from a unary number.

3. NOT is the unary ZEROP function. Another way to test for unary zero is:

Definition of UNARY-ZEROP:

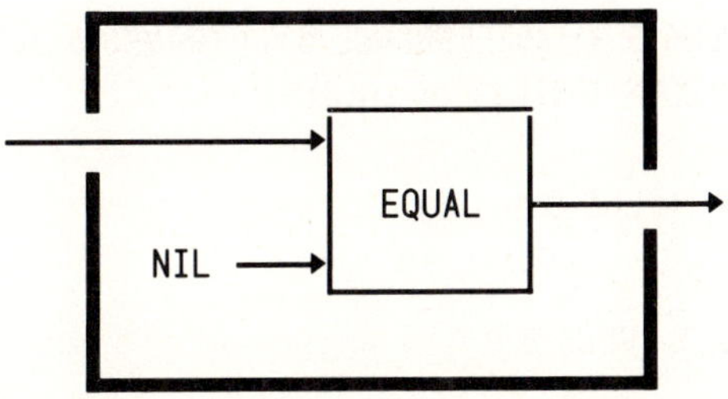

4. Definition of UNARY-GREATERP:

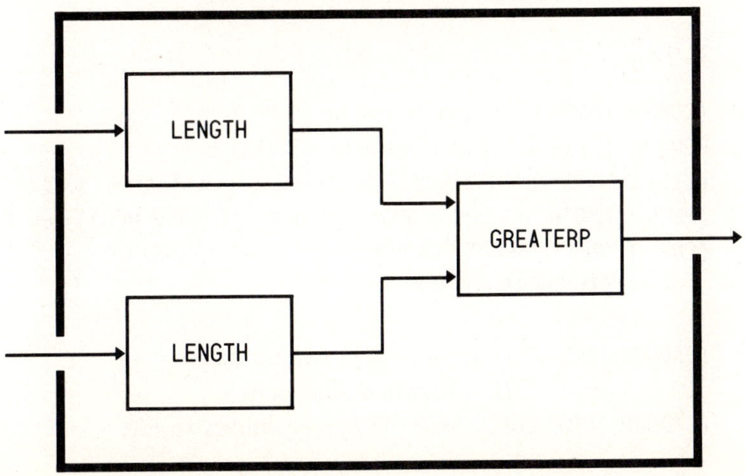

5. CAR is the unary equivalent of the POSITIVEP predicate. It returns NIL (false) for a unary zero and **X** (which is considered true) for any positive unary input.

Chapter 3

page 69

1. `(DIFFERENCE 8 2)` evaluates to `6`
   `(CONS NIL NIL)` evaluates to `(NIL)`
   `(EQUAL 5 (ADD1 4))` evaluates to `T`
   `(NOT (ODDP 4))` evaluates to `T`
   `(LIST (PLUS 5 3) (DIFFERENCE 5 3) (TIMES 5 3))` evaluates to `(8 2 15)`
   `(LENGTH (CONS T NIL))` evaluates to `1`

2. `(QUOTIENT (PLUS 8 12) 2)`

3. `(LIST 1 2 T (PLUS 8 9))`

4. `(PLUS (TIMES 3 3) (TIMES 4 4))`

pages 73–74

1. `(CONS 5 (LIST 6 7))` evaluates to `(5 6 7)`
   `CONS 5 '(LIST 6 7))` evaluates to `(5 LIST 6 7)`
   `(LIST 3 'FROM 9 'GIVES (DIFFERENCE 9 3))` evaluates to `(3 FROM 9 GIVES 6)`
   `(PLUS (LENGTH '(1 FOO 2 MOO)) (CADDR '(1 FOO 2 MOO)))` evaluates to `6`
   `(CDR '(CONS IS SHORT FOR CONSTRUCT))` evaluates to
   `(IS SHORT FOR CONSTRUCT)`

2. `(CADDDR (THE QUICK BROWN FOX))` evaluates to
   error! THE undefined function
   `(CADDDR '(THE QUICK BROWN FOX))` evaluates to `FOX`

`(LIST 2 AND 2 IS 4)` evaluates to *error! AND unbound variable*
`(LIST 2 'AND 2 'IS 4)` evaluates to `(2 AND 2 IS 4)`

`(SUB1 '(LENGTH (LIST T T T T)))` evaluates to *error! wrong type input*
`(SUB1 (LENGTH (LIST T T T T)))` evaluates to 3

`(CONS 'PATRICK (SEYMOUR MARVIN))` evaluates to
error! SEYMOUR undefined function
`(CONS 'PATRICK '(SEYMOUR MARVIN))` evaluates to
`(PATRICK SEYMOUR MARVIN)`

`(CONS 'PATRICK (LIST SEYMOUR MARVIN)` evaluates to
error! SEYMOUR unbound variable
`(CONS 'PATRICK (LIST 'SEYMOUR 'MARVIN))` evaluates to
`(PATRICK SEYMOUR MARVIN)`

pages 75–76

1. `(DEFUN CUBE (X) (TIMES X (TIMES X X)))`

2. `(DEFUN AVERAGE (X Y) (QUOTIENT (PLUS X Y) 2))`

3. `(DEFUN LONGER-THAN (X Y) (GREATERP (LENGTH X) (LENGTH Y)))`

4. `(DEFUN ADDLENGTH (X) (CONS (LENGTH X) X))`

   `(ADDLENGTH (ADDLENGTH '(A B C)))` evaluates to `(4 3 A B C)`

5. CALL-UP requires two arguments. Their names are CALLER and CALLEE. (CALL-UP 'FRED 'WANDA) evaluates to (HELLO WANDA THIS IS FRED CALLING).

6. (CRANK-CALL 'WANDA 'FRED) evaluates to (HELLO CALLEE THIS IS CALLER CALLING). The problem is that the entire list is quoted, so the variables CALLER and CALLEE never get evaluated.

7.
```
(DEFUN MILES-PER-GALLON (INITIAL-ODOMETER-READING
                         FINAL-ODOMETER-READING
                         GALLONS-CONSUMED)
  (QUOTIENT (DIFFERENCE  FINAL-ODOMETER-READING
                         INITIAL-ODOMETER-READING)
            GALLONS CONSUMED))
```

8. Definition of SQUARE:

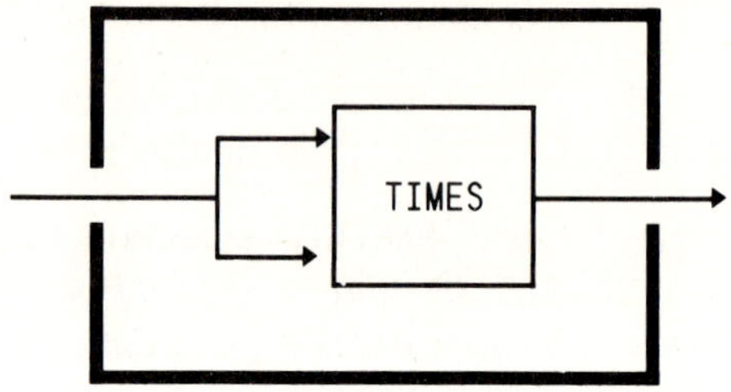

pages 78–79

1. (DEFUN ADD50 (X) (PLUS X 50))

```
X is unbound
   ┌── (ADD50 37)
   │
X = 37          (PLUS X 50) evaluates to 87
   │
   └── ADD50 returns 87
X is unbound again
```

2. WORD is used both as a variable (when it is unquoted) and as a constant (when it is quoted). (SCRABBLE 'AARDVARK) returns (AARDVARK IS A WORD). (SCRABBLE 'WORD) returns (WORD IS A WORD).

3. The variable LARRY is bound to MOE; the variable MOE is bound to CURLY; and the variable CURLY is bound to LARRY. The result of the expression is (MOE (MOE LARRY) LARRY LARRY).

4. Lisp requires that T always evaluate to T and NIL always evaluate to NIL. If T and NIL were used as variables they would have to be bound to the function's inputs; they would not evaluate to themselves.

page 80

1. Functions are easier to type on a computer terminal in EVAL notation than in box notation. EVAL notation supports programming concepts

that are too sophisticated for box notation. EVAL notation makes it possible to use functions as inputs to other functions. Representing functions as data (i.e., lists) is a mathematically elegant thing to do; it lets us use a single notation for both.

2. `(CONS 'GRAPES '(OF WRATH))` evaluates to `(GRAPES OF WRATH)`
   `(LIST T 'IS 'NOT NIL)` evaluates to `(T IS NOT NIL)`
   `(CAR '(LIST MOOSE GOOSE))` evaluates to `LIST`
   `(CAR (LIST 'MOOSE 'GOOSE))` evaluates to `MOOSE`
   `(CADR '(WE HOLD THESE TRUTHS))` evaluates to `HOLD`
   `(CONS 'HOME ('SWEET 'HOME))` evaluates to
   error! 'SWEET undefined function

3. `(MYSTERY '(DANCING BEAR))` evaluates to `(BEAR DANCING)`
   `(MYSTERY 'DANCING 'BEAR)` evaluates to *error! too many inputs*
   `(MYSTERY '(ZOWIE))` evaluates to `(NIL ZOWIE)`
   `(MYSTERY (LIST 'FIRST 'SECOND))` evaluates to `(SECOND FIRST)`

4. `(DEFUN SPEAK (X Y) (LIST 'ALL 'X 'IS 'Y))`
   Variables X and Y should not be quoted.
   `(DEFUN SPEAK (X) (Y) (LIST 'ALL X 'IS Y))`
   Argument list should be (X Y).
   `(DEFUN SPEAK ((X) (Y)) (LIST ALL 'X IS 'Y))`
   Bad argument list. Also, X and Y are variables and should not be quoted in the body. ALL and IS should be quoted but are not.

pages 85–86

1. —

2. `(PLUS 3 5)` evaluates to `8`
   `(3 PLUS 5)` evaluates to *error! 3 undefined function*
   `(PLUS 3 (5 6))` evaluates to *error! 5 undefined function*
   `(PLUS 3 (TIMES 5 6))` evaluates to `33`
   `'(MORNING NOON NIGHT)` evaluates to `(MORNING NOON NIGHT)`
   `('MORNING 'NOON 'NIGHT)` evaluates to
   error! 'MORNING undefined function
   `(LIST 'MORNING 'NOON 'NIGHT)` evaluates to `(MORNING NOON NIGHT)`

`(CAR NIL)` evaluates to `NIL`
`(PLUS 3 FOO)` evaluates to *error! FOO unbound variable*
`(PLUS 3 'FOO)` evaluates to *error! wrong type input*

3. (DEFUN MYFUN (X Y) (LIST (LIST X) Y))

4. (DEFUN FIRSTP (X Y) (EQUAL X (CAR Y)))

5. (DEFUN MID-ADD1 (X)
 (LIST (CAR X) (ADD1 (CADR X)) (CADDR X)))

6. (DEFUN F-TO-C (X)
 (QUOTIENT (TIMES 5 (DIFFERENCE X 32)) 9))

7. ZEROP is going to return either T or NIL; you can't add 1 to that. (FOO 5) gives a wrong-type input error.

8. —

page 87

HALF:	$\lambda x.(x/2)$
SQUARE:	$\lambda x.(x^2)$
ONEMOREP:	$\lambda(x,y).(x=(y+1))$

page 91

```
X, Y, and Z are unbound
  ┌── (ALPHA 2 3)
  │
X = 2     (DIFFERENCE (BRAVO X) (CHARLIE (ADD1 Y) Y))
Y = 3
  │
  │            ┌── BRAVO of 2
  │            │
  │          Y = 2    (TIMES X Y) evaluates to 4
  │            │
  │            └── BRAVO returns 4
  │
Y = 3 again
  │
  │            ┌── CHARLIE of 4 and 3
  │            │
  │          Y = 4
  │          Z = 3    (TIMES Y (SUB1 Z)) evaluates to 8
  │            │
  │            └── CHARLIE returns 8
  │
Y = 3 again
Z is unbound again
  │
  └── ALPHA returns -4
X and Y become unbound again
```

page 93

`(LIST 'CONS T NIL)` evaluates to `(CONS T NIL)`
`(EVAL (LIST 'CONS T NIL))` evaluates to `(T)`
`(EVAL (EVAL (LIST 'CONS T NIL)))` evaluates to
  error! T undefined function
`(APPLY 'CONS '(T NIL))` evaluates to `(T)`
`(EVAL NIL)` evaluates to `NIL`
`(LIST 'EVAL NIL)` evaluates to `(EVAL NIL)`
`(EVAL (LIST 'EVAL NIL))` evaluates to `NIL`

Chapter 4

pages 97–98

1. `(DEFUN MAKE-EVEN (X) (IF (ODDP X) (ADD1 X) X))`

2. `(DEFUN FURTHER (X) (IF (GREATERP X 0) (ADD1 X) (SUB1 X)))`

   This version of **FURTHER** turns 0 into -1.

3. `(DEFUN MY-NOT (X) (IF X NIL T))`

4. `(DEFUN ORDERED (X Y) (IF (LESSP X Y) (LIST X Y) (LIST Y X)))`

page 99

`(COMPARE 9 1)`	*clause 3*
`(COMPARE (PLUS 2 2) 5)`	*clause 2*
`(COMPARE 6 (TIMES 2 3))`	*clause 1*

page 100

```
(DEFUN ABS (X)
  (COND ((LESSP X 0) (MINUS X))
        (T X)))
```

pages 103–104

1.
```
(COND (SYMBOLP X) 'SYMBOL          parens around first clause missing
      (T 'NOT-A-SYMBOL))

(COND ((SYMBOL X) 'SYMBOL)         this is the correct version
      (T 'NOT-A-SYMBOL))

(COND ((SYMBOL X) ('SYMBOL))       should not parenthesize 'SYMBOL
      (T 'NOT-A-SYMBOL))

(COND ((SYMBOLP X) 'SYMBOL)        extra parens around second clause
      ((T 'NOT-A-SYMBOL)))
```

2.
```
(DEFUN EMPHASIZE3 (X)
  (COND ((EQUAL (CAR X) 'GOOD) (CONS 'GREAT (CDR X)))
        ((EQUAL (CAR X) 'BAD) (CONS 'AWFUL (CDR X)))
        (T (CONS 'VERY X))))
```

(EMPHASIZE3 '(VERY LONG DAY)) returns (VERY VERY LONG DAY)

3.
```
(DEFUN EMPHASIZE4 (X)
  (COND ((EQUAL (CAR X) 'GOOD) (CONS 'GREAT (CDR X)))
        ((EQUAL (CAR X) 'BAD) (CONS 'AWFUL (CDR X)))
        ((EQUAL (CAR X) 'NICE) (CONS 'EXCEPTIONAL (CDR X)))
        ((EQUAL (CAR X) 'POOR) (CONS 'ABYSMAL (CDR X)))
        (T (CONS 'VERY X))))
```

4. The definition as typed has (T X) as the first clause instead of the last. Therefore, the second clause will never be reached. The function will always return its input unchanged. Here is a correct version:

```
(DEFUN MAKE-ODD (X)
  (COND ((NOT (ODDP X)) (ADD1 X))
        (T X)))
```

5.
```
(DEFUN FIRSTZERO (X)
  (COND ((ZEROP (CAR X)) 'FIRST)
        ((ZEROP (CADR X)) 'SECOND)
        ((ZEROP (CADDR X)) 'THIRD)
        (T 'NONE)))
```

If you call **FIRSTZERO** with three inputs instead of a list of three numbers, you will get a too-many-inputs error.

6.
```
(DEFUN CYCLE (X)
  (COND ((EQUAL X 99) 1)
        (T (ADD1 X))))
```

7.
```
(DEFUN HOWCOMPUTE (X Y Z)
  (COND ((EQUAL Z (PLUS X Y)) 'SUM-OF)
        ((EQUAL Z (TIMES X Y)) 'PRODUCT-OF)
        (T '(BEATS ME))))
```

We could extend HOWCOMPUTE by adding COND clauses to test for DIFFERENCE, QUOTIENT, and REMAINDER. In the case of QUOTIENT we must first check that Y is not zero, or else the expression (EQUAL Z (QUOTIENT X Y)) could cause a division-by-zero error.

page 106

(AND 'FEE 'FIE 'FOE) evaluates to FOE
(OR 'FEE 'FIE' FOE) evaluates to FEE
(OR NIL 'FOE NIL) evaluates to FOE
(AND 'FEE 'FIE NIL) evaluates to NIL
(AND (EQUAL 'ABC 'ABC) 'YES) evaluates to YES
(OR (EQUAL 'ABC 'ABC) 'YES) evaluates to T

page 108

1.
```
(DEFUN GEQ (X Y)
  (OR (GREATERP X Y) (EQUAL X Y)))
```

2.
```
(DEFUN FOO (X)
  (COND ((AND (ODDP X) (GREATERP X 0)) (TIMES X X))
        ((AND (ODDP X) (LESSP X 0)) (PLUS X X))
        (T (QUOTIENT X 2))))
```

3. This function can be written in many ways. Here are two of them:

```
(DEFUN TEST (X Y)
  (OR (AND (OR (EQUAL X 'BOY) (EQUAL X 'GIRL))
           (EQUAL Y 'CHILD))
      (AND (OR (EQUAL X 'MAN) (EQUAL X 'WOMAN))
           (EQUAL Y 'ADULT))))
```

```
(DEFUN TEST (X Y)
  (COND ((EQUAL Y 'CHILD) (OR (EQUAL X 'BOY) (EQUAL X 'GIRL)))
        ((EQUAL Y 'ADULT) (OR (EQUAL X 'MAN) (EQUAL X 'WOMAN)))
        (T NIL)))
```

4.
```
(DEFUN PLAY (X Y)
  (COND ((EQUAL X Y) 'TIE)
        ((AND (EQUAL X 'ROCK) (EQUAL Y 'SCISSORS)) 'YOU-WIN)
        ((AND (EQUAL X 'SCISSORS) (EQUAL Y 'PAPER)) 'YOU-WIN)
        ((AND (EQUAL X 'PAPER) (EQUAL Y 'ROCK)) 'YOU-WIN)
        (T 'YOU-LOSE)))
```

page 111

1. Remember that (IF A B) is equivalent to (IF A B NIL). Also, (AND X1 X2) is equivalent to (IF X1 X2).

```
(IF X1 (IF X2 (IF X3 X4)))
```

2.
```
(DEFUN COMPARE (X Y)
  (IF (EQUAL X Y) 'NUMBERS-ARE-THE-SAME
      (IF (LESSP X Y) 'FIRST-IS-SMALLER
          (IF (GREATERP X Y) 'FIRST-IS-BIGGER))))
```

```
(DEFUN COMPARE (X Y)
  (OR (AND (EQUAL X Y) 'NUMBERS-ARE-THE-SAME)
      (AND (LESSP X Y) 'FIRST-IS-SMALLER)
      (AND (GREATERP X Y) 'FIRST-IS-BIGGER)))
```

3.
```
(DEFUN GTEST (X Y)
  (IF (GREATERP X Y) T
      (IF (ZEROP X) T
          (IF (ZEROP Y) T NIL))))
```

```
(DEFUN GTEST (X Y)
  (COND ((GREATERP X Y) T)
        ((ZEROP X) T)
        ((ZEROP Y) T)
        (T NIL)))
```

4.
```
(DEFUN BOILINGP (TEMP SCALE)
  (COND ((EQUAL SCALE 'FAHRENHEIT) (GREATERP TEMP 212))
        ((EQUAL SCALE 'CENTIGRADE) (GREATERP TEMP 100))
        (T NIL)))
```

```
(DEFUN BOILINGP (TEMP SCALE)
  (IF (EQUAL SCALE 'FAHRENHEIT) (GREATERP TEMP 212)
      (IF (EQUAL SCALE 'CENTIGRADE) (GREATERP TEMP 100))))

(DEFUN BOILINGP (TEMP SCALE)
  (OR (AND (EQUAL SCALE 'FAHRENHEIT) (GREATERP TEMP 212))
      (AND (EQUAL SCALE 'CENTIGRADE) (GREATERP TEMP 100))))
```

5. If WHERE-IS had eight COND clauses we would need seven nested IFs to write an equivalent function. To solve the problem with AND/OR, we would need one OR and seven ANDs.

page 112

1. Conditionals are important because they allow the computer to make decisions. All nontrivial programs involve some decision making.

2. When IF is given two inputs instead of three, it acts as though the third input (the false-part) were NIL.

3. By writing nested IFs we can handle as many cases as necessary.

4. COND returns NIL when it runs out of clauses. If COND is given no clauses as input it “runs out” immediately, so (COND) returns NIL.

page 114

1.
```
(DEFUN LOGICAL-AND (X Y)
  (IF X (IF Y T)))

(DEFUN LOGICAL-AND (X Y)
  (COND (X (COND (Y T)))))
```

2.
```
(DEFUN LOGICAL-OR (X Y)
  (COND (X T)
        (Y T)
        (T NIL)))
```

3. NOT is not a conditional: it makes no decisions, that is, it cannot choose whether to evaluate an expression. Note that NOT is not a

special form. NOT is a boolean function though. Since it only returns T or NIL, there is no need for a LOGICAL-NOT function.

page 115

1. Truth table for LOGICAL-OR:

X	Y	(LOGICAL-OR X Y)
T	T	T
T	NIL	T
NIL	T	T
NIL	NIL	NIL

2. LOGICAL-IF takes three inputs, each of which can be either T or NIL. This gives 2^3, or eight, combinations, so its truth table has eight lines.

3. Truth table for LOGICAL-IF:

X	Y	Z	(LOGICAL-IF X Y Z)
T	T	T	T
T	T	NIL	T
T	NIL	T	NIL
T	NIL	NIL	NIL
NIL	T	T	T
NIL	T	NIL	NIL
NIL	NIL	T	T
NIL	NIL	NIL	NIL

page 117

1.
```
(AND X Y Z) = (NOT (OR (NOT X) (NOT Y) (NOT Z)))
(OR X Y Z) = (NOT (AND (NOT X) (NOT Y) (NOT Z)))
```

2. Truth table for NAND:

X	Y	(NAND X Y)
T	T	NIL
T	NIL	T
NIL	T	T
NIL	NIL	T

3.
```
(DEFUN AND (X Y) (NAND (NAND X Y) (NAND X Y)))
(DEFUN OR (X Y) (NAND (NAND X X) (NAND Y Y)))
```

4.
```
(DEFUN NOT (X) (NOR X X))

(DEFUN AND (X Y) (NOR (NOR X X) (NOR Y Y)))

(DEFUN NAND (X Y) (NOR (NOR (NOR X X) (NOR Y Y))
                       (NOR (NOR X X) (NOR Y Y))))

(DEFUN OR (X Y) (NOR (NOR X Y) (NOR X Y)))
```

5. AND is not logically complete. Notice that there is no way to put ANDs together to synthesize a NOT function. Therefore we cannot synthesize NAND.

Chapter 5

page 123

If we did not initialize TOTAL, the expression (PLUS TOTAL GLASSES) would cause an unbound variable error the first time we invoked SOLD. If we initialized TOTAL to FOO instead of a number, we would get a wrong-type input error rather than an unbound variable error. Again, the error would only become apparent when we tried to use SOLD.

pages 125–126

1. This version of SOLD sets the global variable TOTAL to zero every time, so values do not accumulate as SOLD is called repeatedly. If we evaluate (SOLD 3) the value of TOTAL is left at 3; after that, (SOLD 5) leaves TOTAL set to 5 rather than 8.

2. The first expression is simply the quoted symbol 'SALE-RECORDED. Since this expression has no side effects and only the value of the *last* expression in a function body is returned, deleting this expression would have no effect on SOLD.

3.
```
(DEFUN FLIP ()
  (SETQ SWITCH (IF (EQUAL SWITCH 'ON) 'OFF 'ON))
  'CLICK)
```

4. There are several ways to write EXCHANGE. Here are three of them:
```
(DEFUN EXCHANGE ()
  (SETQ TEMP A)
  (SETQ A B)
  (SETQ B TEMP))

(DEFUN EXHANGE ()
  (SETQ A (LIST A B))
  (SETQ B (CAR A))
  (SETQ A (CADR A)))

(DEFUN EXHANGE () (EXHANGE1 A B))

(DEFUN EXHANGE1 (A1 B1)
  (SETQ A B1)
  (SETQ B A1))
```

pages 126–127

1. A local variable binding is made when a function is called and goes away when the function returns. A global binding is independent of any function and does not normally go away, although the value of the variable may be changed with SETQ. MAKUNBOUND can be used to remove global bindings.

2. Side effects are actions that a function takes other than returning a value. The side effect of SETQ, for example, is that it changes the value of a variable.

3. SETQ must be a special form so that its first input, the variable name, does not get evaluated.

4. Side effects are indeed possible without global variables. SETQ, for example, can be used to change the value of a local variable. Other functions with side effects will be discussed in later chapters. One

example is the MSG function, whose side effect is to cause things to be printed on the terminal.

pages 127–128

1.
```
(DEFUN INITIALIZE ()
  (SETQ TASKS NIL)
  (SETQ COUNT 0)
  '(SCHEDULER IS INITIALIZED))
```

2.
```
(DEFUN ADD-TASK (X)
  (SETQ TASKS (CONS X TASKS))
  (SETQ COUNT (ADD1 COUNT))
  (LIST 'ADDED X 'TO 'LIST 'OF 'TASKS))
```

3.
```
(DEFUN WHAT-NOW ()
  (IF TASKS (CAR TASKS) 'REST-FOR-A-WHILE))
```

4.
```
(DEFUN HOW-MANY ()
  (LIST (LENGTH TASKS) 'TASKS 'LEFT 'TO 'DO))
```

5.
```
(DEFUN TASK-DONE ()
  (IF TASKS (SETQ COUNT (ADD1 COUNT)))
  (SETQ TASKS (CDR TASKS))
  'CONGRATULATIONS)
```

6.
```
*(initialize)
(SCHEDULER IS INITIALIZED)

*(what-now)
REST-FOR-A-WHILE

*(add-task 'clean-room)
(ADDED CLEAN-ROOM TO LIST OF TASKS)

*(what now)
CLEAN-ROOM

*(add-task 'wash-car)
(ADDED WASH-CAR TO LIST OF TASKS)

*count
2
```

```
*(how many)
(2 TASKS LEFT TO DO)

*(what-now)
WASH-CAR

*(task-done)
CONGRATULATIONS

*count
3

*(what-now)
CLEAN-ROOM

*(task-done)
CONGRATULATIONS

*count
4

*(task-done)
CONGRATULATIONS

*count
4
```

Chapter 6

page 133

(SETQ DOG '(RIN TIN TIN)) evaluates to (RIN TIN TIN)
(LISTP DOG) evaluates to T
(LISTP 'DOG) evaluates to NIL
(ATOM DOG) evaluates to NIL
(ATOM (CAR DOG)) evaluates to T
(CONSP (CDR DOG)) evaluates to T
(CONSP (CDDDR DOG)) evaluates to NIL

(NULL (CDDDR DOG)) evaluates to T
(ATOM (CDDR DOG)) evaluates to NIL
(ATOM (CDR NIL)) evaluates to T

pages 137–138

1. (SETQ LINE '(ROSES ARE RED)) evaluates to (ROSES ARE RED)
   (REVERSE LINE) evaluates to (RED ARE ROSES)
   (CAR (LAST LINE)) evaluates to RED
   (NTH 1 LINE) evaluates to ARE
   (REVERSE (REVERSE LINE)) evaluates to (ROSES ARE RED)
   (APPEND LINE (NCONS (CAR LINE))) evaluates to (ROSES ARE RED ROSES)
   (APPEND (LAST LINE) LINE) evaluates to (RED ROSES ARE RED)
   (LIST (LAST LINE) LINE) evaluates to ((RED) (ROSES ARE RED))
   (CONS (LAST LINE) LINE) evaluates to ((RED) ROSES ARE RED)
   (APPEND LINE '(VIOLETS ARE BLUE)) evaluates to
   (ROSES ARE RED VIOLETS ARE BLUE)
   (SUBST 'CHERRIES 'ROSES LINE) evaluates to (CHERRIES ARE RED)

2. (DEFUN LAST-ELEMENT (X) (CAR (LAST X)))

   (DEFUN LAST-ELEMENT (X) (CAR (REVERSE X)))

   (DEFUN LAST-ELEMENT (X) (NTH (SUB1 (LENGTH X)) X))

3. (DEFUN TACK-ON (X Y) (APPEND X (NCONS Y)))

   (DEFUN TACK-ON (X Y) (REVERSE (CONS Y (REVERSE X))))

4. (DEFUN NEXT-TO-LAST (X) (CADR (REVERSE X)))

5. (DEFUN BUTLAST (X) (REVERSE (CDR (REVERSE X))))

6. MYSTERY is equivalent to CAR.

7. (DEFUN PALINDROMEP (X) (EQUAL X (REVERSE X)))

   (DEFUN MAKE-PALINDROME (X) (APPEND X (REVERSE X)))

8. (DEFUN ROYAL-WE (X) (SUBST 'WE 'I X))

pages 141–142

1. (UNION A '(NO SOAP RADIO)) evaluates to (SOAP WATER NO RADIO)
   (INTERSECTION A (REVERSE A)) evaluates to (SOAP WATER)
   (SETDIFFERENCE A '(STOP FOR WATER)) evaluates to (SOAP)
   (SETDIFFERENCE A A) evaluates to NIL
   (MEMBER 'SOAP A) evaluates to (SOAP WATER)
   (MEMBER 'WATER A) evaluates to (WATER)
   (MEMBER 'WASHCLOTH A) evaluates to NIL

2. The LENGTH function returns the cardinality of a set.

3. (DEFUN ADD-VOWELS (X) (UNION X '(A E I O U)))

4. (DEFUN CONTAINS-ARTICLE-P (X) (INTERSECTION X '(THE A AN)))

```
(DEFUN CONTAINS-ARTICLE-P (X)
  (OR (MEMBER 'THE X) (MEMBER 'A X) (MEMBER 'AN X)))
```

```
(DEFUN CONTAINS-ARTICLE-P (X)
  (NOT (AND (NOT (MEMBER 'THE X))
            (NOT (MEMBER 'A X))
            (NOT (MEMBER 'AN X)))))
```

```
(DEFUN CONTAINS-ARTICLE-P (X)
  (LESSP (LENGTH (UNION X '(THE A AN)))
         (LENGTH (APPEND X '(THE A AN)))))
```

5. (DEFUN SUBSETP (X Y) (NULL (SETDIFFERENCE X Y)))

6. Here are two versions of SET-EQUAL:

```
(DEFUN SET-EQUAL (X Y)
  (AND (SUBSETP X Y) (SUBSETP Y X)))
```

```
(DEFUN SET-EQUAL (X Y)
  (EQUAL (LENGTH (INTERSECTION X Y)) (LENGTH (UNION X Y))))
```

7. (DEFUN PROPER-SUBSETP (X Y)
   (AND (SUBSETP X Y) (NOT (SET-EQUAL X Y))))

pages 144–145

1.
```
(DEFUN RIGHT-SIDE (X) (CDR (MEMBER '-VS- X)))
```

2.
```
(DEFUN LEFT-SIDE (X)
  (REVERSE (RIGHT-SIDE (REVERSE X))))
```

3.
```
(DEFUN COUNT-COMMON (X)
  (LENGTH (INTERSECTION (LEFT-SIDE X) (RIGHT-SIDE X))))
```

4.
```
(DEFUN COMPARE (X)
  (LIST (COUNT-COMMON X) 'COMMON 'FEATURES))
```

5. —

pages 149–150

1. The LENGTH function returns the number of entries in a table.

2.
```
(SETQ BOOKS '((WAR-AND-PEACE LEO-TOLSTOY)
              (GREAT-EXPECTATIONS CHARLES-DICKENS)
              (PRIDE-AND-PREJUDICE JANE-AUSTEN)
              (KIDNAPPED ROBERT-LOUIS-STEVENSON)
              (ROBINSON-CRUSOE DANIEL-DEFOE)))
```

3.
```
(DEFUN WHO-WROTE (TITLE) (CADR (ASSOC TITLE BOOKS)))
```

4. The individual entries in the table BOOKS are unchanged, and ASSOC doesn't care what order a table's elements appear in, so the WHO-WROTE function is unaffected by reversing the value of the variable BOOKS.

5. A WHAT-WROTE function would search the table by author instead of by title. But ASSOC looks at the first element of a table entry, not the second, so we cannot do this using the current table. We would have to reverse each of the elements of BOOKS so that the author came first and the title second.

6.
```
(SETQ ATLAS '((PENNSYLVANIA PITTSBURGH READING)
              (NEW-JERSEY NEWARK PRINCETON TRENTON)
              (OHIO COLUMBUS)))
```

```
(DEFUN WHICH-CITIES (STATE) (CDR (ASSOC STATE ATLAS)))
```

`(WHICH-CITIES 'NEW-JERSEY)` evaluates to `(NEWARK PRINCETON TRENTON)`

page 150

1. A table is the appropriate data structure to use.

```
(SETQ STATE-TABLE
      '((SLEEPING EATING)
        (EATING WAITING-FOR-A-TERMINAL)
        (WAITING-FOR-A-TERMINAL PROGRAMMING)
        (PROGRAMMING DEBUGGING)
        (DEBUGGING SLEEPING)))
```

2. `(DEFUN NEXT-STATE (X) (CADR (ASSOC X STATE-TABLE)))`

3. `(NEXT-STATE 'PROGRAMMING)` evaluates to `DEBUGGING`
   `(NEXT-STATE (NEXT-STATE 'DEBUGGING))` evaluates to `EATING`
   `(NEXT-STATE 'PLAYING-GUITAR)` evaluates to `NIL`

4. `(DEFUN INITIALIZE () (SETQ NERD-STATE 'SLEEPING))`

5.
```
(DEFUN ADVANCE ()
  (SETQ NERD-STATE (NEXT-STATE NERD-STATE))
  (LIST 'THE 'NERD 'IS 'NOW NERD-STATE))
```

page 151

1. Atomic datatypes, such as numbers and symbols, cannot be broken down into smaller components. (The term comes from the Greek *atomos,* meaning "indivisible.") Nonatomic datatypes *can* be broken down. Lists are nonatomic; CAR and CDR are two functions that break them down.

2. LISTP returns T for any list. CONSP returns T for any list built from cons cells, but not for NIL, the empty list.

3. `(DEFUN ROTATE-LEFT (X) (APPEND (CDR X) (NCONS (CAR X))))`

```
(DEFUN ROTATE-RIGHT (X)
  (APPEND (LAST X) (REVERSE (CDR (REVERSE X)))))
```

ROTATE-RIGHT can also be written in terms of ROTATE-LEFT:

```
(DEFUN ROTATE-RIGHT (X)
  (REVERSE (ROTATE-LEFT (REVERSE X))))
```

4. If X and Y are equal, then (SETDIFFERENCE X Y) equals (SET-DIFFERENCE Y X) equals NIL. If X and Y are not equal, their set differences won't be either.

5. The APPEND function performs unary addition.

6. The following table makes ASSOC work like MEMBER would on the list (A B C D).

```
((A B C D)
 (B C D)
 (C D)
 (D))
```

pages 154–155

1. —

2. `(DEFUN CHOICES (X) (CDR (ASSOC X ROOMS)))`

3. `(DEFUN LOOK (X Y) (CADR (ASSOC X (CHOICES Y))))`

4. `(SETQ LOC 'PANTRY)`

5. `(DEFUN HOW-MANY-CHOICES () (LENGTH (CHOICES LOC)))`

6.
```
(DEFUN UPSTAIRSP (X)
  (OR (EQUAL X 'LIBRARY) (EQUAL X 'UPSTAIRS-BEDROOM)))

(DEFUN ONSTAIRSP (X)
  (OR (EQUAL X 'FRONT-STAIRS) (EQUAL X 'BACK-STAIRS)))
```

7.
```
(DEFUN WHERE ()
  (COND ((UPSTAIRSP LOC) (LIST 'ROBBIE 'IS 'UPSTAIRS 'IN 'THE LOC))
        ((ONSTAIRSP LOC) (LIST 'ROBBIE 'IS 'ON 'THE LOC))
        (T (LIST 'ROBBIE 'IS 'DOWNSTAIRS 'IN 'THE LOC))))
```

8.
```
(DEFUN MOVE (X)
  (COND ((LOOK X LOC)
         (SETQ LOC (LOOK X LOC))
         (WHERE))
        (T '(OUCH! ROBBIE HIT A WALL))))
```

9. `(SETQ LOC 'PANTRY)`

`(MOVE 'WEST)`
`(MOVE 'WEST)`
`(MOVE 'NORTH)`
`(WHERE)` evaluates to `(ROBBIE IS ON THE BACK-STAIRS)`
`(MOVE 'NORTH)`
`(WHERE)` evaluates to `(ROBBIE IS UPSTAIRS IN THE LIBRARY)`

`(MOVE 'EAST)`
`(MOVE 'SOUTH)`
`(MOVE 'SOUTH)`
`(MOVE'EAST)`
`(WHERE)` evaluates to `(ROBBIE IS DOWNSTAIRS IN THE KITCHEN)`

pages 162–163

1. If two things are EQ then they have the same address, so they are actually the *same* thing. Thus if two things are EQ they are necessarily EQUAL.

2. `(RPLACA '(FOO BAR) 'BAZ)` evaluates to `(BAZ BAR)`
`(RPLACD '(BEEP) 'MEEP)` evaluates to `(BEEP . MEEP)`
`(NCONC '(A B C) (CDR '(A B C)))` evaluates to `(A B C B C)`

3. `(DEFUN CHOP (X) (RPLACD X NIL))`

4.
```
(DEFUN NTACK (L X)
  (RPLACD (LAST L) (NCONS X))
  L)
```

5. 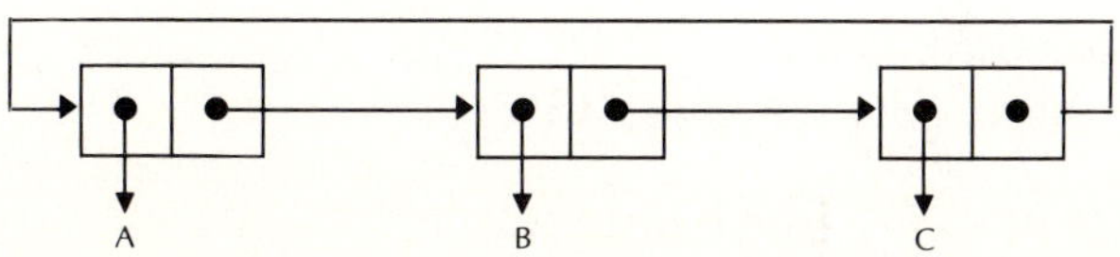

6.

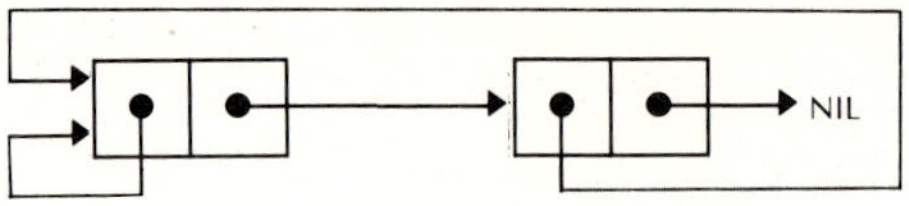

Chapter 7

pages 167–168

1. `(APPLY-TO-ALL 'ADD1 '(1 3 5 7 9))`

2. `(APPLY-TO-ALL 'CADDR DAILY-PLANET)`

3. `(APPLY-TO-ALL 'ZEROP '(2 0 3 4 0 -5 -6))`
   evaluates to `(NIL T NIL NIL T NIL NIL)`

4. `(DEFUN GREATER-THAN-ZEROP (X) (GREATERP X 0))`

   `(APPLY-TO-ALL 'GREATER-THAN-ZEROP '(2 0 3 4 0 -5 -6))`
   evaluates to `(T NIL T T NIL NIL NIL)`

page 169

1. `(LAMBDA (X) (DIFFERENCE X 7))`

2. `(LAMBDA (X) (OR (NULL X) (EQUAL X T)))`

3.
```
(DEFUN FLIP (L)
  (APPLY-TO-ALL
        '(LAMBDA (X) (IF (EQUAL X 'UP) 'DOWN 'UP))
        L))
```

page 171

1.
```
(DEFUN GREATER-THAN-K (X K)
  (FIND-IF '(LAMBDA (X1) (GREATERP X1 K))
           X))
```

2.
```
(DEFUN FIRST-NON-LIST (X)
  (FIND-IF '(LAMBDA (Z) (NOT (LISTP Z)))
           X))
```

pages 171 to 172

1.
```
(SETQ NOTE-TABLE
      '((C 1) (C-SHARP 2) (D 3) (D-SHARP 4)
        (E 5) (F 6) (F-SHARP 7) (G 8)
        (G-SHARP 9) (A 10) (A-SHARP 11) (B 12)))
```

2.
```
(DEFUN NUMBERS (X)
  (APPLY-TO-ALL '(LAMBDA (X1) (CADR (ASSOC X1 NOTE-TABLE))) X))
```

3.
```
(DEFUN NOTE (X)
  (CAR (FIND-IF '(LAMBDA (Z) (EQUAL X (CADR Z)))
                NOTE-TABLE)))

(DEFUN NOTES (X) (APPLY-TO-ALL 'NOTE X))
```

4. (NOTES (NOTES X)) and (NUMBERS (NUMBERS X)) turn lists of numbers or lists of notes into lists of NILs.

5.
```
(DEFUN RAISE (N X)
  (APPLY-TO-ALL '(LAMBDA (X1) (PLUS X1 N)) X))
```

6.
```
(DEFUN NORMALIZE (X)
   (APPLY-TO-ALL
    '(LAMBDA (X1) (COND ((GREATERP X1 12) (DIFFERENCE X1 12))
                        ((LESSP X1 1) (PLUS X1 12))
                        (T X1)))
   X))
```

7.
```
(DEFUN TRANSPOSE (N X)
  (NOTES (NORMALIZE (RAISE N (NUMBERS X)))))
```

Transposing up by 12 half steps has no effect on the song, because after each note value is raised by exactly 12, the NORMALIZE function brings it down again by 12. Transposing up by 11 half steps is equivalent to transposing down by 1 half step. This is another artifact of normalizing the notes.

page 174

1.
```
(DEFUN ONE-FIVE (X)
  (SUBSET '(LAMBDA (X) (AND (GREATERP X 1) (LESSP X 5)))
          X))
```

2.
```
(DEFUN COUNT-THE (X)
  (LENGTH (SUBSET '(LAMBDA (X1) (EQUAL X1 'THE)) X)))
```

3.
```
(DEFUN FIND-PAIRS (X)
  (SUBSET '(LAMBDA (X1) (EQUAL (LENGTH X1) 2)) X))
```

4.
```
(DEFUN MY-INTERSECTION (X Y)
  (SUBSET '(LAMBDA (X1) (MEMBER X1 Y)) X))

(DEFUN MY-UNION (X Y)
  (APPEND X (SUBSET '(LAMBDA (Y1) (NOT (MEMBER Y1 X))) Y)))
```

page 175

1. `(DEFUN ALL-ODD (L) (EVERY 'ODDP L))`

2. `(DEFUN NONE-ODD (L) (EVERY '(LAMBDA (X) (NOT (ODDP X))) L))`

3. `(DEFUN NOT-ALL-ODD (L) (NOT (EVERY 'ODDP L)))`

4.
```
(DEFUN NOT-NONE-ODD (L)
  (NOT (EVERY '(LAMBDA (X) (NOT (ODDP X))) L)))
```

5. All four of these functions are distinct. NOT-ALL-ODD would be better called SOME-EVEN. NOT-NONE-ODD would be better called SOME-ODD. If you have studied the predicate calculus in an introductory logic course, you no doubt see the similarity between these four functions and the effects that various combinations of negation and a universal quantifier can have on the meaning of a formula.

pages 175 to 176

1.
```
(DEFUN RANK (CARD) (CAR CARD))

(DEFUN SUIT (CARD) (CADR CARD))
```

2.
```
(SETQ MY-HAND '((3 HEARTS)
                (5 CLUBS)
                (2 DIAMONDS)
                (4 DIAMONDS)
                (ACE SPADES)))
```

3.
```
(DEFUN COUNT-SUIT (SU HAND)
  (LENGTH (SUBSET '(LAMBDA (CARD) (EQUAL SU (SUIT CARD)))
                  HAND)))
```

4.
```
(SETQ COLORS '((CLUBS BLACK)
               (DIAMONDS RED)
               (HEARTS RED)
               (SPADES BLACK)))
```

5.
```
(DEFUN COLOR-OF (CARD)
  (CADR (ASSOC (SUIT CARD) COLORS)))
```

6.
```
(DEFUN FIRST-RED (HAND)
  (FIND-IF '(LAMBDA (CARD) (EQUAL (COLOR-OF CARD) 'RED))
           HAND))
```

7.
```
(DEFUN ALL-BLACK (HAND)
  (EVERY '(LAMBDA (CARD) (EQUAL (COLOR-OF CARD) 'BLACK))
         HAND))
```

8.
```
(DEFUN WHAT-RANKS (SU HAND)
  (APPLY-TO-ALL
    'RANK
    (SUBSET '(LAMBDA (CARD) (EQUAL (SUIT CARD) SU))
            HAND)))
```

page 177

1. Reduce the list of sets with UNION instead of APPEND.

2.
```
(DEFUN TOTAL-LENGTH (X) (LENGTH (REDUCE 'APPEND X)))

(DEFUN TOTAL-LENGTH (X)
  (REDUCE 'PLUS (APPLY-TO-ALL 'LENGTH X)))
```

3. Zero is the identity value for addition, while one is the identity value for multiplication. See the advanced topics section for further explanation.

page 178

1. An applicative operator is a function that takes another function as input and applies that function to data in some way.

2. Lambda expressions are useful for writing function definitions as part of other functions. One application of this is to derive a one-input function from a function of more than one input. However, if we did not have lambda expressions we could still use DEFUN to separately define each function we needed.

3. `(DEFUN FIND-IF (FN X) (CAR (SUBSET FN X)))`

4. `(DEFUN EVERY (FN X) (EQUAL X (SUBSET FN X)))`

pages 180–183

1. —

2. `(DEFUN MATCH-ELEMENT (ELEM PAT) (OR (EQUAL ELEM PAT) (EQUAL PAT '?)))`

3.
```
(DEFUN MATCH-TRIPLE (ASSERTION PATTERN)
  (AND (MATCH-ELEMENT (CAR ASSERTION) (CAR PATTERN))
       (MATCH-ELEMENT (CADR ASSERTION) (CADR PATTERN))
       (MATCH-ELEMENT (CADDR ASSERTION) (CADDR PATTERN))))
```

4.
```
(DEFUN FETCH (PATTERN)
  (SUBSET '(LAMBDA (ASSERTION) (MATCH-TRIPLE ASSERTION PATTERN))
          DATABASE))
```

5. `(FETCH '(B4 SHAPE ?))` evaluates to `((B4 SHAPE PYRAMID))`

   `(FETCH '(? SHAPE BRICK))` evaluates to
```
                  ((B1 SHAPE BRICK)
                   (B2 SHAPE BRICK)
                   (B3 SHAPE BRICK)
                   (B6 SHAPE BRICK))
```

(FETCH '(B2 ? B3)) evaluates to ((B2 LEFT-OF B3))

(FETCH '(? COLOR ?)) evaluates to

```
((B1 COLOR GREEN)
 (B2 COLOR RED)
 (B3 COLOR RED)
 (B4 COLOR BLUE)
 (B5 COLOR GREEN)
 (B6 COLOR PURPLE))
```

(FETCH '(B4 ? ?)) evaluates to

```
((B4 SHAPE PYRAMID)
 (B4 COLOR BLUE)
 (B4 SIZE LARGE)
 (B4 SUPPORTED-BY B5))
```

6. (DEFUN COLOR-PATTERN (BLOCK) (LIST BLOCK 'COLOR '?))

7.
```
(DEFUN SUPPORTERS (BLOCK)
  (APPLY-TO-ALL 'CAR (FETCH (LIST '? 'SUPPORTS BLOCK))))
```

8.
```
(DEFUN SHAPE-OF (BLOCK)
  (CADDR (CAR (FETCH (LIST BLOCK 'SHAPE '?)))))

(DEFUN SUPP-CUBE (BLOCK)
  (FIND-IF '(LAMBDA (X) (EQUAL (SHAPE-OF X) 'CUBE))
           (SUPPORTERS BLOCK)))
```

9. Building the DESCRIPTION function:

a. (DEFUN DESC1 (BLOCK) (FETCH (LIST BLOCK '? '?)))
b. (DEFUN DESC2 (BLOCK) (APPLY-TO-ALL 'CDR (DESC1 BLOCK)))
c. (DEFUN DESCRIPTION (BLOCK) (REDUCE 'APPEND (DESC2 BLOCK)))
d. (DESCRIPTION 'B1) evaluates to

```
(SHAPE BRICK COLOR GREEN SIZE SMALL
    SUPPORTED-BY B2 SUPPORTED-BY B3)
```

(DESCRIPTION 'B4) evaluates to

```
(SHAPE PYRAMID COLOR BLUE SIZE LARGE
         SUPPORTED-BY B5)
```

10. Add the assertions (B1 MATERIAL WOOD) and (B2 MATERIAL PLASTIC) to the list stored in the global variable DATABASE.

page 184

1. NIL is the identity value for both APPEND and UNION. CONS does not have an identity value.

2. The identity value for set intersection is the set containing everything; in set theory this is sometimes referred to as "the universe." Lisp has no representation for such a set, so the INTERSECTION function does not have an identity value in Lisp.

3. QUOTIENT has a right identity of 1.

4. AND has a left identity of T. LOGICAL-AND has T as both a left and right identity. OR and LOGICAL-OR have NIL as both a left and right identity.

5. Suppose a function has a left identity I_L and a right identity I_R. By the definition of an identity element, (FN I_L X) equals X and (FN X I_R) equals X. Therefore (FN I_L I_R) equals both I_R and I_L, so the left and right identities are the same.

6. T is the identity value for EQUAL over the domain {T,NIL}.

page 186

1. For XL, five successive CARs get us to the symbol A. One CADR gets us to F. For XR, one CAR gets us to A; five CADRs get us to F.

2. Yes, because APPEND is an associative function.

3. In general, using LEFT-REDUCE on a list X does not yield the same result as RIGHT-REDUCE on (REVERSE X). However, if the reducing function is commutative, it does. A commutative function is one where (FN X Y) equals (FN Y X). PLUS is an example of a commutative function. DIFFERENCE is a noncommutative function.

4.
```
(DEFUN ODD-PARITY (L)
  (AND L
       (REDUCE '(LAMBDA (X Y) (NOT (EQUAL X Y)))
               L)))
```

The lambda expression implements the XOR (exclusive or) truth function, which is both associative and commutative. Therefore it does not matter whether left or right reduction is used to compute parity.

page 187

```
(APPLY-TO-ALL
     '(LAMBDA (ENTRY SPWORD) (APPEND ENTRY (LIST SPWORD)))
     WORDS
     '(UNO DOS TRES QUATRO CINCO))
```

evaluates to the list

```
((ONE UN UNO)
 (TWO DEUX DOS)
 (THREE TROIS TRES)
 (FOUR QUATRE QUATRO)
 (FIVE CINQ CINCO))
```

page 189

```
(DEFUN MAPAPPEND (FN L)
  (REDUCE 'APPEND (APPLY-TO-ALL FN L)))
```

Chapter 8

page 202

```
(DEFUN LAUGH (N)
  (COND ((ZEROP N) NIL)
        (T (CONS 'HA (LAUGH (SUB1 N))))))
```

(LAUGH 0) returns NIL, "the empty laugh." If given an input of −1, LAUGH will invoke itself recursively on larger and larger negative numbers and never return a value. This is called infinite recursion. Infinite recursion is discussed in more detail later in the chapter.

pages 202–203

1. The single step is to add the CAR of the list to the sum of the elements in the CDR.

2. (ADD-UP (CDR X))

3. We stop at the empty list, the sum of whose elements is zero. Here is the complete definition of ADD-UP:

```
(DEFUN ADD-UP (X)
  (COND ((NULL X) 0)
        (T (PLUS (CAR X) (ADD-UP (CDR X))))))
```

page 203

1.
```
(DEFUN ALLODDP (X)
  (COND ((NULL X) T)
        ((ODDP (CAR X)) (ALLODDP (CDR X)))
        (T NIL)))
```

2.
```
(DEFUN REC-MEMBER (X L)
  (COND ((NULL L) NIL)
        ((EQUAL X (CAR L)) L)
        (T (REC-MEMBER X (CDR L)))))
```

3.
```
(DEFUN REC-ASSOC (KEY TABLE)
  (COND ((NULL TABLE) NIL)
        ((EQUAL KEY (CAAR TABLE)) (CAR TABLE))
        (T (REC-ASSOC KEY (CDR TABLE)))))
```

4.
```
(DEFUN REC-NTH (N L)
  (COND ((ZEROP N) (CAR L))
        (T (REC-NTH (SUB1 N) (CDR L)))))
```

5.
```
(DEFUN REC-PLUS (X Y)
  (COND ((ZEROP Y) X)
        (T (REC-PLUS (ADD1 X) (SUB1 Y)))))
```

pages 206–207

1.
```
(DEFUN FIB (N)
  (COND ((EQUAL N 0) 1)
        ((EQUAL N 1) 1)
        (T (PLUS (FIB (DIFFERENCE N 1))
                 (FIB (DIFFERENCE N 2))))))
```

2. If the input to ANY-7-P contains a 7, ANY-7-P will return T. If the input does not contain a 7, then ANY-7-P will recurse infinitely because there is no check for a null list as input.

3. Giving FACT a negative number as input will cause it to recurse infinitely.

4. `(DEFUN SHORTY () (SHORTY))`

5. The CAR of the list is the symbol FOO. The CDR is the list itself. COUNT-SLICES will recurse infinitely when given this circular list as input.

page 209

1. `(DEFUN FACT (N) (REDUCE 'TIMES (COUNTUP N)))`

2.
```
(DEFUN MAKE-LOAF (N)
  (COND ((ZEROP N) NIL)
        (T (CONS 'X (MAKE-LOAF (SUB1 N))))))
```

3.
```
(DEFUN PAIRINGS (X Y)
  (COND ((NULL X) NIL)
        (T (CONS (LIST (CAR X) (CAR Y))
                 (PAIRINGS (CDR X) (CDR Y))))))
```

4.
```
(DEFUN SUBLISTS (X)
  (COND ((NULL X) NIL)
        (T (CONS X (SUBLISTS (CDR X))))))
```

5.
```
(DEFUN REC-REVERSE (L)
  (COND ((NULL L) NIL)
        (T (APPEND (REC-REVERSE (CDR L)) (LIST (CAR L))))))
```

page 212

1.
```
(DEFUN REC-REVERSE (X) (REC-REV1 X NIL))

(DEFUN REC-REV1 (X RX)
  (COND ((NULL X) RX)
        (T (REC-REV1 (CDR X) (CONS (CAR X) RX)))))
```

2.
```
(DEFUN LARGEST (L) (LARGE1 L 0))

(DEFUN LARGE1 (L CONTENDER)
  (COND ((NULL L) CONTENDER)
        ((GREATERP (CAR L) CONTENDER) (LARGE1 (CDR L) (CAR L)))
        (T (LARGE1 (CDR L) CONTENDER))))
```

3.
```
(DEFUN HUGE (N) (IF (ZEROP N) 0 (HUGE1 N 1)))

(DEFUN HUGE1 (N CNT)
  (COND ((EQUAL N CNT) N)
        (T (TIMES N (HUGE1 N (ADD1 CNT))))))
```

pages 213–214

1. A recursive function contains a reference to itself within its definition. Functions that invoke themselves are recursive.

2.
```
(DEFUN REC-LAST (L)
  (COND ((NULL (CDR L)) L)
        (T (REC-LAST (CDR L)))))
```

3.
```
(DEFUN EVERY-OTHER (L)
  (COND ((NULL L) NIL)
        (T (CONS (CAR L) (EVERY-OTHER (CDDR L))))))
```

4.
```
(DEFUN LEFT-HALF (X) (LEFT1 X NIL))

(DEFUN LEFT1 (X L)
  (COND ((EQUAL (LENGTH X) (LENGTH L)) L)
        (T (LEFT1 (CDR X) (APPEND L (LIST (CAR X)))))))
```

5.
```
(DEFUN FACT (N)
  (COND ((ZEROP N) 1)
        (T (QUOTIENT (FACT (ADD1 N)) (ADD1 N)))))
```

The definition is a valid recursive definition, but it does not lead to a good function because it causes us to violate the second rule of recursion. The second rule says to break each journey down to one step plus a *smaller* journey, but this definition generates a *larger* journey with each step we take. The function that implements this definition will work correctly only when given an input of 0. To compute a factorial using the definition, we have to solve the equations backward. For example, to compute factorial 4, we write:

```
FACTORIAL(0) = 1
= FACTORIAL(1)/1
= (FACTORIAL(2)/2)/1
= (FACTORIAL(3)/3)/2/1
= (FACTORIAL(4)/4)/3/2/1
```

So we have

```
1 = (FACTORIAL(4)/4)/3/2/1
```

which can be solved to yield

```
FACTORIAL(4) = 4×3×2×1 = 24
```

pages 216–218

1. —

2.
```
(DEFUN FATHER (X) (CADR (ASSOC X FAMILY)))

(DEFUN MOTHER (X) (CADDR (ASSOC X FAMILY)))

(DEFUN PARENTS (X)
  (UNION (AND (FATHER X) (LIST (FATHER X)))
         (AND (MOTHER X) (LIST (MOTHER X)))))
```

```
(DEFUN CHILDREN (PARENT)
  (AND PARENT
       (APPLY-TO-ALL
           'CAR
           (SUBSET '(LAMBDA (ENTRY) (MEMBER PARENT (CDR ENTRY)))
                   FAMILY))))
```

3.
```
(DEFUN SIBLINGS (X)
  (SETDIFFERENCE (UNION (CHILDREN (FATHER X))
                        (CHILDREN (MOTHER X)))
                 (LIST X)))
```

4.
```
(DEFUN MAPUNION (FN L) (REDUCE 'UNION (APPLY-TO-ALL FN L)))
```

5.
```
(DEFUN GRANDPARENTS (X) (MAPUNION 'PARENTS (PARENTS X)))
```

6.
```
(DEFUN COUSINS (X)
  (MAPUNION 'CHILDREN (MAPUNION 'SIBLINGS (PARENTS X))))
```

7.
```
(DEFUN DESCENDED-FROM (P1 P2)
  (COND ((NULL P1) NIL)
        ((MEMBER P2 (PARENTS P1)) T)
        (T (OR (DESCENDED-FROM (FATHER P1) P2)
               (DESCENDED-FROM (MOTHER P1) P2)))))
```

8.
```
(DEFUN ANCESTORS (X)
  (COND ((NULL X) NIL)
        (T (UNION (PARENTS X)
                  (UNION (ANCESTORS (FATHER X))
                         (ANCESTORS (MOTHER X)))))))
```

9.
```
(DEFUN GENERATION-GAP (X Y) (G-GAP1 X Y 0))

(DEFUN G-GAP1 (X Y N)
  (COND ((NULL X) NIL)
        ((EQUAL X Y) N)
        (T (OR (G-GAP1 (FATHER X) Y (ADD1 N))
               (G-GAP1 (MOTHER X) Y (ADD1 N))))))
```

10. Answers to genealogy questions:

a. `(DESCENDED-FROM 'ROBERT 'DEIRDRE)` evaluates to `NIL`

b. `(ANCESTORS 'YVETTE)` evaluates to

```
(ROBERT ZELDA QUENTIN JULIE GEORGE ELLEN
 FRANK LINDA ARTHUR KATE VINCENT WANDA BRUCE
 SUZANNE COLIN DEIRDRE)
```

c. `(GENERATION-GAP 'OLIVIA 'FRANK)` evaluates to `3`

d. `(COUSINS 'PETER)` evaluates to `(JOSHUA ROBERT)`

e. `(GRANDPARENTS 'OLIVIA)` evaluates to `(ANDRE HILLARY GEORGE ELLEN)`

pages 221–222

1.
```
(DEFUN COUNT-SYMBOLS (X)
  (COND ((NULL X) 0)
        ((SYMBOLP X) 1)
        (T (PLUS (COUNT-SYMBOLS (CAR X))
                 (COUNT-SYMBOLS (CDR X))))))
```

2.
```
(DEFUN REMOVE-ALL (X L)
  (COND ((SYMBOLP L) L)
        ((EQUAL X (CAR L)) (REMOVE-ALL X (CDR L)))
        (T (CONS (REMOVE-ALL X (CAR L))
                 (REMOVE-ALL X (CDR L))))))
```

3.
```
(DEFUN REC-SUBST (X Y L)
  (COND ((EQUAL L Y) X)
        ((SYMBOLP L) L)
        (T (CONS (REC-SUBST X Y (CAR L))
                 (REC-SUBST X Y (CDR L))))))
```

4.
```
(DEFUN MAX (X Y) (IF (GREATERP X Y) X Y))

(DEFUN MAXDEPTH (X) (MAXDEPTH1 X 0))

(DEFUN MAXDEPTH1 (X DEPTH)
  (COND ((SYMBOLP X) DEPTH)
        (T (MAX (MAXDEPTH1 (CAR X) (ADD1 DEPTH))
                (MAXDEPTH1 (CDR X) DEPTH)))))
```

5.
```
(DEFUN COUNT-CONS (X)
  (COND ((CONSP X) (ADD1 (PLUS (COUNT-CONS (CAR X))
                               (COUNT-CONS (CDR X)))))
        (T 0)))
```

6.
```
(DEFUN FLATTEN (X)
  (COND ((NULL X) NIL)
        (( ATOM X) (LIST X))
        (T (APPEND (FLATTEN (CAR X)) (FLATTEN (CDR X))))))
```

pages 224–225

1.
```
(DEFUN TR-COUNTP (N) (TR-CNT1 N NIL))

(DEFUN TR-CNT1 (N X)
  (COND ((ZEROP N) X)
        (T (TR-CNT1 (SUB1 N) (CONS N X)))))
```

2.
```
(DEFUN TR-FACT (N) (TR-FACT1 N 1))

(DEFUN TR-FACT1 (N RES)
  (COND ((ZEROP N) RES)
        (T (TR-FACT1 (SUB1 N) (TIMES N RES)))))
```

3.
```
(DEFUN TR-UNION (X Y)
  (COND ((NULL X) Y)
        ((MEMBER (CAR X) Y) (TR-UNION (CDR X) Y))
        (T (TR-UNION (CDR X) (CONS (CAR X) Y)))))

(DEFUN TR-INTERSECTION (X Y) (TR-INT1 X Y NIL))

(DEFUN TR-INT1 (X Y RES)
  (COND ((NULL X) RES)
        ((MEMBER (CAR X) Y)
         (TR-INT1 (CDR X) Y (CONS (CAR X) RES)))
        (T (TR-INT1 (CDR X) Y RES))))

(DEFUN TR-SETDIFF (X Y) TR-DIFF1 X Y NIL))

(DEFUN TR-DIFF1 (X Y RES)
  (COND ((NULL X) RES)
        ((MEMBER (CAR X) Y) (TR-DIFF1 (CDR X) Y RES))
        (T (TR-DIFF1 (CDR X) Y (CONS (CAR X) RES)))))
```

4. ```
   (DEFUN TR-NTH (N X)
     (COND ((ZEROP N) (CAR X))
           (T (TR-NTH (SUB1 N) (CDR X)))))
   ```

pages 226–227

1. ```
   (DEFUN ARITH-EVAL (X)
     (COND ((NUMBERP X) X)
           (T (APPLY-OP (CADR X)
                        (ARITH-EVAL (CAR X))
                        (ARITH-EVAL (CADDR X))))))

   (DEFUN APPLY-OP (OP X Y)
     (COND ((EQUAL OP '+) (PLUS X Y))
           ((EQUAL OP '-) (DIFFERENCE X Y))
           ((EQUAL OP '*) (TIMES X Y))
           ((EQUAL OP '%) (QUOTIENT X Y))))
   ```

2. ```
   (DEFUN LEGALP (X)
     (OR (NUMBERP X)
         (AND (LISTP X)
              (EQUAL (LENGTH X) 3)
              (LEGALP (CAR X))
              (MEMBER (CADR X) '(+ - * %))
              (LEGALP (CADDR X)))))
   ```

3. A sentence is in the set if it is the sentence "John hit the ball," or if it begins with the words "He said that" followed by a sentence that is in the set.

4. A positive integer greater than one is either a prime or the product of a prime and a positive integer greater than one.
   ```

5. The terminal nodes are the symbols A, B, C, D, E, and NIL. The nonterminal nodes are the cons cells.

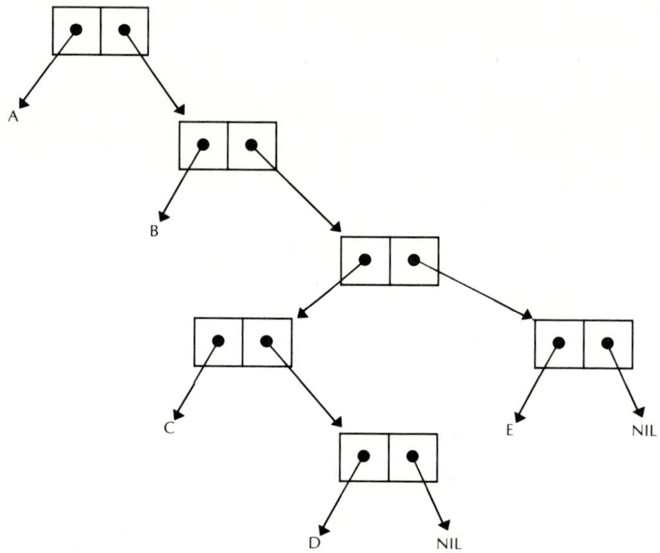

6. A book can be viewed as a tree structure whose levels correspond to parts, chapters, sections, subsections, paragraphs, subparagraphs, sentences, words, and letters. Letters are the terminal nodes of the tree.

Chapter 9

pages 232 to 233

1.
```
(DEFUN MARY ()
   (MSG "Mary had a little lamb," T)
   (MSG "Its fleece was white as snow." T)
   (MSG "And everywhere that Mary went" T)
   (MSG "The lamb was sure to go." T))
```

2.
```
(DEFUN DRAW-LINE (N)
  (COND ((ZEROP N) (MSG T))
        (T (MSG "*") (DRAW-LINE (SUB1 N)))))
```

3.
```
(DEFUN DRAW-BOX (COLS ROWS)
  (COND ((ZEROP ROWS) (MSG T))
        (T (DRAW-LINE COLS) (DRAW-BOX COLS (SUB1 ROWS)))))
```

4.
```
(DEFUN NINETY-NINE-BOTTLES (N)
  (COND ((ZEROP N) (MSG "Awww, no more beer!" T T))
        (T (MSG N " bottles of beer on the wall," T)
           (MSG N " bottles of beer!" T)
           (MSG "Take one down," T "Pass it around," T)
           (MSG (SUB1 N) " bottles of beer on the wall." T T)
           (NINETY-NINE-BOTTLES (SUB1 N)))))
```

5.
```
(DEFUN PRINT-SQUARE (SQ)
  (COND ((EQUAL SQ 'O) (MSG " o "))
        ((EQUAL SQ 'X) (MSG " x "))
        (T (MSG "   "))))

(DEFUN PRINT-ROW (X)
  (PRINT-SQUARE (CAR X))
  (MSG " | ")
  (PRINT-SQUARE (CADR X))
  (MSG " | ")
  (PRINT-SQUARE (CADDR X))
  (MSG T))

(DEFUN PRINT-BOARD (X)
  (PRINT-ROW X)
  (MSG "-----------" T)
  (PRINT-ROW (CDDDR X))
  (MSG "-----------" T)
  (PRINT-ROW (CDDDR (CDDDR X))))
```

page 234

1.
```
(DEFUN GROSS-PAY ()
  (MSG "What is the worker's hourly wage in dollars?")
  (SETQ RATE (READ))
  (MSG "How many hours did the worker put in?")
  (SETQ HOURS (READ))
  (MSG "The worker earned "(TIMES RATE HOURS)" dollars." T))
```

2.
```
(DEFUN COOKIE-MONSTER ()
  (MSG "Give me cookie!!!" T "Cookie?")
  (SETQ GIFT (READ))
  (COND ((EQUAL GIFT 'COOKIE)
         (MSG "Thank you! . . . Munch munch munch . . . BURP" T))
        (T (MSG "No want" GIFT ". . ." T T)
           (COOKIE-MONSTER))))
```

page 235

1. Strings are enclosed by quotation marks. They are not converted to uppercase on input. Strings evaluate to themselves.

2.
```
*(msg "a" "b")
abT

*(msg "a" " " "b")
a bT

*(msg "a" t "b")
a
bT
```

3. (MSG "X") prints a capital **X** on the terminal. (MSG X) prints the value of the variable **X** on the terminal.

4. The side effect of **READ** is that the computer stops and waits for you to type something on the terminal. The program cannot continue until you have typed in a piece of data.

pages 236–237

1.
```
(DEFUN SPACE (N)
  (COND ((LESSP N 0) (MSG "Error!" T) NIL)
        ((ZEROP N) NIL)
        (T (MSG " ") (SPACE (SUB1 N)))))
```

2.
```
(DEFUN PLOT-ONE-POINT (SYM YVAL) (SPACE YVAL) (MSG SYM T))
```

3.
```
(DEFUN PLOT-POINTS (SYM YVALS)
  (APPLY-TO-ALL '(LAMBDA (Y) (PLOT-ONE-POINT SYM Y)) YVALS))
```

4.
```
(DEFUN GENERATE (M N)
  (COND ((GREATERP M N) NIL)
        (T (CONS M (GENERATE (ADD1 M) N)))))
```

5.
```
(DEFUN MAKE-GRAPH NIL
  (MSG "Function to graph? ")
  (SETQ FUNC (READ))
  (MSG "Starting x value? ")
  (SETQ START (READ))
  (MSG "Ending x value? ")
  (SETQ END (READ))
  (MSG "Plotting symbol? ")
  (SETQ SYM (READ))
  (PLOT-POINTS SYM (APPLY-TO-ALL FUNC (GENERATE START END)))
  T)
```

6.
```
(DEFUN SQUARE (X) (TIMES X X))
```

pages 239–240

1.
```
(DEFUN DOT-PRIN1 (X)
  (COND ((NOT (CONSP X)) (MSG X))
        (T (MSG "(")
           (DOT-PRIN1 (CAR X))
           (MSG " . ")
           (DOT-PRIN1 (CDR X))
           (MSG ")"))))
```

2. ```
   *(dot-prin1 '(a (b) c))
   (A . ((B . NIL) . (C . NIL)))T
   ```

3. ```
   *(dot-prin1 '((((a)))))
   ((((A . NIL) . NIL) . NIL) . NIL)T
   ```

4. ```
   *(dot-prin1 '(a . (b . c)))
   (A . (B . C))T
   ```

5. When you type in '(**A . B**) Lisp types back (**A . B**). This is a dotted pair; it has no representation in ordinary list notation.

6. For the first one DOT-PRIN1 would print

   (FOO . (FOO . (FOO . (FOO . (FOO . *etc.*

   For the second it would print

   ((((((((((((((((((*etc.*

page 240

```
(DEFUN HYBRID-PRIN1 (X)
  (COND ((NOT (CONSP X)) (MSG X))
        (T (MSG "(")
           (HYBRID-PRIN1 (CAR X))
           (HYBRID-PRIN2 (CDR X))
           (MSG ")"))))

(DEFUN HYBRID-PRIN2 (X)
  (COND ((NULL X) NIL)
        ((CONSP X) (MSG " ")
                   (HYBRID-PRIN1 (CAR X))
                   (HYBRID-PRIN2 (CDR X)))
        (T (MSG " . " X))))
```
```

Chapter 10

pages 249–250

1.
```
(DEFUN COUNT-SLICES (L)
  (PROG (CNT)
        (SETQ CNT 0)
    LOOP
        (IF (NULL L) (RETURN CNT))
        (SETQ L (CDR L))
        (SETQ CNT (ADD1 CNT))
        (GO LOOP)))
```

2.
```
(DEFUN IT-NTH (N X)
  (PROG ()
    LOOP
        (IF (ZEROP N) (RETURN (CAR X)))
        (SETQ N (SUB1 N))
        (SETQ X (CDR X))
        (GO LOOP)))
```

3. `(PROG () LOOP (GO LOOP))`

4. The errors are: (1) the prog variable CNT was not initialized to 0 before entering the loop, and (2) GO was not used to send control back to the point in the body where the tag appears. Since there is no GO, when PROG reaches the end of the body it will simply return NIL. Here is the corrected function:

```
(DEFUN MAKE-LOAF (N)
  (PROG (CNT LOAF)
        (SETQ CNT 0)
    LOOP
        (IF (EQUAL CNT N) (RETURN LOAF))
        (SETQ LOAF (CONS 'X LOAF))
        (SETQ CNT (ADD1 CNT))
        (GO LOOP)))
```

5.
```
(DEFUN ISOLATED-PRINT (X)
  (PROG ()
   LOOP
       (IF (NULL X) (RETURN NIL))
       (MSG (CAR X) T)
       (SETQ X (CDR X))
       (GO LOOP)))
```

```
(DEFUN ISOLATED-PRINT (X)
  (COND ((NULL X) NIL)
       (T (MSG (CAR X) T) (ISOLATED-PRINT (CDR X)))))
```

```
(DEFUN ISOLATED-PRINT (X)
  (APPLY-TO-ALL '(LAMBDA (X1) (MSG X1 T)) X))
```

The applicative version is the shortest as well as the simplest. This is because all its control structure details are handled by APPLY-TO-ALL, while the iterative and recursive versions require us to explicitly state how to exit the loop and how to continue looping.

6.
```
(DEFUN IT-MEMBER (X L)
  (PROG ()
   LOOP
       (COND ((NULL L) (RETURN NIL))
             ((EQUAL X (CAR L)) (RETURN L))
             (T (SETQ L (CDR L)) (GO LOOP)))))
```

7. The action of the first COND clause should be (RETURN NIL) rather than simply NIL. The action part of the second clause should be (RETURN (CAR L)) rather than simply (CAR L). You must use RETURN to get out of a PROG anywhere other than at the end of the body; you must *always* use RETURN if you want the PROG to return a value other than NIL.

8.
```
(DEFUN IT-UNION (X Y)
  (PROG ()
   LOOP
       (IF (NULL X) (RETURN Y))
       (IF (NOT (MEMBER (CAR X) Y))
           (SETQ Y (CONS (CAR X) Y)))
       (SETQ X (CDR X))
       (GO LOOP)))
```

9.
```
(DEFUN IT-REVERSE (X)
  (PROG (Y)
    LOOP
        (IF (NULL X) (RETURN Y))
        (SETQ Y (CONS (CAR X) Y))
        (SETQ X (CDR X))
        (GO LOOP)))
```

10. IT-INTERSECTION goes through the elements of X one at a time and, if a given element appears in Y, it is added to the *beginning* of RESULT. This means the elements of RESULT will appear in the reverse of the order they appear in the list X. One way to counter this reversal is with another reversal at the end—for example, change the first IF expression to read (IF (NULL X) (RETURN (REVERSE RESULT))). Another way would be to replace the expression (CONS (CAR X) RESULT) with (APPEND RESULT (LIST (CAR X))), so that elements are added to the *end* of RESULT instead of to the beginning.

page 253

```
(DEFUN ADDUP (X)
  (DO ((SUM 0 (PLUS (CAR L) SUM))
       (L X (CDR L)))
      ((NULL L) SUM)))

(DEFUN MAKE-LOAF (X)
  (DO ((LOAF NIL (CONS 'X LOAF))
       (N X (SUB1 N)))
      ((ZEROP N) LOAF)))

(DEFUN FACT (N)
  (DO ((RESULT 1 (TIMES CNT RESULT))
       (CNT 1 (ADD1 CNT)))
      ((GREATERP CNT N) RESULT)))
```

page 255

1. PROG's variable list is simply a list of symbols, like the argument list of a function. Prog variables are bound to NIL when the PROG is entered. LET's variable list is a list of pairs of form (*var value*). Each

variable *var* in the list is initialized according to its corresponding expression *value*. DO's variable list is the most complex of the three. It is a list of triples of form (*var init upd*). Each variable *var* is initialized according to the expression *init* upon entering the DO; on succeeding times through the loop the variable's value is updated according to the expression *upd*. If *upd* is omitted the variable is not updated.

2. If a form in the body of a PROG is a symbol, then it is a tag and will not be evaluated. If it is not a symbol, then it is treated as an expression and will be evaluated if the PROG reaches that point.

3.
```
(DEFUN FOO (X L)
  (LET ((A (ASSOC X L)))
    (LIST (CADDR A) (CAR A) (CADR A))))
```

4.
```
(DEFUN ANYODDP (X)
  (DO ((Z X (CDR Z)))
      ((NULL Z) NIL)
      (IF (ODDP (CAR Z)) (RETURN T))))
```

5.
```
(DEFUN FIB (N)
  (PROG (CNT R1 R2 RESULT)
        (SETQ CNT 0)
        (SETQ R1 1)
        (SETQ R2 0)
        (SETQ RESULT 1)
    LOOP
        (IF (EQUAL CNT N) (RETURN RESULT))
        (SETQ RESULT (PLUS R1 R2))
        (SETQ R2 R1)
        (SETQ R1 RESULT)
        (SETQ CNT (ADD1 CNT))
        (GO LOOP)))
```

pages 257–258

Two versions are given for each iterative function, one with PROG and one with DO.

1.
```
(DEFUN COMPLEMENT-BASE (B)
  (CADR (ASSOC B '((A T) (T A) (G C) (C G)))))
```

2.
```
(DEFUN COMPLEMENT-STRAND (STRAND1)
  (PROG (STRAND2)
    LOOP
      (OR STRAND1 (RETURN (REVERSE STRAND2)))
      (SETQ STRAND2 (CONS (COMPLEMENT-BASE (CAR STRAND1))
                          STRAND2))
      (SETQ STRAND1 (CDR STRAND1))
      (GO LOOP)))

(DEFUN COMPLEMENT-STRAND (STRAND)
  (DO ((STRAND1 STRAND (CDR STRAND1))
       (STRAND2 NIL))
      ((NULL STRAND1) (REVERSE STRAND2))
    (SETQ STRAND2 (CONS (COMPLEMENT-BASE (CAR STRAND1))
                        STRAND2))))
```

3.
```
(DEFUN MAKE-DOUBLE (STRAND)
  (PROG (RESULT)
    LOOP
        (OR STRAND (RETURN (REVERSE RESULT)))
        (SETQ RESULT
              (CONS (LIST (CAR STRAND)
                          (COMPLEMENT-BASE (CAR STRAND)))
                    RESULT))
        (SETQ STRAND (CDR STRAND))
        (GO LOOP)))

(DEFUN MAKE-DOUBLE (STRAND)
  (DO ((STRAND1 STRAND (CDR STRAND1))
       (RESULT NIL))
      ((NULL STRAND1) (REVERSE RESULT))
    (SETQ RESULT (CONS (LIST (CAR STRAND1)
                             (COMPLEMENT-BASE (CAR STRAND1)))
                       RESULT))))
```

4.
```
(DEFUN COUNT-BASES (DNA)
  (PROG (ACNT TCNT GCNT CCNT)
        (SETQ ACNT 0)
        (SETQ TCNT 0)
        (SETQ GCNT 0)
        (SETQ CCNT 0)
    LOOP
        (OR DNA (RETURN (LIST (LIST 'A ACNT)
                              (LIST 'T TANT)
                              (LIST 'G GCNT)
                              (LIST 'C CCNT))))
        (COND ((ATOM (CAR DNA)) (COUNT-ONE-BASE (CAR DNA)))
              (T (COUNT-ONE-BASE (CAAR DNA))
                 (COUNT-ONE-BASE (CADAR DNA))))
        (SETQ DNA (CDR DNA))
        (GO LOOP)))

(DEFUN COUNT-ONE-BASE (N)
  (COND ((EQUAL N 'A) (SETQ ACNT (PLUS 1 ACNT)))
        ((EQUAL N 'T) (SETQ TCNT (PLUS 1 TCNT)))
        ((EQUAL N 'G) (SETQ GCNT (PLUS 1 GCNT)))
        ((EQUAL N 'C) (SETQ CCNT (PLUS 1 CCNT)))))

(DEFUN COUNT-BASES (DNA)
  (DO ((X DNA (CDR X)) (ACNT 0) (TCNT 0) (GCNT 0) (CCNT 0))
      ((NULL X) (LIST (LIST 'A ACNT)
                      (LIST 'T TCNT)
                      (LIST 'G GCNT)
                      (LIST 'C CCNT)))
    (COND ((ATOM (CAR X)) (COUNT-ONE-BASE (CAR X)))
          (T (COUNT-ONE-BASE (CAAR X))
             (COUNT-ONE-BASE (CADAR X))))))
```

`(COUNT-BASES (MAKE-DOUBLE '(A G G T C A T T G)))` evaluates to

```
((A 5) (T 5) (G 4) (C 4))
```

5.
```
(DEFUN PREFIXP (STRAND1 STRAND2)
  (PROG ()
    LOOP
        (OR STRAND1 (RETURN T))
        (OR (EQUAL (CAR STRAND1) (CAR STRAND2)) (RETURN NIL))
        (SETQ STRAND1 (CDR STRAND1))
        (SETQ STRAND2 (CDR STRAND2))
        (GO LOOP)))

(DEFUN PREFIXP (STRAND1 STRAND2)
  (DO ((S1 STRAND1 (CDR S1))
       (S2 STRAND2 (CDR S2)))
      ((NULL S1) T)
    (OR (EQUAL (CAR S1) (CAR S2)) (RETURN NIL))))
```

6.
```
(DEFUN APPEARSP (STRAND1 STRAND2)
  (PROG ()
    LOOP
        (IF (GREATERP (LENGTH STRAND1) (LENGTH STRAND2))
            (RETURN NIL))
        (IF (PREFIXP STRAND1 STRAND2) (RETURN T))
        (SETQ STRAND2 (CDR STRAND2))
        (GO LOOP)))

(DEFUN APPEARSP (STRAND1 STRAND2)
  (DO ((S2 STRAND2 (CDR S2)))
      ((GREATERP (LENGTH STRAND1) (LENGTH S2)) NIL)
    (IF (PREFIXP STRAND1 S2) (RETURN T))))
```

7.
```
(DEFUN COVERP (STRAND1 STRAND2)
  (PROG ()
    LOOP
      (OR STRAND2 (RETURN T))
      (OR (PREFIXP STRAND1 STRAND2) (RETURN NIL))
      (SETQ STRAND2 (NTHCDR (LENGTH STRAND1) STRAND2))
      (GO LOOP)))

(DEFUN COVERP (STRAND1 STRAND2)
  (DO ((S2 STRAND2 (NTHCDR (LENGTH STRAND1) S2)))
      ((NULL S2) T)
    (OR (PREFIXP STRAND1 S2) (RETURN NIL))))
```

8.
```
(DEFUN PREFIX (N STRAND)
  (PROG (RESULT)
    LOOP
        (IF (ZEROP N) (RETURN (REVERSE RESULT)))
        (SETQ RESULT (CONS (CAR STRAND) RESULT))
        (SETQ STRAND (CDR STRAND))
        (SETQ N (SUB1 N))
        (GO LOOP)))

(DEFUN PREFIX (N STRAND)
  (DO ((RESULT NIL (CONS (CAR S) RESULT))
       (S STRAND (CDR S)))
      ((ZEROP N) (REVERSE RESULT))
    (SETQ N (SUB1 N))))
```

9.
```
(DEFUN KERNEL (STRAND)
  (PROG (CNT)
        (SETQ CNT 1)
    LOOP
        (IF (COVERP (PREFIX CNT STRAND) STRAND)
            (RETURN (PREFIX CNT STRAND)))
        (SETQ CNT (ADD1 CNT))
        (GO LOOP)))

(DEFUN KERNEL (STRAND)
  (DO ((CNT 1 (ADD1 CNT)))
      ((COVERP (PREFIX CNT STRAND) STRAND)
       (PREFIX CNT STRAND))))
```

10.
```
(DEFUN DRAW-DNA (STRAND1)
  (LET ((N (LENGTH STRAND1)))
    (DRAW-STRING N "-----")
    (DRAW-STRING N "  !  ")
    (DRAW-BASES STRAND1)
    (DRAW-STRING N "  .  ")
    (DRAW-STRING N "  .  ")
    (DRAW-BASES (COMPLEMENT-STRAND STRAND1))
    (DRAW-STRING N "  !  ")
    (DRAW-STRING N "-----")))
```

```
(DEFUN DRAW-STRING (CNT STRING)
  (PROG ()
    LOOP
        (IF (ZEROP CNT) (RETURN (MSG T)))
        (MSG STRING)
        (SETQ CNT (SUB1 CNT))
        (GO LOOP)))

(DEFUN DRAW-STRING (CNT STRING)
  (DO ((I 1 (ADD1 I)))
      ((GREATERP I CNT) (MSG T))
    (MSG STRING)))

(DEFUN DRAW-BASES (SEQ)
  (PROG ()
    LOOP
        (IF (NULL SEQ) (RETURN (MSG T)))
        (MSG "   " (CAR SEQ) "   ")
        (SETQ SEQ (CDR SEQ))
        (GO LOOP)))

(DEFUN DRAW-BASES (SEQ)
  (DO ((S1 SEQ (CDR S1)))
      ((NULL S1) (MSG T))
    (MSG "   " (CAR S1) "   ")))
```

page 261

```
(DEFUN SETQ MACRO (X)
  (LIST 'SET (LIST 'QUOTE (CADR X)) (CADDR X)))
```

page 262

```
(DEFUN PROG1 NARGS
  (AND (GREATERP NARGS 0) (ARG 1)))

(DEFUN PROGN NARGS
  (AND (GREATERP NARGS 0) (ARG NARGS)))
```

```
(DEFUN LIST NARGS
  (PROG (CNT RES)
        (SETQ CNT NARGS)
    LOOP
        (IF (ZEROP CNT) (RETURN RES))
        (SETQ RES (CONS (ARG CNT) RES))
        (SETQ CNT (SUB1 CNT))
        (GO LOOP)))
```

Chapter 11

page 267

1.
```
(DEFUN SUBPROP (SYM ELEM PROP)
  (PUTPROP SYM
           (SETDIFFERENCE (GET SYM PROP) (LIST ELEM))
           PROP))
```

2.
```
(DEFUN FORGET-MEETING (X Y)
  (SUBPROP X Y 'MET)
  (SUBPROP Y X 'MET)
  T)
```

3.
```
(DEFUN HASPROP (SYM PROP) (HAS1 PROP (PLIST SYM)))

(DEFUN HAS1 (X L)
  (COND ((NULL L) NIL)
        ((EQUAL X (CAR L)) T)
        (T (HAS1 X (CDDR L)))))
```

HAS1 recurses on the property list of SYM, taking the CDDR of the list each time. It takes the CDDR rather than the CDR so that it checks only the property names, not the values. This is important because if we are checking whether a symbol has a property named FOO, we don't want to be fooled by its having a property named BAR whose *value* is FOO.

4.
```
(DEFUN GET (SYM PROP) (GET1 PROP (PLIST SYM)))

(DEFUN GET1 (X L)
  (COND ((NULL L) NIL)
        ((EQUAL X (CAR L)) (CADR L))
        (T (GET1 X (CDDR L)))))
```

5.
```
(DEFUN REMPROPS (SYM)
  (AND (PLIST SYM)
       (REMPROP SYM (CAR (PLIST SYM)))
       (REMPROPS SYM)))
```

pages 270–273

1.
```
(SETQ ALPHABET
      '(A B C D E F G H I J K L M N O P Q R S T U V W X Y Z))

(SETQ C1
      '(ZJ ZE KLJJLS JF SLAPZI EZVLIJ PIB KL JUFWXUJ P HFFV JUPI
        JF ENLPO PIB SLAFML PVV BFWKJ))
```

2. —

3.
```
(DEFUN WORDS-TO-LIST (WORDS)
  (REVERSE (CDR (REVERSE
    (REDUCE 'APPEND
            (APPLY-TO-ALL '(LAMBDA (WORD)
                             (APPEND (EXPLODE WORD) (LIST NIL)))
                          WORDS))))))
```

4.
```
(DEFUN GROUP-TEXT (TEXT)
  (DO ((TEXTLINES NIL) (LINE NIL) (CNT 0 (ADD1 CNT)))
    ((NULL TEXT) (APPEND TEXTLINES (AND LINE (LIST LINE))))
    (SETQ LINE (NCONC LINE (NCONS (CAR TEXT))))
    (COND ((AND (GREATERP CNT 60) (NULL (CAR TEXT)))
           (SETQ TEXTLINES (APPEND TEXTLINES (LIST LINE)))
           (SETQ LINE NIL)
           (SETQ CNT 0)))
    (SETQ TEXT (CDR TEXT))))
```

5.
```
(DEFUN MAKE-SUBSTITUTION (LETTER1 LETTER2)
  (PUTPROP LETTER1 LETTER2 'DECIPHERS)
  (PUTPROP LETTER2 LETTER1 'ENCIPHERS))
```

6.
```
(DEFUN UNDO-SUBSTITUTION (LETTER)
  (REMPROP (GET LETTER 'DECIPHERS) 'ENCIPHERS)
  (REMPROP LETTER 'DECIPHERS))
```

7.
```
(DEFUN CLEAR NIL
  (APPLY-TO-ALL '(LAMBDA (LETTER)
                   (REMPROP LETTER 'DECIPHERS)
                   (REMPROP LETTER 'ENCIPHERS))
                ALPHABET))
```

8.
```
(DEFUN SHOW-LINE (LINE)
  (APPLY-TO-ALL '(LAMBDA (LETTER) (SHOW-CHAR LETTER)) LINE)
  (MSG T)
  (APPLY-TO-ALL '(LAMBDA (LETTER)
                   (SHOW-CHAR (GET LETTER 'DECIPHERS)))
                LINE)
  (MSG T T))

(DEFUN SHOW-CHAR (CHAR)
  (COND (CHAR (MSG CHAR))
        (T (MSG " "))))
```

9.
```
(DEFUN SHOW-TEXT (TEXTLINES)
  (MSG "--------------------" T)
  (APPLY-TO-ALL 'SHOW-LINE TEXTLINES)
  (MSG "--------------------" T))
```

10.
```
(DEFUN SUB-LETTER (LETTER)
  (PROG (L2)
    (AND (GET LETTER 'DECIPHERS)
         (MSG LETTER " has already been deciphered as "
              (GET LETTER 'DECIPHER) "!" T)
         (RETURN NIL))
    (MSG "What does " LETTER " decipher to? ")
    (SETQ L2 (READ))
    (COND ((NOT (MEMBER L2 ALPHABET))
           (MSG L2 " is not a letter!" T)
           (RETURN NIL))
          ((GET L2 'ENCIPHER)
           (MSG "But " (GET L2 'ENCIPHER)
                " already deciphers to " L2 "!" T)
           (RETURN T))
          (T (MAKE-SUBSTITUTION LETTER L2)))))
```

11.
```
(DEFUN UNDO-LETTER NIL
  (PROG (LETTER)
    (MSG "Undo which letter? ")
    (SETQ LETTER (READ))
    (OR (MEMBER LETTER ALPHABET) (RETURN NIL))
    (COND ((NULL (GET LETTER 'DECIPHERS))
           (MSG LETTER " wasn't deciphered!" T))
          (T (UNDO-SUBSTITUTION LETTER)))))
```

12.
```
(DEFUN SOLVE (CRYPT)
  (CLEAR)
  (DO ((TEXT (GROUP-TEXT (WORDS-TO-LIST CRYPT))) (X NIL))
    ((EQUAL X 'END) T)
    (SHOW-TEXT TEXT)
    (MSG "Substitute which letter? ")
    (SETQ X (READ))
    (COND ((MEMBER X ALPHABET) (SUB-LETTER X))
          ((EQUAL X 'UNDO) (UNDO-LETTER))
          ((EQUAL X 'END))
          (T (MSG "I don't understand " X T T)))))
```

13. **Solution to cryptogram:**

```
IT IS BETTER TO REMAIN SILENT AND BE THOUGHT A FOOL THAN
TO SPEAK AND REMOVE ALL DOUBT
```

Index